A present to Bobby from Tony and the Baurns.
Xmas 1995.

KU-166-653

EMERGENCY RESCUE

EMERGENCY RESCUE

BLITZ EDITIONS

Copyright © Bookmart Ltd 1995

All rights reserved. No part of this publication may be reproduced,
stored in a retrieval system, or transmitted in any form or by any
means, electronic, mechanical, photocopying, recording or otherwise,
without prior written permission from the publishers.

Published by Blitz Editions
an imprint of Bookmart Ltd
Registered Number 2372865
Trading as Bookmart Ltd
Desford Road
Enderby
Leicester LE9 5AD

ISBN 1 85605 271 0

Every effort has been made to contact the copyright holders for the pictures.
In some cases they have been untraceable, for which we offer our apologies.
Special thanks to the Hulton-Deutsch Collection, who supplied the majority of pictures,
and thanks also to the following libraries and picture agencies:
Popperfotos, Syndication International, Range/UPI Bettman, Press Association,
AFP/EPA, Associated Press, Frank Spooner, Rex Features, Assignments, SWNS,
Peter Lomas, PA Photos, Portfolio Pictures, The John Frost Collection,
Joanna Nathan-Ayres, Pat Morris, Jerry Young.

The Authors
Allan Hall is the American correspondent for a major U.K. newspaper.
He has written several books on crime, the paranormal and the unexplained.

Nick Constable wrote the chapter 'Dial Rescue'.
He is a writer and journalist whose work for national newspapers has involved many
dramatic rescue stories – from major disasters such as Zeebrugge to individual tales
of courage and heroism.

This book was produced by Amazon Publishing Limited
Designed by Wilson Design Associates
Edited by Graham McColl

Printed in the Czech Republic
51783

Contents

EMERGENCY RESCUE

These tales are of life lived on the edge, sometimes by accident, sometimes by design. They cover tales of stranded individuals clinging on to life as the elements take their toll, daring rescuers who are willing to risk everything to save the lives of their fellow human beings and evil villains with no concern for anything other than their own self-preservation.

Sometimes the setting for human heroics is a life-or-death struggle in a steamy jungle, a volcano, a raging sea, an earthquake-ridden city or a nuclear power station in the throes of its destruction. Sometimes the action will take place in a courtroom, sometimes in a police station, as the forces of law and order battle bravely on behalf of justice.

In this volume you will find a host of heartwarming tales of ordinary people who step out of anonymity for a few hours or days after performing their own small-scale heroics – mothers who risk life and limb for their children and animal lovers who go to extraordinary lengths to ensure the survival of helpless creatures. And it takes a fresh look at people made famous by other motives – greed, revenge, a quest for power – such as Mike Tyson's rape case, Lorena Bobbit's desperate action, the assassination of the Russian Royal family and the gangster John Dillinger. It also looks at how the law has battled determinedly to keep a step ahead of criminals through advances in forensic detection.

This is a book that rides the peaks and troughs of human behaviour. That behaviour may shock and stun or bring a smile to the lips. It is never dull.

OPERATION RESCUE

CHERNOBYL
Nuclear Horror

It was the disaster that that bastion of secrecy, the USSR, couldn't cover up. After the Chernobyl reactor blew up, a cloud of fear drifted over Europe in the late 1980s. The radiation scares terrified the West but the most awful price was paid by the locals.

The first warning blips ripped across the screens on that fateful, terrible morning. At 9.00am on Monday April 28 1986, scientists at the Forsmark nuclear power station, 60 miles from the Swedish capital of Stockholm, noticed disturbing signals bleeping on their ghost-green screens.

Miles away in the Ukraine the force that had sent out those signals had melted down a nuclear reactor and caused the worst radiation poisoning since the atomic bombs were dropped on Japan. The signals were measures of radiation and at first the horrified boffins feared a major reactor leak at their own power plant. A careful and methodical check of all equipment and monitoring gauges showed no leakage – and yet the sensors indicated that the air they breathed in was four and five times the ordained safe limit. Geiger counters were hurridly deployed for swift checks on all 600 workers. The readings were haywire, showing virtually every employee had been exposed to radiation way above safe limits. Outside it was the same story – samples taken from soil and plant life showed extraordinarily high deposits of radioactive material.

It dawned on the scientists that Sweden and much of Europe was being infected by a silent, unseen killer that could not be sniffed on the wind or seen with the naked eye. Yet its effects are still being felt to this day.

While the Forsmark technicians saw the effects of what had taken place in the Ukraine at a safer distance hours later, a dedicated band of men became heroes

Opposite: The remains of the Chernobyl nuclear power plant almost six months after the reactor blew, giving mankind its worst atomic plant disaster.

CHERNOBYL PRODUCED THE WORST RADIATION POISONING SINCE NUCLEAR BOMBS WERE DROPPED ON JAPAN

Below: The front page of the New York Post the morning the news of the disaster filtered out.

Left: The burnt-out shell of the reactor itself, where brave firemen equipped with just hoses and no protective clothes sought to stem the ravages of nuclear catastrophe.

Right: *A satellite picture showing the doomed Chernobyl plant, located to the left of the large cooling pond, used in more normal times to keep the reactor fuel rods at a stable working temperature.*

AT THE EYE OF THE STORM, THE HEROES OF CHERNOBYL ATTEMPTED THE GRIMMEST RESCUE MISSION IN HISTORY

THEY SAVED OTHERS WHILE LITERALLY PLACING THEMSELVES IN THE JAWS OF DEATH — JAWS WHICH CONTINUE TO CLAMP SHUT

at the eye of the nuclear storm as they attempted the grimmest rescue mission in history. They were the heroes of Chernobyl who saved others while literally placing themselves in the jaws of death – jaws which continue to clamp shut on them months and years after the disaster.

Lt. Col. Leonid Telyatnikov was one of those who had been enjoying a few well-earned days off when the telephone rang at his home 75 miles outside Kiev in the Soviet Ukraine at 1.32am on April 26. A breathless voice informed him that there had been an "incident" at the Chernobyl nuclear power plant 80 miles from Kiev. It was a bright, starlit night as

Right: *Technician Jorgen Reed at a Danish atomic research facility testing for air and water contamination as the cloud of atomic infection spreads across Europe.*

Telyatnikov, leading his crew of 28 firefighters, raced to the scene. Soon there appeared on the horizon a bright, orange glow. "I had no idea what had happened or what we were heading into," recalled Telyatnikov, then 33.

"But as I approached the plant I could see debris on fire all around like sparklers. Then I noticed a bluish glow above the wreckage of reactor four and pockets of fire on surrounding buildings. It was absolutely silent and eerie."

PITIFUL PROTECTION

He and his brave men were protected by no more than Wellington boots and hard hats. And how would they have known better anyway? The Soviet Union had long shrouded its nuclear programme in secrecy. The kind of disaster that he was facing that night would later ensure his honour as a Hero of the Soviet Union, but he knew little of gamma rays, x-rays and the myriad other pulsing, unseen death beams emitting from the meltdown of the plant, save that they were dangerous and prolonged exposure to them increased that danger.

Since the time that Telyatnikov and his men trained their hoses on the burning debris untold thousands have died from tumours and cancer caused by the explosion. Cattle and livestock, together with human beings, have given birth to nightmarish offspring, deformed and mutated by the effects of the radiation. The earth has been scarred forever and mankind left to ponder whether the benefits of nuclear energy are not outweighed by the spectre of such a disaster ever re-occurring. But on that night the only resource that Telyatnikov and his fire-fighters had in abundance was courage.

Telyatnikov was one of the few in the first hours who came to realise the enormity of the disaster. "I sensed it was not an ordinary situation as soon as I passed through the gate," he said. "There was just the noise of machines and the fire crackling. The fire fighters knew what they had to do and proceeded quietly, on the run. The radiation-measuring meters which we had on the trucks had frozen on their highest level. Thoughts of my family would flash through my mind and be gone. No-one would discuss the radiation risk. The most frightening thought was that we

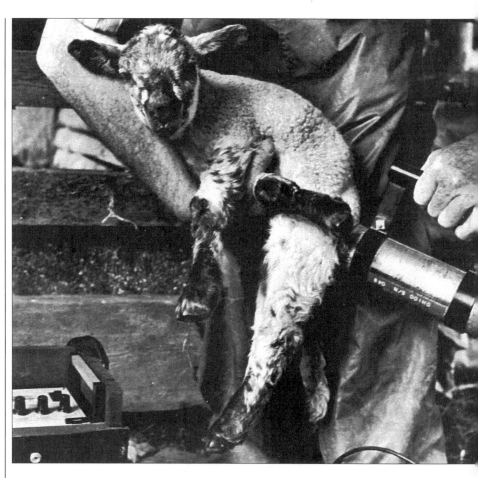

wouldn't have enough strength to hold out until reserves came. About an hour after the fire began a group of fire-fighters with symptoms of radiation exposure were taken down from a rooftop close to the damaged reactor. When I approached five men to take up the position they rushed to the rooftop almost before I could get the words out of my mouth. They are all dead now, from radioactive poisoning."

NARROW ESCAPES

The sacrifices of the initial team enabled technicians, maintenance men and security staff at the plant to escape – some without overexposure to the deadly radiation. One maintenance crew were trapped by a wall of radioactive flames in a tool bunker 500 yards from the explosion's core. Gerady Kolisnya, who was saved that night, recalls: "We piled sandbags against the metal door as the hot wind blowing sparks underneath roared towards us. The walls began to leach a blood-red liquid – they were literally 'bleeding' in the massive heat. We felt the hot blast of the flames as they licked under the sill of the door and

Above: *Welsh lambs were just one species of animal forced to undergo quarantine and testing following the spread of radiation.*

GAMMA RAYS, X-RAYS AND MYRIAD OTHER PULSING, UNSEEN DEATH BEAMS WERE EMITTING FROM THE MELTDOWN OF THE PLANT

Left: *Soviet leader Mikhail Gorbachev initially attempted to play down the accident at Chernobyl but proof of the disaster soon spread across Europe, making any attempt at public relations futile.*

HE BEGAN VOMITING AS HE FOUGHT THE FLAMES AND SINCE THEN HE HAS BATTLED CANCER LIKE THOUSANDS OF OTHERS

Below: *A mountain of lettuces rots in Austria, victim of the toxic cloud from Chernobyl.*

singed the canvas of the sandbags. Eventually two of the other men – there were four of us altogether – cried out that we should make a run for it, but I counselled against it. Finally there was a hiss like that of cold water on hot metal, which was exactly what it was. A hose from the firefighters was playing on the door. They kept the flames back from it long enough for us to get out, although the two guys that wanted to make a break for it have since died from cancer."

Telyatnikov too is one of what the Ukraines call "the living dead". He began vomiting even as he fought the flames and since then has battled cancer, like thousands of others. The burning white-hot graphite core of the reactor blazed at 5,000 degrees fahrenheit – twice the temperature of molten steel – and thrust millions of cubic feet of radioactive gas into the atmosphere. Pictures taken by a CIA satellite 400 miles above the earth were on President Ronald Reagan's desk 48 hours after the red alert was sounded by the Forsmark scientists. They showed a picture of hell that

embarrassed, technologically inept Soviets, refused to publicly admit.

Moscow kept silent to the world but in reality mobilised an army to deal with the initial blazes and the chaos that followed in their wake. Workers and soldiers – most of them now dead or suffering from the effects of prolonged exposure to such massive doseages of radiation – were drafted in by truck and trains. Helicopters carrying tons of wet sand and lead flew over the site and dumped their loads directly on to the blazing reactor. Tons of the element boron, which absorbs neutrons, was also dumped on to the smouldering fires. Over days, entire colonies of workers sprouted on ships moored in a nearby river and were hosed down at the end of every mission over the ruined reactor. But experts say that approximately four percent of all the radiation contained in the reactor escaped – some ten times the amount of radiation released by the atomic bombs exploded on Hiroshima and Nagasaki towards the end of World War Two. Hoses alone would not wash away the unseen killer.

By the time the Forsmark scientists had discovered the presence of massive amounts of radiation in the atmosphere, strong winds were carrying it all over Europe. Light rain fell on the salt marshes of Brittany, making the milk in cows' udders toxic. Heavier rain thundered on to the Welsh hillsides, making the tender lamb forbidden flesh. Snow in Finland, Sweden and West Germany was infected too. The Swedish scientists told their government

that they believed the source for this nuclear volcano, spewing its lethal residue into the skies, was the Soviet Union. But communist Russia in the hours afterwards remained silent.

It was not until 9.00pm Moscow time that night when the Kremlin finally admitted that something HAD happened – but they gave no indication of the gravity of the mishap. A terse four-sentence statement was read on the nightly news in Moscow. Almost grudging in its admission, the statement said: "An accident has taken place at the Chernobyl power station and one of the

Right: *The Three Mile Island plant in America, scene of that country's closest-ever brush with nuclear catastrophe.*

Below: *A researcher from the Russian Atomic Energy Ministry uses an advanced geiger counter in Siberia after a 1993 accident sent radiation leaking into the atmosphere.*

reactors was damaged. Measures are being taken to eliminate the consequences of the accident. Those affected by it are being given assistance. A government commission has been set up." The announcer then picked up another sheaf of paper and continued to read a story about a Soviet peace fund.

POLITE PRESSURE

Western governments began to exert diplomatic pressure on the Soviet Union for details of exactly what had happened. In the immediate hours after the tragedy Per Olof Sjostedt, technical and scientific adviser for the Swedish embassy in Moscow, contacted officials of the Soviet nuclear energy programme armed with the information given to him via the Forsmark scientists. He was curtly told that there was no information to be had. Swedish Ambassador Torsten Orn made a smiliar request to the foreign ministry. He was fobbed off with a polite: "We will look into it." It took Soviet politican Boris Yeltsin to step forward several days later to lend gravity to his government's casual response to the disaster. He said: "It is serious. Very serious. The cause apparently lies in human error. We are undertaking measures to make sure this doesn't happen again."

Those measures included the biggest forced evacuation of Soviet territories since World War Two when entire factories,

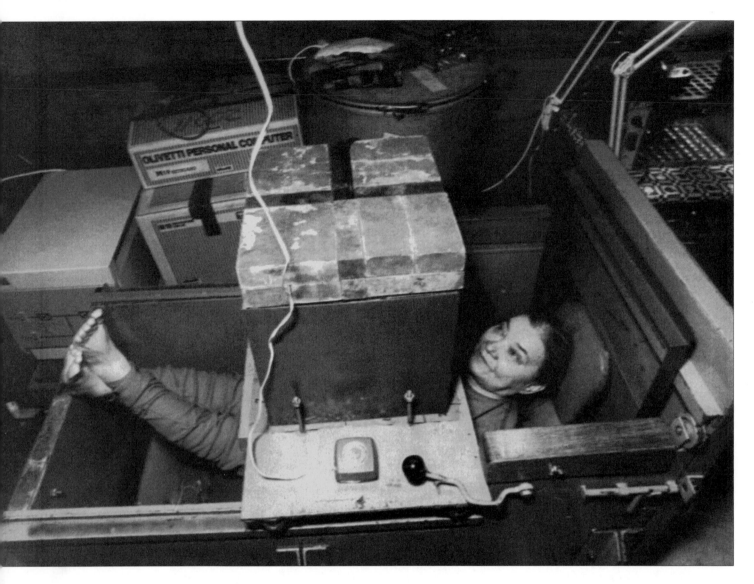

Above: *Iada Fofanoff from Lapland subjects herself to undignified but necessary tests in Helsinki for radiation a year after the Chernobyl accident.*

"THERE ARE MANY HUNDREDS OF DEAD AND WOUNDED... YOU CAN'T IMAGINE IT... PLEASE TELL THE WORLD TO HELP US"

towns and cities had uprooted and headed east away from the path of the advancing Nazi armies. An 18 mile radius around Chernobyl was evacuated and declared an unfit zone, where cattle, drinking water and vegetation were all deemed to be unfit for consumption.

This was more than a mere evacuation – harsh though it was, and chaotic though conditions were, the exodus undoubtedly saved untold hundreds of thousands of lives. The area around and about was – and in many places still is – a nuclear dead zone where unseen radiation proved deadly. A great number of the peasants around and about required more than a little persuasion to move, but the movement itself saved a great many lives.

A graphic example of the misery in those chaotic days after the explosion was provided by a Dutch radio ham called Annis Kofman who turned into another

wireless enthusiast living near Chernobyl. The man cried over the airwaves: "There are many hundreds of dead and wounded. We heard heavy explosions. You can't imagine what is happening here with all the deaths and fire. I'm here 20 miles from it and in fact I don't know what to do. I don't know if our leaders know what to do because this is a real disaster. Please tell the world to help us."

A SCIENTIFIC EXPLANATION

Nuclear physicists began to theorise about what had happened at the Chernobyl reactor and came up with a likely scenario. The Chernobyl reactor used uranium fuel rods to generate heat used to boil water to steam. The steam in turn powers turbine generators for power. Cooling water is essential to stop the fuel rods from super-heating, causing a melt-down, or burn-up, in which the core virtually turns itself into a nuclear bomb. It seems that the water circulation system to provide the cooling liquid failed, causing the temperature in the reactor core to hit 5,000 degrees. The uranium fuel rods melted and produced radioactive steam that reacted with the zirconium alloy cladding of the rods to produce explosive hydrogen gas. A second reaction between the steam and graphite core produced free hydrogen and carbon oxides which, mixed with oxygen, blew off the top of the concrete structure housing the reactor and caused the graphite to burst into flames. The incoming cool air acted like a perfect chimney for the nuclear gas to escape into the atmosphere.

Soviet officials proved reluctant in seeking outside assistance while still trying to pretend that not much had happened. But a Soviet scientific officer attached to their embassy in Bonn did approach the West German nuclear power industry with a request for information on fighting graphite core fires. A similar request went out the same day to Swedish authorities and Moscow invited Californian bone-marrow expert Dr. Robert Gale to provide medical aid to Chernobyl victims.

A TERRIBLE LEGACY

By the end of the week the fire was out – but so was the radiation, incalcuable amounts of it, speading an ominous pall over Europe and the western half of the Soviet Union. On the ground, near to the site, the victims began dying of haemorrhaging and brain seizures. They were often the lucky ones – the lingering deaths, the mutated stillborn babies, the cancer which racks heroes like fireman Telyatnikov, were yet to come. In a bid to clean up some of the debris the Soviets dug a huge pit and filled it with shattered remnants of the reactor, twisted metal and broken concrete from the plant and clothes worn by disaster workers. Some two million cubic feet of concrete was mixed over the next six weeks and poured on the reactor, sealing it forever.

As the rescuers struggled, President Reagan became angrier with Moscow and said so in a nationwide radio address. He told America in his usual Saturday speech: "The Soviets owe the world an explanation.

A full accounting of what happened at Chernobyl and what is happening now is the least the world community has a right to expect." In Europe the Swedish energy minister demanded that the Soviet atomic energy network be placed into the hands of an international watchdog committee. In Poland all children aged between nine and 16 were given iodine solutions to keep their bodies from absorbing the element in radioactive form and all milk produced by grass-fed cows was banned from sale.

Nuclear experts said the RBMK-1000 reactors at Chernobyl were mighty but outdated machines. "It was a crude technology," said a senior administration official in America. Its design features dated back to

INCALCULABLE AMOUNTS OF RADIATION SPREAD AN OMINOUS PALL OVER EUROPE AND THE WESTERN SOVIET UNION

Below: *Children, such as Igor Pavioviec, were born with defects caused by radiation.*

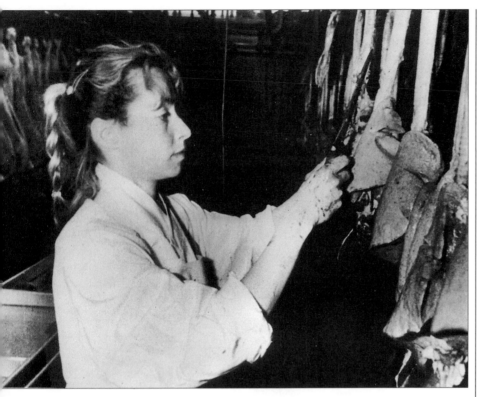

Above: Carcasses are checked at a slaughterhouse in Germany as the radioactivity spreads westward.

deformed plant life that is unlike anything else found on earth. "We still aren't sure exactly what Chernobyl is responsible for," said Valerie Kaleetnschker a former communist party health official in the blighted region, "but we know that things are much, much worse than we thought."

The Soviet Parliament in 1989 voted a belated 15 billion pounds worth of aid to the victims through check-ups, disability benefits and re-location expenses, but critics contend it was far too little too late. For in all some 600,000 people passed through Chernobyl during its clean-up and each and every one of them may be carrying the cancers caused by the radioactive cloud.

NUCLEAR ILLNESSES

Dr Gale, who provided much of the medical expertise the Soviets needed for bone marrow transplants on victims predicts as many as 150,000 new cancer cases in the next ten years as a direct result of the Chernobyl fall-out. In Minsk alone the incidences of leukaemia have doubled in five years from 41 million sufferers five years ago to 93 million today. Due to the outdated technology and stagnant economy of the Soviet Union, just a fraction of these people will be cured.

Chernobyl's most lasting legacy will be the mistrust felt by the former Soviet Union's own citizens about a workers' paradise that condemned people to die with disinformation, disorganisation and stupidity.

"The problems will unfold well into the next century," said Igor Ignatchey, a radiation expert from the University of Orel, Ukraine. "It could be 50 years or more before we see the real, lasting effects of this catastrophe unfolding before our eyes. Mental retardation and genetic effects could lie dormant in some generations only to re-occur in others, like black-haired children being born to blonde parents."

The Soviets were quick to find scapegoats. Former director of the plant Viktor Bryukhanov and the former chief engineer Anatoly Dyatlov, in charge of doomed reactor number four, were both asleep when the cooling system failed and blew up at 1.23am. and consequently were jailed for dereliction of duty. Two others received three-year prison terms and two more suspended sentences.

the very earliest nuclear power units where graphite was first used to regulate the nuclear reaction instead of water, as used in most American and British reactors. But most glaringly, said the experts, the Soviets showed a distinct lack of care about safety by not building the reactor with a concrete outer structure that could have contained most of the fire and the subsequent radiation. Such an outer structure was in place in 1978 at the Harrisburg, Pennsylvania plant known as Three Mile Island that suffered a partial meltdown. Because of the outer shell there was no fire, minimal leakage and no deaths.

Gradually, over weeks, months and finally years, the full story of what occurred began to take shape. It was, of course, far worse than the one the Soviets intially peddled to the world. It is now known that over 100,000 people were evacuated from the region and 200,000 more will have to leave because of gross underestimation of the effects of the radiation. Even the government newspaper Izvestia admitted in 1988 that as many as three million people are still living on irradiated land, selling as well as devouring their produce. After close to eight years of bureacratic book-cooking, newly released *Glasnost* health statistics show an increase in blood disorders, freak offspring and

> STATISTICS SHOW AN INCREASE IN BLOOD DISORDERS, FREAK OFFSPRING AND DEFORMED PLANT LIFE

As a macabre postscript to the tragedy of Chernobyl, the Kiev authorities are offering to take death-wish tourists on a tour of the devastated nuclear power plant! Ever-hungry for hard currency, the local tourist bureau apparatchiks are hoping to lure westerners to the dead zone with advertising that promises fairground-type thrills.

And as if to prove their social responsibility, the organisers behind this macabre voyeurism promise takers on the tour a full medical examination afterwards to check for radiation poisoning. Part of the tour which will cost up to £200 for a single day – includes visits to the farms and homes where comrades have defied the Kremlin and returned to the land after the explosion. "Is there a place where people do not die sooner or later?" said Olga Chikolovits, who moved back to her deserted home last November. "Tourists come here all the time with guides who know the region. Now the government is greedy for the money too. Soon we will be animals in a cage and they will be throwing us apples to eat." The Kiev local authority says it sees the trips as "brisk, quick visits"... instead of lingering too long in the dead zone. An official told a New York newspaper: "On hand will be special radiation monitoring equipment and treatment available for anyone who needs it."

A DEAD ZONE

But it is highly unlikely that the land and buildings are completely free from radioactivity. Some scientists believe that it could be up to 100 years before the radiation levels have dropped sufficiently for it not to pose a potential health threat.

Thirty seven died in the reactor explosion and fire. But thousands more have died from radiation poisoning and cancers triggered by the fall-out. Scientist Dr. David Abrhamovitz said: "If tourists were to go there, say, after a rainfall, there would be more chance of a higher radiation level registering than if they went when it was dry because the water would release more toxins in the dry earth. It is not a visit that I would be queuing up to go on. Excursion officials say they will also take in the little town of Slavutich, a radiation-workers' colony that is home to the people who monitor the dead zone and ensure that the radioactive pile is not leaking from its concrete tomb.

> AS A MACABRE POSTSCRIPT, KIEV AUTHORITIES OFFER DEATH-WISH TOURISTS A TOUR OF THE PLANT!

Below: *Major Leonid Telyatnikov, one of the first firefighters on the scene of the Chernobyl disaster, hugs his wife Larisa in the grounds of the hospital where he was treated for radiation cancer.*

The motto of the town is: "Life is good – but too short!"

American writer Francis Clines said: "The notion has the virtue of dark candor, of daring to think the outside world might like to at least leer, if not memorialize, an historic outrage upon one of the earth's humbler landscapes."

Of the 100,000 men who built the concrete vault that now encases the dead reactor, some 25,000 are dead from radiation poisoning. Those that are left alive are classified as heroes in society, entitled to ride free on subways and buses, with 50 per cent discounts on their rents and pay-bonuses on their retirement benefits. They were called "liquidators" by the Soviet government of the day and were every bit as heroic as the firefighters who first tackled the blaze. "They called us heroes," said Serafim Bulkagov who was a supervisor on the Chernobyl sarcophagus. "Yet all the time my friends were dying from radiation. I cannot walk more than ten minutes without feeling exhausted.

"Some heroes. We did what they told us to while the countryside for miles around was polluted. It was a tragedy, yet in all the time I worked for the nuclear industry there were hundreds of mini-Chernobyls. And while the new governments of the Ukraine and Russia build more and more reactors, I fear that there may still be worse to come."

TOWERS OF FEAR
America Tastes Terror

When Arab terrorists planted a bomb that devastated the World Trade Centre in New York they shook not only the victims of the explosion. The entire American nation was shocked that such an atrocity could happen on their home territory.

Terrorists could not have picked a better target for their dual aims of publicity and misery. The twin towers of the World Trade Centre stand at the bottom of the island of Manhattan as the new symbols of New York wealth and power; higher than the Empire State Building, these shimmering, mirror-glass sentinels were a perfect choice by the fanatics who chose a chill February day in 1993 to bring home to America the kind of bloodshed that had been exported to European countries, Israel and the Middle East.

At 12:18a.m. on Friday February 26 a car packed with explosives detonated in an underground garage beneath tower 1, the north tower. The force of the blast was so strong that four levels of the multi-tiered parking complex collapsed like a deck of cards and the roof of the subway station deep underground was blown out. As the earthquake-like shock reverberated through the towers – home to 130,000 workers and visitors each day – it dawned on all inside the leviathan building that something had gone terribly wrong. And it sparked emergency rescue efforts the like of which the battered and bruised Big Apple had never before witnessed.

EARLY WARNINGS

"What the hell was that?" yelled 28-year-old Joseph Gibney, a government lawyer, in his office on the 37th floor of the tower as the low rumble beneath shook everything around him. The phone in his hand went dead and he remembers seeing his office rolling like a wave. Far below him in the basement Joseph Cacciatore, 24, was checking on refrigeration equipment when the blast hit him. The force was so great that it blew out his contact lenses and shattered an

Opposite: The twin towers of the World Trade Centre – to fanatical Arab terrorists they were symbols of a "satanic culture".

TERRORISTS COULD NOT HAVE PICKED A BETTER TARGET FOR THEIR DUAL AIMS OF PUBLICITY AND MISERY

AMERICA EXPERIENCED THE KIND OF BLOODSHED THAT HAD BEEN EXPORTED TO EUROPE, ISRAEL AND THE MIDDLE EAST

Left: *Officials of the FBI and the New York police department sift through the twisted bricks and steel of the World Trade Centre for clues to the bombers.*

eye socket. Covered in blood, he stumbled around in the pitch darkness trying to make sense of a world gone mad. All around him in the pitch darkness he heard the screams of office workers who suddenly thought they were in a war zone. "God help us," they shrieked. "God help us."

Beneath these men and thousands of others lay six bodies in the twisted steel and concrete wreckage. But they couldn't know that – all that they concentrated on was survival as thick acrid smoke began barrelling up through the tower like it was a giant chimeneystack. All emergency lighting systems failed, there were no alarm bells,

> COVERED IN BLOOD, HE STUMBLED AROUND IN THE PITCH DARKNESS TRYING TO MAKE SENSE OF A WORLD GONE MAD

Below: *Rubble outside the World Trade Centre, the tower that fanatical Islamic militants damaged but failed to topple.*

elevators jammed with children stuck in the mammoth lift shafts and panic began coursing through the floors of the second highest building in the world. It was to be the longest day in New York history for rescued and rescuers alike.

Every rescue company in the city's Fire Department raced to the scene. People who still had working phone lines rang into the city's news channels, providing perhaps the world's first running commentary on a disaster while it was unfolding. Lunchtime news viewers heard the descriptions from office workers as they tried to describe the panic, the fear and the desperation which had beset them. A businessman trapped on the 51st floor of the World Trade Centre made a dramatic telephone call to a news show describing the plight of victims in the building. John Cune told the NBC News network: "People are choking in the smoke and breaking windows. The power is out and the building intercom system doesn't seem to be working. I was on a higher floor when the explosion happened and was moved down but there was too much smoke in the emergency stairwells to proceed. People are lying on the ground with napkins on their faces but there's no panic yet. We need help up here." Al Pursell, a businessman who got out, said: "We were like a human crocodile snaking in the darkness. We couldn't see each other so we had to hold on to the person in front. It was a very scary experience." All that day tiny acts of heroism and courage would be played out on all floors of the crippled structure.

A SPIRITED REACTION

Anna Marie Tesoriero will never forget the nightmare. A teacher from Brooklyn, she had just shepherded 17 kindergarten schoolchildren into an elevator from the observation deck and was descending when the lift jammed in total darkness between the 35th and 36th floors. Smoke billowed into the elevator but there was nothing she could do except tell the children to breathe through their scarves and sing nursery rhymes to keep their spirits up. "We told them not to worry but the little ones really missed the light," she said. "I took out a rosary that glowed in the dark and led all the children in prayers and Hail Marys." In the end she was stuck in the elevator for five terrifying hours, saved only when the soot-blackened faces of firemen appeared through a hole they chopped in the side of the lift with their axes.

For Geralyn Hearne, a 28-year-old accountant, the ordeal was just as fearsome. A week short of seven months pregnant, she was terrified for the life of her unborn child as the oily black smoke filled her office on the 43rd floor. She began feeling violently sick, praying for the rescuers whom she feared wouldn't arrive before she and her baby were suffocated in the smoke. Ambulancemen wearing oxygen masks fought their way up an emergency stairwell with firefighters and strapped her to a gurney. Using superhuman strength they carried her down step by step. Rushed to hospital once at ground level, her baby was born by Caesarian section just two hours later. Both were in a serious condition – but both recovered and will live to tell the tale.

BASIC SURVIVAL

As firefighters struggled upwards through the building a human crocodile of frightened workers and visitors poured down the stairwells. Unable to see in front of them they snaked down with one hand on the shoulder of the person in front, the other holding handkerchiefs and rags over their faces in an attempt to breathe easier.

Those who were too frightened to go into the blackened stairwells began smashing the windows high over the streets of New York with their chairs and desks, sending huge shards of glass crashing in a deadly rain to the streets below. The rescue services who heard and saw the pleas of the trapped on the radio and TV used the reporters interviewing the trapped to plead with them to stop breaking the glass as some of it was ripping through hoses playing on the blaze beneath.

There was also a much more serious danger from the broken windows; with the air conditioning and heating ducts not working the smoke was travelling slowly. Breaking the glass had the effect of drawing the smoke up much more rapidly. "We really feared that they would be burned to death instead of just suffering breathing difficulties," said firefighter Jack Mason. "Yet it is hard to tell people in pitch darkness and thick smoke what is best for them. They

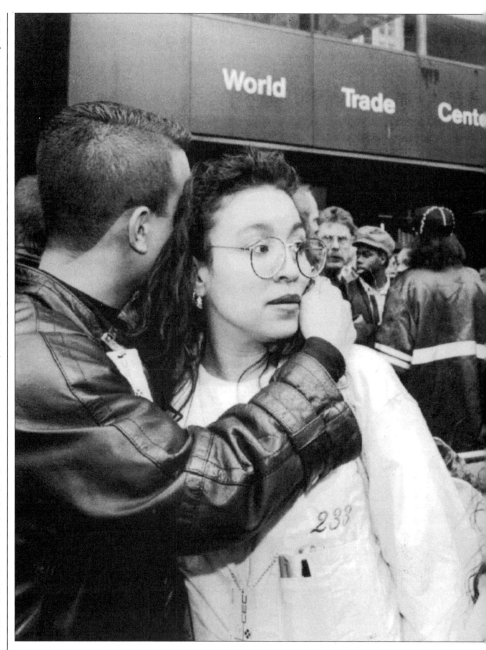

Above: The victims of terror gather in the street outside while hundreds of others remain trapped in the minutes and hours after the blast.

A HUMAN CROCODILE OF FRIGHTENED WORKERS AND SOME VISITORS POURED DOWN THE STAIRWELLS

were all overcome with the instinct to survive at any cost."

One man who could testify to that was David Deshane, a 25-year-old computer specialist trapped on the 105th floor. He said: "I felt the explosion beneath as soon as it had gone off – it was a low rumble that growled through the building steadily. All the computers instantly shut down and then the phones in this office went dead too. Suddenly there was smoke everywhere – thick, black smoke like if you were burning a tyre or something with a lot of plastic on it. I ran to hit the fire emergency button – nothing happened. Someone smashed out a window and we managed to breathe fresh air. I later heard that they wanted people not to break any windows. But did the fire guys know

Right: *A car parked outside the garage of the World Trade Centre that was utterly destroyed by the force of the bomb from within.*

A FLEET OF AMBULANCES STACKED WITH RESPIRATOR BOTTLES WERE LINED UP OUTSIDE THE TOWERS DISPENSING OXYGEN

Below: *The minute inch-by-inch search of the blast area eventually led to clues about the bomb, the van it was in and, ultimately, the villains who had assembled it.*

what trouble we were having just trying to stay alive? It was no small problem."

Firefighters had their own problems too in the confusion. The force of the bomb had blown out a pit 200 feet across in which glowed burning cars and sparking electricity cables. Kevin Shea, 33-year-old member of Rescue Company Number One, was inching his way across the garage floor in the pitch dark when he plunged into the abyss. He landed on a pile of office room dividers that had dropped into the wreckage with the force of the blast. The force of the fall broke his left knee and right foot as hot cinders and rocks caused him serious back and face injuries. He lay wounded for three hours until colleagues came to his rescue. Lt. Joe Ward, 56, of Ladder Co. Six, heard the low moans coming through the smoke and stench and crept to the edge. A powerful beam of light pinpointed his comrade and soon a team of six firefighters hoisted their buddy to safety. The crippled Cacciatore, still blinded and in great pain, was found by the same rescue team on their way back to the surface. He had been spraying himself with water from a shattered main to fend off the heat and was carried out, by two firemen. He made a full recovery.

INSTANT HEROES

One of the most strength-draining and inspiring rescues was carried out by two attorneys known as Jack and Andy. Both decided to lift wheelchair-bound lawyer Gibney down to the ground. He weighed close to 200lbs but the young men went 400 steps with him draped over their shoulders before collapsing in the fresh air outside. "I don't know what would have happened to me if these good samaritans hadn't happened along," said Gibney.

In sleet and snow outside, a fleet of ambulances stacked with respirator bottles were lined up outside the towers dispensing life-giving bursts of oxygen. The tired, terrified, blackened faces of the office girls and dark-suited fund managers said it all. They were all tired and despairing, but nothing could disguise the delight in their eyes that they had made it out alive. Over a thousand workers and visitors were rushed to hospitals in the metropolitan area for treatment, although most of them were released after several hours.

In the searing heat beneath the towers, at the bomb's epicentre, a casualty of the blast were the Secret Service limousines used to shuttle the president around on his travels in the New York area. President Clinton's customised £150,000 armoured Secret Service Lincoln Continental was one of several of the agency's cars destroyed. Exploding ammunition in the Secret Service limousines added to the effects of the bomb which destroyed a huge underground area – the wreckage in which the only fatalities of the disaster were located.

"This was a cowardly, criminal, callous act," said Raymond Kelly, New York's Police Commissioner as he visited the wreckage of New York's crown jewel. "All resources are being channelled into finding those responsible and bringing them to justice." President Clinton received hourly briefings from FBI, police and forensic experts labouring to piece together the jigsaw puzzle of clues left behind by the massive blast. "It is a sign of how seriously the investigation is being taken in Washington," said a Justice Department spokesman in the wake of the explosion "We have set up a War Room – a War Room in every sense of the word because America is now at war with persons aiming to disrupt or destroy our way of life. There will be no let-up until those responsible are found."

The main fear for law enforcers was that a well-trained cell of terrorists was in place in America with the dedication and logistical back up to commit further outrages. A unit called the Serbian Liberation Front – hitherto unheard of – was one of the groups which claimed responsibility for the blast. A caller, one of 19 who telephoned police emergency lines on the day, phoned in 75 minutes after detonation saying the explosion was in retaliation for the American airlift of food to Bosnian Moslem foes which

> NOTHING COULD DISGUISE THE DELIGHT IN THE EYES OF THOSE WHO HAD MANAGED TO MAKE IT OUT ALIVE

Below: *Firemen and rescue crews lower a woman from the upper reaches of the 110-storey tower after the blast plunged the skyscraper into darkness, chaos and terror.*

Above: *A scene repeated many times in the aftermath of the explosion – rescue workers dragging victims, their mouths and noses blackened by smoke, into the fresh air and safety.*

WITH THE AID OF AN EGYPTIAN INFORMER, THE POLICE FOUND THE CULPRITS WITHIN WEEKS

began that weekend. This caller identified precisely where the bomb had detonated.

Yet dogged police work, with the aid of an Egyptian informer named Emad Salem, fingered those responsible within weeks. The men behind the bombing were Middle Eastern fanatics, children of terror raised in the cauldron of the ongoing war between Israel and Arab states who looked to Moslem fundamentalism as their future – and regarded America as the Great Satan which stood in their way. They were linked with a group caught mixing bombs in March 1993 – devices with which they intended to devastate New York in the summer of the same year. World leaders, landmark buildings and headquarters of crimefighters were all to be targeted by the fanatical killers. Eight people were arrested – Egyptians, Palestinians and one American – in midnight swoops in the Queens section of the city and the follow-

ing day FBI boss William Sessions said that the arrests prevented a "bloodbath" on the streets of New York.

EVIL PLANS

A death list found by FBI agents had Egyptian premier Hosni Mubarak on it, earmarked for assassination during his visit to the city's United Nations HQ in September. United nations cheif Boutros Boutros Ghali, also an Egyptian, was marked for death too. And there were plans for a massive bomb to devastate the U.N. building situated on Manhattan's East River. One of the most macabre acts planned was the bombing of the Lincoln Tunnel at the height of the rush hour. The tunnel connects Manhattan with New Jersey and is used by hundreds of thousands of commuters daily. The FBI building in the city was also on the list of targets and a local politician, Senator Alfonse D'Amato, was marked for assassination. A Justice Department spokesman said he was "staggered" by the scope and size of the terror plot. Referring to the plot to bomb the Lincoln Tunnel he said: Can you imagine the Hudson River pouring in at rush hour? It would have been loss of life on a staggering scale. Several of the men seized were mixing bombs with commercially available chemicals when FBI SWAT teams broke into their lairs. Found with them were schematic drawings of all the locations that were targetted, together with the names of those to be murdered.

LIFE SENTENCES

In March 1994, screaming abuse at jurors and proclaiming the justness of their cause, four fanatics who sought to turn New York into a kind of terrorist playground like Beirut or Belfast, were found guilty on numerous terrorist charges that put them behind bars for most of their lives. The five month trial ended almost exactly one year after the single most destructive act of terrorism America had ever endured – the stunning World Trade Centre explosion which not only took life, but shattered America's belief that it was remote from merciless terror which has been part of other nations' experience for decades.

At the trial it was revealed that the bomb which destroyed the tower basement was in a parked van and weighed 1,200lbs. The FBI, using thousands of man hours, managed to re-build the van from its shattered carcass and piece together vital bomb pieces, even locating parts of the detonator. The nitrate traces left over from the explosion were later matched with the bomb making equipment found at the homes of two of the seized men.

The court heard testimony how four of the N.Y. Port Authority workers whose offices and locker rooms were in the basement where the bomb exploded were literally blown to smithereens while the other two victims – people who had innocently parked their cars there – died from concussion. But it was also clear that the carnage could have been 1,000 times worse. A bomb expert told the trial: "Another few pounds of explosives, or the more strategic positionining of the van which contained the device,

might have resulted in a significant weakening of the structure which could have rendered stairwells useless and left thousands of people choking in the acrid smoke which filtered upwards through the tower."

Yet such humane sentiments were lost on defendants Mohammed Salameh, Mahmud Aboulhalima, Ahmed Ajaj and Nidal Ayyad. They were on a mission from God, warriors in the war to spread Moslem fundamentalism to their own country – Egypt – and to other Arab countries. They went to the cells shouting defiance and obscenities in the face of overwhelming evidence, each one receiving life sentences.

Several others have yet to stand trial, including Sheik Omar Abdel-Rahman, a blind Egyptian cleric said to be the spiritual leader of the gang. It is a supreme irony for him that his trial will take place in the Manhattan courthouse which stands in the shadow of the gigantic building his followers swore to raze to the ground.

THE FOUR FANATICS WERE FOUND GUILTY ON CHARGES THAT PUT THEM BEHIND BARS FOR MOST OF THEIR LIVES

Below: *He may look like a harmless old cleric, but blind Sheik Omar Abdel Rahman was the spiritual leader of those who murdered innocents in the World Trade Centre.*

THE SUNSET LTD
Amtrak's Nightmare

What should have been a luxurious trip became unforgettable for all the wrong reasons when the coaches of The Sunset Limited plunged off a bridge in Florida. Some passengers met their deaths by drowning, others faced alligators.

For the passengers aboard the luxury train The Sunset Limited it was supposed to be a night to remember – a ride through some of the most beautiful countryside in America on an express ranked as one of the best in the world. The passengers on board, many of them British tourists en route to the sunshine of Florida, drank and sang with friends as the train rolled effortlessly through the southern states. Others dozed, chatted or simply enjoyed the lingering southern night which extended the light on the bayous and creeks of the wetlands, replete with exotic wildlife including alligators and flamingoes. For 20th century travellers the comfort and serenity of the train was a throwback to a more golden, more refined age of travel.

And it was to become a night to remember – although not in any way that the innocent passengers could have forseen or wanted. In the early hours of September 22 1993 the Sunset Limited crashed, exploded and plunged into an alligator-infested creek near Mobile, Alabama, after the bridge spanning the water had been weakened due to a barge collision in dense fog. In the next few hours there were untold acts of heroism played out in the darkness as the best in man surfaced to help those suffering and in danger.

For many, in those first seconds in the oil-slicked water, illuminated by the fierce fires of the blazing double-headed locomotive, the screams of the dying pierced the still night air as alligators swarmed around the victims. Survivors thrashed in the water as they escaped from submerged coaches, desperately trying to reach shore in a nighttime scene lit with the flames of the disaster. "It was an unreal scene from Hades," said Mobile Fire Department spokesman Steve Huffman. "It was foggy, there was noise, there was fire, there were screams, there were 'gators, there was panic. It was a nightmare scenario. It must be every

Opposite: *The broken bridge and wrecked carriages left in the aftermath of the Sunset Limited disaster.*

Below: *The scene on the morning following the crash.*

Above: An unassuming hero, Cliff Hurst from London, found superhuman stamina and courage to work throughout the night rescuing survivors from the murky waters of the bayou.

THE NIGHT WATER REFLECTED BACK DOZENS OF PAIRS OF RED EYES — EYES OF THE 'GATORS IN THE RIVER

person's fear to be in water with alligators that you can't see."

Briton Simon Grant, 25, from Reading, Berkshire, who was in a coach towards the back of the eight-car train heading for Miami from Los Angeles, gave a dramatic description on American TV of his ordeal. He said: "It was a nightmare. I was just dozing off in the rear coach. I woke up and the train was like a roller coaster slowing down. We came to a complete standstill like a car hitting a brick wall. I felt like I was in an airline seat. My head hit the seat in front and dazed me. I got up and people were screaming. It was dark because all the power had gone. The electric door wouldn't open and people began to panic. Eventually one of these Amtrak chaps smashed a window for us to get out of. I was one of the fortunate ones because I was in the rear.

The front of the train, two coaches on, were on a bridge and the bridge collapsed in the middle and went straight into the water. The front car and engines were just alight, and completely exploded in a big orange ball across the sky. I saw people in the water, or swamp, or whatever it was, swimming to get to shore."

Londoner Cliff Hurst survived the carnage in Mobile along with Ayrshire man Brian McConnell. Hurst said: "The train had gone into the water and was burning but we couldn't get down there to help. No way could we get to it so we went down the bank a bit further along. I waded out to the people in the water and helped drag them in. They stank from the stagnant water and from the diesel fuel which burned their eyes and made them feel sick. There was near panic among many in the water who couldn't swim or who felt they weren't strong enough to attempt to make it to shore. I just did my bit for everyone I could. I could see some girls in their nightdresses treading water, but they managed to make it back under their own steam. It was a hellish night."

ALLIGATOR ALERT

The Sunset Limited plunged into a spur of the Mobile River on the outskirts of Mobile after jumping the tracks on the wooden bridge over Cabot Bayou. The tracks had been dislocated due to the barge collision and the weight of the train collapsed the weakened structure. The river is composed of the brown, slow-flowing, brackish water that alligators thrive on. As survivors trod water and attempted to get to shore the night water reflected back dozens of pairs of red eyes – the eyes of the 'gators that traditionally lay claim to the river.

In all, 47 would die in the wreckage, including a mother and father who pushed their handicapped son to safety through a broken window while they were left behind to drown in their sinking compartment. Aside from the professional rescuers, the firemen and policemen and divers who selflessly worked through the night and following day to help the stricken, the single biggest hero of the disaster emerged as 26-year-old Michael Dopheide, credited with saving 30 of the 163 survivors. A soft-spoken graduate in law, he was taking a few well-earned months' rest before embarking on his legal career. The Omaha native had boarded the Sunset Limited two days earlier in Los Angeles and was, like many other tourists on board, en route for the sunshine and beaches of Florida.

At 3.00am his world and that of his fellow passengers came to a devastating halt. "People were screaming and moaning and groaning," he recalled. "I couldn't see much because of the near-total darkness. One woman shouted: 'Oh my God, we're all gonna die!'

"My coach was sixth from the front in the 11-car train and was tilted in the air at a 45-degree angle, hanging off the bridge."

The double-decker train had hit the bridge at 70mph, enough force to bury the lead locomotive 57 feet deep into the bayou bank. As he struggled to see he could make out that four cars, including two of the passenger coaches, lay strewn in the water while four others, including his own, teetered on the remnants of the bridge.

Without thinking of himself – "there was no time to think, I was really one of the only people in the car who could have done what needed to be done" – he struggled to an emergency exit and gazed at the 25-feet-deep water six feet below. The bridge was in danger of imminent collapse and the car was filling with choking smoke from the burning loco's diesel fuel. "I coaxed people out," he said, "and made them form a chain in the water. I towed those who couldn't swim and guided them

Above: *Two survivors huddle together – shattered, cold and weary but alive.*

Below: *The passengers of coach 34040 were luckiest of all... if it had travelled another foot it would have plunged into the water.*

Coach 34040

Above: *The grimmest task of all came to rescue divers and police boatmen, who pulled bodies from the water throughout the day.*

to a metal girder ten feet away where they could hang on. A tow boat from a barge came on the scene and was able to drop a line to an old woman and a couple of kids before it got beaten back by the smoke and flames. Some I towed to the roof of one of the cars in the water, the others we got to shore in a human chain. I just did what had to be done." But Donnie Hughes, 54, is one survivor who looks on him as a saint. She said after she was rescued: "I am covered in diesel, I can't swim, my eyes are on fire and this boy's arms are pulling me up to safety. I didn't even know his name then. But I do now, and I will never forget him."

LIFE OR DEATH

"He coaxed me into the water when I really didn't want to go, and yet I knew I had to if I wanted to live. I was on the metal frame of the window before I jumped in and I started having flashbacks to when I was eight and I nearly drowned. The only light is from the fires of the locomotive and the flames are spreading closer. This boy, this

THERE WERE HEROIC ACTS AND SUPREME MOMENTS OF COURAGE IN THE HOURS FOLLOWING THE CRASH

beautiful boy with his arms outstretched below me, looked up and said: 'Come on, it's OK, I got ya, I got ya.' I jumped down and my whole life flashed before me. And then he saved me. I will remember him until the day I die."

For George Simpson, a 73-year-old man who was saved, along with his wife Carole, words will never adequately express his gratitude. "He was a hero," he said. "If there is one hero in all of this it is Michael." Michael was also the man who tugged 11-year-old cerebral palsy victim Andrea Chancey to safety when her parents perished in the flooded carriage they had been sharing moments earlier.

Of course there were other heroic acts and supreme moments of courage in the hours following the crash. Because of the remoteness of the scene, miles from any major town or highway, help was slow in getting to those who were in the water. Luckily the noise of the crash and the explosions and subsequent flames had driven away any alligators that usually lurked in the water. But in the eerie pre-dawn darkness, as smoke and fog clogged the air and the wails of the injured filled the sky, that seemed little consolation.

Police divers were among the first at the scene, the water lit for them by helicopters using searchlights which also played a part in keeping the alligators at bay. Police chief Harold Johnson said: "All rescue efforts were hampered by the burning diesel fuel, the fog and the natural murkiness of the water. At times visibility was a mere six inches. And there was no way to get heavy lifting equipment to the scene. It was a hell of a night."

ELEGANCE WASTED

The doomed train that now lay wrecked was put in service by the American passenger company Amtrak in April 1993 to bring back the 'age of elegance' to rail travel. The Sunset Limited provided gourmet food, white linen tablecloths, silver tableware, crystal glasses and fine sleeping cabins for passengers – although souvenir hunters stole most of the china after the

BODIES WERE LAID ALONG THE RAILWAY EMBANKMENT, COVERED IN COATS AND IN BODY-BAGS SUPPLIED BY A LOCAL MORGUE

Below: *Huge barge cranes had to be deployed to lift the carriages and locos weighing hundreds of tons.*

inaugural trip. It is the first scheduled trans-continental train in 163 years with stops at 50 stations en route – places with such evocative names as Biloxi, New Orleans, Pensecola, El Paso and Phoenix. Amtrak sold the train as a romantic way to travel in the age of sterile airplanes and airports, emphasising the breathtaking scenery on the way of Pine Forests, dogwood plants, crawdad ponds, the smoke-spewing oil stacks of Houston and the tumbleweed desolateness of Arizona.

It was often compared to the Orient Express, although its luxury was far more affordable. But the only service that it proved capable of rendering by first light on September 22 was as a safe haven for some non-swimmers to cling to until help came. With the dawn came the full realisation of the disaster with the sight of bodies laid along the railway embankment, covered in coats and in body-bags supplied by a local morgue.

As the survivors slept or wept on the embankment, waiting to be attended to by dozens of doctors and nurses who donned

clothes over their pyjamas and nighties to attend to the wounded, those still able to talk told news reporters at the scene the stories of their escape. Elizabeth Watts, from Califoria, remembered being catapaulted out of her seat and clambering to safety as water poured into the half-submerged car. She said: "It was like a combination of the worst roller coaster and the worst horror show you have ever experienced. It looked like the Pirates of the Caribbean show at Disneyworld, black with all these fires and electrical wires

dark water, a testament to the horror below, bobbed babies' milk bottles, a pushchair, suitcases, diaries, books that people had been reading with the page folded down at their place. There would be many among the passengers who would never get to read those final pages.

For Mark Dowers, a police diver, the worst was yet to come. By the time he began looking for survivors beneath the water – operating on the slim chance that some people might be trapped in air pockets – he knew in his heart of hearts that he would

Above: *A portion of The Sunset Limited lies like a twisted snake of steel in the water.*

snapping. And we all thought, every one of us, that we were goners. I managed to slither out of a window like a fish escaping from a cracked goldfish bowl. It was utter terror and I thank God I am alive.

"Myself and three others made it to some logs, but they were too close to burning diesel fuel that looked like spreading our way, so we struck out for the shore and came to rest among some cypress trees and magnolia. It was three hours before any help reached us." On the surface of the

only find corpses. But that didn't make his job any easier: "There were some people sleeping, some still in their nightclothes. Some were dressed up, some were naked. I pulled out 33 bodies in all. I didn't pull up any live people at all. There was one old lady, she had her hands up in front of her face, and her eyes open like she was trying to fight the water. When rigor mortis sets in the last state they were in is what they are for eternity. I was operating totally automatically down there. It was like stacking the bodies in a bucket. It was like war and that is what I compared it to in my mind." It was later determined that most of the victims had drowned, overwhelmed in the first two cars by the massive inrush of water when the train plunged into the bayou.

Edward Mouton, a 20-year-old passenger from Los Angeles, provided a graphic account of the panic that broke out in some carriages after the crash. He said: "Many went crazy with fear because there was simply no-one around from the railroad company to help them. I think if there had been the sight of someone in uniform or someone able to offer words of comfort that might have helped. But obviously the engine crew were dead and there was no sign of anyone else.

"It really was a case of every man for himself and in a situation which even the most hardened would have found hard to bear. I was in a car that didn't go into the water and was throwing out of the window sheets and blankets down to the riverside to those people who had. Some people were hysterical, like in the movies.

There were a lot of old people on the train and they were in a state of fear and bewilderment too. It was a very unpleasant and unnerving experience. You could smell the smoke from the fires burning in the engine car and see ash falling from the sky. But it was so foggy you really couldn't see the water."

By the end of the day the crash of the Sunset Limited had gone down in U.S. history as one of the worst. It became clear that a barge licensed to ply the waters of the Mobile River had cut down the spur of the Cabot Bayou for a rest and hit one of the bridge's supporting pillars. An enquiry is still underway in America regarding the captain of the towboat pulling the barge. The railway tracks were moved out of line, but because sensors on the rail only give a warning if the tracks are severed completely, there was no way for the driver of the express to know that he was rattling towards his own doom and that of so many innocent others. In the wake of the crash there are ongoing reviews of the safety devices deployed on American railroads and calls for tougher bridges to be built along the hundreds of thousands of miles of track. Yet such innovations will be of little comfort to the relatives of those who loved lost ones on a night they hoped to remember for the rest of their lives.

THE CRASH OF THE SUNSET LIMITED HAS GONE DOWN IN AMERICAN HISTORY AS ONE OF THE WORST TRAIN DISASTERS

Below: *A policeman stands guard while some of his colleagues identify bodies before they are taken to the mortuary.*

CARRIAGE CARNAGE
Commuter Hell

Few journeys appear as risk-free as a ride home to the suburbs after work in the city. But on one evening in New York, what should have been a routine train trip turned into terror as a crazed gunman fired a hail of bullets into his fellow passengers.

No one noticed the sullen black man sitting in the corner of the train, hunched furtively over, or if they did they quickly looked away. This was New York, after all, and it doesn't do to stare too long at an individual for fear he may be drunk, or deranged, or drug addict-ed, or armed or all four at once. Besides, the crowds pouring into his carriage on the night of Tuesday December 7 at the city's Penn Station were pre-occupied with get-ting home to friends and loved ones, their arms weighed down with more baggage than usual as early Christmas shopping had been done in their lunch breaks and imme-diately after work.

So Colin Ferguson sat silently in the cor-ner of the train, brooding over what he felt was his slighted life and bracing himself for the ultimate revenge. The 5.35 pm train jolted out of the station into the cool night air, the commuters aboard burying them-selves in their usual travel habits – some reading books, others newspapers, still more sitting silently or nodding off for a snooze on the journey out to Long Island. The Island, as most New Yorkers refer to it, is a suburban sprawl of commuter homes that are far more affordable to most than the skyscraper penthouses of Manhattan. All those aboard the train bound for Hicksville were so wrapped up in their own routines that they failed to notice Ferguson stir in his seat, bring out a Ruger semi-

Opposite: *Colin Ferguson, the man who gave a new meaning to rush hour hell when he pumped bullets into innocents on their way home from offices.*

THEY FAILED TO NOTICE FERGUSON STIR IN HIS SEAT AND BRING OUT A RUGER SEMI-AUTOMATIC PISTOL

Below: *A police officer examines one of the bodies left from Ferguson's grim harvest of death on the Long Island Railroad.*

Above: *Police stand outside car three of the Long Island Railroad Train where Ferguson went berserk.*

Hell on wheels is too banal a phrase to describe what happened next in the railway car. Rising from his seat in car number three, after the train had left New Hyde Park station en route for Merillon Avenue, Ferguson calmly walked from the seat and began his human harvest. Survivors later described him as "cool and methodical", as he aimed directly at the heads of the passengers and began squeezing off the lethal .9 mm rounds – of which he had over 100. In seconds a car full of people anticipating nothing more adventurous than a midweek movie and a quiet dinner were plunged into a life or death lottery.

Ferguson, a 35-year-old Jamaican immigrant with a warped and seething resentment for whites, and also those blacks who he viewed as subservient to whites, capitalised on the horror of the passengers to continue his massacre unhindered. Crack! crack! The shots rang out in the car. David Farrell, 23, who was sitting near him ini-

automatic pistol and begin loading it with bullets for his brief shining moments of revenge against the white race. Within 30 minutes the fury that had boiled within this disturbed individual for years would spill over into one of the worst incidents of handgun violence in American history.

> HE AIMED DIRECTLY AT THE HEADS OF THE PASSENGERS AND BEGAN SQUEEZING OFF THE LETHAL ROUNDS

Right: *The grim task of removing those passengers who couldn't walk out was left to firemen and police officers.*

tially in the rear of the carriage, said: "I thought that it was the sounds of a cap gun, like a starting pistol. It was only after the fourth or fifth shot that I started hearing the screams. And I said: 'Holy s**t! That is no cap gun.' Two women dived on to the floor at my feet and I saw that the surface of the floor had become slick with a thick red goo – it was blood. I put my hands on my head and dived for the floor. After that a couple of guys jumped on top of me. There was mass panic in the car. People were jumping every which way to get away from the shooter, but there was nowhere to go."

The victims fell forward in their seats,

bundles of paperwork inside would save him if Ferguson got him in his sights. He said: "As I sat there I could feel him walk past me as he was shooting, but I wasn't hit. I think that if I had run up the aisle I would have been a goner. I just lay very still and tried not to draw attention to myself. It was a nightmare scenario – helpless as this man is gunning to death people like me all around."

So deliberate yet so casual, Ferguson even paused in the middle of the massacre to re-load his gun. He turned and began walking back to his seat when Zaleskie heard the shouts of "grab him, grab him!" It was the

THE VICTIMS FELL FORWARD IN THEIR SEATS, FLOPPING CRAZILY LIKE STORE MANNEQUINS PUSHED INTO POSITION

Left: *Colin Ferguson is equipped with a bullet-proof vest for his first court appearances. Feelings were running so high it was believed someone might assassinate him.*

flopping crazily like store mannequins pushed casually into position. Ferguson had chosen lethally efficient Black Talon hollow-point bullets – ammo expressly designed to do the maximum amount of damage to the victim.

On and on he moved down the aisleway, firing mostly at whites. Some commuters managed to open the doors connecting the carriages, but others just fell to the floor and tried feebly to hide under seats and pray that the grim reaper wouldn't target them. Kevin Zaleskie, 39, pulled his briefcase up over his head, hoping that thick

heroic actions of three men who undoubtedly saved every single person in the carriage from becoming a corpse. As he ambled back Kevin Blum, 42, Michael O'Connor, 32, and Mark McEntee, 34, piled on him and forced him down into a seat. The gunman, in a moment of remorse, looked at them, dropped his gun, and said: "Oh my God, what have I done, what have I done? Whatever happens I deserve what I get." One man, weeping with fear, yelled at him: "You son of a bitch, you deserve a thousand times more than whatever you get."

O'Connor, who said he had no inten-

SO DELIBERATE YET SO CASUAL, FERGUSON EVEN PAUSED IN THE MIDDLE OF THE MASSACRE TO RE-LOAD HIS GUN

tions of being a hero, said the decision to rush Ferguson was a simple matter of choosing life over death. He said: "It was obvious that if we didn't get him he would get us and every other person in the coach. He was slow and deliberate in his aim and there was no compassion, no look of regret in his eyes for what he was doing. He just aimed, pulled the trigger and moved on. I heard this guy Kevin – who I had only got talking to minutes earlier and had never met – shout: 'Let's get him' and we did. We pushed him on to a seat with his face up and his back to the wall of the coach. Blum had his knees on the guy's chest and I his right arm and the other guy his left. He kept saying: 'I deserve whatever I get... I deserve whatever I get.' He also said: 'God will treat me well.' It was all gibberish. But he basically collapsed like a sack of potatoes.

> THERE WAS SO MUCH
> BLOOD THAT PEOPLE FELL
> IN POOLS OF IT AND
> SMEARED IT OVER THE
> GLASS DOORS

To O'Connor and the others it seemed "like an eternity" while they waited for someone in authority to come along and take the gunman into custody. Eventually LIRR police officer Andrew Roderick arrived, cuffed Ferguson and marched him off. O'Connor's mother Patty, who heard and saw of her son's bravery on the nightly news broadcast, said proudly: "To this moment, I don't think he realises how close he came to being a victim or how brave he was. I have nothing but admiration for him, which I am sure is shared by all of New York, if not the entire United States."

AN AWFUL SIGHT

Lying on the floor of the carriage, slumped on seats, arranged at awkward angles, were the dead, dying and injured. There was so much blood that people fell in pools of it

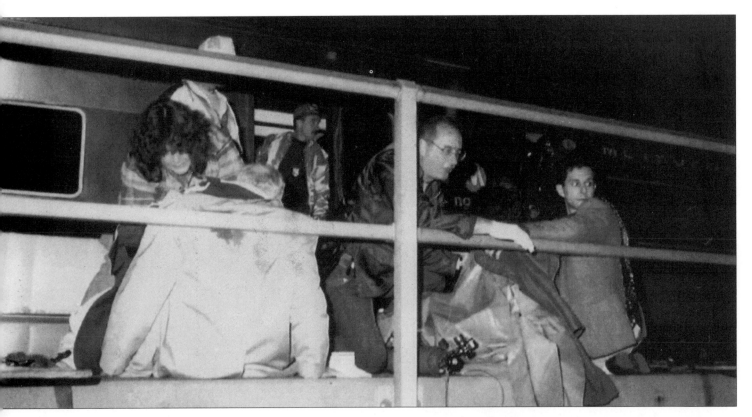

"He was a big guy and he could have put up far more of a struggle, but it was like he was glad in a way it was all over. I don't feel heroic for what happened, it was just something that had to be done. The doors of the train were still closed and there was the potential right there for him to kill every last one of us. It was a survival instinct taking over, pure and simple."

Above: First aid was administered to the wounded before ambulances could come to race them to local hospitals.

and smeared it over the glass doors they prised apart to scream for help. Among the casualties was Dennis McCarthy of Minneola, who had only recently started taking the train to and from the city with his son Kevin. Now Dennis lay dead and his son was severely wounded with brain damage. His widow Carolyn sobbed later: "My husband had been taking the 42

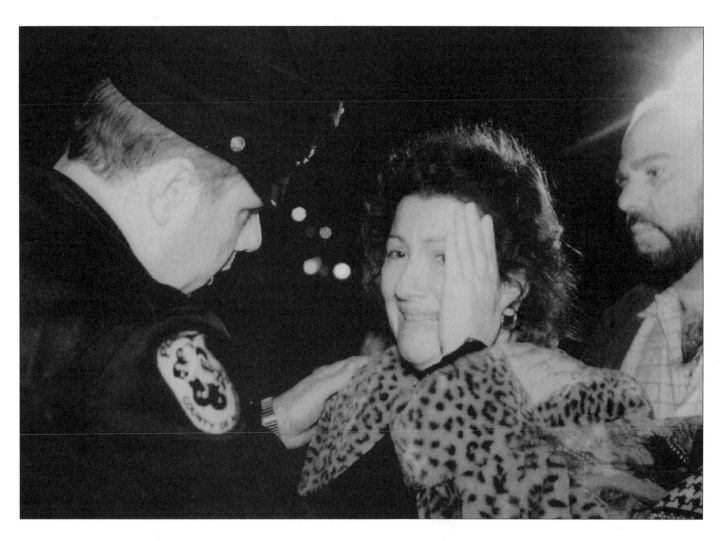

minute train ride for twenty years. My son had only just begun riding the line after getting a job. It was real quality time for them both – my husband really enjoyed the bonding with our son. Now Kevin, who is only 26, is paralysed and will probably remain so. How could someone do this to my family? Why, why, why?"

A FATAL DECISION

For the Gorycki family the question was the same. James Gorycki had worked for 15 years on the island and had only recently begun to take the train after a promotion meant re-location into the city. His weeping widow Joyce said: "For years I worried about him driving in all the traffic. Then he finally decides to take the train and I feel good for him and now this happens. He was a wonderful, gentle man. He did everything by the book. He didn't deserve to be gunned down like some mad dog by a crazy with a gun." In all six people were killed and 25 wounded.

Above: *A police officer comforts one of the victims who survived Ferguson's crusade of death.*

A FLEET OF AMBULANCES
FERRIED THE WOUNDED
AND THE MENTALLY
TRAUMATISED SURVIVORS
TO HOSPITALS

One of the wounded was lawyer Thomas McDermott, 50, a Vietnam veteran who survived some of the worst battles of that terrible conflict only to be hit in the shoulder by one of the first rounds loosed off by Ferguson. He recalled: "I had a flak jacket, helmet and rifle in Vietnam. Here I was dressed in slacks and a blazer. I felt the pain of the bullet and went down on the floor, certain that I was going to take another one. It was a feeling of wonderment and helplessness. I was just amazed at the powerlessness I felt. God's good graces saved me. This experience is absolutely going to change my life. I thought about it and now I have more of an appreciation and knowledge that life is so fleeting."

After the massacre a fleet of ambulances ferried the wounded and the mentally traumatised survivors to hospitals. People living by the railway opened their homes as relief stations for the commuters to calm their nerves and ring frightened loved ones who had learned of the massacre due to the instantaneous local TV news reports. Joan

Right: *A Long Island Railroad train identical to the one which Colin Ferguson boarded at New York's Penn Station for his bloody ride.*

FERGUSON HAD DELUSIONS FOR YEARS, A PARANOID SCHIZOPHRENIC WHO BELIEVED IT WAS HIM AGAINST THE WORLD

HIS PROLONGED UNEMPLOYMENT IN THE BIG APPLE WAS WHAT FINALLY LIT THE FUSE OF THIS TICKING TIME BOMB

Caryle, whose home bordered the rail line, was praised as a heroine by the police, but she said: "I only did what any human being would do. I comforted them and gave them a drink, let them use the phone. God, I hope someone would do the same for me if I was in a similar situation. It is common humanity, the thread that binds us all together."

A MURDER MYSTERY

Ferguson was led away in handcuffs, his bloody night's work behind him. Who was he – what was his motive? At first police could only go on the items he possessed as he refused to tell them anything. Among the deranged notes police found on him and later at his home were these:

"NYC was spared because of my respect for Mayor David Dinkins and Commissioner Raymond Kelly, officially still in office. Nassau County is the venue. Also that Chinese mother f***er Sue will never put me to shame again without cause.

Reasons for this: Adelphi University's Racism, the EEOC's racism, workers' compensation racism, NYC transit police, NYC police, the racism of Governor Cuomo's staff and execution chamber. The racism of the Lt. Governor's staff and execution chamber. This includes Susan Whitley and Carol Goestel. Additional reasons for this:

The sloppy running of the no. 2 train. It is racism by Caucasians and Uncle Tom

negroes. Also, the false allegations against me by the filthy caucasian racist female on the no. 1 train. Also the racism of Mark Martin and the legal aid society and court system. Also those filthy swines who live at 226 Martense Street Brooklyn. Once they hear of this they will loot all the evidence in my room such as documents and tapes. I hate them with a passion. In case of emergency call. Also for those corrupt black attorneys who not only refused to help me but who tried to steal my car. Also those so-called civil rights leaders such as the Rev. Herbert Vernon Mason and Calvin Butts."

Ferguson's incoherent ramblings were the key to a tormented soul who blamed anyone and anything for his problems in life other than himself. Born in January 1958 in Kingston, Jamaica, his life from childhood onwards deteriorated into a succession of disappointments, each one greater than the last – in school, in college, in work, in marriage until finally he snapped. He had delusions for years, a paranoid schizophrenic who believed it was him against the world. James Fox, co-author of *Mass Murder: America's Growing Menace* and an authority on random spree-killings, said that Ferguson's prolonged unemployment in the Big Apple was what finally lit the fuse of his ticking time bomb. He said: "This train was full of commuters with jobs with money in their back pockets and with families who loved them waiting at home –

everything that he didn't have. He carried these enormous resentments around with him, functioning apparently normally, but all the while with the rage growing and growing and getting harder and harder to contain. Stung by disappointments, he had convinced himself that what was wrong with his life was caused by everyone around who impinged on it; in his twisted reasoning they were all to blame and so they had to die."

HATE-FILLED HEROES

Such reasoning caught on with some. A fanatical black leader – a disciple of the late Malcolm X – dubbed the mad gunman a hero. Hate-filled followers at a rally cheered when he called Ferguson "brave", and "on a mission from God". Nation of Islam leader Khalid Muhammad fuelled racial tensions in the Big Apple with his praise for Ferguson. He chose a black university in Washington to deliver his hate-filled sermon.

Two thousand cheering students at Howard University heard him scream: "Colin Ferguson killed all those white people on the Long Island train. I love Colin Ferguson!" Describing his actions as "heroic" he went on: "God spoke to Colin Ferguson and said: 'Catch the train, Colin, catch the train!'" In a further rant against Jews he said: "I am going to be like a pit bull. That is the way I am going to be against Jews. I am going to bite the tail of the honkies."

He singled out the government for funding the Holocaust Museum in Washington which chronicles the extermination of the Jews saying: "Not one dollar has been put aside for our holocaust, which is still taking place." Joyce Gorycki, whose husband James was among Ferguson's victims on the railway, said: "I am outraged and disgusted. What would he have said if a relative of his had been killed on the train?"

Since his capture the defence being put forward by his lawyers has become as controversial as the crime he committed. His lawyer Ronald Kuby says: "Nobody is saying that Colin Ferguson did a good thing. Nobody is saying that he was justified. We are not saying that people should name their children after him or follow in his footsteps. We are just saying that he is not responsible for his own conduct – that white racism was to blame." This defence strategy has not gone down with the cell block inmates sharing hard-time with Ferguson while he is on remand awaiting trial. In March 1994 five of them beat him severely, breaking his nose and smashing his ribs in a frenzied assault.

"Let him tell the fancy lawyers that it was rage," said one. "In here he's lower than a child molester. What he did on that train was unforgivable. If it hadn't been for those three guys, there would have been so many more dead. Even the cons think those guys are heroes."

Above: *The New York Post screams news of the appalling massacre on its front page the next day.*

FIVE INMATES BEAT HIM SEVERELY, BREAKING HIS NOSE AND SMASHING HIS RIBS IN A FRENZIED ASSAULT

THE LA QUAKE
Californian Tears

Los Angeles, one of the world's wealthiest cities, had no protection against a natural disaster that swept in in the night and destroyed lives, property and dreams. The only consolation was the heroism some LA citizens showed under pressure.

The City of Angels slept peacefully on that January night, slumbering beneath a billion desert stars. On the freeways rolled the early morning trucks bringing goods into the sprawling southern Californian metropolis, their passage marked by a low rumble that spread through the neighbourhoods all across the great city. Yet the scene of peacefulness was shattered when a 45-second earthquake plunged America's second city of Los Angeles into death and destruction on a massive scale. The city which had been quiet and tranquil one moment reeled in the next under the hammer blow from the earth's core which sparked raging fires, buckled motorways and destroyed homes and offices with lightning speed.

NATURAL FORCE

Cement and steel designed to withstand the worst kind of earthquake collapsed like a Chinese lantern in seconds. Six freeways were out of action by the time the trembling had ceased and police helicopters circled the crippled arteries of the city and silhouetted the carnage with their searchlights. But in neighbourhoods where fire turned wooden houses into barbecue pits in seconds, no artificial light was needed to see the damage. Eighty seven homes in Granada Hills – near the quake's epicentre – were engulfed in a firestorm fuelled by the vicious Santa Anna winds which late in 1992 had fanned the brush fires which

destroyed so much of the countryside around L.A. At Sylmar, 40 mobile homes were also destroyed due to exploding gas lines while in the neighbourhood of Balboa was one of the eeriest sights of all – a 40-foot-high wall of flame erupting from the centre of a surging two-foot deep river of water running down the main street. The water had come from a reservoir whose banks were shattered, releasing hundreds of millions of gallons of water, and the flames from a ruptured gas main.

President Clinton received hourly updates on the disaster in the Big Orange as daybreak on January 17 revealed yet more scenes of appalling devastation. From the

Opposite: It struck like a hammer blow from hell... Dozens died in the quake that ripped through America's second city in seconds.

Below: Brett Whiston is one of the lucky ones, still able to jack his car up after it almost plunged through a fissure in the highway. Many were not so lucky.

millionaire mansions of Hollywood and Beverly Hills to the ghettos of South Central Los Angeles, the "big one" didn't discriminate between rich and poor. The quake was so big its ripples caused power failures as far north as Portland, Oregon, almost 1,800 miles away. Power was out in most of L.A. by daylight. It struck, as one survivor recalled, "like a hammer blow from hell," at 4.31 a.m. as the city slept beneath a starlit sky. It was a public holiday – Martin Luther King Day – and many had been looking forward to a relaxing time off. At least 50 fires erupted in the tinder-dry city and suburbs, draining the resources of every single fire station in a 50 mile radius of the city centre. And powerful

> LOOTERS ON SUNSET BOULEVARD LURKED UNDER COVER OF DARKNESS TO PILLAGE SHOPS AND STORES

Below: *It was as if a giant hand had taken southern California and shaken it like a rag doll. Here workers kneel in a supermarket at Big Bear City to re-stock the shelves after the tremors had passed.*

aftershocks continued to shake the region, adding to the confusion and fear.

As Mayor Richard Riordan declared the area a disaster zone within 30 minutes of the quake – and appeals for blood donors and emergency volunteers were made on local radio stations – predators took to the streets to take advantage of the chaos. Looters on Sunset Boulevard and in Sherman Oaks lurked under cover of darkness to pillage shops and liquor stores in a re-run of the 1992 riots. With phone lines down, resources stretched to the limit and emergency services' computers useless, there was little police could do to stop the pillaging.

STARS HIT

The quake centred in the residential district of the San Fernando Valley, its ripples shook the earth out to the stars' homes at Malibu, back through Hollywood, down to South Central L.A., the downtown area of the city and out into the desert leading to Las Vegas. At the mansions of Jack Nicholson, Marlon Brando and Sharon Stone the swimming pools were suddenly emptied, along with thousands of others, sending a chlorinated waterfall tumbling down the Hollywood Hills.

In downtown Hollywood the art deco buildings lining the Walk of Fame cracked and crumbled, showering the golden stars of celebrities with debris. South of the city the Santa Monica freeway collapsed under the gigantic roller coaster of rippling earth. Mother Nature's force twisted steel reinforced concrete like plasticine, destroying in seconds a freeway section that took nine months to build. For the rescuers there could only be anxiety for the living. The dead were dead and there could be no time for mourning while the clock ticked down on those still trapped in the wreckage of shattered buildings.

The biggest single loss of life occurred in an apartment block where 15 died as a whole floor was literally wiped out when the building collapsed. The same day it was turned into a shrine when bouquets began arriving in the early afternoon, a sad floral farewell to innocents crushed to death in their own homes. Nothing summed up the savage intensity, the unfathomable fury of Mother Nature, than the squat apartment block which collapsed killing innocent people.

dazed residents in the pre-dawn gloom to save the screaming survivors.

One hundred and fifty people were saved from the precarious second and third stories, shinning to safety on firehoses stretched from a balcony adjoining the undamaged block next door and climbing down ladders held by burly men at their base. "People were screaming," said Erik. "They were crawling all over each other. People came down in front and between your legs. We went from floor to floor in the dark with flashlights and hollered to anyone still alive that we were looking for them. The worst thing I saw was a woman lying face down on her king size bed, still alive, with a beam that had fallen right across her. I was unable to move it and ran to get help. When I came back she was dead."

Chris Taga, a 46-year-old firefighter with 19 years service, wept after surveying the scene. "This is the worst I have seen, the very worst. It is just devastating." Tons of rubble did terrible things to the people

Roses, bunches of lilies, mixed sprays with ribbons and simple cards with messages of grief were left for those whose lives ended at 4.31 a.m. on Monday January 17 1994 in what newspapers termed the Sandwich of Death.

MISERABLE MEMORIES

The memories of the tremor will continue to haunt survivors of the single biggest killer in the L.A. quake. "I kind of felt like a bomb was going off," said Susan Pearson, who was sleeping with her husband Erik on the third floor of the Northridge Meadows apartments. "It tossed me up in the air and when I came back down it tossed me up again." "We were airborne, thrown from our beds," said Erik, 26. "It was one big explosive jolt that slammed up and down and then pitched the whole building diagonally about 12 feet."

They were the lucky ones. Their building had concertinaed in the quake, falling in on itself so that the ground floor had telescoped to just 18 inches. And in that crawl space were the crushed remnants of what had moments earlier been human beings. Many more might have died had it not been for the impromptu rescue efforts of the Pearsons and others like them. Having leaped 14 feet from the balcony of their wrecked apartment to safety, emergency medical worker Erik mobilised other

*Above: **Carrie Newman weeps at the devastation of her home in suburban Landers.***

*Below: **How the newspapers reported the disaster, together with graphic pictures.***

Los Angeles Times

CIRCULATION: LUR DULY DAILY 1,523,197 SUNDAY

TUESDAY, JANUARY 18, 1994
COPYRIGHT 1994: THE TIMES MIRROR COMPANY CCN: 362-4232

DAILY
DESIGNATED AREAS HIGHER

33 Die, Many Hurt in 6.6 Quake
L.A. Area Freeways Buckle, Buildings Topple

Sylmar Jolted by Ghosts of Horror Past

■ **History:** The city that crumpled under a 6.5 quake in 1971 remembers well the terror that came when the earth gave way. On Monday, it seemed like it was cursed.

By CRAIG TURNER and RICHARD E. MEYER
TIMES STAFF WRITERS

■ **Disaster:** Epicenter is in Northridge, where three-story apartment complex pancakes. Ruptured gas lines erupt in fire in strongest temblor in city's modern history.

BY TRACEY KAPLAN and GREG KRIKORIAN
TIMES STAFF WRITERS

The body of LAPD Officer Clarence W. Dean lies near his motorcycle, which plunged off the Antelope Valley Freeway overpass that collapsed onto the Golden State Freeway during Monday's earthquake. The 6.6 temblor closed at least 11 major freeways at interchanges.

Thrust Faults Pose Brutal
Commuters Will Face Nightmare for Months
Questions on Reinforcing of

Above: *Where there was once a road there was only a gaping chasm for a Los Angeles policeman who plunged to his death as he raced to help quake victims.*

ALL OVER, IN THE PRE-DAWN DARKNESS, THE STORY IN LOS ANGELES WAS ONE OF CHAOS AND DESTRUCTION

---

who were directly in its path. And pets. One cat was flattened like a tiger rug in an antique shop by a heavy oak chest of drawers which fell on it. Outside, as the corpses were brought out one by one by firemen throughout the day, two distraught young women displayed a birthday picture of a handsome young man holding a birthday cake. They flashed it vainly in the grime-smeared faces of the firemen and paramedics, but they could only shake their heads from side to side as the women hugged each other for comfort.

A 13-year-old boy was among the dead. Survivors and onlookers who saw the covered body brought out knew it was a child as the blanket draping his small body lay flat on the end of the stretcher. Martha Quispe, who was on the ground floor with her fiancé, miraculously survived as her apartment was on a corner and a supporting beam allowed several feet of clearance. "It was a miracle," she said. "You know, we were screaming and pushing at the wall.

Your instincts in this are just to survive, whatever it takes. Our cars were outside and flattened like pancakes. But they are material things, along with everything else we have lost. But we survived. Thank God, we survived." Annette Gross, a 76-year-old pensioner who woke up to find her first floor apartment sitting at ground level, said: "What can I tell you? I was lucky. I felt like it was the end of the world. Luckily, the good Lord wasn't looking for me that day."

THE TERRIBLE AFTERMATH

All over, in the pre-dawn darkness, the story was one of chaos and destruction. The poor area of Balboa was the scene of a huge inferno which broke out in wooden apartment buildings after a gas main ruptured. Eighty foot flames leaped into the air, resembling a Kuwaiti oilfield fire. In the financial district of Los Angeles – virtually the only part of the metropolis with high-rise buildings – the streets were littered with downed power lines, bricks, rubble, shattered glass and felled lampposts. Fortunately the skyscrapers are built to quake-proof specifications – massive structures that sit on skis deep in the earth. This "give" allows the buildings to sway but stay upright in the event of a quake.

RESCUE SERVICES

The emergency sirens of the police and fire departments wailed through the twilight as city authorities struggled to determine the extent of the destruction. Mingling with their eerie requiem were the screaming of thousands of car alarms triggered by the force of the initial shock.

Flashes lit the skyline as power lines collapsed and generators fused out, cloaking huge tracts of the city in darkness. Los Angelinos – used to earthquakes over the years due to their city's location on an extension of the notorious San Andreas Fault – were hurled from their beds when it struck in the pre-dawn hours. In hotel rooms from Beverly Hills to Burbank guests were evacuated in their night clothes. Many had their buckled doors hacked open by fire axes before they could be led to safety. Yellow school buses, usually used to transport thousands of children daily along L.A.'s massive freeway network, were instantly deployed to rescue people whose neighbourhoods were turned into infernos. In one San Fernando housing area an underground oil line fractured in the initial shock and erupted into an uncontrollable fire. Fleets of buses took away stunned and shocked residents as their homes burned behind them.

"They gotta let 'em burn, there ain't nothing they can do about it," said Paul Abrams, who drove one of the buses to safety. "We're the cavalry around here," he added. "The whole place is in chaos." Brough Copper, a single woman living in the San Fernando Valley, told of the moment that the quake struck. She said: "It was like something out of a horror movie. I couldn't sleep so I was in my kitchen having a glass of water when all of a sudden the lights went off and I was aware that the whole of the room was full of flying, shattering glass. Then in total blackness I was aware that the fridge was rolling towards me. It pinned my arm to the wall. Outside it

MINGLING WITH THE SIRENS' EERIE REQUIEM WAS THE SCREAMING OF THOUSANDS OF CAR ALARMS

Below: *A stunning aerial shot showing the full awesome power of Mother Nature. Several vehicles were stranded in the middle of this freeway section after it was sliced in two places.*

Left: *The crunch came for this row of residents' cars when the earth moved, collapsing the apartment block above on to them.*

HUGE CONCRETE BLOCKS WERE PINNING HIM ALONE IN THE EERIE DARKNESS, HIS LEGS CRUSHED BENEATH ONE SLAB

Below: *It was like a war zone as doctors struggled in the open air when hospital wards bulging with the wounded could take no more.*

was as if all hell had let loose. There was a huge chorus of car alarms going off."

One of the most heroic rescues was carried out by firemen on a desperate worker dubbed The Miracle Man – a 23-year-old trapped in a car crushed under the weight of hundreds of tons of concrete blocks and twisted steel. For six hours the man known only as Salvador was kept alive with air pumped from a compressor into his mangled vehicle. He had been sweeping up in the basement of a 30-foot high garage when the quake struck and his mini-tractor was crushed as the structure was reduced to just seven feet in seconds.

Huge 20-ton concrete blocks were scattered like children's building blocks, pinning him alone in the eerie darkness. He lay in the twisted truck with his legs crushed beneath one slab of concrete, another slab just inches from his face.

FEARFUL SOUNDS

As the hours wore on all Salvador heard from the world outside was the blare of sirens as emergency vehicles raced to quake

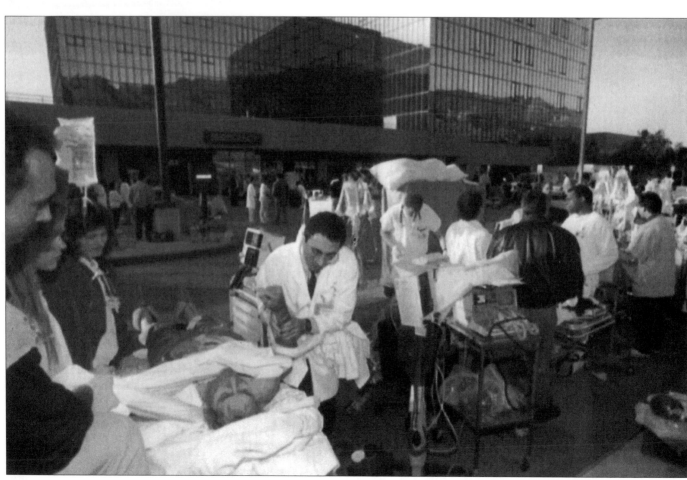

disaster centres. None seemed to be coming for him. He licked moisture caused by his own body heat from the concrete above his head and prayed in Spanish for a merciful end to his plight. After 90 minutes, employees at the Northridge Fashion Centre shopping mall told firefighters they had heard a man screaming in Spanish for help from the destroyed parking garage. Then it had gone silent. Using borrowed jackhammers and special airbags capable of lifting 74 tons at

HE LICKED MOISTURE CAUSED BY HIS OWN BODY HEAT AND PRAYED IN SPANISH FOR A MERCIFUL END TO HIS PLIGHT

screams pierced the ruined labyrinthine, lit by sodium arc lamps dragged into the ruins by the firefighters. He complained that his arms and legs had gone numb with pain. But Fire Captain Tom Burau said: "He never lost the will to live and that was important. He was one helluva brave guy. He told Trujillo he had a wife, but when he asked whether he had any children he began screaming. Nothing makes much sense when you're in a concrete tomb like

Above: "Why me? Why me?" The grief and pain in one LA resident's face as flames consume his home.

a time, 18 firefighters burrowed through the debris, shoring it up with two-by-two pit props as they went. As they drew nearer to Salvador, Fire Department volunteer Lorenzo Trujillo approached the stricken man to pray with him.

"Come, come and pray with me" begged the gravely wounded man, a silver crucifix bearing the image of the Virgin Mary dangling from his neck. "He thought he was dying," said Trujillo, "and wanted someone to be there when he finally slipped away. I told him we weren't there to pray, that we had come to get him out and, by God, that was what we were going to do." Salvador's

that. You see two arms and legs and he's breathing and screaming and that's the best we can hope for."

The firefighters felt like miners in an underground disaster especially as aftershock followed aftershock, shaking loose concrete and other debris in the dust-clogged atmosphere. Several times they were forced to retreat, trying to communicate to the terrified man that they would be back for him. "There was a lot of emotion when we were down there," said Burau. "We had to be so careful, so surgical in every step we took. There were a lot of men's lives, not just Salvador's, hanging in

Above: *Flames shoot like a geyser from a ruptured gas main near Balboa Boulevard in Los Angeles.*

PARAMEDICS RUSHED HIM MOANING, BUT CONSCIOUS, TO A WAITING AMBULANCE WHICH TOOK HIM TO A HELICOPTER

Right: *The wooden frame houses that dot Los Angeles and the surrounding areas were no match for the quake.*

the balance of every step we took." Finally, about noon, metal jaws capable of slicing through the steel plate of American big rigs in highway accidents, ate through the twisted steel of his sweeper as airbags simultaneously pushed the concrete pillars off his legs. Paramedics rushed him moaning, but still conscious, to a waiting ambulance which took him in turn to a helicopter. He was flown by chopper to the University of California Hospital for emergency surgery on his crushed limbs. Trujillo, who has risked his life in other rescues, said: "Of all the things I have ever done, this was the scariest. He was a brave man."

Another brave man who never got a chance to help the people he was racing to the aid of was Californian Highway Patrol officer Clarence Dean, 46. He was racing along a collapsed freeway answering the first of numerous emergency calls that day when his motorbike plunged through a gaping hole on a collapsed freeway.

He had been en route to a woman six months pregnant trapped in her car on the freeway when it buckled in the quake. Hero highway worker Mark Sumner managed to save her life – and the life of her unborn child – moments after seeing the policeman die. He said: "The woman was OK, just badly shaken. She was driving when the road suddenly buckled like a carpet. We got her to safety. But the California Highway Patrolman died on the road. I saw his flashing lights and he hit a lot of rubble in the middle of the highway. He was bleeding badly from the mouth and nose. He had obviously sustained severe head injuries." The tragedy happened on Highway 14 which fell on to Interstate 5 at Sylmar.

THE PRESIDENT'S COMMENTS

President Clinton spoke to America at noon on the day of the tragedy in Los Angeles. He used a luncheon on economic planning at the White House as the occasion to comment on the quake which ripped through L.A. 2,500 miles away. He promised federal aid for the state – and asked Americans to pray for the victims of the disaster. The president said: "I have spoken with Governor Pete Wilson and Mayor Riordan and assured them that we will do everything we possibly can to help the people of L.A. deal with the earthquake and its aftermath. We have done everything we can to provide resources and back-up they need.

"I believe later in the day we can issue the appropriate federal emergency declaration for California. I have been very impressed with the work that has been done since the early morning hours. We do know that many people have lost their homes, some have lost their lives. I ask the American People to remember the people of L.A. in their thoughts and prayers today."

Firefighters, police, ambulancemen, paramedics and ordinary people who showed exrtraordinary courage in the face of adversity were the real heroes of the disaster. When it was totalled up there had been over 50 deaths, from heart attacks, to the people crushed in the apartment building, to deaths on freeways and in collapsed homes. Damage totalled out at £50 billion, the single most expensive item needing re-building the 16-lane Santa Monica Freeway, the busiest highway in the world.

Yet not all the damage was physical – thousands of school children are still undergoing psychological counselling because of the disaster. "It was something that mom and dad couldn't make stop," said child development expert Lawrence Balter PhD. "The world of these children has suddenly become less stable. It is just one more effect of Mother Nature's most terrible power."

Below: *The scene at the Northridge apartment complex where people were crushed to death when one floor disappeared beneath the weight of those above it.*

PIPER ALPHA
The Tower of Fire

Only the bravest souls took jobs on the North Sea oil rigs. And those on the Piper Alpha rig on the night of July 6, 1988 needed all their bravery when their worst fears were realised and fire erupted, a fire from which there was no escape except into the iciest of waters.

There was big money to be made working the oil rigs of the grey, cold North Sea in the 1980s. A new breed of frontiersman, earning upwards of £1,000 a week, was lured to the steel outposts standing like sentinels in the wild, wild water. The work was hard and dirty, completed in tours of duty. Like soldiers, the men who worked the rigs put up with long spells away from home and sweethearts, but when they went ashore for leave it was with their pockets bulging with cash and the knowledge that they had between a fortnight and a month before going back to the gruelling 12-hours-on 12-hours-off shift system.

Yet no-one could claim it was the safest job in the world. There were numerous accidents associated with any heavy engineering job, while the divers who worked beneath the waves of the angry sea faced death and injury daily. There had already been a disaster on an enormous scale in 1980 when the rig Alexander Kielland, a four-year-old platform, turned over in hellish weather 164 miles off 0 Stavanger, Norway. The rig had been converted into an accommodation platform solely for workers. But 130mph winds began to buffet the rig badly, and in the middle of the night it tipped over. Within 15 minutes the 10,000 ton structure was upside down in the savage seas. Of the 213 men aboard, 123 were lost. It sent shock waves throughout the drilling industry and basic flaws in the rig design – found to exist on at least five other platforms – were corrected in the following months.

DEADLY EXPLOSION

But in 1988 came the disaster which would eclipse the Kielland tragedy, not only in numbers of lives lost, but also because of the horrifying way in which men died. For the rig named Piper Alpha was devastated by fire and explosion which claimed many of the tough workers before they even had a chance to dive into the swirling water below. It was a night of hell on an unparalleled scale, the worst ever offshore oil rig disaster. A banshee wail of escaping gas was the only signal for the workers that something had gone wrong and, in the minutes that followed, fire and explosions turned the steel structure into a crippled tomb that claimed the lives of 167 men.

Derek Ellington was one of the lucky ones who lived. "I have never heard anything like it nor will I ever forget it," he said, referring to the screaming noise of the gas. "There were two gas leaks within seconds of each other and literally 30 seconds later came the first explosion. There was just nothing anyone could do." In such a situation, with the elements battering the rig and the men aboard knowing they could

Opposite: *The twisted, burning wreckage of the Piper Alpha rig, scene of the worst disaster ever to befall Britain's North Sea oil and gas industry.*

PIPER ALPHA WAS DEVASTATED BY FIRE AND EXPLOSION WHICH CLAIMED MANY OF THE TOUGH WORKERS

Below: *Wives and loved ones back home were forced to endure images like this on their TV sets, unsure whether their menfolk had been claimed in the terrible tragedy.*

"fry and die – or jump and try," many pitched themselves into the swirling ocean. Their own courage in trying to stay alive in those desperate hours of July 6 1988 was matched only by that of the rescue armada that struck out to try to save them.

Before describing their heroism it is worth mentioning the "jinx" that many of the men who worked aboard Piper Alpha thought hung over their rig. It was, by the time of the disaster, thought to be one of the most unsafe platforms, having been constructed without anti-corrosive

THE RIGGERS' OWN COURAGE WAS MATCHED ONLY BY THAT OF THE RESCUE ARMADA TRYING TO SAVE THEM

Above: *The scarred metal and twisted steel of the rig that blew.*

measures – and to have withstood the battering of the North Sea for nine years. Underwater inspections had routinely showed up a number of significant faults. There had been an explosion on it in 1984 and several deaths in accidents. Sabotage had also been attempted, leading the men aboard to think their platform was cursed.

At about 9.45pm on July 6 1988 a problem occurred with the system that burned off the inflammable gases produced in the extraction of the crude oil. A safety-release

gas flare started to burn furiously and much more intensely than usual. What was happening was a build-up of gas that the flame was not able to cope with and at 9.58pm it exploded, fuelled further by rupturing diesel tanks – the fuel which operated most of the rig's heavy equipment. There was the sound of tearing metal, the ear-splitting roard of explosion after explosion and, too soon, the sound of men dying in agony. At 10.20pm a major gas jet running through the centre of the rig blew and released gas at pressure close to 2,000lbs per square inch. When this was ignited the fireball ripped through the rig, forcing most of the men to risk everything by jumping into the water. At 10.52 pm there was an even greater fireball which was so intense that it literally melted some of the deck plates of the rescue ships which had come to aid the desperate workers.

INTOLERABLE HEAT

Father-of-three Roy Carey, a 45-year-old instrument technician, coined the phrase "fry and die or jump and try". "The flames were billowing above us," he said, "and I had to jump. When I was in the water I found my head was being cooked by the intensity of the heat. I had to keep ducking it under. I must have been half an hour at least in the water with two or three others. There was a lot of bouyancy foam from a smashed lifeboat and we desperately wanted to get hold of it but couldn't. Four of us managed in the end to get to part of a lifeboat but I couldn't get a foothold and I didn't want to drag another guy off of it back into the water."

As he bobbed in the water veteran rigger James McDonald bravely risked the flames to save himself and three of his workmates. He later recalled: "You couldn't get out of any of the doors for the flames. I tried to get into the helideck but I knew it was a waste of time. The stairwells were tightly jammed with people and the boys at the exits were too afraid to move. For about 45 minutes we were huddled inside the reception area but the heat was too intense. But I decided I wasn't going to wait to get burned to death so eventually I rallied the others and we got out through the drill deck to a lower level which took us to the foghorn platform."

Left: *A low-flying helicopter scouts over the skeletal, still smouldering, remains of Piper Alpha.*

Bachelor Iain Letham was among the rescuers who nearly lost his life trying to save the stricken workers, many of whom screamed in the water with massive burns. In an inflatable boat launched from another vessel that had raced to the scene after receiving Mayday messages from the crippled Alpha's radio room, Iain, 27, recalled: "We went right in under the rig and picked up four crewmen. We went back in again to pick up another two, but then there was this colossal explosion and the boat was engulfed in flames. My hard hat and jacket just melted in the heat. I never saw the two we picked up again – they were gone." Diver Edward Amaria saw other rescuers vapourised in one of the explosions that continued to wrack the rig: "We just saw a bunch of guys blown to bits. They died risking their lives to save others." Squadron Leader Garfield Porter, among the 40 helicopter pilots who ferried the wounded back to Aberdeen 120 miles away, said of the rescue ships: "Their bravery was incredible. Time and time again they went back into that heat. We could feel the heat from a mile away as we flew in."

Some 36 vessels in the area had gathered as a rescue armada for the doomed rig. Again and gain these little boats bobbed amid the legs of the crippled structure, risking everything to drag the blackened and burned men to safety. Some of them were fishing trawlers that had been casting their nets not far away when the night sky was lit by the explosions. One worker, Ed Punchard, 31, felt burned after he had shinned down an emergency ladder to sea level where a vessel was waiting. He clambered on board the fishing smack just as another explosion ripped behind his back. He said: "The heat was so bad that I felt I just had to find cover, even though we must have been 100 yards away from the thing. I saw a rope hanging over the trawler's side so I grabbed hold and just jumped into the sea. The skipper just opened up both engines full to get away and I was dragged through the sea like a human sledge, clutching hold of the rope for grim death. At times I was dragged underneath the surface but I just held on until we were away from the heat and then they dragged me back on board again. We can't thank those boats enough. I saw one inflatable dinghy pay the price though – it had its tanks ignited by the heat and exploded into flames, leaving only a melted stretch of rubber on the sea."

A SAD SIGHT

The most poignant and tragic sight of all was for the men aboard the accommodation platform Tharos that was several hundred yards away in the sea from Piper Alpha. Andrew McBain, a Glasgow shot blaster,

VESSELS THAT HAPPENED TO BE IN THE AREA HAD GATHERED AS A RESCUE ARMADA FOR THE DOOMED RIG

AGAIN AND AGAIN THESE LITTLE BOATS BOBBED AMID THE LEGS OF THE CRIPPLED STRUCTURE, RISKING EVERYTHING

Above: *From the nearby rig the full devastation of Piper Alpha is seen in a maelstrom of smoke and fire.*

was dozing in bed when the alarm rang out. Even now the memory of what he saw haunts him: "I could see through the smoke these men, ten or twelve of them, standing on the heli-deck. They were waving their arms, pleading to be taken off. But no-one could get to them. It took 20 minutes before the whole thing blew. I saw men climbing down the legs, jumping into the water. The heat was unbearable. There was men with their faces burned off. All I wanted to do was help. To do something. And myself and the others with me could do nothing except stand around like sheep as those men died."

Survivors said most of the 167 men who died were burned to death on the rig. One hundred of them were trapped in the smoke-filled living and galley quarters, pleading for a miracle to save them from being roasted alive. It never came. Shocked survivor Harry Calder, the helicopter landing officer and a father of two, said: "Men

THE SURVIVORS SAID THAT MOST OF THE MEN WHO DIED IN THE FIRE WERE BURNED TO DEATH ON THE RIG

were shouting into their radios: 'We need breathing apparatus. What's happening? Is there anyone out there? We are all going to die.' It was sheer panic. A lot of the guys were just lying on the floor trying to breathe. We had towels and were just dipping them in anything to help us to breathe. I would have perished in the flames with them if I hadn't jumped. It was 100 feet into the sea and I barely missed the flames from the burning oil on the surface. But at least I made it."

REAL HORROR

Blasting foreman William Lobban was among many of the crew watching the horror film *Carrie* when their own nightmare took over from movie fiction. Married just four weeks before the disaster, he just had time to grab his boots and run when the walls of the cinema began melting and buckling. Outside, he could hear the sizzle of his friends' hands as they cooked whenever they touched twisted hot metal. "I got into the water – I was a lucky one. A supply boat picked us up, God bless him. The rig had tilted thirty degrees off centre by the time I jumped. From the boat it looked as if it would topple into the water at any moment."

ACTS OF BRAVERY

Back in Aberdeen the hospitals worked flat out to cope with the appalling number of injured. Hospitals issued an immediate SOS for blood and volunteers flooded the wards. Throughout the night the helicopters landed with the most serious casualties, sometimes picking them up from the little ships that would take too long to make the journey back to port. It was only on land that the superhuman acts of bravery that constitute the most brilliant side of the human spirit were fully revealed. Acts like the younger men on board giving up lifejackets to the older men before leaping into the water. Diver Christoper Niven 23, from Portsmouth, said: "There were 20 lifejackets where I was for 40 men. We gave the older men preference. The heat was so intense we had to get into the water. Me and five other men clung on to a ladder but four of them had to give up in the end. They let go and just drifted away. Me and

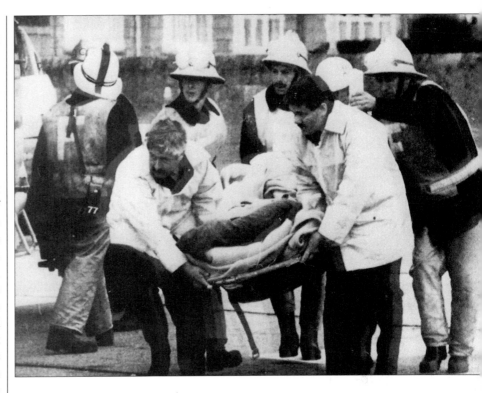

Above: *The lucky ones – scarred mentally but still survivors.*

Below: *Another victim is helped off a helicopter.*

another bloke managed to hang on for more than half an hour when a rescue boat turned up but couldn't get us on board because of the danger of falling debris. We kicked our boots off and managed to swim to it. There were bodies all around us in the water badly burned, with strips of skin coming off them. It was horrible." Other acts of bravery were carried out far above the shattered 34,000 ton platform. Canadian Air Force Major Gary Barth, aboard an RAF Nimrod plane that co-ordinated the rescue effort, spent seven hours in the air circling the rig... all the while knowing one more massive fireball would soar into the sky quicker than the craft could climb and vapourise it.

A NATO naval force was in the area at the time and the American commander ordered all of his vessels at full speed ahead into the disaster zone.

One rigger said: "They looked like the Seventh Cavalry coming into view – and to us they were. It was a welcome sight."

By dawn the sea was an eerie sight. Flames were

BACK IN ABERDEEN, THE
HOSPITALS WORKED FLAT
OUT TO COPE WITH THE
APPALLING NUMBER OF
INJURED

Below: *Dr Armand
Hammer, whose corporation
owned the doomed rig, chats
in hospital with a badly
burned man rescued from
the flaming sea.*

shooting straight from the water, the crippled, smoking rig lay at a crazy angle and
in the water, slick with thick oil, bobbed
men who had been burned to death or
drowned. It was a sight that many men
would need years of intensive psychiatric
therapy to overcome. Plastic Surgeon
Anthony Roberts, head of Stoke
Mandeville Hospital's burns unit, who led
doctors caring for the victims of the 1985
Bradford City football stadium fire, said:
"One of the first things these men will feel
is terrible guilt. They will feel guilty that so
many men died while they survived. Then
they will probably relive the night over and
over again. Another factor they face is that
they suddenly find they have become disabled and dependent. These men are not
used to that. It will be hard."

After the final death count was in and the
tours of hospitals had been completed by
government ministers and royalty, there still
remained the problem of putting out the
raging fire aboard Piper Alpha. There were
men who came cheaper than Red Adair, the
legendary Texan who had spent all his life
with his famous "hellfighters" fighting
blazes at oil and gas wells around the globe
– but none better. When he was hired to
douse the flames he was, in effect, coming
to the rescue of the entire oil and gas industry in the North Sea. Piper Alpha was connected to many of the other rigs in the area,
linked by an extraordinary undersea network of pipes carrying billions of cubic feet
of inflammable substances. A blowback or
a spark would have decimated the region
and polluted the sea for years.

Adair was supremely confident that he
could tackle Piper Alpha... but was under
no illusions about the extent of the task facing him and his men. "It's one hell of a
mess," he said. "The worst I have ever seen.
But nobody has yet drilled the well I can't
tame and this baby is going to have to learn
to do as I tell her."

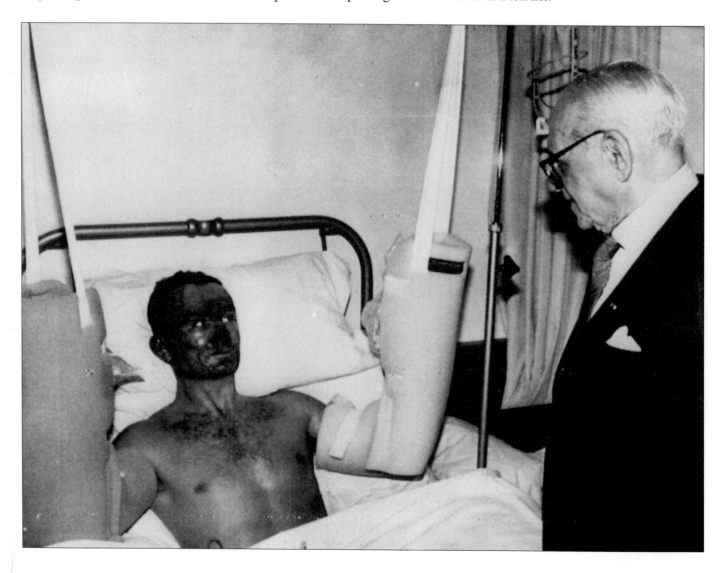

then grasped exactly what their men had been through.

Dave Tumelty, of a survivor's support group called Piper Outreach, said: "It was a shocking video. The families had a strange feeling of wanting to be there to watch it, but at the same time not wanting to be there. It was upsetting. Most alarming of all was the din of the blaze, sounding like the roar of jet engines."

A DAMNING CONCLUSION

The enquiry laid the blame of the disaster upon equipment failure and poor communications. There were extensive recommendations to ensure it would never happen...but for 167 men they were measures that came too little, too late.

Left: *A wife tearfully hugs the husband she thought she might never see again.*

Below: *Red Adair, the maverick but expert Texas oilman whose skills eventually conquered the flaming funeral pyre that was once Piper Alpha.*

Adair, who was being paid £2 million for his efforts, was faced with extinguishing the rig's six leaking wellheads. The worst part for him and his men when they boarded the ugly hulk of the rig was the dead still on board. He said: "It is tough walking among the dead, the toughest part of all. We are walking on men's graves. But this is our job and we have got to do it. This thing must be tamed." The flames continued for four days until Adair and his hellfighters managed to extinguish them, but the damage they had done had scorched Piper Alpha into the collective British conscience and became forever a symbol of heroism and suffering. An unwelcome taste of what it was like was seen by the relatives almost a year later at the public enquiry into the disaster. Ole Andersen, a Danish officer aboard a supply ship which had picked up survivors, videotaped the first hours of the blaze. Stunned relatives

KINGS CROSS
Stairway to Hell

Years of negligence, carelessness and ignorance of basic safety standards conspired, one deadly night, to create one of Britain's most fearsome disasters. Kings Cross, one of London's most famous stations, was the venue for a terrible fire.

The London Underground complex at Kings Cross that fateful night in November 1987 was as busy as anyone could remember, the subterranean tunnels crammed with office workers going home, young lovers going on the town, students going to concerts and the myriad other pursuits of people bustling to and fro in the city. Yet 31 people would never make it home again after the events of that terrible night had been played out.

A fire broke out on the wooden escalators that connected the booking hall of the station with the Piccadilly Line hundreds of feet below. Within minutes the station was turned into a charnel house of misery and death, where people died from poisonous fumes and horrendous burns as the smoke from plastic fixtures and tiles billowed through the station, being sucked upwards by the draught of air which fuelled the flames to intense 2,000 degree heat. It was a night of suffering and supreme courage, heroism and tragedy. After it would come laws and rules designed to never let it be repeated. But for those who lived through it, life could not, would not ever be the same again.

Mariella Santello was one of those innocents who was not meant to be there at all on November 18… She was walking with her boyfriend Marco Liberati, a 24-year-old philosophy student from Bologna, Italy, trying to prise out of him what sort of secret gift he had bought for her 21st birthday the next day. She had come back to London a month earlier for a third time, to take

singing lessons and improve on her English. "It was an impulse and Marco came to join me," she said. "Now he is dead and I will never forget that night."

A LUCKY IMPULSE

Friends in Italy had clubbed together to pay for Marco to join her. They were on their way from Wood Green, where she had been staying with friends, to her new room in London's East End. She intended to try several bus and tube routes to find the best way of getting there and when the train stopped at Kings Cross she decided on a snap impulse to get off. Her gripping testimony as to what happened is among the most graphic of the survivors. She said: "The doors were already closing when we got off. I smelled smoke as soon as we stepped on the platform. But it was mid-November,

after fireworks night, kids still playing around with fireworks, so I didn't think it was too important. Even the policeman directing people didn't show any alarm. I was facing Marco on the escalator with my back to the ticket hall. We were teasing each other – 'I've got a surprise for you' and this and that. As I turned near the top of the escalator a huge flame spread right across the ticket hall. It just filled the whole space.

"I don't remember anyone screaming. Panic sometimes makes you shut off. I don't know why we simply didn't run back down the escalator. The way out seemed to

Opposite: *People died in a sea of fire when a carelessly tossed cigarette butt ignited refuse behind a main escalator at Kings Cross station.*

WITHIN MINUTES, KINGS CROSS STATION WAS TURNED INTO A CHARNEL HOUSE OF MISERY AND DEATH

Above: *Quaint old wooden escalators like these were lethal firetraps that went up like matchwood when the Kings Cross spark was applied.*

Above: *Brave rescuers toiled throughout the night, putting their own lives at risk in a fog of poisoned smoke and flames.*

"THE HEAT WAS ENORMOUS AND WAS MELTING MY SKIN, I THOUGHT 'I AM GOING TO DIE HERE AND THERE IS NOTHING I CAN DO'"

Right: *Inside the ticket hall after the flames had gone out and the full scale of the disaster became known.*

be up and into the air. I didn't think of smoke being the killer. I could see a gap beneath the flames and I dived for it. As I went underneath I shook myself and my hair and threw away my black plastic jacket and bag. I turned round to see if Marco had followed me but I couldn't open my eyes. I tried to shout his name but couldn't even open my mouth. I knew later that everyone behind me had died. The heat was enormous and was melting my skin. I must have put my right arm over my head because that was burned more than my left one. I thought then and there: 'I am going to die here and there is nothing that I can do about it.' What came to my mind was my mother, my friends, how far away they all were as I was about to die in those flames. I cannot remember

over her face and buckets of cooling water being sloshed over her legs. She remembers giving a friend's name and telephone number at University College Hospital before she passed out into the coma that lasted for the next 24 days.

DEADLY FLAMES

Her boyfriend was among those claimed in the flames that had erupted in seconds. While emergency services poured in from all over the capital the possibilities as to the cause seemed endless – everything from terrorism to a mad arsonist. In fact, the wooden escalator had caught alight 18 times in the past, the creaking machinery, accumulated grease, overheated electrical circuits and mounds of tinder-dry rubbish dropped by millions of daily passengers all waiting for the "big one" to ignite it. When it came, the air rushing through the underground tunnels had the effect of turning the entrance to the escalator into a searing blowtorch that incinerated people where they stood. Fire, police and ambulancemen who struggled to rescue the victims that night had no time to ponder the causes – it

Left: *Fireman Colin Townsley – a selfless hero who gave his own life in the line of duty.*

THE AIR RUSHING THROUGH THE TUNNELS TURNED THE ENTRANCE TO THE ESCALATOR INTO A SEARING BLOWTORCH

feeling pain or fear, just sadness. Then I thought: 'I can't die – I am too young. There are so many things I want to do.'"

She managed to claw her way out to the St. Pancras steps side of the station. She remembers an oxygen mask being placed

Below: *Burned but happy, fire hero Steve Hanson gets a kiss from daughter Katie.*

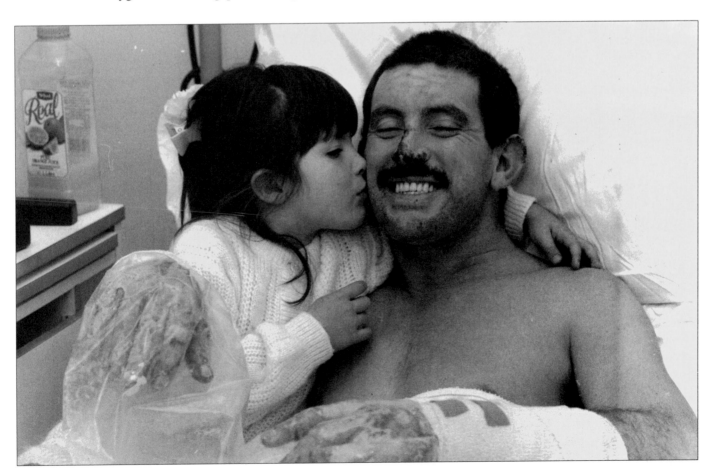

was all they could do to brave the searing heat in a bid to get to the victims.

Yet a series of human errors – later aired at a marathon public enquiry which lasted five months – compounded the suffering of the doomed. London Underground staff were woefully deficient in safety training to evacuate the station. When firemen turned up there was no-one to point the way to the fire, point out underground fire fighting equipment and hydrants or produce vital maps showing the layout of the web of tunnels below. In such circumstances the very best in human resourcefulness and courage came to the fore in individuals – often with tragic results.

Police Constable Steve Hanson literally watched his hands melt in front of his eyes as he clawed at victims and dragged them from the fire. Again and again he reached out to pull choking, burning people from the centre of the flames, even though he could smell his own flesh "barbecuing" in his nostrils. He survived, but hero fireman, Station Officer Colin Townsley, did not. S.O. Townsley was the only fireman to die at the scene, the victim of cyanide poisoning caused by burning paint. He was the first fireman on the scene and laid down his life helping others. As he and his colleagues attempted to shepherd the innocents away from the flames he was caught by a huge fireball at 7.45pm – the time frozen forever on a digital clock that stopped when the fire "flashover", its critical point, occurred.

A SPECIAL INDIVIDUAL

Anthony Palmer, a businessman who showed supreme courage at the time, was later singled out for special praise by coroner Dr. Douglas Chambers at the inquest into the deaths. He said: "He maintained his presence of mind and behaved very, very bravely in the circumstances. Company director Mr. Palmer, from Sheffield, had left St. Pancras Station on the night of the blaze and saw a crowd gathering at the Kings Cross exit. Smoke was pouring out of the underground station stairwell and he saw several people with blackened faces, coughing and spluttering for breath. "Then there was a roar," he recalled, "followed by a thick black jet of smoke that billowed from the exit. I noticed a further person trying to get out of the stair-

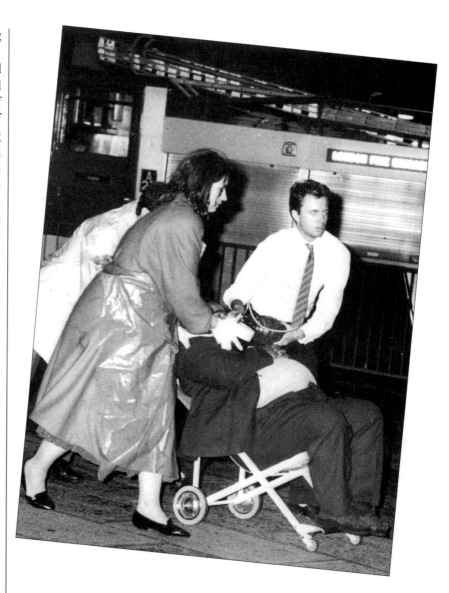

Above: *Oxygen was the most precious and rare commodity of all for the survivors.*

Opposite: *The unbelievable scene of destruction after the blaze. Plastics, wood and electrical wiring proved a lethal mix for the flames.*

well. At this point I couldn't tell whether it was male or female. I got hold of his right hand and could feel it was red hot. Some of the skin came off in my hand. I got hold of his right arm and started to lead him from the smoke. I went back to the underground entrance and at the top of the stairwell a woman was semi-crawling and she was obviously very seriously injured. I put my arms around the woman's back and assisted her from the stairwell." Palmer then tried to enter the stairwell but was driven back by smoke and heat. He asked a fireman for permission to take a rope from his vehicle, tied a loop at the end of it and threw it down the stairwell. "I threw the rope in several times, but to no avail," he said.

Many of the survivors endured horrendous burns to their hands and arms, the result of the body's natural instincts to cover the head and face in such searing heat. Ron Lipsius was a classically trained

guitarist whose playing days ended as a result of the blaze. Ron, 27, was at Kings Cross with a friend's mother, 65-year-old Mrs. Natalie Falco, who died in the blaze. He was en route to play basketball with some pals when he ran into the wall of flame spreading across the top of the doomed escalator.

He said: "I knew the station and I made for the tunnel which comes up outside St. Pancras after I lost Natalie. I must have looked like a blackened alien because the tramps who sit there said: 'Jesus Christ, where has that come from?'" Skin hung from his hands in ribbons. His wounds were so severe he would need several skin grafts, one of them a delicate procedure which literally carved pockets out of his body into which his raw hands were placed by surgeons for three weeks. "Sometimes I thought it would have been better if I had died in the fire," he said. "I hate moaning about it but the pain was excruciating. They gave me heroin in hospital but sometimes the pain even came through that. I remain

very bitter about the fire. One of the survivors said that Jesus got her out that night, but I think that he was notably absent. Why didn't he get Natalie out? Why didn't he get so many out? Why did I survive?"

A WALL OF FIRE

Kwasi Arari-Minta, a business studies student, ran into the flames when he came up the Victoria Line escalator, parallel to the one engulfed by fire. "As I reached the top I saw a tremendous flash of flame," he said. I saw the flames hit the man who was directing us out, who turned and ran towards the exit with his hand over his face. The flames by this time had spread completely over the booking hall and seemed to be just over my head. At the same time, all the lights went out. People were screaming and shouting in fear. I dived head-first underneath the flames towards the exit barrier and crashed into what I think was the ticket collector's box. The whole area was in flames. I realised

"PEOPLE WERE SCREAMING AND SHOUTING IN FEAR. I DIVED HEAD-FIRST UNDERNEATH THE FLAMES"

Below: *These steps became a chimney for the smoke billowing from the flames below.*

that I couldn't use that exit so I turned and ran down the stairs to the Circle Line platforms. There I ran into two women, one of whom shouted: 'My God, you're on fire!' She started to tear my clothes off and probably saved me from even worse injuries." Richard Bates, a journalist for the Guardian newspaper, was also severely burned in the booking hall. He dived back down an escalator and was squirted with a fire extinguisher held by a London Transport worker at the bottom. But when his rescuer tried to move him along a corridor connecting the Underground network with a British Rail platform he found the door blocked in two places by locked doors. It took ten minutes to get the first door open and even longer to get the second one open – another blunder on a night full of them. Desmond McLean, a music teacher from Islington, North London, told the inquest into the deaths that he didn't understand why the escalators were not switched off when the fire was at full force. "The escalator was still moving," he said,

"feeding the passengers in front of me into the flames. I could see them burning. I could hear them screaming...."

Through that chill November night the streets of London echoed to the wails and screeching of sirens as fire engines raced to

Above: *Chaos in the streets around Kings Cross.*

Below: *Flowers for the dead.*

the blaze and ambulances ferried the wounded to hospitals. The station manager at Kings Cross, Mr. Joseph Worrell, had not been trained in the use of fire-fighting equipment and it was later discovered that a number of closed circuit safety monitors and a loudspeaker system were not working properly. Neither had any staff had training in fire drill or evacuation. As a result of this and other human errors he was not informed of the blaze until ten minutes after it had started!

Below: *Flowers strewn at the entrance to the doomed station say more than a million words of sorrow could for the dead.*

The timetable of disaster went like this: at 7.29pm a passenger travelling on the up-escalator of the Piccadilly Line noticed a small fire underneath a step at the right-hand side of the upper part of the escalator. He reported it at the ticket office to the booking clerk. At 7.32pm some further alarm was raised by another passenger and PC Terry Bebbington telephoned the British Transport Police HQ to raise the alarm. At 7.38pm the relief Station Inspector Christopher Hayes entered the machine room beneath escalator no.5 and saw smoke and flames beneath no.4 adjoining it. He was unable to get near enough to the flames with an extinguisher. At 7.39pm the police officers at the station decided to evacuate the area. At 7.42pm the first fire engine arrived with S.O. Townsley, who lost his life trying to lead people to safety. At 7.45pm came the "flashover", or fire-ball, which claimed Townsley's life and many of the victims, as they sucked in super-heated air which roasted their lungs and caused their breathing tubes to seal. It wasn't until 1.46am the following morning that firemen were able to relay their "stop" message to headquarters, indicating that the fire was out.

POOR PROCEDURES

The enquiry into the aftermath did not look for scapegoats, although there was damning evidence of slackness and negligent safety procedures. Experts who sifted through the wreckage estimated that there was half-a-ton of grease underneath the escalator that became a deathtrap. Most of the London Underground staff were unable to help because they had not been trained in any emergency procedures. In fact, the official report said they hadn't splashed a single drop of water on to the fire in its early stages. But there were no criminal prosecutions of anyone, a fact that Dave Matthews, of the Fire Brigades Union, found "damnable". He added: "How can they say there is insufficient evidence when 31 people lost their lives? It is totally unacceptable. I am not surpised but I am bitterly disappointed. Once again it shows that eminent people in positions of power and on good salaries seem on occasions to be beyond the law." Six firemen however who were wounded on the night, or suffered heat stress, received compensation ranging from £4,500 to £10,000.

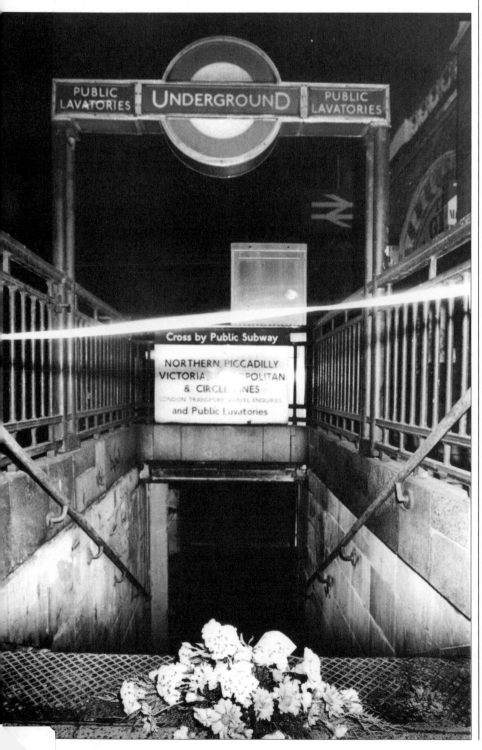

When it was all over, the paperwork from the enquiry filed away in faceless Whitehall offices, the promises of "never again" repeated by fire chiefs and London Transport officials, the nightmares continued for the survivors and their rescuers. For one hero the bleak memories were triggered by yet another fire on the underground, albeit a small one. And he fears that they will be with him for the rest of his life.

"I just can't cope with the nightmares," said PC Hanson, whose hands had literally melted in the intensity of the blaze. "The stress is unbearable. I have to get out now for the sake of my sanity. I returned to duty in 1989 after two years of being on sick pay. Having won the Queen's Gallantry Medal I had met a load of celebrities and even went to a reception at 10 Downing Street. But I was reduced to a wreck when I took up my career again. As I approached Kings Cross on my first day I had a terrible sense of doom. My hands sweated and I shook uncontrollably. When I walked down the platform the smell of charred flesh was in my nostrils. Terrible images from that night flashed up before my eyes. I saw

Above: *Prime Minister Margaret Thatcher and transport secretary Paul Channon visit the disaster site the morning after.*

A HERO'S BLEAK MEMORIES WERE TRIGGERED BY ANOTHER FIRE ON THE UNDERGROUND, ALBEIT A SMALL ONE

those dreadful burning bodies once more. To me, the place was just a graveyard... the place where so many had died. Then one day a fire broke out on the Victoria Line. It turned out to be trivial – but I didn't know that at the time. Me and a colleague rushed down to evacuate the area. But as we got close I felt a terrible, stifling claustrophobia. I couldn't breathe. The sweat was pouring down me and I was shaking violently. I just turned and ran. I rushed past the passengers I was supposed to be helping and ran blindly out the exit. I had to get out. It was like that awful night in 1987 all over again. When I got back to the office I sent a radio message for more police to attend the scene. Then I calmly took off my uniform and folded it away, put on some casual clothes and went home. My shift hadn't finished, but I couldn't stay a moment longer. I had served in Northern Ireland as a Coldstream Guardsman. I did three tours of duty. I saw death first hand as my mates were shot and kids were blown up. But nothing prepared me for Kings Cross. That awful nightmare will be with me forever."

AUSSIE BUSHFIRES
Sydney Suffers

They came from nowhere and within hours and days transformed a whole section of Australia into a charred mass of cinders. Animals, homes and humans fell prey to the uncontrollable blazes – blazes that only a huge effort conquered.

Australians say it takes a certain kind of individual to live in the continent's inhospitable Bush, the bone-dry tundra that is home to wildlife and hardship and precious little else. But the Bush has a special place in the hearts of people down under; it is the repository of the nation's abundance of wildlife, the home to Aborigines and an environmental gem that has been preserved and nurtured for the last half-century when it seemed man would devour this national treasure.

Yet despite the best efforts of conservationists the Bush – and many homes and businesses built in and around it – vanished forever in savage fires in 1994 that even threatened the country's greatest city, Sydney. Fuelled by high winds and aided by tinder-dry trees and undergrowth, only the valiant efforts of heroic individuals in the fire and emergency services finally extinguished the flames and saved the city from total devastation. At times their courage was supreme, prompting Queen Elizabeth to send a personal message to the governor of New South Wales in which she praised the "magnificent work" of all those who stood in the front line of the disaster.

The continent down under has long lived with the threat of bushfire like some nations learn to live with periodic drought or flood; the very nature of the climate there means that fire is always a risk. Yet, for the most part, it has been a containable one – indeed, often started by bush rangers to burn off dense undergrowth in order to

encourage new life. Yet the fires that erupted around Sydney in January 1994 were stoked into an uncontainable maelstrom of heat that sometimes approached 2,000 degrees centigrade. Whole communities faced destruction from walls of flame that devoured everything in their path. Around the world prime-time TV viewers watched the fires advance on Sydney... but, for that city, the hell was just beginning.

What started as one blaze in the north-eastern suburbs of Sydney soon developed into two, three, four and finally a dozen – most of them copycat blazes set by demented arsonists. The fires advanced over a ten-day period until at one time it was darkness at noon in the magnificent city and the 200ft high flames could be seen from the top of the Opera House just five miles away.

One of the first casualties was the wilderness itself. Bone-dry land vapourised in seconds with the oven-hot winds blowing the

Opposite: *The bushfires do their worst.*

THE FIRES ADVANCED OVER A TEN-DAY PERIOD UNTIL AT ONE TIME IT WAS DARKNESS AT NOON IN THE MAGNIFICENT CITY

Below: *It's only a boat this time but much more, including irreplaceable wildlife, would perish before the flames had finally been beaten.*

Above: *The scarred landscape in the Como area of Sydney where the firestorm wiped out numerous homes in its path.*

WHEN FIREMEN TURNED THEIR HOSES ON TO THE INTENSE WALLS OF HEAT THEY FOUND THAT THE WATER TURNED TO STEAM

flames along at 45 miles-per-hour. The 38,000 acre Royal National Park, the nation's first park, was the first to go. After seven days just ten per-cent of it was left intact – the rest reduced to a smoking husk littered with the charred carcasses of wildlife.

But it was, after all, human life and property that was the first concern of the rescuers – and the task was daunting. When firemen turned their hoses on to the intense walls of heat they found that the water turned to steam before a drop of it could douse any flames. They reasoned that they could fight the fires behind six-lane highways. But the flames literally leap-frogged these and other man-made obstacles. Small whirlwinds within the fires blew burning embers almost two miles ahead of the main heart of the inferno. At the peak of the blazes the firefighters and troops called in to aid in the massive task, some 7,000 volunteers in all, were like a retreating army whose only aim became evacuating people before the unstoppable fires got to threatened properties.

Tony Purves, a homeowner at Pittwater on Sydney's smart North Shore, failed to get out before the flames struck. He said:

"We jumped in the swimming pool and kept going under as the fireballs raced straight over our heads. There was nothing we could do. We just stayed there and kept ducking under and when I came up for the last time my house and everything in it had gone."

A MERCY DASH

At the exclusive residential area of Jannali, perched on a rocky escarpment overlooking oyster beds and rugged coves, firemen arrived just in time to alert homeowners as a 20-mile-wide wall of flames was about to sweep down. "Get out and get out now," raged fireman Peter Smith, his face blackened, his eyes red from smoke and lack of sleep. One woman on the outskirts of town died as she dived into a swimming pool to escape the flames and suffered a heart attack. Another woman died when her car was engulfed in flames as she drove along a road that was suddenly hit by a fireball that appeared from nowhere. Thirty homes were destroyed in Jannali in seconds, although the utter randomness of the flames left some standing where others had been completely annihalated. "Rarely do I use the word catastrophic," said Terry Griffiths, state minister for emergency services, "but we are at catastrophic conditions now."

At no. 8 Lincoln Crescent in Jannali Barry Brewer was woken up by another fireman moving house-to-house. "He just knocked at the door," said Barry, "and said if we didn't want to be barbecued to a frazzle we had better move. My wife Rhoda and I jumped into the car with the flames snapping at us as we drove. Yet when we came back the next day we found that our house had survived – largely due to all the watering my wife had done on the back garden. It was very green and the flames

the boots of their cars or strapped on to the roof. Million pound homes at places like Broken Bay and Lindfield were turned into torches while catamaran boats on the Hawkesbury River became a high-powered armada to rescue citizens of the trapped communities along its banks. Time and again these vessels, which usually operated in the bright sunshine-speckled waters between Sydney and Manly, became floating hospital ships that took off the trapped and wounded as thick smoke blanketed the whole area. One refugee, Wally Regan, said: "These guys were operating in terrible conditions with just wet towels around their faces. But they had no thought for themselves – they came right up to the burning

> "HE KNOCKED AT THE DOOR AND SAID IF WE DIDN'T WANT TO BE BARBECUED TO A FRAZZLE WE HAD BETTER MOVE"

just went right around it." The Brewers were lucky – in all, the town lost 89 residences, burned to a cinder.

Winds swung wildly in that second week of the fires, whipping the blazes lethally from suburb to suburb, forcing a pitiful mass evacuation of families who hit the road with their most treasured belongings stuffed in

riverbanks to pull us off. And if they hadn't we would have fried or drowned."

In Gosford, a city of 250,000 people, the outer suburbs were swamped with flames. Fire chief John Costello ordered the evacuation of the local hospital by helicopter, although all others had to take their chances by road or on foot. "We urged

Above: *A solitary man against nature's fury. A trickle of water, a wall of fire and a plucky Aussie resolutely standing in its path.*

Sea. The fire was so intense that it super-heated the oil in the predominant eucalyptus trees, causing them to literally explode as if someone had strapped hand grenades to them. Two million acres across the state were ablaze, thousands of homes had been destroyed but miraculously just four lives had been lost – largely due to the round-the-clock efforts of the firefighters.

TRYING CONDITIONS

David Sandford was typical of the valiant firefighters. A married man with two children, he had five hours sleep in five days, and was still on duty in Jannali. The problem was that the fire, whipped by winds in different directions, would scorch an area, turn around, and come back through a suburb for a second scorching. "What can you do but go on?" he said.

The men, when they were captured on TV film, looked like a wild-eyed army of wraiths, like the old-before-their-time soldiers returning from a World War One battlefield. But none of them ever deserted their posts. Phil Robinson, a district fire officer who set up his post in Jannali's burned-out school building, said: "It was absolute mayhem, destruction and misery all around. And down the road in Waterfall the same story. It has been a case of getting to the people before the fires and hoping we can get them out."

As the fires lapped at the very edges of Sydney the roads from the outer suburbs were choked with refugees. From the Queensland border in the north down almost to Victoria in the south, Australia resembled a gigantic, berserk barbecue that no-one seemed able to extinguish. Hope for rain or a change in the winds seemed the only solution to the disaster. At their height there were 150 major firestorms raging out of control.

Journalist James Morgan, writing for the Times, described vividly the destruction of a wealthy suburb called Lindfield. "A young woman runs ahead of a 40ft high wall of flame crying: 'Where's my dad? I've lost my dad.' From inside the firestorm a terrible scream rings out – human or animal, it is impossible to tell against the crackle of burning wood. Everyone is running from the flames and choking smoke as a ring of fire moves ever closer to the heart of Sydney.

everyone to make for open spaces like the beaches," he said. "There was no need for panic but things didn't look good." As it was, the city was spared, but not before looters had added to the misery of the flames. As police and firefighters moved residents out the thieves moved in, braving the flames to steal from jewellery, electrical and furniture stores.

By this second week of the blaze the ash from the fires was blowing over New Zealand, 940 miles east across the Tasman

Above: *Controlled burning of tinder-dry scrub was one way of cheating the flames out of more fuel. Here a firefighter becomes a firestarter in a bid to save Sydney.*

"Dozens of homes have already been destroyed on the outskirts of Sydney, exploding in the intense heat with thousands forced to flee. Mark Peters, 47, running down the road with his dog, said: 'I hung on until the end, firing the hose at the roof, but it had no effect. The fire jumped across the road and that was it. My wife is at work, thank God. But what kind of home will she be coming back to? I know there's going to be nothing left.'

"The Bush fires are the worst in the state in half a century… They are like a monster, devouring everything in its path, old and new, animal and vegetable. Last night the horizon around Sydney – which only months ago was celebrating its success in being awarded the 2000 Olympics was a red glow. White ash rained down and the smell of smoke pervaded every home. The terrified public, hearing that two million acres across the state was ablaze, asked: 'When will it end? What will stop it?'"

Right: *An Australian army soldier called in to fight the flames runs in a gas mask from the terror of the advancing wall of fire.*

HOMES ON THE OUTSKIRTS OF SYDNEY EXPLODED IN THE INTENSE HEAT WITH THOUSANDS FORCED TO FLEE

Below: *Dale Egan watches his beloved car collection burn after the firestorm swept over his home.*

Those closest to Sydney considered themselves the safest – often with lasting regret. Mito Curic on the North Shore side of the city, said: "I watched my house burn to the ground and I always considered that

Above: *Barry McAlpine's home is destroyed by the flames.*

Below: *Planes dropped water from above but on the ground it was trench-warfare against the fires.*

I live 'in' Sydney. I always thought we were safe here, so close to everything, I never thought about hosing the house down. It wouldn't have done any good anyway – it was over in minutes. One second everything was fine and the next the flames were upon us. Flames 60 feet high jumped from treetop to treetop." Firefighters had to drag one young woman from her home nearby when she refused to leave. The property was vapourised minutes later.

THE END OF THE FIRE

In the end it was a combination of weather, ingenuity and the sheer guts of the volunteer army standing in its path that conquered the great blaze of '94. A massive "back-burning" effort was instigated around Sydney and outlying suburbs which consisted of the controlled-burning of the back gardens of homes close to the flames, leaving nothing for the advancing tide of fire to devour. That, coupled with a change in wind direction and a drop in temperature undoubteldy saved one of the loveliest cities in the world from utter devastation. And there was a new breed of hero to rank alongside the outlaw and the athlete in Oz – the firefighter. The courage shown by these men, and the hours they put in, earned them a place of eternal gratitude in the nation's heart. "Stories of their bravery abound," said one commentator. "One group of them had to hide in a hole in the ground covered with blankets and earth when their escape route was cut off. They emerged, singed and sorry for themselves, but they never stopped to complain. They carried on and got the job done. Undoubtedly, many owe their lives to these men." At one time the firefighters' chiefs considered that the loss of 2-3,000 homes around Sydney would be acceptable – in the end there were just under 100 homes lost; an incredible feat. Also swallowed up were three blocks of flats, ten cars, two petrol stations, five small factories, two shops, one church. In all 24,864 people were evacuated by the firefighters to safety.

ANIMALS IN DANGER

In the end 100 fires raged – but they were containable and away from the populated areas. It was the wildlife that suffered the most. The greatest casualty of the blaze was thought to be the koala bear population. Next to the kangaroo the best-known symbol of Australia, thousands of these cute mammals were wiped out, many thousands more badly burned or too traumatised to eat.

Before the disaster, colonies of koalas numbering between 50 and 100 thrived in the bushland. When the flames had died down their losses were revealed to be collosal. Up to two-thirds of them were wiped out, bringing their numbers down to less than 100,000. Even those that survived the firestorm were in peril – their only natural source of food was the eucalyptus tree, the leaves of which are their staple diet. Rescuers who went to their aid found the wide-eyed creatures too shocked and frightened to take food from them.

Audrey Koosmen, who runs the Friends of Koala group at Toronto near Sydney, said: "We have been into the ruins of the bush and seen many of the surviving koalas sitting at the tops of trees, some with their young clinging to them, too frightened to come down. They have survived, many of them with scorched fur, because the fire has not gone all the way up the tree. But they are in danger of perishing unless we can get them down to get food. God knows how many of them have died." Many of the baby koalas which were rescued had severe burns to their faces, despite being in the relative safety of their mothers' pouches. All around Sydney refuge centres opened to take in animals of all species that had been wounded, displaced or left in deep shock by the blazes – everything from cats and dogs to wild lizards, exotic birds like cockatoos, wombats and kangaroos.

Charles Wright, the chief executive officer of the Royal Society for the Prevention of Cruelty to Animals in Sydney, estimates that it will be some 30 to 40 years before the animal populations reach those of the pre-fire levels. Wild animals had no salvation at all from the inferno. The annihalated zones cover an area that is too large to imagine."

Hundreds of people were hospitalised for everything from burns to breathing difficulties – the "smoke" legacy has left many with bronchial difficulties. But Sydney still stands, the homes are being re-built and the wildlife will, with time, return to the scorched Bush. Queen Elizabeth sent her personal regards to the firefighters – a breed of men who turned out as tough as anything nature could throw at them.

Commmissioner Phil Koperberg, Bush Fire Services chief for the whole of New South Wales, said of his men: "I felt for the firefighters on the ground because I knew what they were going through. I realised the enormity of their task. I knew that many of them would risk their lives and many of them would be injured. The emotion I felt as the effort was being scaled down was numbness and exhaustion. We all shared this feeling. Exhausted by the effort, numbed by the ferocity of nature. The fires of '94 should never be forgotten as a warning of the danger that lurks in the Australian Bush."

THOUSANDS OF CUTE KOALA BEARS WERE WIPED OUT, MANY THOUSANDS MORE WERE BADLY BURNED

Below: *Sandra Chung embraces her daughter Olivia amid the ruins of their home in a Sydney suburb. The fires were so intense at one point that they threatened to devour the entire city completely.*

HILLSBOROUGH
Football's Black Day

The 1989 FA Cup semi-final was ready to be graced in 1989 by two of the country's finest teams. Fans expected a fun afternoon but 95 of them were to die, crushed against the barriers that had been erected to protect them.

It was meant to be a football game that the fans would remember for a long time to come. On April 15 1989, a warm and sunny spring day, Liverpool were to play Nottingham Forest in the semi-final of the FA Cup, a match scheduled for the neutral ground of Hillsborough Stadium in Sheffield. The game was a 54,000 ticket sell-out and the police presence purposely heavy in a bid to announce to one and all that Sheffield was well equipped to deal with mob violence should anyone be considering it. Yet it was a day that was to end in terrible tragedy, the cages on the terrace that were meant to contain hooligans becoming death chambers for innocent fans out to enjoy the best that soccer could offer. Before the final whistle blew on that day 95 people were dead, 170 injured. It was a catastrophe that touched every heart in the nation and of feeling people around the world. For the police on that day it was of paramount importance to keep the rival fans from being near to each other inside the stadium. The last thing they wanted was the kind of violence on the terraces that has brought the name of English soccer fans so low around the world. The kick-off was timed for 3.00pm and it was police practice to avoid delaying this if at all humanly possible.

Parents, many of them with young children, began arriving at the ground around 1.00pm, getting to positions at the front of the terraces, pressed up close to the wire net

Opposite: *The image that will haunt football in Britain for as long as it remains the national game.*

THE CAGES ON THE TERRACES MEANT TO CONTAIN HOOLIGANS BECAME DEATH CHAMBERS FOR INNOCENT FANS

Below: *Fans joined in with police in ripping down advertising hoardings ringing the pitch to fashion makeshift stretchers for the wounded.*

tide swelled. It was a well intentioned gamble that the police took – and one that would end up costing 95 people their lives. Superintendent Roger Marshall obtained permission to open the 14ft wide Gate C allowing hundreds of fans to swarm through towards the 12ft wide entrance to the terrace five minutes before kick-off.

From where they were the fans could see the pitch but had no idea that Pen 3 was full already. They rushed for it without signs or information to tell them to head for the emptier pens either side. Several people died in this mad, initial lemming-like rush for the stand. But at 3.04pm, when Beardsley struck the crossbar for Liverpool with a powerhouse shot, the fans surged forward and the nightmare massacre had

ting that bordered the pitch. At the Leppings Lane entrance the Liverpool faithful filed in, children on their shoulders, jostling for the best positions. The terrace areas were divided into pens, which in theory allowed police and ground stewards to divide and control the distribution and flow of the crowd, preventing the kind of mass-movement of fans once inside the ground that could lead to trouble after kick-off. At midday it was decided to let fans choose any pen they wished on the Liverpool side; they would not be directed into any single one. Pens three and four were directly behind the goal-mouth and so extra popular. As the magic hour of kick-off approached the turnstile figures showed only 12,000 Liverpool fans had passed through when all indications from ticket sales, trains and police intelligence in town told them there were over 18,000 expected.

A FATAL RUSH

Suddenly, with less than a quarter-of-an-hour to go before the whistle blew, thousands of fans turned up at the entrance, far too many to quckly access the ground through the seven available turnstiles. As the minutes passed they grew increasingly impatient. The police were faced with a dilemma; let them in quickly or risk serious injuries and disorder outside as the human

Above: *The agony of the dead and dying was a human tragedy on a colossal scale.*

Top: *The strong arm of the law helps one lucky fan to get away from the carnage.*

begun. The crush was so powerful that people had the life squeezed out of them where they stood – and the players and spectators in other areas of the ground were oblivious to the unfolding tragedy. Police initially feared a pitch invasion... and then the contorted faces of agony, of women crushed up close against the wire, were seen and it became a desperate race against time to save as many as possible.

At 3.06pm a senior police officer gave the orders for the ref to stop the game. Doctors in the crowd rushed to the scene as quickly as they could. One of them, Dr. John Ashton, a Liverpool supporter, left his two children behind as he vaulted on to the turf and sprinted towards the sea of humanity slowly being squeezed to death. "When I got there I had the awful experience of going along a row of bodies certifying people dead. It was like a scene from M*A*S*H just too awful to describe."

Hero ambulanceman Peter Wells, in charge of 30 St. John volunteers, stuck his hands through the cage to try to force open the mouths of crushed fans gasping for breath. "I just tried to keep their airways open because their arms were trapped at their sides. But people were choking to death in front of me. One young girl was looking at me when her eyes just rolled up into her head and she died in front of me. I had a large cylinder of oxygen and tried to feed it to some of those directly accessible. But people were literally dying for want of a pair of wire cutters. If only we could have cut that wire we could have saved some lives by getting people out quicker. Our people, one of whom was only 12, worked like mad to save lives. We did everything we could. My wife Kathy was working on a little boy about ten. His father was watching as she did everything she could to revive him. But a doctor walked past and said: 'There's nothing more you can do for him. Try to save the others.' We could not have done any more if we had had 200 doctors there."

Ian Clarke, a 16-year-old Liverpool schoolboy who would be the youngest

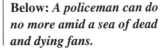

Right: The grief of a solitary spectator sums up the sadness of an afternoon of sport that turned into mass death.

"ALL IN FRONT OF ME WAS A MASS OF BODIES ENTANGLED IN EACH OTHER. PEOPLE WERE CLIMBING OVER THEM…"

Below: A policeman can do no more amid a sea of dead and dying fans.

person to give evidence at the enquiry that would ultimately follow, later gave this account of the tragedy:

"All in front of me was like a mass of bodies entangled in each other. People were climbing over them to try and get out over the fence on to the pitch. I could hear that some of them were crying for help and, together with a couple of fans and a police officer who had arrived, I started pulling people out of the tangle. I don't know which were dead or were just passed out and injured, but we were helping them and giving them the kiss of life. As we moved one body of a man from the tangle near the middle of pen three I saw the body of a little boy still on his shoulders. His arm was reaching out towards the gate.

"Just after this we were taking more bodies across to where they had pulled open the fencing to get them out and I remember that there was another push from the back. I was just lifting up a dead man as the push developed. It pushed me into a pile of dead bodies and I took the man's place. The other bodies were pushed on top

Above: *The Kop End of Liverpool football ground transformed into a shrine of flowers for the dead.*

Top: *The empty stands, showing, from the viewpoint of those who died, the futility of trying to struggle against the steel railings.*

callous, but Paul Brooks, a Fleet Street professional, said: "A couple of fans did ask me to stop taking pictures but maybe photos like these will get something done. I had this feeling of complete disbelief. I came to photograph a football match and this just erupted. It was bloody awful."

George Fendwick, a 19-year-old fan who received serious leg injuries in the crush, said: "We were stuck right at the front of the terraces by the safety barriers and I remember begging and pleading with the police to let us on to the pitch, but they wouldn't. I saw a girl of 15 or so beside me. Her face went red and her head started shaking. She couldn't breathe. The police caused the disaster. They let the fans in at the back and wouldn't let us out when it became too crowded."

Thomas Byrne was a 37-year-old fan who had survived the crush in the Belgian stadium of Heysel several years before, only to almost lose his life again at

of me and I blacked out." He was one of the lucky ones, pulled from beneath the corpses stacking up like cordwood by a policeman and other fans.

Fans on the pitch tore down the cheery advertising hoardings surrounding the field to use as makeshift stretchers. Around them were press photographers, continuing to record the tragedy as it unfolded. Many of them were criticised as being unfeeling and

Hillsborough. He said: "People stood on top of people's heads and shoulders to try to find a way to escape on to the pitch. I was only about eight feet from the pitch but it might as well have been eight miles. It was a continuous pressure. There was no way out and I just remember all this moaning and above it the sound of people praying." He was one of the lucky ones too. But Brian Anderson got separated from his 62-year-old dad John in the melee – and the next time he saw him he was lying down in a row of bodies. "He was among the bodies lying outside the ground," said Brian, 32. The police had laid him there. They said he didn't stand a chance."

The pitch became a scene out of a war zone with the most hardened fans helping out to try to save the wounded. John Ashton, a senior lecturer in community medicine at Liverpool University, assumed an overall command of the situation. He said: "There was nobody in charge, no plan, no organisation at all. I had to assume control of the casualty situation myself. I had to make sure the people who were still alive and most seriously injured were got

off to hospital first. People were being put into ambulances in any order when I got there." He had harsh words for the police and the football authorities: "The whole thing from beginning to end had incompe-

Above: A simple sign from former sworn enemies.

Below: Scene of chaos at Hillsborough.

the next few days the pitch was transformed into a sea of wreathes and crosses, the goalposts shrouded in scarves and notes of remembrance of sons and daughters, mothers and fathers, uncles and aunts. It was a fitting tribute to people who had gone to enjoy a good game of soccer and ended up never coming home again.

CONSIDERED COMMENTS

Schoolmaster David Wilson gave this eloquent and measured account of what happened that terrifying day on the eve of the inquiry opened by Lord Justice Taylor. Delivered in the form of a letter to a national newspaper, Mr. Wilson told concisely and simply of the chaos and bungles which he believes led to the tragic loss of life. He said: "May I speak for the survivors of the tragic events at Hillsborough, whose views will never be sought by tribunals but who were in the Leppings Lane end. I am a primary school headteacher and, together with my 24-year-old son, set off from Cheshire at 11.00am for Sheffield. Because of traffic jams outside Manchester we did not reach the ground until 2:45pm by which time conditions at the turnstiles were incredible. The turnstiles could have operated until 4:00pm and would still not have moved the crowd. The resulting despair for supporters desperate to see the start of play, and the arrival of still more people, caused a situation which a handful of constables on foot could never have hoped to cope with. No wonder a senior officer feels justified in defending his undoubtedly wrong decision to open the exit gate. The crisis was already in the making.

"To add to the confusion the entrances to Hillsborough are not logically marked. We waited in what we thought was the right area until we saw supporters turned away from the turnstiles because they had the wrong tickets. We were directed by a policeman to the B turnstiles and it was here that we found the gate open. May I say here that the supporters making their way into that very dimly lit passageway under the stands – no stewards were there to advise otherwise – were not drunk, not aggressive, not crazed as one newspaper suggested.

"But they were entering a death trap. Once entering that central area behind the Liverpool goal there was no escape. But my son and I were among the lucky ones. Why?

tence running through it. I think it is about time we started to ask questions about the accountability of some of the senior officers in the F.A. They treated our people here like animals and it resulted in their deaths. I am outraged."

Glyn Phillips, a GP and Liverpool supporter, was also on hand and criticised the lack of life-saving equipment at the stadium. He said: "It was sheer mayhem. We spent ten minutes resuscitating one man and succeeded, but I don't know what it did to his brain. I asked for a defribrillator – a machine that sends out electric shocks to a heart that has gone out of rhythm – and there was not a single one in the whole ground, which was appalling for a major event like this. It was an absolute disgrace."

The tally at the end of the disaster was horrendous. In addition to the 95 dead – only three of the victims were over 50 and the majority aged between 20 and 29 – were 400 seriously injured. The dead had all succumbed to asphyxiation, the life squeezed from them by the remorseless crush. For the people of Liverpool, the grieving was just about to begin. A dark shroud of mourning settled over the city where football is a second religion. At the Anfield Ground over

Above: *Police helmets in a bunch, discarded at the end of a day which everyone wanted to forget but which no-one can.*

"THE FA TREATED OUR PEOPLE HERE LIKE ANIMALS AND IT RESULTED IN THEIR DEATHS. I AM OUTRAGED"

Because we were not among the early arrivals crushed at the front of the terrace. Because we were not among the later arrivals, some of whom I understand died in the tunnel. Because, though almost 60, I am 16 stone and therefore able to look after myself. Because my son is agile and was able to get across to the railing and, after helping many escape, clamber over the fence and on to the pitch. It was 50 minutes before we confirmed each other's safety – a period of time I will never forget. Meanwhile, others were dying amid scenes of increasing anger. And when the fans caged on terraces know that supporters are dying and demand action they are not impressed by a policeman clambering on to a fence and pleading weakly with spectators 'move back'. Movement is not possible when you have 3,000 people pressing on you from behind.

"It was 15 to 20 minutes before the crowd's demands for the perimeter fencing to be dismantled were answered. By this

"IT WAS THE FANS WHO OPENED THE PERIMETER FENCE. IT WAS THE FANS WHO STRETCHERED THE DYING AWAY"

Below: *One of the lucky ones – he would live to see another game, if he ever wanted to.*

time people had already died. No wonder the crowd near to me responded with the observation that it was a 'bit bloody late'. Time means nothing when you have a young boy dying of suffocation near you and your only intention is to survive. But you do retain certain impressions and the noise level was one.

"Even when the pressure was off, the public address system pleading with people to empty the terrace could not be understood. But when Kenny Dalglish spoke to the crowd we could hear every syllable. Someone could take a few lessons in crowd psychology and control from that. Finally – and for those who do care for football supporters please note – it was the fans who opened the perimeter fence. It was the fans who stretchered the dying away on advertising boards. It was the fans who, with modest first aid skills, helped the injured. In spite of what our critics may say, I saw public conscience respond to the crisis at Hillsborough

Right: *Honouring the dead – a memorial to those who died from those who will always remember them.*

"JOYOUS SINGING WENT ROUND THE REST OF THE GROUND WHILE THOSE CRUSHED AND TRAPPED SLOWLY EXPIRED"

IT IS CLEAR THAT THE MENTAL SCARS OF HILLSBOROUGH WILL TAKE LONGER TO HEAL THAN THE PHYSICAL ONES

to a degree which leads me to believe all is not lost in our society."

"The football continued to joyous shouting and singing round the rest of the ground while those crushed and trapped slowly expired." So said Lord Justice Taylor at the end of the official enquiry into the tragedy.

He laid the blame on the failure of police control and voiced his hope that football in general might, one day, become a sport again where steel cages and pens are not needed to keep apart fans for what is supposed to harmless fun.

The final victims of the disaster are ironically its survivors. Five years after the slaughter more than 200 people who were there suffer from panic attacks, nausea and nightmares. Beareavement counsellors waiting at the end of special phone lines after a TV documentary in 1994 screened details of what happened that day were staggered by the number of callers who rang. Others are suffering acute guilt complexes, feeling they could have done more to help the fans crushed on the terraces. The mental scars of Hillsborough will take longer to heal than the physical ones.

DIAL
RESCUE

AIR RESCUE
Winged Wonders

He was perhaps the greatest pilot of postwar years, and certainly one of the bravest. Throughout an extraordinary life American Don Sheldon saved the lives of dozens of fellow adventurers with barely a thought for the risk to his own neck. Even the boys' storybook hero Biggles could have learned a few tricks from him.

Sheldon was a Bush Pilot, one of that rugged breed who flew the world's jungles, mountains and wildernesses wherever a contract took them. They traced their history back to the ice wastes of Alaska in the 1920s, when string-and-glue aircraft helped connect a network of remote settlements by ferrying mail, medicines, food and emergency aid. There was a glut of old World War One planes on the market then and many well-trained ex-service pilots eager to buy them. These men flew to make a living – but also because they were hooked on the thrills of the air.

Born in 1922, into a farming family in Wyoming, Don Sheldon followed the exploits of the young aviators with relish. He dreamt of living in Alaska, lured by its cold beauty and remoteness, and at 17 struck out to discover it for himself. Work as a dairyman, trapper and gold miner – plus a stint as a tail gunner in a World War Two B-17 – finally led to him starting his own air charter business in Alaska.

CALCULATED RISKS

By the early 1950s he had more work than he could handle. A growing proportion involved ferrying mountaineers and prospectors out to some God-forsaken spot of their choice. Sheldon adopted the classic Bush Pilot's philosophy: "If you'll ride there, I'll fly there." But his carefree attitude did not extend to recklessness. He knew how good he was but he also had a healthy respect for the awesome Alaska Range of mountains and its unforgiving weather. If he dropped a party off somewhere he would try to overfly their intended route a day or so later. It was all part of the service.

In 1955, soldiers from the US Army Search and Rescue Section based at Fort Richardson in Anchorage announced plans to chart the navigable waters of the river Susitna. It would mean having to shoot a five-mile length of "white water", known as the Devil's Canyon rapids. Sheldon thought they were mad.

DEADLY RAPIDS

He'd flown close to the 50-70 yard sheer canyon and he knew the ferocity of the waters. When he took a short detour above the river, just 36 hours into the expedition, his worst fears were confirmed. He spotted chunks of the boat's yellow hull being tossed around the river along with a mass of other debris. Then he saw seven of the original party of eight, their life jackets shredded, huddled together on a narrow spray-soaked platform next to the northern edge of the sheer cliffs. Even if they had had the strength, the upward climb was suicidal. He realised that the party risked being washed away as their mental and physical reserves drained. The simple option was to fly to the nearest air base to raise the alarm.

Opposite: Rescue operations carried out by air usually require great skill and present huge personal risk to those involved.

> THESE MEN FLEW TO MAKE
> A LIVING — BUT ALSO
> BECAUSE THEY WERE
> HOOKED ON THE THRILLS
> OF THE AIR

Below: *Sheldon and friends pose outside their makeshift camp. "If you'll ride there, I'll fly there," he told customers.*

But Sheldon knew there was no one else in Alaska with his skill and knowledge of mountain flying. Besides, by the time help arrived the men could be dead.

There was only one thing for it. He dropped his passengers – a couple of fishermen – at nearby Otter Lake. Then he headed his Aeronca Sedan plane into the wind and took off for Devil's Canyon. One of the greatest single-handed rescues in history was about to take place. Sheldon knew that it would be impossible to land on the swirling torrent immediately beneath the men. Even if he put the plane down successfully its pontoon floats would be almost certain to hit an underwater boulder. If he didn't have total control of the aircraft he would be swept to oblivion.

A couple of practice fly-pasts revealed a calmer stretch of the river a quarter of a mile upstream. With scarcely believable daring, Sheldon overflew the white water and touched down on a smoother stretch, his pontoons pointing straight into the oncoming current. Then, throttling up to give the tiny aircraft stability, he allowed himself to drift backwards at 20 mph.

WATER MEETS AIR

Later he recalled his feelings: "As the plane backed into the first of the combers I felt it lurch heavily fore and aft. It was like a damned roller coaster. The water was rolling up higher than my wing tips, beating at the struts, and I could barely see because of the spray and water on the windows.

The engine was beginning to sputter and choke, and I knew it was getting wet down pretty good. If it had quit, I'd have been a goner. But it didn't."

As the Aeronca bobbed madly along like a cork, Sheldon saw the drenched soldiers looming behind him. The hardest part of the whole, fantastic operation was now upon him.

"I had to stop the airplane's backward motion, which I did with full throttle," he said. "But I knew my problems had only begun. Without damaging a wing on the rocks, I had to get the airplane close enough to the ledge for the guys to jump out onto the float and get aboard. If they missed, in their condition, they'd drown for sure. I jockeyed around and finally got the wing angled just enough to get one of them on the left float and still keep myself from running downstream."

RAPID ACTION

Sheldon allowed his aircraft to ride the rapids over 2,500 yards – "one of the longest rides on a river that I've ever taken" was how he later described it. Once the current slackened into calm water he manoeuvred the plane around and headed propellor-first downstream for take-off. Most pilots in his place would have been happy to have performed that miracle and gone to get help.

But Sheldon was no ordinary pilot. After landing one soldier safely he persuaded himself he could get the rest out, taking a man on each pontoon every trip. Such an operation was madness, danger and bravado rolled into one. Sheldon pulled it off.

Not only that, but he also spotted the missing eighth member of the expedition lying battered, bruised and barely conscious downstream. All the men recovered.

Such heroics earned the lanky aviator a rare civilian citation from the U.S. Army. It read: "Seeking neither acclaim nor reward Mr Sheldon willingly and voluntarily pitted his skill and aircraft against odds. His intrepid feat adds lustre to the memory of those stalwart pilots whose rare courage and indomitable spirit have conquered the vastness of the Alaskan Territory." Sadly, Sheldon was only 53 when he died of cancer in 1975. In an earlier interview he summed up the lives of the Bush Pilots in their heyday of the 1920s and 1930s.

"The hours are too long and the pay's not

IF HE DIDN'T HAVE TOTAL CONTROL OF THE AIRCRAFT HE WOULD BE SWEPT TO OBLIVION

Below: *Pilot Don Sheldon with one of his early planes. His company was one of the first to open up the inhospitable Alaskan mountains.*

good enough," he said. "If you make it everyone says hooray! When you don't, you shouldn't have been doing the damn stunt anyway. But whoopee boy, you just can't sit around like a vegetable. You got to do something."

Just as the 1920s saw aeroplanes opening up Alaska, so they helped connect the remote homesteads and sheep stations of the sun-parched Australian Outback.

Some of these farmers were so cut off they had never even heard of the Wright Brothers and had no concept of powered flight. One legendary young pilot, Hudson Fysh, dined out for years on the story of how he once landed at a far-flung sheep station to find the owner twisting his hat in his hands and murmuring respectfully: "Hello God, my name is Smith."

One of the ranchers' greatest enemies was isolation. Few women were prepared to accept their proposals of marriage and the boredom, loneliness and strength-sapping 130 degree heat that went with it. The women were also conscious of the dangers of pregnancy. With the nearest hospitals a ten-day cart ride away, any complications could be disastrous. Cases of death in childbirth among Outback wives was frighteningly high.

The early flying doctors, later to become the Royal Flying Doctor Service, changed all that. On February 21 1924, Hudson Fysh performed one of the first medical missions when he was called to rescue a Mrs Armstrong, the wife of a sheep station manager, in Queensland. She was about to have her first baby and needed to be taken to hospital. But land transport was impossible.

The wet season had turned most of the state into a lake. An emergency call was telegraphed to Fysh, who gamely managed to land near the farm on a road that was still intact. He quickly found out why Mr Armstrong was close to a breakdown. The farmer's first wife had died in childbirth when flooding cut off all medical help. Now he feared the same would happen again. Despite convincing himself that the woman would have her baby in the air, Fysh gently lifted her into the passenger seat and took off for the nearest hospital. Thanks to him she survived childbirth and produced a healthy little girl.

MAKING ENDS MEET

Some medical rescue flights involved the most bizarre arrangements. In 1925 the Father of the flying doctors, Dr Frederic A. Hope Michod, was anxious to get a desperately ill and crippled woman patient from

Above: *A warm welcome. Outback families gather for the arrival of the Flying Doctor aircraft, their only link with the outside world.*

"BUT WHOOPEE BOY, YOU JUST CAN'T SIT AROUND LIKE A VEGETABLE. YOU GOT TO DO SOMETHING"

his basic small-town hospital at Longreach to distant Brisbane. The ideal Qantas plane was a de Havilland 50, which had enough cabin space to take a stretcher. Unfortunately this had not returned from a previous assignment. All that was available was an open-cockpit D.H.9C, into which the incapacitated woman could not possibly be expected to climb.

The solution to the quandary was provided by Qantas's chief mechanic, Arthur Baird. He hoisted the woman, strapped into a seat, high in the air on a block and tackle. The aircraft was then wheeled beneath her and she was lowered into the cockpit. The same procedure was followed when she landed. The Outback pilots on missions such as this needed very special skills. Not only flying skills but an ability to inspire faith and trust in those they were trying to help. The classic example of this came one stormy night in 1951 during the rescue of Vera Anning, a Queensland grazier's wife who was haemorrhaging badly after a miscarriage. Husband Bev radioed his nearest airbase at Cairns, north of Brisbane, correctly predicting that her life hung in the balance.

DRASTIC CONDITIONS

The Cairns controller felt helpless. His bulky de Havilland Rapide air ambulance had no hope of landing near the Anning's sheep station which, like the rest of the state, was completely waterlogged. There was just one faint chance that a lighter plane could get down on a hilly, well drained slope ten

Above: *Queen Elizabeth II has been one of the most active supporters of the Australian Flying Doctor Service. In 1963 she addressed listening posts throughout the country from the Alice Springs Flying Doctor Station.*

HE HOISTED THE WOMAN, STRAPPED INTO A SEAT, HIGH IN THE AIR ON A BLOCK AND TACKLE

---

miles away at Reedy Springs. It was a chance worth taking.

Luckily, a former Royal Australian Air Force Pilot called Bob Norman had put down in Cairns where he learned of the emergency. He reckoned his Tiger Moth was as good as any for the job and he set about planning the mission. Vera's husband Bev was meanwhile instructed to make for Reedy Springs with some farm hands to prepare a crude landing strip. He set off with the men and his wife in a station wagon. The car ride took 36 agonising hours.

The Annings successfully linked up with Norman, only for Vera to lose her nerve. "That thing," she moaned, "will never get off the ground if it's heading uphill and carrying two people." Norman decided that there was only one thing for it. He grabbed her husband and persuaded him to come for a joy-ride. Once she'd seen them take off, Bev consented to climbing into the Tiger Moth. She was rushed to hospital at Hughenden where a series of blood transfusions saved her life.

Afterwards Bev Anning was so grateful to Norman that he invested £300 in helping the flier start up a company called Bush Pilots Airways. The business rapidly expanded as the demand for air charter services grew and later emerged as the successful Air Queensland, which served dozens of small airports and landing strips in the Australian Outback.

HEROES OF THE SKY

There are countless other tales of heroism which surround these pioneering aviators. Occasionally there were also moments when a brush with death would spill over into a glorious, mouth-watering piece of comedy. One such incident is credited to another of the great early Bush Pilots, Ray Parer. This blunt-speaking, diminutive Aussie was renowned for his legendary bad luck in a career spiced with frequent crashes. Nonetheless, his flying helped open up the hostile terrain of New Guinea, still largely unexplored in the 1920s.

The story goes that, despite his unenviable record, Parer persuaded the British Lieutenant Governor of Papua New Guinea, Sir Hubert Murray, to go for a spin in his spanking new DH9C plane. It was Sir Hubert's first experience of flying but a

British public school education, and the traditional stiff upper lip philosophy of the British gentry, ensured he displayed not a trace of nerves.

Deliberately, impassively, Sir Hubert clambered into the plane with his niece, a Miss Morrison. Only seconds into the flight the curse of Parer struck and the engine seized up. Realising the only chance of rescuing his esteemed passengers was to perform a jungle-style crash landing, Parer glided towards trees at the end of the runway and smashed into the foliage, shearing off both wings simultaneously. The aircraft ploughed through the ground, every joint and rivet in its structure shrieking in violent death-throes. When it stopped, Parer scrambled out of his seat and rushed back to see how his two flying companions had fared.

A COMICAL SCENE

Miss Morrison had already stumbled out, eyes glazed, clothes rumpled and dumb with shock. Above her and Parer Sir Hubert gazed down owlishly, as though awaiting instructions. He looked like a Punch cartoonist's impression of the British aristocracy. The exchange between pilot and passenger was priceless.

"Excuse me sir," ventured Parer, "don't you think you ought to get out?"

"Is it all over then?" asked Sir Hubert.

"We've had a crash," said Parer.

"Oh," replied the Lieutenant Governor seriously. "I thought it was one of those stunts you chaps get up to."

Air travel may have become much safer in terms of technical advances. But it doesn't follow that the number of accidents and close shaves has been reduced.

On the contrary, the increase in airline traffic, and a boom in the use of small, private planes has led to many an inspired life-or-death rescue.

In British air space alone, four such incidents between 1990 and 1993 show there is still adventure aplenty for those who take to the skies. In the case of 27-year-old Alan Anderson from South Wales, adventure was just about the last thing he wanted.

It was a balmy April evening in 1992 when Alan met his father-in-law Les Rhoades at Cardiff Airport. He had flown as a passenger only once before and was looking forward to his joyride over the glittering

Above: *Les Rhoades, whose untimely death in the cockpit of his private plane led to one of the most dramatic air rescues ever seen in European skies.*

waters of Cardiff Bay with a mixture of nervousness and excitement.

Mr Rhoades, who held a full private pilot's license, helped strap him into the two-seater Rallye Minerva plane and at 6.03 air traffic controllers gave them clearance for take off. Flight Golf Delta Golf was exactly 44 minutes away from a drama, both tragic and triumphant, which would grip the nation.

At precisely 6.47, Mr Rhoades collapsed at the controls of the plane from a massive heart attack. A terrified Alan tried desperately to revive him but he could see it was useless.

Above: *Alan Anderson and 'guardian angel' Robert Legge.*

Below: *Alan and the plane he landed successfully.*

His father-in-law was dead and it looked likely that he would soon follow. He was at 2,000ft and without the faintest clue how to get down.

At Cardiff airport the frightened voice emerging from the radio told the whole story in 20 words: "Mayday! Mayday! Mayday! I'm in trouble and I'm scared.

"The pilot has had a heart attack. What can I do?"

It was a good question. As controllers activated the "major emergency" routine a radio operator coaxed crucial information out of Alan. The plane's height, position and state of fuel tanks were key importance. The operator didn't mention that seven fire engines had lined up on the runway.

CAREFUL INSTRUCTIONS

At 6.55 Alan's guardian angel, in the form of flying instructor Robert Legge, made visual contact. Legge had been cruising nearby with one of his pupils, Martin Leighton, and had responded immediately when Cardiff control explained the crisis. He hailed Alan on the radio and began explaining basic handling techniques. A few moments later he eased his Piper Warrior plane alongside.

Alan was still scared – but he could see he was no longer alone. A radio ham from nearby Barry Island, Howard Drone, taped the following extracts from the conversation between the two men.

Legge: Forward on the controls. That's fine. Let the aeroplane fly itself.

Anderson: I wish it would.

Legge: Read the air speed.

Anderson: The air speed is about 105.

Legge: I'm on your right hand side. Just relax. We're bringing you down to land. I would like you to fly straight over the runway. What's the speed?

Anderson: 102.

Legge: That's fine as long as it doesn't get much less. We're going to do a left-hand circuit. Try to keep that height. A nice gentle turn to the left.

Keep the turn going all the way round again.

Anderson: Is there anyone down there who can get in contact with Les's wife and my wife?

Legge: Don't worry about that. We'll get that sorted out for you. Just concentrate on my instructions at this time.

Anderson: We are going down aren't we?

Legge: We are shortly, yes. Bank gently to the right. We're aiming for the wide tarmac strip to the right of the white and red lights. Can you see it?

Anderson: Affirmative.

Legge: I would like you to reduce the power slightly now. What's your airspeed?

Anderson: 100

Legge: Pull back very gently on the control column. Close the throttle… just hold it there. Pull gently back on the control column and hold it there.

Hold it! Hold it! Hold it!

(The plane touches down)

Legge: Hold the control column back. Relax. OK. On the rudder pedals – press the top of the rudder pedals. You'll find the brakes. Press both pedals together.

Anderson: I can't find the brakes.

Legge: Don't worry. The emergency vehicles are coming up behind you. Just sit in the aircraft. You just sit in the aircraft and leave the engine running. In fact, can you see the red lever next to the throttle?

Anderson: I can't.

Legge: Pull the red lever towards you.

Anderson: I've got to unstrap myself. I can't see anything.

Legge: Can you see some keys in the ignition?

Anderson: Affirmative

Legge: Turn the key to off and the engine should stop.

DON'T WORRY. THE EMERGENCY VEHICLES ARE COMING UP BEHIND YOU. JUST SIT IN THE AIRCRAFT

Below: *Back in the air. Alan Anderson managed to overcome the memory of a terrifying ordeal to continue with flying tuition. Here he makes his first flight after the celebrated talk-down.*

Right: *Parachute instructor Ronnie O'Brien turned himself into a human dart to save two skydivers who became tangled in their ropes. "There was only one chance to get it right," he said later.*

Below: *Ronnie O'Brien's feat turned him into an instant celebrity. Millions, including football manager Brian Clough (right), marvelled at his daring – faithfully recorded by a video camera on his helmet.*

Anderson: It's stopping now.

Legge: Unstrap yourself and the emergency services will see you.

Anderson: Thank God.

Legge: You're welcome. It's all in a day's work.

If that drama tested Robert Legge's teaching skills to the limit, pity parachute instructor Ronnie O'Brien.

In May 1991 he was jumping with a group of skydivers near Sibson airfield, Peterborough, England. Ronnie, the 44-

on his video camera and relaxed, ready to enjoy the 125 mph descent.

A LIFESAVER

It was then he realised something had gone very wrong below. Instead of adopting the classic spread eagle position, Smith and Maynard were locked in an uncontrollable spin. A small drag chute had tangled around Smith's neck, cutting off his air supply. Within a few seconds he was unconscious, although

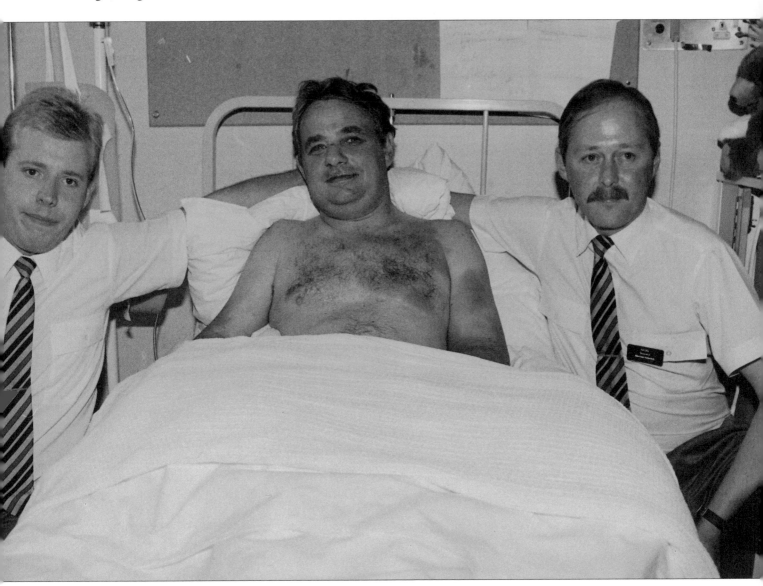

year-old chief instructor at Peterborough Parachute Club, planned to film his own jump and that of fellow instructor Mike Smith and first-time rookie Richard Maynard, who were strapped together.

As the men stepped out at 12,000 ft there was no hint that anything was amiss. Ronnie, some 300ft above them, switched

pupil Maynard was blissfully unaware of the peril both men were in. He assumed the spin was all part of the fun. Ronnie said: "I saw Mike try initially to cut away the bridle line from around his neck. But it was hopeless. Then he dropped the knife and blacked out. I formed my body into a dart allowing me to accelerate towards them.

Above: *Pilot Tim Lancaster with two of the cabin crew who saved his life at 23,000 feet. But for their determination he would have been sucked out of a shattered windscreen.*

"The timing had to be right for me to intercept them. There was only one chance to get it right."

With just 10 seconds before the pair faced certain death, Ronnie managed to halt the spin and release Mike's reserve chute. He then floated down alongside to alert ground support crew. Later, British Parachuting Association spokesman Tony Butler said:

Below: *A fully recovered Tim Lancaster attends a press reception in honour of his crew. "I knew I could die if whoever was holding me couldn't hang on," he said.*

"None of us has ever heard of anything like this. It was an utterly freak accident.

"Ronnie was magnificent. He undoubtedly saved the lives of these two men."

There is no textbook advice on how to handle air rescues of this nature. Survival is down to the reactions and skills of those close by, plus a large dose of luck.

Like many other airline captains, Tim Lancaster had often asked himself what he would do in a crisis. Procedures for engine failure, aborted take-offs and forced landings were all clear in his mind. Never in a million years did he expect to be sucked out of his cabin window at 23,000 feet.

Yet that is exactly what happened in July 1990 as Captain Lancaster piloted a British Airways BAC 1-11 holiday jet from Birmingham to Spain. The aircraft was over Southampton when two cabin windows shattered, depressurising the cockpit. The captain found himself clinging to the nose of his aeroplane at 400 mph. A crewman inside fought frantically to hold on to his legs. The ordeal lasted 20 minutes. For most of the time, Lancaster was unconscious.

Steward Simon Rogers, 29, from Solihull, Birmingham, led the rescue operation.

He strapped himself into the captain's seat and held on for dear life as co-pilot Andrew Atchison brought the plane down to Eastleigh airport, Southampton. Behind them, in the main fuselage, cabin crew worked out of their skins to calm the 81 holidaymakers aboard.

Later Captain Lancaster said: "I just remember this almighty bang and the horror of realising I was outside the aircraft. It must have been minus 30 Centigrade and, though I wasn't conscious throughout, I knew I could die if whoever was holding me couldn't hang on."

CAPTAIN COURAGEOUS

A British Airways spokesman said: "Every one of the crew did BA proud, and that includes Captain Lancaster. We have nothing but praise for all of them. It was a tremendous example of alertness and bravery."

Captain Ed Wyer – nicknamed Captain Cool by British newspapers – also fought a potentially catastrophic mid-air accident to win through. In June 1993 he found himself at 5,000 ft, flying at 200 mph, when both engines of his Piper Navajo aircraft failed.

The plane, on a scheduled flight between Birmingham and Norwich, tumbled into a corkscrew 3,500ft dive above Gayton, Norfolk, with Ed wrestling the controls in the hope of gliding to an emergency landing. After a heart-stopping minute he succeeded, and put the aircraft down in a barley field. Within seconds his passengers were all over him hugging and kissing. "Unfortunately," he joked later, "some of them were blokes."

Farmer Peter Burman, who saw it all happen, said: "He did a miraculous job. I have nothing but praise for his skill. I was absolutely amazed to see the passengers get out."

And Squadron leader Jack Love, who led a helicopter rescue operation from RAF Coltishall, said: "What a feat of airmanship! It's remarkable. The passengers had no qualms about getting into the helicopter – that shows what a good landing he made."

ENGINE FAILURE

Ed, from Barnham, near Thetford, Norfolk, later recalled his adventure: "I heard this almighty bang and realised the starboard engine had sheared away from the main frame. The propellor sliced through the nose

Above: *The man with nerves of steel, Ed Wyer relaxes at home with his wife Wendy. One eye-witness to the plane drama said: "He did a miraculous job."*

Left: *Pilot Ed Wyer saved all his passengers after watching the propeller from one engine sheer off and smash the other to shreds.*

of the aircraft and hit the left-hand engine. We had no power and were spinning down. I thought that was it. It was like piloting a block of flats.

"Finally I managed to get the aircraft gliding and then had to look for somewhere suitable to land. I had to avoid a few high-tension cables and trees. I had no power and I gave it an awful lot of left rudder.

"I spotted a field of barley and thought that might be a good place for a crash landing because it would cushion us. Just before we landed I looked round and all the passengers were bracing themselves."

He added: "I knew it wasn't going to be my day when I nearly got run over crossing the road on the way to work."

ANIMAL RESCUE
Pet Mates

The rottweiler's name was Trudi and her story ranks among the most extraordinary animal rescues on record. To anyone who ever loses a pet dog, her survival represents an enduring symbol of hope.

I n May 1990 a heavily pregnant Trudi set off on a sailing holiday with her owners, the Williamsons of Paraparaumu, North Island, New Zealand. Robert Williamson, a single father, was skippering the yacht with sons Aaron, 12, and Ben, 5, acting as crew. Their plan was to set a course between the straits of North and South Island, an area notorious for its treacherous currents and heavy Pacific swells.

During the early part of the voyage Trudi went into a long and exhausting labour, eventually producing eight lively, hungry puppies. Already weakened by the births, she now faced an insatiable demand for milk and her condition weakened further. Then, disastrously, as her puppies played safely below deck, Trudi was tipped off the boat by a large wave. Though she was well used to life as a salty dog, she had neither the strength nor the will to hang on. Death should have been a formality.

DISCOVERING THE TRUTH

At first the Williamsons refused to accept that she had fallen overboard. They searched the yacht from bow to stern, always expecting to see her big, brown eyes staring up at them. When it at last became obvious that she had been washed away, they mapped out a search area and steered the yacht in circles. The children screamed her name as loud as they could, but there was no answering bark.

The family was grief-stricken, yet they could not allow themselves the luxury of retreating into mourning. They had eight hungry mouths to feed and had no Trudi to supply the milk. They certainly didn't have

a baby's bottle or a supply of teats and so the boys had to painstakingly direct milk into the puppies' mouths using an eye-dropper. At least these desperate measures kept their minds off the dog that they had loved and lost.

The pups all survived and two weeks later they were safely back at the Williamsons home. The family did its best to settle back into life without Trudi.

Then the miracle happened.

The captain of a fishing boat which had been cruising off the Chetwode island group telephoned Robert to say he'd rescued Trudi from a tiny, wave-spattered rock miles from the usual sea lanes. She had lost half her original weight and could hardly

SHE HAD NEITHER THE STRENGTH NOR THE WILL TO HANG ON. DEATH SHOULD HAVE BEEN A FORMALITY

Opposite: *Even the most gentle of animals can show determined resilience under tough conditions.*

Below: *Aaron Williamson and his miracle-dog Trudi.*

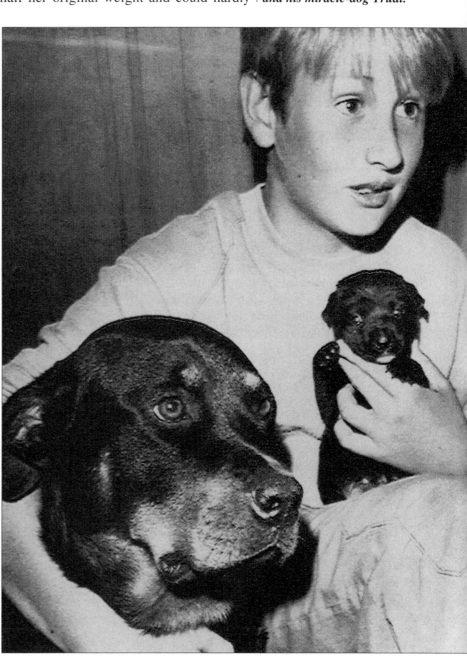

walk. But she still wore her collar and the tag bearing her owners' telephone number.

Robert said: "I almost fainted when I heard the news of how she had been found on the island. The boys were beside themselves with happiness. We went to meet the fishermen and I cried as I thanked them. Trudi was licking my hand like she'd never been away."

To this day, no one knows how a severely-weakened Trudi made it to safety. One theory is that a school of dolphins guided her to the nearest land. But New Zealand vet Murray Gibb has the most likely explanation. "The animal's fatty tissues around the mammary glands – enlarged after giving birth – probably helped to keep her afloat and to keep her warm.

PADDLING FOR SURVIVAL

"Somehow, by paddling and with the help of a current, she made it to the island. Dogs can go without food for a long time. Nonetheless, Trudi's survival is a miracle."

Pets like her – and her pups – seem born to adventure. But few dogs can ever expect to lead the kind of all-action devil-may-care lifestyle enjoyed by Antis the alsation. For much of World War Two he was either being rescued or rescuing others.

It was late 1939 and in the skies above the shell-cratered stretch of no man's land between France and Germany a Soviet-built ANT-40 bomber was spluttering towards the ground, its engines shot to pieces by ack-ack fire. Somehow the six-man crew – members of Czech resistance flying with the First Bomber Reconnaissance Squadron of the French air force – crawled out of the wreckage. Dazed and terrified of discovery they stumbled a few hundred yards into the ruins of a farmhouse to debate their next move.

As they huddled together the bomber crew were startled to hear a whimpering sound coming from the rubble. They saw a tiny puppy, half starved and obviously abandoned. He was crying out for affection and one of the gunners, Jan Bozdech, picked him up and started cuddling him. In that moment a bond was made between them.

The airman voted to trek south, away from the German forces. One man challenged Jan about the wisdom of bringing the pup with them. Might he not bark or

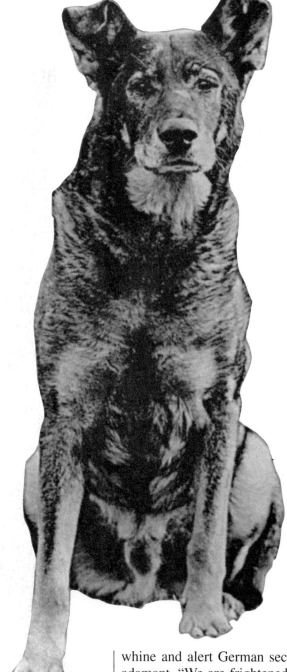

Above: *The canine war hero Antis, who cheated death time and again with his Free Czech unit.*

whine and alert German security? Jan was adamant. "We are frightened and so is he," he said. "The dog is coming with us."

But what about a name. Someone suggested calling him Ant, after the bombers they had flown. "Too undignified," ruled Jan. Antis he became.

Weeks later, the air crew were billeted in Southern France. There they were asked to fly some French officers to Algeria and readily accepted the chance to be back in action. Jan took his place in the rear gunner's turret along with the debutante flier Antis. For the puppy, it was going to be a memorable first flight.

Just past the island of Majorca, the plane was struck by anti-aircraft fire and ditched in the sea. Everyone escaped alive, only to be hauled aboard a German cargo boat as prisoners of war.

Yet Antis seemed to attract good luck just when he needed it most. The following day, a British Royal Navy flotilla sighted the German convoy and immediately engaged it. Jan and Antis dived into an oily, fiery sea to escape the shells and were later picked up by a British vessel. Next stop; Britain via Gibralter.

JAN'S PLAN

Antis had to be smuggled on board. The Czechs realised that they would be in trouble if they were caught but, as one of them said: "We cannot desert him any more than we could desert one another." When they eventually arrived in Britain Jan spoke no English and just hoped his pet would be shown kindness.

In fact Antis received all the tender, loving care that he needed from the Peoples' Dispensary for Sick Animals. Soon he was back at Jan's side, navigating Wellingtons for an RAF Czech squadron. The dog was even fitted out with his own special custom-built oxygen mask.

Twice Antis was struck by flying shrapnel. On one occasion half his ear was blown off and he lay mournfully in a pool of blood for four hours until the Wellington landed and medical help arrived.

Before the war ended, Antis got his chance to be the rescuer rather than the rescued. One evening he was walking with Jan back to their barracks in Speke, Merseyside, when German bombs suddenly rained down, demolishing the street. As soon as the dust cleared Antis was pawing at the rubble, helping to locate and dig out survivors. He worked tirelessly until rescue marshals decided no one could be left alive. Then he disappeared.

At first Jan panicked, believing the dog had got himself trapped or crushed under falling rubble. He need not have worried. After ten minutes Antis was heard whining and Jan rounded a corner to see him standing guard over the collapsed brickwork that was once a house. The digging gangs arrived and work began furiously. Minutes later a baby was found, still alive, in its cot.

After the war, Antis performed one last act of courage to repay the man who had once saved his life. By now he and his master were back in Czechoslovakia, where Czech airmen who had fought with

Above: *Antis' Dickin Medal. He was the first non-British dog to receive it.*

JAN AND ANTIS DIVED INTO AN OILY, FIERY SEA TO ESCAPE THE SHELLS AND WERE LATER PICKED UP BY A BRITISH VESSEL

ANTIS WENT FOR HIM, THE GUARD WAS KNOCKED BACKWARDS AND HE AND JAN DASHED ACROSS THE BORDER TO FREEDOM

the Western Allies were regarded suspiciously by the pro-Soviet government.

Man and dog fled towards the German border with another escapee and on a dark, misty night they found themselves staring towards territory still occupied by the Allies. At that moment a Czech border guard appeared, gun in hand. Antis went for him, the guard was knocked backwards and he and Jan then dashed across the border to freedom.

HIGH RECOGNITION

Months later, Antis became the first foreign-born dog to be awarded the British Dickin Medal, the animal equivalent of the Victoria Cross. The canine hero's citation read: "For outstanding courage, devotion to duty and life-saving on several occasions while serving in England and overseas with the RAF and the French Air Force from 1939 to 1945."

Antis died in 1953. Jan married an English wife, Maureen, and settled in England. He died of a stroke in 1980.

The couple decided it was impossible to replace Antis. "That dog really had an extraordinary intelligence," said Maureen. "Jan had promised Antis that he would never have another dog.

"He kept his promise."

Dog lovers like Jan Bozdech are a rare jewel. The wartime bonding between Antis and he was special in that both lived their lives on a knife-edge. In a world fraught

Above: Sandra Rodriguez, 22 months-old, in her mother's arms. Her dog Rambo was the little girl's sole protection while being lost in the forests of Quiroga, Northern Spain, for an entire night.

"WHEN I SAVED TESSA SHE HAD SHRUNK INTO A LITTLE BALL ABOUT HALF HER NORMAL SIZE... I DIDN'T THINK OF MY OWN SAFETY"

with danger, risks were easy to take for an animal you loved.

Yet even in peacetime, it seems dogs in distress bring out the best in their masters.

Take Steve Shimell and his springer spaniel bitch Tessa. In 1992 the 20-year-old carpenter was out hunting rabbits near Newton Abbott, Devon, south-west England, when Tessa discovered a disused well. Curious to see what was inside, she strained her neck, overbalanced and plunged 20 feet to the bottom. When a frantic Steve peered down he could see her trying desperately to tread water. The sound of her terrified whimpering cut through him like a knife.

A friend hunting with them ran to raise the alarm and Steve concentrated his efforts on reassuring Tessa and making sure she could see him. But as no assistance materialised, it became obvious she would not last much longer. Her head kept disappearing into the freezing, black water.

"I could see she was in trouble," he said, "and I didn't think twice about jumping in because there was no time to waste. I could not stand by and watch her drown and she must have been treading water for ages before we got back to her. Luckily there was a wooden crossbeam down the well I could hang on to as I grabbed her, but it was impossible to get out without help.

"I was very cold and wet down there and when I saved Tessa she had shrunk into a

little ball about half her normal size.

At the time I didn't think about my own safety but looking back I could see how dangerous it was and I'm glad we both got out safely."

The two of them were huddled together for 15 minutes until another member of the hunting party, lifeboatman Jim Trout, returned with ropes from the boot of his car. Both were then pulled to safety.

A local vet, Allan Birchby, said later: "When Tessa arrived here she was suffering from hypothermia and was barely conscious. We wrapped her in blankets and gave her intense heat treatment. She would certainly have died if it had not been for Steve."

Curiosity was, quite literally, Tessa's downfall, although dogs are strictly amateur-league when it comes to being nosey. Cats – and especially kittens – are the pets guaranteed to raise any owner's stress level by embroiling themselves in some hair-raising escapade.

A VANISHING ACT

Pity poor postman David Tedder. On October 21 1993 his 14-week-old puss Jess scrambled up the chimney in Londonderry Street, Silksworth, Sunderland, north-east England and vanished. David and his wife Lorraine at first assumed she must have escaped from the house. It was only at 11pm that night, when they heard muffled cries behind the brickwork that the awful truth dawned. A cat-lover's nightmare that was to obsess the entire street had begun.

Jess, named after the black and white cat owned by the children's TV and book character Postman Pat, had been bought for the couple's two-year-old daughter Megan. David, 25, didn't want to alarm the little girl, but he had few options. While Megan slept, he began ripping bricks out of his sitting room wall to create a big enough escape hole. Then he and Lorraine set out dishes of her favourite tuna in the hope that the smell would entice her out.

It didn't work. The following morning the tuna remained untouched. So, with a resigned look on his face, David began demolishing a dining room wall, the area where miaows had been heard most recently. By Friday evening there was still no sign of Jess. So he started knocking down part of a bedroom.

CURIOSITY OVER A CAT

By now neighbours were dropping by to give advice. The story of the curious cat was spreading like wildfire and everyone in the street began anxiously waiting for news. The Tedders were beside themselves. They realised they couldn't go on demolishing walls indefinitely. It was time to call in the experts. At tea time on the Saturday night they telephoned their local fire station.

"I felt a bit daft calling out the fire brigade," said David afterwards, "but it was the only option left. We couldn't bear to leave her to die. There were two engines here most of the time. Every now and then, one had to go and fight a fire, but they kept coming back. There was always at least one outside the door."

A total of 15 firemen were now taking turns to search for Jess. At midnight they called in a third engine equipped with an endoscope, normally used to locate earthquake victims. There was also other sophisticated looking and listening equipment.

At midnight Jess was located in the chimney of the house next door. "My neighbour wasn't too pleased," David admitted ruefully. "But she let them remove the fire to get her out."

Sooty and subdued, a miserable Jess was gently lifted to freedom amid cheers from the fire crews. Outside, a crowd which had gathered in the street burst into spontaneous applause. David burst into tears.

"It must have been the worst four days of my life," he confessed afterwards. "We didn't eat and we couldn't sleep because we could hear Jess's crying."

Perhaps they shouldn't have worried quite so much. Cats are able to live for long stretches without food and can survive on the barest minimum of water, such as licked-off condensation. In the spring of 1994, three young cats – Sciff, Floyd and Passport – each proved the point after they were rescued in three quite separate incidents.

Passport was a trans-Atlantic stowaway discovered by staff at the Glen Keith distillery, Keith, in the very north of Scotland.

She was released from a whisky cask, part of a shipment originating from Kentucky, and had survived on nothing more than whisky fumes. Fortunately for her, managers at Chivas Brothers, which owns the distillery, agreed to pay for her quarantine and give her a full-time job as official mouser. Director John Watson said: "We couldn't let anything happen to her after all she'd been through."

UNWANTED WEIGHT LOSS

Floyd was another puss who placed himself on an unintentional crash diet. When his owner, Janet Turner of Gosport, southern England, put the tabby out for his usual evening stroll he vanished into thin air. Her three children were heartbroken and for a month Janet searched the area daily, even appealing on local radio.

Floyd was finally saved when a family friend, who was viewing a new house, was told by builders that plaintive miaows were coming from beneath the floorboards. Although they had cut a hole in the boards, the puss refused to budge.

At last Floyd was coaxed out, wobbly on his feet and desperately thin, having stayed

> DAVID BEGAN DEMOLISHING A DINING ROOM WALL, THE AREA WHERE MIAOWS HAD BEEN HEARD MOST RECENTLY

Above: *Postman David Tedder and his troublesome cat Jess.*

alive on rainwater and mice. He soon recovered enough to resume his evening walks... but he stayed close to his garden.

A "lucky" black cat called Sciff knows just how Floyd feels. Except Sciff's prison was much more escape-proof.

Sciff, from Exmouth on England's south coast, found her way into the foundations of a house which was being constructed at nearby Brackendale. Unfortunately for her, her only available exit was blocked up as she took a nap. For four weeks she was confined to a concrete tomb until prospective homebuyers heard her cries and raised the

alarm. Builders released her after demolishing brickwork and removing an air vent.

Owner Norma Warner said afterwards: "I couldn't believe it when we got a phone call from the vet to say she had been found. My 10-year-old son Lee was over the moon. He had gone to the window every day to see if she had come home."

If cats can be a pain in the tail, they can also be life-savers themselves.

In 1991 cat-lover Evelyn Robinson of Batley, West Yorkshire, England, collapsed in a diabetic coma. All standard medical techniques failed to bring her round.

Then doctors and nurses at Dewsbury District Hospital decided to see if her greatest love Sandy, the 10-year-old tomcat she rescued from the streets, could make a difference. Sandy leapt onto her bed, played with the tubes feeding her body with nutrients and pawed her nose. "When I came round I just cuddled Sandy and cried," said Evelyn. "He saved my life."

Even more dramatic was the intervention of alley-cat Max. In May 1994 she heard her owner, a 34-year-old disabled woman, calling to him from the passage next to her home in Bracknell, Berkshire, England. It was evening and the unlit alley was in darkness.

Suddenly a man leapt out from the shadows, grabbed her from behind and began punching her face, arms, ribs and legs. It was a violent and unprovoked attack from a

Below: *This puss called Patty survived for 25 days inside a cargo container shipped from America to South Korea in 1981.*

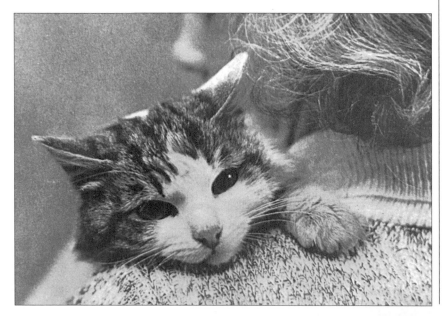

Right: *Tabatha, a cat from Pasadena, is reunited with her owners after escaping from her cage in a 747 jet. In 1994 she travelled as an air stowaway for 30,000 miles and over 13 days.*

Left: *A young woman pours sea water over a beached baby whale on Farewell Spit, New Zealand. The apparent determination of the whales to kill themselves is a mystery.*

cowardly would-be rapist and it seemed that there could be only one winner. The woman, who was never at any stage identified by police at her own request, was helpless to hit back.

At this point a mean and moody Max decided it was time to even the odds. She gave the mugger the shock of his miserable life by jumping onto his head, scratching his neck and embedding razor-sharp claws into his face. The terrified rapist stopped tearing at his victim's clothes and tried to shake off the cat. He failed. Then he ran away as fast as he could.

POLICE PRAISE

Afterwards Detective Constable Steven Gilkes told newsmen: "It was a most unusual incident and the first time I can ever remember a cat going to the aid of someone being attacked. The woman screamed and shouted but the assault continued until her cat suddenly became the heroine of the hour. Had the woman not fought so hard, and the cat not intervened, then we could have been dealing with a more serious matter."

The rescue of any animal is usually perfect material for newspapers. Somehow, there is a feel-good factor associated with these stories – both for everyone involved in the rescue and those reading about it. There is something about the helplessness of an animal in trauma that makes people forget their everyday worries.

In New Zealand they know all about this phenomenon. The most common manifestation of it occurs when "pods" of whales beach themselves and begin thrashing about hopelessly in the shallows. Without proper assistance, the noble mammals then die a slow death, their breathing increasingly laboured. Once a beaching is publicized however, volunteer helpers come from miles around to lend a hand.

In recent years there have been numerous examples of spontaneous whale-aid. In 1993 hundreds of New Zealanders and foreign tourists flocked to Farewell Spit beach on the northern tip of South Island to carry 100 pilot whales back into deeper water. Some were no more than 3ft-long babies.

> SHE SHOCKED THE MUGGER BY JUMPING ONTO HIS HEAD AND EMBEDDING RAZOR-SHARP CLAWS INTO HIS FACE

Below: *The scene at Golden Bay, New Zealand, when a pod of pilot whales stranded themselves on New Year's Eve, 1992.*

Left: *Another Farewell Spit rescue. This incident in January 1991 involved 270 pilot whales in one of the biggest mass-strandings for half a century.*

Below: *A pilot takes to the skies! This pilot whale was rescued from Key West, Florida, where it became stranded in March 1991. It was taken by helicopter to waters 150 miles off the coast.*

That rescue proved to be a repeat of an incident two years previously when a staggering 285 pilot whales had beached on Farewell Spit. All but 20 of the whales were saved on that occasion, but the exhausting operation was extended when 50 which had been returned to the deep promptly swam back to the shallows. Again, an army of holidaymakers and locals worked devotedly throughout the night, hosing the whales down at low tide, to keep them alive. The pilots also had to be kept apart in order to prevent the adults thrashing around and crushing the younger ones.

WASTED ENERGY

"Once they come on to land, whales become like deflated balloons," said Chris Stroud of the Whale and Dolphin Conservation Society. "They use up a lot of energy just trying to breathe."

One of the worst Canadian instances of "suicide" pilot whales occurred in August 1990 when 50 beached themselves on the

rocky Atlantic coastline of Nova Scotia. Around 200 people from the nearby fishing village of Cheticamp turned out to help in the rescue and all but two of the whales died. These two resisted all efforts to force them out to sea. "It was like they wanted to die and nobody was going to interfere," said one villager.

The Cheticamp incident provoked a huge debate among marine and wildlife experts as to why pilots put themselves through such risks. One idea is that they are driven ashore by killer whales hunting for food further out. Another is that, for some unknown reason, certain coastlines affect the whales' navigational systems. Yet another theory has it that a single, stranded whale emits a distress signal to which the rest of the pod responds.

Then again, the antics of humans must be almost as baffling to the mammals themselves. What must two short-finned pilot whales have been thinking after they were rescued off Key West, Miami, in 1991, and then returned to the sea 150 miles off-shore a year later? The whales were unceremoniously tipped out of two American air force helicopters hovering 40ft above the waves. The headline writers had a field day. "Pilot takes to the skies" was the favourite.

The thought processes of these beautiful creatures remain an enigma to scientists, a constant reminder of how little we really know about the oceans of the world.

Dolphins are equally puzzling, not just because they are probably the second most intelligent life-form on earth (some individuals would be able to argue quite convincingly that they are the most intelligent) but also because of their powerful desire to help other creatures. Examples of dolphins rescuing human beings are now cropping up almost every year.

TERRIFYING WEATHER

In October 1993 a Frenchman, Jean-Francois Colombier, was out fishing along with his son Julien, 16, and one of their friends, when one of the Bay of Biscay's ferocious autumn storms erupted without any warning at all. Jean-Francois, from the town of Brest, was convinced that their rubber dinghy would capsize and that they would be left to drown.

Above: *One of three California grey whales trapped beneath ice off the Alaskan coast. Rescuers cut blow holes to keep them alive.*

Below: *Too late to help. These pilot whales were found dead or dying on a Tasmanian beach.*

"What happened next was barely credible," he said. "They [the dolphins] encompassed the boat, two at the stern and one each side of us. If we hadn't been so afraid, we could have reached out and stroked them. I felt them exerting pressure on the boat and pulling it in a particular direction, out of danger and away from the rocks."

The amazing convoy continued for 30 minutes. Only when the dinghy was close to a safe landing point did the dolphins swim away, their rescue operation complete.

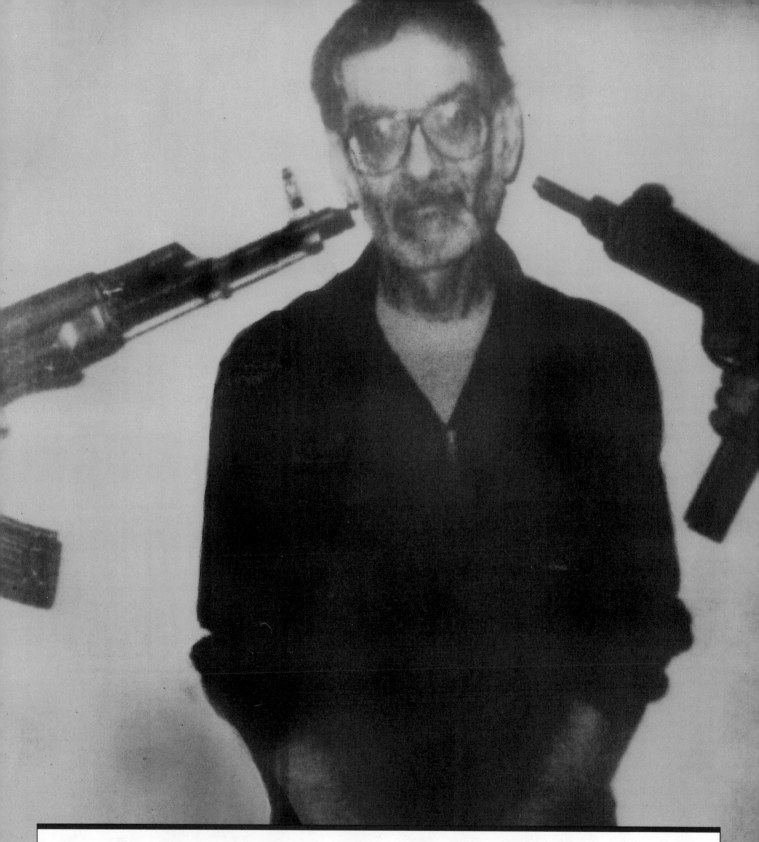

TROUBLE ABROAD
Difficult Territory

Think of daring rescues, and your mind reaches out to dramatic stories of courage, selflessness and determination. Those qualities are required of anyone who encounters danger or disaster in a strange land.

Just occasionally, a particular chain of events demands superhuman qualities of resilience. Where the combined barriers of foreign laws, bureaucracy, diplomatic niceties, and double-dealing opponents can tie the innocent up in knots and where months or even years can pass with no hint of a result one false step can sentence an innocent man to death.

This was just the scenario which emerged from the Beirut hostage crisis of the 1980s. Journalists and academics, whose only crime was to be Westerners, were seized and held to ransom by terrorists with the intention of advancing Islamic terrorist causes. Freeing them by military means was impossible. Apart from any political factors, it was impossible to know exactly where they were being held at any one time. The only hope was negotiation and persuasion.

Into this cauldron of intrigue stepped a young woman from Yorkshire, northern England, who once wouldn't have said boo to a goose. Her name was Jill Morrell and she was to become a reluctant symbol of the international fight against Middle Eastern fanaticism. The force that drove her on was a determination to rescue the man she loved.

INTO THIN AIR

He was John McCarthy, a well-respected journalist based in London with Worldwide Television News. They had met in 1983 while he was a telex operator and she was a secretary. Two years later they were sharing a flat and making plans for their future together. On April 17 1988, those dreams vanished in a single phone call to 27-year-old Jill from Roby Burke, a senior manager at WTN. She had taken the day off so that she could pick John up at Heathrow after his month-long stint on the news beat in Beirut. Now Burke's words

*Opposite: **Professor Robert Polhill, kidnapped by Islamic extremists. Photographs like this were designed to increase pressure on Western governments.***

BUREAUCRACY, DIPLOMATIC NICETIES, AND DOUBLE-DEALING OPPONENTS CAN TIE THE INNOCENT UP IN KNOTS

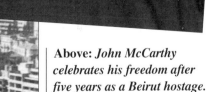

Above: *John McCarthy celebrates his freedom after five years as a Beirut hostage.*

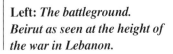

Left: *The battleground. Beirut as seen at the height of the war in Lebanon.*

Above: *A relaxed Jill Morell with a copy of the book she and John wrote from very different perspectives.*

THE CAPTORS WOULD PLAY CRUEL TRICKS, TELLING THE PRISONERS THEY WERE ABOUT TO BE RELEASED

Western governments to get any reliable intelligence on the hostages.

In the mid-1980s the hostage crisis was reaching its apex. John found himself sharing dark, damp cells with the likes of Americans Terry Anderson, another journalist, and Thomas Sutherland, a university lecturer. And there was his fellow Briton, the Anglican envoy Terry Waite, and Brian Keenan, the Irish lecturer who was to become his close friend. In all, 17 Westerners were abducted and held between 1985 and 1987. Not all escaped alive.

Very often the captors would play cruel tricks, telling their prisoners they were about to be released when in fact they were merely being moved to a new safe house or cell to avoid the attentions of the occupying Syrian army. It was a nightmare scenario. To Jill Morrell it was a nightmare without end.

For the first six months Jill was content to remain silent. She accepted the advice of the British Foreign Office that "making a fuss" would only serve to elevate John's importance in the eyes of the kidnappers. "Keep quiet," said the men from the ministry, "it's the best way."

A NEW OUTLOOK

But as the months rolled by with no news, Jill began to question this advice. With the active support of John's friends and family, and their colleagues at WTN, she arranged her first fund-raising party to pay for a trip to the Lebanon. "I felt that we had to act; to go out to the Middle East and see what was happening for ourselves, to talk to people," Jill said later. "I just wanted to be closer physically to where John was."

From this modest start grew a pressure group called "The Friends of John McCarthy". At last, Jill had an independent voice with powerful sympathisers in the British media. Gradually she came to realise that to win, she had to fight.

Nine months after the kidnap the change in her was apparent. From a woman content to take a back seat, and with a seemingly low level of personal confidence, she had transformed into a no-nonsense, steely campaigner with a healthy disrespect for protocol. One evening in London's St Bride's Church, Fleet Street, prayers had just ended for Terry Waite. The rector, Canon John Oates, suddenly became aware

were to leave her speechless: "Jill, I have some bad news. John's been kidnapped. He was on his way to the airport when some gunmen stopped the car and ordered him out. We're doing our best to discover what's happened."

Jill could not have known then that she was embarking on a 1,942-day quest which would eventually rank among the greatest love stories of our time.

John, 30, had been taken by Islamic Jihad, one of the fundamentalist terror groups with a powerbase amid the maze of shrapnel-spattered streets and bombed-out buildings that was West Beirut. Jihad was not a unified force. It was made up of a number of warlords, each with his own private army and each nurturing an agenda of his own. Faced with this kind of rambling hierarchy it was almost impossible for

of a diminutive stranger haranguing him as he bade farewell to worshippers.

"You're the journalists' church aren't you?" said Jill. "John McCarthy's a journalist. What are you doing about it?"

Canon Oates recalled: "She left me in no doubt that I'd better get on and do something about it. "From the moment I saw her I knew this was a very determined lady."

One of Jill's colleagues at WTN, reporter Sian Lloyd said: "She'd been a very shy and nervous girl but she blossomed as a result of having to hold forth. It was almost a total change in personality."

The Foreign Office would have echoed that view. Jill and "The Friends" launched an unremitting campaign against it, demanding to know what had been done, what further efforts were being made, and what new tactics tried.

Was the Prime Minister, Margaret Thatcher, fully informed? Was SIS (the British Secret Intelligence Service) pulling its weight? And all the time Jill kept up the pressure with a constant round of rallies and TV and radio interviews. No stone was left unturned. Even PLO leader Yasser Arafat did not escape her zeal at a face-to-face meeting.

In the dark days of 1988 and 1989, when it seemed John was being forgotten, Jill refocused attention on his plight. She helped promote one of the most powerful pieces of TV and cinema "advertising" ever seen in Britain – black and white pictures of all the Western hostages, together with the date of their kidnap, rolled slowly across the screens. The accompanying music was to move thousands of viewers to tears. It was the song "Homeward Bound" by Simon and Garfunkel.

A WANTED MAN

Similarly, a nationwide poster campaign reminded politicians that they would never be allowed to quietly ditch the hostage issue. Underneath a close-up black and white portrait of John, a single word succinctly rammed home the aims of the Friends of John McCarthy. It blared out from tube stations, bus stops, car parks and airports. "WANTED", it read.

On April 23 1990 it seemed the long fight was nearing its end. Jihad released American business studies lecturer Professor Robert Polhill, 55, one of three American academics kidnapped from the University of Beirut on January 24 1987. The terrorists handed him over to a Syrian general, Brigadier General Ghazi Kenaan, and within three hours he was re-united with his Lebanese-born wife Feryal at the American embassy in Damascas. "I am very sorry to have kept you waiting so long," he joked to officials.

The fact that Americans, rather than Britons, were released first is an indication of the problems Jill Morell faced. American President George Bush had carefully oiled

"SHE'D BEEN A VERY SHY AND NERVOUS GIRL BUT SHE BLOSSOMED AS A RESULT OF HAVING TO HOLD FORTH"

A NATIONWIDE POSTER CAMPAIGN REMINDED POLITICIANS THEY WOULD NEVER BE ALLOWED TO QUIETLY DITCH THE ISSUE

Below: *Party Time. The "Friends of John McCarthy" organisation celebrates confirmation of his freedom. Its dogged campaign was a crucial factor in his release.*

Above: *The wave and the smile said it all. John McCarthy pictured on his arrival home at RAF Lyneham in England. Jill told reporters: "I have thought a million times what I might say when I finally see him."*

" I WAS ANGRY AT WHAT WAS DONE TO ME... IF I BEGAN TO LOSE THAT ANGER I WOULD JUST BECOME A VEGETABLE"

---

his diplomatic links with Syria, whose highly professional army was now squeezing out the Beirut terror groups. Bush had even offered the Syrians intelligence information in exchange for their help.

Britain on the other hand had broken off its diplomatic links with Syria following an alleged Syrian plot to bomb an Israeli jumbo jet at London's Heathrow Airport in 1986. Britain had only two junior officials in Damascas, both working out of the Australian embassy.

On his release Mr Polhill revealed his formula for handling the years of captivity: "I was angry at what was done to me," he said, "at being taken away from my wife and family, my friends and students. So I strived to continue to be angry, knowing at

all times that if I began to lose that anger I would just become a vegetable."

It was 16 months before John McCarthy's turn for repatriation arrived and the hostage crisis entered its end-game phase. Thanks largely to Jill's campaign, Britain had begun talking to Syria once more and the Syrians obliged by turning the screw on Jihad. On August 8 1991 John was flown home to RAF Lyneham and a reunion with the woman that he prayed still loved him. In their book *Some Other Rainbow*, they told of the awkwardness of the moment – the need to get to know each other again before committing themselves to a serious relationship. As she waited for the plane to land Jill said: "I have thought a million times what I might say when I

*Left: **Robert Polhill with fellow American hostages Jesse Turner (centre) and Alan Steen (right).***

THE HOSTAGE CRISIS
REMINDED TERROR
GROUPS JUST HOW
EFFECTIVE KIDNAPPING
COULD BE

---

*Below: **St Bride's Church, Fleet Street, London, became a centre for prayers on behalf of the Beirut hostages.***

finally see him. I can only come up with the most banal greetings possible."

It was not until March 1993 that the couple felt strong enough to tell the world how their love had conquered the horrors of Beirut. "We're back where we were when I was kidnapped," said John. "Yes, we love each other."

Although the hostage crisis ended peacefully, it reminded terror groups around the globe just how effective kidnapping could be as a propaganda weapon. Abducting Westerners guaranteed publicity for the cause. It was an easy crime to carry out and there was little chance of meeting resistance. Best of all, there was even less chance of getting caught.

INNOCENT VICTIMS

Australian nurse Tania Miller and her British boyfriend, engineer David Rowbottom, discovered this to their cost in the summer of 1993. They were on a round-the-world cycling trip when, in the desolate mountains of eastern Turkey, they took a short detour to see the dormant volcano Mount Nemrut. On their way back they were stopped by two gun-toting Kurds walking near Lake Van.

At first the men were friendly, shaking hands and indicating that Tania and David should come with them to enjoy some local hospitality. When the couple politely refused however, the men quickly turned

aggressive and threatened them. They then had to endure four days of forced marches to reach the remote mountain village which would become their prison.

The men were members of the Kurdistan Workers' Party a separatist group fighting for Kurdish independence from Turkey. For years the Kurds had waged a terrorist campaign against the government in Ankara, planting bombs in major towns and cities and ambushing Turkish troops on patrol in the mountains. Now they wanted world recognition for their cause. Tania and David were seen as a gift from God.

Soon after the kidnapping in early July 1993, the Kurds issued a statement confirming their role. The statement promised that the couple would come to no harm, that they were being well treated and that they were being used to draw attention to the Kurdish armed struggle. As the news flashed around the world it seemed the exercise had succeeded.

The problem for the British and Australian governments was that they could not be seen to be negotiating with terrorists.

Above: *Australian nurse Tania Miller and her British boyfriend David Rowbottom celebrate freedom after weeks of secret negotiations with Kurdish rebels.*

THEY THEN HAD TO ENDURE FOUR DAYS OF FORCED MARCHES TO REACH THE VILLAGE THAT WOULD BE THEIR PRISON

Contact with the kidnappers had to be established through moderate Kurds on an unofficial basis. And yet the kidnappers had to be sufficiently flattered to believe their plight was being taken seriously.

British contacts in the region were reasonably strong. Britain was perceived as a friendly state by the Kurds, not least because of a comradeship built up during the Gulf War. British SAS (Special Air Service) troops helped supply and train Kurdish resistance forces in their battle with Saddam Hussein. And after the war, when millions of Kurds fled Iraq to seek refuge in the Turkish mountains, units of the Royal Marines helped organise aid distribution, clean water and sanitation.

For five weeks the secret negotiations went on. The British Foreign Office, and the Australian Foreign Affairs Department, used a carrot-and-stick approach in talks with the captors. The Kurds were assured that their demand for statehood would be pursued with Turkey, and that alleged Turkish atrocities against the tribesmen would be pursued. But the kidnappers were also given a robust reminder of the consequences in the event that Tania and David were not released quickly. The Kurds would alienate themselves from previously friendly powers. They would lose sympathy at the United Nations.

A PLEASANT SURPRISE

Above all they risked turning themselves into international pariahs. At last, on August 10, the couple were freed. Without warning they were driven to a forest close to where they had been snatched and left by a roadside. A lorry driver gave them a lift to the nearby town of Guroymak where Tania and David strolled into the local police station and calmly announced: "We think we're the people you've been looking for." A couple of hours later they celebrated with cold beer.

At their respective homes – in Brisbane and Stockport – there was jubilation. David's father Alan said: "It is a strange feeling. We're hardly daring to believe it. We have had so many ups and downs over the past few weeks."

Although the pair's ordeal paled in comparison to that of John McCarthy, it was nonetheless terrifying. They had to rough it on open mountain tops, walk everywhere at gunpoint and listen to discussions on their fate conducted in a totally alien language. At one point they even came under air attack from Turkish forces trying to flush out rebel Kurdish factions.

SECRET SERVICE

When their freedom was secured, the British and Australian authorities could have revealed more about the role each played in the rescue. Yet little was forthcoming. A spokesman for the Foreign Office acknowledged only: "We are absolutely delighted they have both been released in good health. We would however point out that it is intolerable that innocent tourists should be kidnapped."

David and Tania were fortunate that some channels, however tenuous, were open between their kidnappers and their governments. For some hostages the chance of a negotiated release may depend solely on the courage and initiative of their loved ones.

The abduction in 1994 of British tourists Kim Housego, a 16-year-schoolboy, and David Mackie, 36, a former video company director, is a case in point.

They had never met until fate threw them together to endure 17 days as hostages of the Kashmiri rebel force Harkut-ul-Ansark. The Islamic group's aims were cessation from India and union with Pakistan. For Kim and David it was hardly the kind of sightseeing trip envisaged from their holiday brochures.

The drama began on June 5. Kim was on a trekking holiday with his father, David Housego, a former Indian correspondent of the Financial Times, and his mother Jenny. David Mackie and his wife Cathy were in the midst of a two-year trip around the world. Both parties knew of the risks of travelling in Kashmir but official advice from the Indian tourism authorities was that the chances of rebel action were slight.

The Mackies were robbed at gunpoint by the Kashmiris as they slept in a small hotel at Aru. They were held prisoner and were joined the following day by the Housegos, who had been escorted down the mountain by a second group of rebels. That evening Kim and David Mackie were separated and taken hostage.

Above: *Prime Minister Margaret Thatcher's oft-declared policy was never to negotiate with terrorists.*

THE MACKIES WERE ROBBED AT GUNPOINT AS THEY SLEPT IN A SMALL HOTEL... THEY WERE THEN HELD PRISONER

It was immediately clear to the three who had been left behind that the rescue of Kim and David was down to them. The Indian police and military authorities were regarded as an occupying force by the locals. No one would lift a finger to help them. British intervention at diplomatic level was also a non-starter.

Even if they had wanted to negotiate with the rebels, embassy staff hadn't a clue where to begin.

The Mackies and the Housegos decided they must make things happen. They lobbied the local military commanders, pleading that no action should be taken which might jeopardize the lives of the hostages. Then, in a

Above: *Palestinian Liberation Organisation leader Yasser Arafat.*

Above Right: *Tania Miller and David Rowbottom pose for a publicity photograph set up by the Kurds in Southeastern Turkey.*

THEIR CAPTORS HAD A HIERARCHY BASED ON GUNS – THE MORE MODERN THE GREATER ITS OWNER'S IMPORTANCE

daring initiative, they arranged to have dozens of leaflets printed in Urdu appealing for news. These were distributed in Pahlgam, a village 60 miles east of Srinagar near the spot where the rebels struck.

Speaking ten days after the kidnapping David Housego said: "We have been working hard to get the militants to release Kim and David. There is a danger that if we do nothing we will lose the momentum. If we let things drift, the kidnappers might feel compelled to move Kim and David elsewhere. We shall wait at Pahlgam for about three days and we shall set up a tent outside the village. We will sit there so that people can feel safer in coming to see us."

Meanwhile Kim and David Mackie were concentrating on survival. They learned that their captors had developed a hierarchy based on possession of guns – the more modern the greater its owner's importance.

The youngest rebel, who was aged about 16, had no weapon and was constantly teased by the others with the nickname "Commando". He was clearly expected to fulfil some kind of apprenticeship before he would be considered fit to handle an ageing Kalashnikov rifle.

The Britons realised that three of the group spoke English and would eavesdrop on their conversation. To guard against this they invented a crude code in which the Indian Army was referred to as "Charlie", Pakistan as "Paul", Kashmir as "Kevin" and India as "Ian". They also gave nicknames to their captors, the leader of whom they dubbed "Duffy".

DEVOUT INDIVIDUALS

Religion was the focus of the rebels' lives. "They were annoyed when I shaved," David would recall later. "They told me that our own prophet had not shaved and they did not think I should. They talked a lot about religion. It was the main subject of their conversation. They started praying at four in the morning and would take time to pray even when they were in a hurry.

"The group's leader was an impressive man, always first to cross a river or climb a difficult slope. At night he made sure the men were comfortable and took trouble to see that we had enough blankets. On our last night with him he cooked and served the evening meal.

"Group morale was high and I was surprised they kept so buoyant considering the hard conditions in the mountains."

Neither he nor Kim made any serious bid to run away. "We thought about escape early on," Kim said, "but it soon became clear that our lives were not threatened. Dave had an injured knee and we couldn't have moved very quickly anyway. They were fitter and faster."

As the two of them continued their daily treks along snowbound Himalayan paths, their relatives were celebrating a break-through. A leading local Muslim cleric, Dr Qazi Nisar, 42, had agreed that he would act as a mediator in negotiations with the Kashmiris. He sent a note to the tent at Pahlgam and on Friday, June 17, David Housego drove 30 miles south to meet him in the town of Anantnag.

After an hour's wait, Dr Nisar, a well-built, genial man, arrived and drove him to another address where he was told to wait alone. A further hour passed before the cleric returned with four masked men from Harkut-ul-Ansark. Their leader told how they had risked death to reach the rendezvous – the mountains were apparently crawling with state troops. After promising that the two Britons were safe and would be returned, the men shook hands and left. Dr Nisar told David: "I think it will be about four days."

A BREAKTHROUGH

Three days later, on the afternoon of June 22, the Housegos and Cathy Mackie received a message that a "development" was under way. David Housego had lobbied local military commanders for days, urging them to cut troop activity to a minimum allowing the captors a clear run in and out of the mountains. He prayed the soldiers had kept their word.

That evening the two families had an ecstatic reunion in Srinagar. The rescue had been accomplished through patience, pleading and a dogged determination to succeed. Privately, the Indian authorities recognised that they could never have ended the crisis so speedily.

It was a happy ending... except for one sickening event. The cleric who had done so much to free the Britons paid a heavy price for his intervention. Some powerful

"WE THOUGHT ABOUT ESCAPE EARLY ON BUT IT SOON BECAME CLEAR THAT OUR LIVES WERE NOT THREATENED"

Below: *Once perceived by Westerners as the individual behind much of Middle Eastern terrorism, PLO leader Yasser Arafat sealed his growing reputation as a statesman with the signing of the Israeli-PLO peace accord at the White House in September 1993.*

Above: *American Michael Fay is freed following his caning. The Singapore government came under intense pressure from the Americans to spare him.*

HE WAS SUMMONED TO A "MEETING"... THERE, AN ASSASSIN PUT TWO BULLETS THROUGH HIS HEAD

faction within the rebel Kashmiris decided he had abused his position as a man of God. The Sunday before the release of the hostages he was summoned to a "meeting" a few miles from his home. There, an assassin put two bullets through his head.

FAMILY HELP

The influence of close relatives, as opposed to governments, cannot be over-stated in the world of international diplomacy. Governments intervening on behalf of one of their nationals often present a picture of secrecy, distortion, double-dealing and bureaucracy. A parent has the simple motive of wanting to help the child he or she loves. For those in control of a hostage or prisoner the public relations advantage of this is obvious. Sometimes a parent and State working in consort can be effective.

In early 1994 an 18-year-old American student, Michael Fay, was caught spray-painting cars in Singapore. Corporal pun-

ishment for serious vandalism was mandatory and the courts could not be seen to show favouritism to a Westerner.

Fay pleaded guilty and on March 3 was sentenced to six strokes of a bamboo cane and four months in prison. The case focused world attention on Singapore's draconian punishments, with liberals and human rights activists leading the clamour. The fact that dozens of Singapore's own teenage nationals were caned each year was by the by. Fay was an American... and that meant certain publicity.

The American President, Bill Clinton, led the pleas for clemency along with the teenager's divorced parents, George Fay of Ohio, and Randy Chan, who was based in Singapore. Yet this was not a cause that attracted wide public support.

Public opinion in America was sceptical of Michael Fay's claim that he had been coerced into a confession. Many of the older generation felt a short, sharp dose of the cane was just what their own country needed to hit back at young criminals. And Singaporeans were emphatically against pandering to the American government.

This public perception changed little throughout the 81 days during which Fay was kept in detention awaiting his punishment. Yet behind the scenes the Singapore government was doing its best to find a compromise. The efforts of George Fay had certainly concentrated the minds of ministers. Mr Fay had obtained enormous worldwide news coverage by accusing the government of being a "narrow-minded dictatorship". Now he was threatening to campaign for an end to Singapore's "favoured trade status" with America. Michael's mother Randy was just as forthright, describing the whipping as a "horrendous, barbaric form of torture."

This parental pressure, combined with the Clinton Administration's veiled warnings, had its effect. Singapore was particularly mindful of Clinton's suggestion that, in future, Americans planning to visit Singapore would be warned about the harsh and severe punishments in force. This was hardly in keeping with its image as the perfect relocation base for wealthy multinational companies.

On May 5, the flogging of Fay was carried out. He was stripped naked, bent over a wooden A-frame and tied down. A cushion was strapped over his lower back to prevent any permanent damage from a misdirected stroke. The flogger then whipped him four times across his buttocks.

A DIPLOMATIC GESTURE

It was a reduction of two strokes, a gesture, the Singapore government claimed later, acknowledging "the constructive economic and security role of the U.S. in the region". Though it may not have seemed to be a great deal in Western eyes, commuting the sentence by one third was an act of some political bravery. Singaporeans hated the thought that spoiled American teenagers should be accorded preferential treatment over their own.

As for Michael Fay, he was released on June 22 and flew immediately to his father's home in Dayton, Ohio. He spoke with bitterness at the coercion tactics allegedly used by police but bore no ill-will towards the man who beat him.

"The flogger himself did not come voluntarily, he came under government orders, so I went over afterwards and shook his hand. I wanted to keep my pride.

"I keep my pride with me and I don't ever want to lose it."

> HE WAS STRIPPED NAKED, BENT OVER A WOODEN A-FRAME... THE FLOGGER WHIPPED HIM FOUR TIMES ACROSS HIS BUTTOCKS

Below: *A Singaporean prison officer demonstrates his caning technique on a dummy inside Changi jail. For his punishment Michael Fay was stripped naked. Afterwards he shook his flogger's hand.*

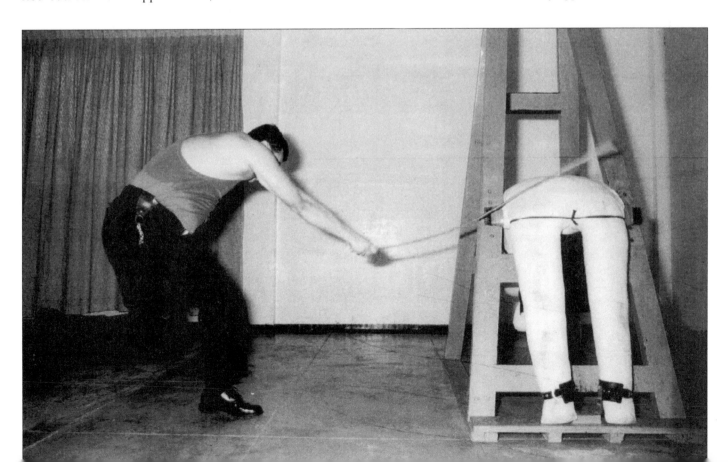

MOUNTAIN PANIC
Peaks of Heroism

Mountain ranges provide man with one of his greatest challenges. Even in a sophisticated age of satellite photography, aerial mapping and computer-aided navigation, jungle-cloaked slopes and icy caps have stubbornly refused to yield their secrets. They have, more often than not, rebuffed attempts by explorers to conquer them, sparking off intensive mountain searches and rescue operations.

An exploration team led by Lieutenant Colonel Robert Neill, 46, of the British Army's Royal Logistics Corps, set out for the mountains of northern Borneo in spring 1994. His right-hand man was Major Ronald Foster, 54, an officer who had been seconded to Britain's part-time Territorial Army. They shared a burning ambition to conquer one of the most forbidding places on earth.

Low's Gully is a 2,000 ft-deep ravine slashed down northern Borneo's glacial mountain ridge. No one has ever climbed down it, though several men have lost their lives trying. It is so deep it can't be mapped from the air. Some scientists believe it could be a treasure chest of undiscovered life forms. There are rumours of giant butterflies, fantastic tropical plants, huge insects. Even the local tribesmen are scared to enter. They believe a ferocious dragon guards a giant pearl at its entrance.

Some headway in the exploration of the gully was made in 1991. Two British mountaineers – Robert New and Stephen Pinfield – succeeded in navigating a route down the upper stages. Like so many before them, they were forced to abandon the project while still far from their goal. They encountered a series of cascading waterfalls, each hundreds of feet high, which fed a seemingly unending stretch of white-water rapids. The river wound its way between sheer cliffs, towering rock spires, fathomless pools, massive granite boulders and a streaming, impenetrable jungle. The whole scene could have come straight from a Jules Verne adventure story.

AN ADVENTUROUS EXPEDITION

Foster and Neill were fascinated by the mountaineers' account and resolved to make a fresh assault on Low's Gully. Neill, a qualified army mountain leader, had

*Opposite: **Helicopter rescue teams make the difference between life and death for mountaineers.***

LOCAL TRIBESMEN BELIEVE A FEROCIOUS DRAGON GUARDS A GIANT PEARL AT THE ENTRANCE TO LOW'S GULLY

*Below: **The search begins for the five lost mountaineers. Malaysian forces are briefed on which area to cover.***

Above: *The brooding mass of the 13,450 ft Mount Kinabalu. From its summit the doomed Neill/Foster expedition began its descent into the unknown.*

ON EACH OCCASION THE MEN WERE BEATEN BY A COMBINATION OF ATROCIOUS WEATHER AND EXHAUSTION

already tried twice and failed. Foster, a services abseil instructor, had separately made three previous attempts. On each occasion the men were beaten by a combination of atrocious weather and exhaustion. Now it seemed New and Pinfield had made their task fractionally easier.

Neill obtained funding from the British Army's adventure training board and set about gathering a ten-man expedition team around him. He chose a group of young, fit, non-commissioned officers from various units in the RLC. There were also three Hong Kong-based soldiers from his old regiment, the Supply Corps, who had no experience of mountaineering. These three only joined the group for the final stage of the flight to Borneo. They missed the advance training weekends in England, held on the wilds of Dartmoor and at Ripon.

TOUGH GOING

The expedition's aim was to descend into the gully from the top of the 13,450ft Mount Kinabalu. Yet well before they reached even this point they had encountered trouble. The three Hong Kong soldiers kept lagging behind, ultimately abandoning items of kit to lighten their load. Foster, too, was feeling the strain and had to have his pack carried by a local guide, David Powell.

Powell had joined them at the start of the mission convinced they would have to abandon it. He tried to persuade Neill to look at other routes which were less hazardous than the gully but which would still test the men. "I explained numerous times how difficult it was going to be," he said. It made no difference. On February 22 Neill ordered a rest day in a hut just short of the summit. This enabled some of the party to walk back down the ascent path in search of abandoned items.

A BEAUTIFUL SIGHT

The following morning everyone climbed the last 450ft in time to watch the sunrise. It was decided that the five younger British soldiers should press on ahead, leaving Neill and Foster to supervise the less experienced Hong Kong troops. The declared reason for this was so that the five could find suitable abseiling points and leave ropes for their colleagues travelling behind. In fact a rift had opened up exposing the frustrations of the younger men.

For the first couple of days 25-year-old Richard Mayfield was despatched by the advance party to run messages between the two groups. But as the distance between them widened, so the feeling of team spirit diminished. Mayfield complained that the younger men were spending too much time waiting around, "burning fuel" as he put it. Finally, at a point called Lonely Tree, the advance forged ahead with a 1,500ft abseil into a sheer valley. As the last man dropped down he caught sight of Neill and Foster's group high above him. The date was March 1. It was to be the last confirmed sighting of the stragglers for weeks.

Over the next few days the front five men negotiated a spectacular succession of waterfalls, often wading through rapids in the process. They reasoned that as the route grew more treacherous so the men behind them would be certain to give up the expedition and return to civilisation via the slopes of Kinabalu.

BACKTRACKING

By the time they reached a waterfall so high they could not see over it – a spot fittingly known as "the point of no return" among mountain tribesmen – the advance party itself abandoned the mission. They struck out of the gully, hacking their way through thick jungle with machetes, and eight days later made it to safety. In doing so they had split up again, this time into groups of two and three, losing their rations and specialist Gortex survival sleeping bags in the process.

Neill and Foster, meanwhile, were continuing a slow and steady descent with the three Chinese. They successfully abseiled the sheer cliffs at Lonely Tree and managed to traverse the massive glacial boulders which littered the valley below. Then they reached the point of no return and Neill made the fateful decision that they were all fit enough to descend. It was a disastrous move. As one rescuer put it later: "Once they went down there there was just no way back. The cliffs are unclimbable. They were like spiders in a bath tub."

As the weather worsened, with torrential tropical storms a constant feature, Neill gradually realised there was no escape. Attempts to scale the heights around them ended in potentially lethal rock falls. The jungle around was too thick and the river too fast. Neill had seen a new cascade of waterfalls ahead and knew they would soon be fed by the heavy rains. He and Foster decided that further descent into the gully was beyond their limitations.

They resolved to stay put, take cover in a cave, conserve rations and review escape routes. In their hearts they knew that only outside help could save them. On March 5,

> THEY RESOLVED TO STAY PUT... IN THEIR HEARTS THEY KNEW THAT ONLY OUTSIDE HELP COULD SAVE THEM

Above: *The view from the door of the Malaysian air force rescue helicopter that found Neill and Foster. The SOS sign was made from white pebbles.*

Left: *A Sea King helicopter similar to the one used to winch the trapped adventurers to safety. The pilot hovered within inches of the rock face, braving unpredictable crosswinds.*

Above: *A Chinese member of the expedition is carried to hospital for medical checks. He had eked out his meagre rations for three weeks.*

NEILL PROUDLY DISPLAYED A "LUCKY CHARM"... A SIGN ADVERTISING A SHOP SALE AND IT READ: "HOW LOW DARE WE GO"

eleven days into the expedition, Neill wrote this entry in his log:

"Rescue situation now?" For the next 20 days he and his men would launch a desperate fight against starvation.

Later, he described his feelings: "The nights were certainly the worst because they were 12 hours of darkness," he said. "When darkness comes it brings all sorts of unknowns, but all the time your mind remains in escape mode, even when you are asleep. You find yourself physically climbing in your sleeping bag, clambering over rocks and stones and slipping, always slipping.

"You imagine yourself on the end of a rope, hanging on as the rain sweeps over you, and suddenly you wake to find yourself upside down in your twisted sleeping bag. Then you notice the comforting glow of a chemically operated nightlight. It brings back some stability, so you go back to sleep – and in no time you are climbing again."

EMERGENCY ACTION

The following day they spent hours rigging up extra protection around the cave using waterproof items from their kit bags. They strictly rationed the remainder of their food – a few biscuits, sweets and stock cubes – because they had carried supplies to last only until March 4. They formed the giant letters SOS in white pebbles on a nearby rock and stretched out silver foil and red cloth in the

hope that they would attract rescue planes and helicopters. Fires were impossible because the vegetation was too wet.

When their spirits sank they would tell stories and sing games and songs. Neill proudly displayed a "lucky charm" he'd picked up at Heathrow Airport the day the expedition party got together. It was a sign advertising a shop sale and it read: "How Low Dare We Go".

Later he was to insist: "Don't get the impression that we sat on our rapidly disappearing backsides doing nothing. We didn't. We kept going because we didn't want to die and because we wanted to see our loved ones again.

THE PARTY'S GAMES

"When we weren't doing anything physically, we kept our minds occupied. We had a chess set and Scrabble. I wrote notes for three or four hours a day and drew up plans for a new conservatory. As our food ran low and we found ourselves with one beef cube, say, to last the day we'd keep it to have in water before we bedded down so we had a feeling of something in our stomachs."

Several times the party saw helicopters flying in the gully, giving them reassurance that a rescue operation was underway. But the choppers passed agonisingly close without seeing them.

In fact a 400-strong army of Malaysian soldiers, police, park rangers, water scouts, tribesmen, British and Australian mountaineers and UK Royal Air Force mountain rescue squads had been combing Low's Gully for days. By Friday, March 25 they had largely lost hope. There was just one, last desperate throw of the dice. It involved dropping teams of climbers and pot holers in the lower reaches of the gully so that they could scale the series of waterfalls.

At 10am that Friday morning Malaysian air force pilot Michael Izhar took off from Baru in his ultra-light Alouette IIB helicopter. His mission was to look for a suitable place to land one of the search parties and he cruised slowly up the gully, constantly battling against the powerful updrafts and buffeting winds.

Then, at 10.10am, he saw them. Together with crewman Sgt Mohammed Salleh, Izhar spotted two figures moving along the SOS lettering. Salleh had seen flashes in the same area two days earlier but senior officers had told him it was a Malaysian search team. Now there could be no mistake. The airmen's frustration was palpable. For one thing their helicopter was too lightweight to carry the party off, especially in such poor weather. For another they could not relay the good news to their base because of the mountains looming all around them. They decided to descend low enough for the men to know they had been found and then return to Baru for help.

Izhar said: "We only had a second or two to look into a narrow part of the gully and then we were past it. But in that second we saw some figures on the rock and when I turned to go back we saw the SOS sign. This time we knew for sure it was them. I tell you, my heart missed a beat."

Salleh added: "It was difficult to make out who was who but as we got lower we could see three men. They were wearing dark clothing and they were waving.

One of them held up two fingers to indicate two more men, pointed into the jungle behind them and then patted their stomachs. We realised they were telling us that the other two, who were out of sight, were still alive but they had stomach problems. We thought the best thing was to go back to the landing area as quickly as possible and relay this wonderful news.

"It was a chance sighting because we had written off that part of the gully. But oh my God I can't tell you how happy I am."

BACK TO BASE

Izhar returned to Baru, jumped from his helicopter and rushed up to a group of British officers. "We've found them, we've found them," he cried. The amazed officers hurriedly grabbed a 24-hour army ration pack and urged him to return with it. Izhar obliged, and then flew a third mission with a paramedic to assess the condition of the party.

By now the Malaysian authorities had ordered in a Sea King chopper, larger and far more powerful than the Alouette. It hovered between the walls of the gully, buffeted by breezes, its rotor-blades whirring only a couple of feet from the rock on either side. In an amazing piece of airmanship the pilot kept the craft steady while Col. Neill and the Chinese soldier Lam Ywai Ki were winched aboard. These

were the two men considered most urgently in need of medical help. The three other members of the party, Foster, Chen Wai Keung and Cheung Yiu Keung had to wait another night until the weather eased and the chopper could return.

THE TASTE OF FAILURE

The ordeal faced by the survivors, and the circumstances of their rescue, goes down as one of the greatest tales in the annals of world exploration. It also provided a salutary lesson for Col. Neill. He said later: "I failed. I obviously came very close to death and that is not acceptable. I personally think that the gully is not possible – but we did our damnedest. I'm a humbler man than when I went in. We will not be the same people ever again."

The same sentiments were no doubt shared by Hollywood film photographer Michael Benson and two colleagues after they were pulled to safety from the lip of a live Hawaiian volcano in November 1992. Benson, 42-year-old director of photography at Paramount, had chartered a helicopter to shoot scenes for the thriller *Sliver*, starring Sharon Stone and William Baldwin. The shoot ended in a drama which mirrored the film classic *Ace in the Hole*, starring Kirk Douglas. Benson, fellow cameraman

> "THIS TIME WE KNEW FOR SURE IT WAS THEM. I TELL YOU, MY HEART MISSED A BEAT"

Above: *Lt. Col. Robert Neill (second left) and his co-leader Major Ronald Foster are re-united with wives Fiona (far left) and Janette.*

Chris Duddy and chopper pilot Craig Hosking smashed into the sheer-sided Puu Oo vent of the huge Kilauea volcano. It is thought gases from the volcano stifled the Bell Jet Ranger's engines causing sudden and total loss of power.

Above: *Actress Sharon Stone at an awards ceremony. She was filming* **Sliver** *in Hawaii in 1992 when cameraman Michael Benson crashed inside a live volcano.*

A CLOSE SHAVE

Puu Oo was some 11 miles from the main crater, which had last erupted six years earlier. Nevertheless, the three men crash-landed an uncomfortable 250 ft from a boiling lava pool below. Above them lay a daunting 60ft climb through an atmosphere of poisonous sulphur dioxide and hydrogen sulphide gases.

Hosking was too badly injured to attempt an escape. But Benson and Duddy realised they somehow had to try to raise

---

THE PILOT WAS FORCED TO HOVER JUST ABOVE THE LAVA POOLS, HIS CRAFT SWINGING DANGEROUSLY IN THE GAS UPDRAFTS

---

the alarm. They successfully rigged their damaged radio to a battery and managed to send out a distress signal.

It was picked up later that day, November 22, by a passing helicopter flying a tourist jaunt and a rescue chopper was called in. The pilot, Don Shearer, was forced to hover just 50ft above lava pools, his craft swinging dangerously in the gas updrafts.

Shearer winched Hosking aboard but then lost Benson and Duddy in a fog that descended suddenly. He knew he had to get out fast if he wasn't to crash as well. Beneath him the two men shouted despairingly as they heard the helicopter take off.

CLINGING ON TO LIFE

Now they began the long, slow crawl up the vent. Duddy took the lead, although with visibility down to three feet it was impossible for him to know exactly how his colleague was progressing. At one point Duddy stopped to rest for 24 hours on a ledge with Benson clinging on some 30ft below him. Both men knew that one wrong move could send them tumbling down on to the red hot lava bed below.

Duddy at last made it to the top and fell into the welcoming hands of rescuers. He was suffering from exhaustion, and his lungs were badly blistered from inhaling hot gases, but at least he had survived. Before he was rushed to hospital he told how a desperation for oxygen had forced him to keep crawling up.

Of Benson there was still no sign. Almost 48 hours after the crash his film colleagues were close to despair. Nothing, it seemed, could be done.

Park rangers had ruled out a helicopter rescue because of a blanketing fog. They also feared the chopper blades could stir up volcanic ash, risking the lives of both the airmen and Benson himself. Even lowering a man in a basket was considered too risky.

The rangers and Benson's friends felt completely helpless. But they knew they had to try something. One by one they jumped to their feet and began walking around the vent rim screaming down words of encouragement and reassurance. They also hurled down blankets, chocolate bars and fresh water to the point where Benson was thought to be sheltering.

Ranger Mardie Lane said: "If the weather had been fine this would have been over by now. But with these gases we can't allow anyone to go down there. It's too dangerous. We are in the same position as yesterday. We desperately need a break in the weather so that we can see the position Mr Benson is in. We have not been able to get voice contact with him and he must be weakening."

At last, on the third day, the prayed-for improvement in the weather finally arrived. Benson was spotted huddling 60ft below the crater rim by a team of firemen, rangers and U.S. Marines. They rigged up a rescue helicopter with a winch and basket and pilot Tom Hauptman, from Maui, agreed that he would attempt the treacherous flight. With him was park ranger Jeffrey Judd, who volunteered to be winched down to the stricken man.

Judd got to him and helped him, semi-conscious, into the basket. Seconds later the chopper was climbing out of the vent and heading at top speed for Hilo hospital.

The flying ability of Hauptman and Don Shearer in the Kilauea rescue was quite breathtaking. Yet such bravery and skill is typical of those men and women who fly mountain rescue missions. Pilot Don Sheldon, for example (see also the air rescue chapter), has now become a legendary figure in the mountains of Alaska where, during the 1950s and the 1960s he earned a living by ferrying climbers, scientists, explorers and prospectors across some of the most forbidding territory to be found anywhere in the world.

A HELPING HAND

In the summer of 1960 Sheldon was called in by the army's 10th Rescue Division at Anchorage. It had received a distress signal seeking assistance for a party of mountaineers led by Oregon farmer John Day. The men had been edging their way down a frozen granite slope below the summit of the 20,320ft Mt McKinley, North America's highest peak, when one of them slipped and fell. Although all were roped together, no one could halt their 400ft slide. Ice picks were useless on the rock.

Below Day's group some mountaineers from Anchorage witnessed the accident and despatched three men to help. But they had troubles of their own. Almost 1,000ft further down the mountain one of their number, Helga Bading, was holed up in a tent

THE FLYING ABILITY OF HAUPTMAN AND DON SHEARER IN THE KILAUEA RESCUE WAS QUITE BREATHTAKING

Below: *Kirk Douglas whose film* **Ace in the Hole** *mirrored the real-life drama on a Hawaiian volcano.*

suffering from oxygen depletion. She was becoming incoherent. One of the Anchorage team, Paul Crews, reckoned both she and the injured climbers above had to be brought off the mountain fast.

Senior officers at 10th Rescue had no hesitation in alerting Sheldon. For one thing he was much nearer McKinley than them. For another, his knowledge of the area was incredibly detailed.

Sheldon had, in fact, ferried both sets of climbers to the mountain. He'd been checking on their progress while engaged on other chartered flights in the area but could not have known of Helga Bading's plight. Now he hurled some emergency supplies into his Piper Super Cub plane, packed an oxygen mask, and headed for the cloud-swathed peak to make food drops.

Over the next two days he ferried five teams of rescuers to the lower slopes. Then, just as it seemed he could leave them to complete the operation, word came that Helga Bading would die in hours unless she was brought off the mountain. Her fellow-climbers could get her down to 14,000ft on a sled.

Could Sheldon pick her up from there?

It was a mind-boggling mission for any pilot, even one as experienced as Sheldon. No one had ever landed so high on the mountain before. That in itself was a chal-

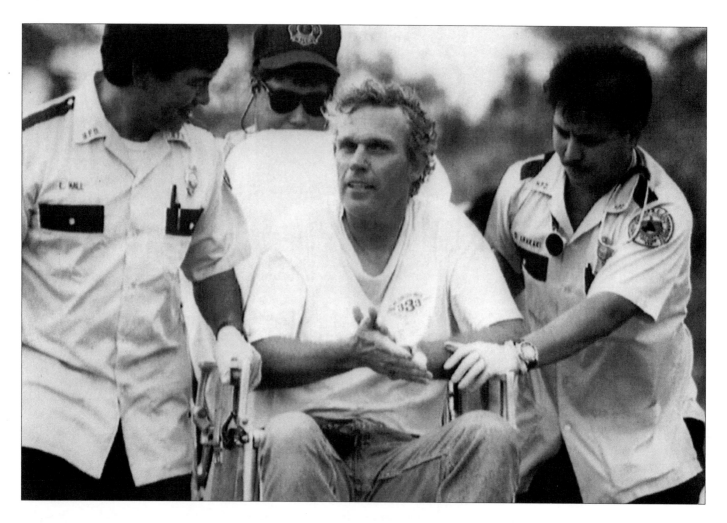

Above: *Hollywood cameraman Michael Benson after he was miraculously rescued from the Puu Oo vent of Hawaii's Kilauea volcano. For 48 hours he braved acrid hot gases.*

A MISJUDGEMENT WOULD SEND HIM CRASHING INTO THE MOUNTAIN'S NORTH FACE OR PLUMMETING DOWN CREVASSES

lenge Sheldon could not resist and with the help of a friend, Boston mountaineer and scientist Bradford Washburn, he began poring over maps and photographs to find a possible landing point.

HIGH-RISK ACTION

Washburn it was who found the only site possible – the West Buttress – a narrow 700-yard long shelf of crusty snow slanted at a ridiculous angle for an air-strip. Landing would be difficult enough; take-off a huge gamble. At 14,000 ft. the Super Cub's engines sustained a 45% power loss. The aircraft would have to be stripped of all unnecessary weight.

Sheldon realised he had to get it right first time. A misjudgement would either send him crashing into the mountain's North Face or plummeting down crevasses at the lower end of the "runway". The thought concentrated his mind wonderfully and he executed a superb landing at full throttle, swinging the airplane's tail around at the last minute to park it with skis at a

right-angle to the slope. Three hours later a rendezvous was made with the climbers carrying Helga Bading. She was strapped into the plane, Sheldon revved the throttle to maximum and sped away on a downhill takeoff. He glided into the air within yards of the crevasses.

Bading was flown to Talkeetna where she was transferred onto an Air Force transport waiting to take her to hospital in Anchorage. She later made a full recovery.

But Sheldon refused to rest until he had finished what he had started. He assisted in rescuing Day's four mountaineers and then flew 18 continuous missions to bring out the rescue teams he had dropped earlier. By the time that it was all over, he had become a living legend in Alaska.

By their very nature, most successful mountain rescue operations demand the skills of dedicated fliers such as Sheldon. Yet because flying light aircraft in mountainous zones is such a hugely risky business, pilots of his calibre are hard to find. The chances of crashing are too high; the financial rewards too low.

So when, in December 1941, the residents of New Guinea found themselves trapped in mountain villages at the mercy of Japanese bombers, they were fortunate that a number of extraordinary Australian fliers were on hand to help.

In the wake of Pearl Harbor, Australia was ready and willing to take as many refugees as possible from New Guinea. The idea was to ferry women and children to Port Moresby, the island's capital and an important Allied base, from where they could board boats to the Australian mainland. The trouble was getting the mountain people to Moresby without them being blown to bits on the open roads.

Of the many acts of bravery in this Dunkirk-style operation, two in particular stand out. One involved an old time miner called Norman Wilde who happened to come across an abandoned and dilapidated de Havilland Moth rusting away in Port Moresby. "I didn't know what condition the engine was in," he admitted later, "but I filled her up with petrol and hoped for the best. In that Moth I took 11 Chinese from Salamaua to Port Moresby in one hop."

He then performed a second risky mission, dodging Japanese fighter planes in the island's cloud-swathed peaks as he went about rescuing women and children from the hilltop settlement of Wau.

WARTIME HEROICS

In another feat of daring an Australian Catholic missionary, Father John Glover, teamed up with an engineer called Karl Nagy to perform one of the great civilian wartime rescues. Glover and Nagy managed to navigate their plane safely across New Guinea's highland ridges to ferry life-saving drugs and provisions to a mountain village where 77 sick soldiers and tribespeople were being looked after by a single nurse.

On the return flight the two men did not possess enough fuel to make Thursday Island, the extreme tip of Northern Australia, and so had to put down on New Guinea's southern coast. From here they were transported in a native canoe across the Torres Straits until a friendly passing merchant ship took them aboard.

Undeterred by this setback, Glover then persuaded the Australian military controllers that he could take two unarmed

Qantas D.H.86 biplane airliners back to the village where the 77 refugees were hiding out. It seemed the act of a madman to fly two such enormous sitting ducks over unfriendly territory.

Glover put his faith in his God and thought no more of the risks. Whether it was luck or an act of Providence mattered little. All 77 were saved.

Luck or – depending on your particular viewpoint – divine intervention usually has some part to play in a successful mountain rescue. No matter how well the search party is trained, or its level of air support, the chances of finding missing persons alive are often no better than evens. Where the search area is snow-covered the chances of success drop dramatically.

In 1994 two separate incidents, both involving British women, highlighted the fine line between life and death in a hostile

Above: *Dr Stephen Caswell and his wife Pamela, from Plymouth, England. They were climbing Mont Blanc when he fell more than 100 ft to his death.*

WILDE THEN PERFORMED A SECOND RISKY MISSION, DODGING JAPANESE FIGHTERS IN THE ISLAND'S CLOUD-SWATHED PEAKS

mountain environment. In August of that year 37-year-old Pam Caswell, a teacher from Plymouth, England, had been climbing Mont Blanc along with her husband, Stephen, who was also 37, and her 16-year-old son Simon. The Caswells were experienced climbers who were well-attuned to the hidden dangers.

The journey up took longer than they had expected. With air temperatures rising, melting ice had turned many normally reliable routes into treacherous slipways. Severe electrical storms were also building over the western Alps.

A TRICKY ROUTE

The family decided to head down the mountain on the Italian side, choosing to negotiate a glacier instead of a rocky, ice-bound ridge. But as they trudged across a snow "bridge" over a crevasse it suddenly gave way, sending them tumbling 100ft. Although all three were roped together, none of them could halt the slide.

Mother and son survived largely unscathed, but Mr Caswell had broken his

> THE TWO SURVIVORS FACED A NIGHTMARISH ORDEAL... TWO NIGHTS TRAPPED AT THE BOTTOM OF THE ICE-CHASM

Below: *Pam Caswell and her son Simon recovering in hospital after their rescue on Mont Blanc. They tried desperately to keep Dr Stephen Caswell alive, but he was bleeding too badly.*

leg and was bleeding badly. His wife made a rough splint and tried to keep him warm but her efforts were in vain. He died some six hours later.

The two survivors faced a nightmarish ordeal in which they spent two nights trapped at the bottom of the ice-chasm, the body lying next to them. During daylight hours they regularly blew six blasts on a whistle – the internationally recognised rescue signal – and flashed their torch. Just as their hopes were fading, they were at last spotted by another group of mountaineers.

"We knew they had heard us," said Mrs Caswell. "I managed to say 'mon mari est mort' so that they would realise it was serious and that we needed the helicopter. We just realised how cold we were and could not stop shaking."

Mountain rescue co-ordinator Rudolfo Bornei said: "They were very, very lucky. It is not normal to stay two nights in a crevasse and survive."

The second incident occurred in the Scottish Highlands some six months earlier. School secretary Jacqueline Greaves, 51, became separated from two fellow

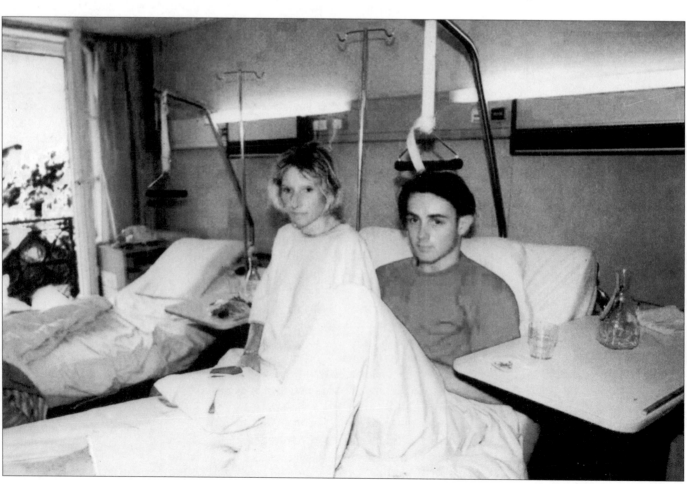

Scout leader Andrew Pascall. In June 1993 he and three friends were ascending the 13,600ft Jungfrau in the Alps when an ice ledge gave way and sent them toppling down the perilous slope. Three of the men, including Andrew, came to a halt safely, but the fourth, Andy Hindley, lay stranded 600 feet below them.

With little thought for his own safety Andrew clambered down to help his friend, unaware that Hindley was already dead. Just as he reached the body the snow again gave way and he tumbled an incredible 3,000 metres before at last coming to a standstill. Then, knowing that two more lives depended on him, he spent ten hours painfully hauling his way to a mountain hut to raise the alarm. Considering his skull was fractured, both his elbows were smashed, his knees were injured and he had a broken nose, it was a genuinely heroic feat.

Afterwards he said: "I fell over hard rocks and scree and started to pray. I prayed and I prayed as I fell, finally landing in deep snow. I prayed I would live and I prayed to Jesus that the others would remain safe."

His prayers were answered.

climbers in a blinding blizzard on the 3,788ft Derry Cairngorm and then wandered for 41 hours, hopelessly lost. A standard survival technique kept her alive through two nights – she dug herself into a peat bog – but she had no supplies and had began to suffer hallucinations. At one point she even heard the voices of those searching for her, but they could neither hear nor see her in the appalling conditions.

AN AMAZING SURVIVAL

Just in time, a rescue dog called Solo led an RAF search party to her. Its leader, Corporal Alan Sylvester said: "When we got to Jacqueline the first thing she said was: 'I am looking forward to a pint of Guinness. But before that, when she saw us, she stopped walking, sat down and there were tears of pure relief and emotion. It was a memorable moment. We gave Jacqueline hot drinks, Mars bars, chocolate and Ribena. Then, as we waited for the helicopter to arrive, she cracked jokes."

Of all the climbers who have counted themselves lucky to be alive, few can match the experience of British Assistant

Above: *School secretary Jacqueline Greaves became separated from her fellow climbers amid blizzards on Scotland's 3,788ft Derry Cairngorm. She was rescued alive after digging herself into a peat bog.*

Right: *Andrew Pascall at a bravery awards ceremony in London. He slid more than 3,000ft to bring help for his friends stranded in the Alps.*

SEA RESCUE
Splash Headlines

For centuries the sea has proved an irresistible lure to the adventurous, the restless and the downright daring. Like a jealous mistress, its calm caresses can erupt into murderous rage without warning.

The danger of the sea is great enough, even for those who have learned respect. Those who treat the ocean with disdain should, sooner or later, expect to pay with their lives.

No wonder that maritime history is littered with extraordinary tales of rescue and heroism. Author Peter Benchley has a theory for the phenomenal success of his novel *Jaws*, one of the biggest-selling in history. It is that the terrors of the deep play upon a primeval fear within us all – a fear that can emerge even in the shallows of a holiday beach. Certainly, Benchley's great white shark with a taste for human prey is not the stuff of fiction. Several hundred attacks by man-eaters around the world have now been closely documented. Of the victims rescued alive, few can boast a story to rival that of MacIntyre William Shark Schaumann.

Little MacIntyre is probably the youngest person in the world to survive a shark attack. So young, in fact, that he will never remember a thing about it. As the ferocious monster closed in on his mother Dawn, MacIntyre was blissfully curled up in her womb – still three months away from his birth day.

A DANGEROUS DECISION

It was October 1993 and Dawn, an American champion in the speed division of beach life-guarding, decided to take a plunge into the surf at Treasure Shores Beach near her home in Florida. While on duty earlier that day she had hoisted red flags to warn swimmers that sharks were cruising off shore. But she didn't sense any danger. An attack was always something that happened to others.

Opposite: *Some of the first women lifesavers to go on duty at Sydney's Bondi Beach.*

THOSE WHO TREAT THE OCEAN WITH DISRESPECT SHOULD, SOONER OR LATER, EXPECT TO PAY WITH THEIR LIVES

Below: *Terror of the seas. With their razor-sharp teeth and awesome power, sharks are among nature's most ruthless killers.*

Above: *Author Peter Benchley. His bestseller* **Jaws** *introduced millions to the great white shark – a species blamed for the string of attacks off America's Atlantic coast in 1916.*

sand, her life ebbing away. But her plight had been seen by two elderly holidaymakers and now her life-guard partner Chris Henderson leapt to the rescue. The first call he made was to an EMT (emergency medical technician) medic... who just happened to be Dawn's husband Bill.

Bill said: "I was the first EMT on the scene and took over the treatment from Chris. I shuddered when I saw the bone-deep bite on Dawn's thigh. Her pulse was weak and her heart was racing out of control."

Fighting back his own emotional instincts, Bill concentrated on stemming the blood flow and trying to calm his wife. He didn't dare risk painkillers – apart from any other considerations Dawn was insisting she wouldn't have them in case they harmed her baby. Later, when surgeons began an operation to insert 100 stitches in her wound, she was persuaded to have an anaesthetic tested as safe for unborn infants.

NO FEAR

After many scares and false labours, MacIntyre was born a bonny 7lbs 1oz on January 19 1994. His mother insisted that "Sharkey", as he was already nicknamed, would be swimming in the sea just as soon as she could teach him. She didn't want him to have any complexes about the ocean.

At least Dawn Schaumann had a chance of making it to shore. Any yacht crew which sinks in shark-infested waters knows that survival is down to chance.

That said, there have been some remarkable rescues against the odds. In August 1989 a Miami couple, 60-year-old William Butler and his wife Simone, 52, were found

She was 100 yards out when a sudden, jarring pain seared through her limbs. Instantly, she knew what had happened.

"A shark hit me so hard it felt like a huge truck," she recalled. "The sea turned red around me and my first thought was 'my time has come'. Then I realised my husband Bill was going to lose me and our baby, all because I'd ignored his warnings of swimming that day. He'd seen baitfish close to the shore, a sign sharks were in the surf. I knew my only chance was to get out of that water pretty fast."

The shark's teeth had closed over her left hand, which had been trailing at her side in the middle of a free-style stroke, and her left thigh next to her femoral artery. Despite the cold of the water, the pain was intense.

"I swam faster than I'd ever swum before," she said, "amazingly the shark didn't finish us off. I was losing a lot of blood and had to get help."

Dawn was flung on to the beach by a wave and lay helpless in the reddening

> A SUDDEN JARRING PAIN SEARED THROUGH HER LIMBS. INSTANTLY SHE KNEW WHAT HAD HAPPENED

barely alive in their rubber lifeboat by Costa Rican coast guards. Their 40ft sloop had been sunk by a whale 1,200 miles off Costa Rica in waters known to be heavily populated by sharks. Incredibly, they survived for 66 days with the help of two vital pieces of equipment – a salt-water purifier and some fishing line salvaged from the wreckage of their boat.

William told his rescuers: "We survived on three litres of water a day and fish we caught with our bare hands as they took the bait."

Every bit as fortunate were yachtsmen Larry Myers and Dennis Hampton who in 1991 survived five days adrift in shark-filled seas off Florida. Myers, 42, and Hampton, 46, had set off from Port Crystal with their boat already leaking. By the time they realised the extent of the problem the vessel had shipped 10ft of water and was already far out to see. Their SOS message, using smoke signals, only made matters worse. Flames spread throughout the yacht and sank it.

A LIFESAVING CREATION

The two men refused to give up hope and managed to lash together a makeshift raft from a few buoyant containers floating around the wreck. They stayed alive by rationing their fresh water and eating peanut butter. Even so, Myers was suffering shark bite wounds when they were picked up by a passing yacht.

Once the advice for fending off sharks was to kick, shout and splash the water in the hope of scaring them away. Now experts differ. Some say that these actions can be interpreted by man-eaters as a signal that their prey is injured or in trouble. They argue that the best policy is to make slow deliberate movements in the water.

The fact is that very little is known about sharks, especially monsters such as the Carcharadon carcharias or great white. Some game fishermen believe that these fish patrol huge territorial areas of the sea and will home in on any prey they encounter using their highly developed sense of smell. Beneath the sea, they have no natural enemies.

In the early 20th century it was believed sharks were harmless. But in July 1916 a series of attacks along a 65-mile stretch of America's Atlantic coast, south of New York, changed that view completely. A

"WE SURVIVED ON THREE LITRES OF WATER A DAY AND FISH WE CAUGHT WITH OUR BARE HANDS AS THEY TOOK THE BAIT"

Above: *A marine biologist with the jawbone of a great white. This one was thought to have been some 16ft long.*

"rogue" shark – believed to be a great white – killed four people and would have savaged a fifth to death. The lucky survivor was 12-year-old John Dunn, pulled by rescuers out of the very jaws of the killer.

On July 12, John had been swimming with his brother William in the waters of Matawan Creek, some 20 miles inland from the New Jersey coast where a few days earlier two swimmers had died from shark bites. That morning a retired mariner, Captain James Cottrell, was taking his morning stroll along the creek when he spotted a massive, dark grey shape moving through the waters.

Recalling the coastal attacks, he rushed into town to spread word that a shark was cruising in local waters.

He was laughed at. Nobody could believe a shark had swum 20 miles from the ocean through Raritan Bay. Families flocked as usual for their daily swim in the creek.

The fish's first victim was Lester Stilwell, aged ten. He suddenly began thrashing about in the water and screaming,

Above: *Man-eating sharks investigate a party of divers off the Bahamas. Despite their reputation, sharks will not always attack without warning.*

STANLEY DIVED TWICE DEEP INTO THE CREEK AND EMERGED WITH THE BLOODSTAINED BODY OF LITTLE LESTER IN HIS ARMS

---

his body swirling around in the water. A local man, Stanley Fisher, raced to his aid convinced the boy was suffering from a fit. When a terrified by-stander told Fisher about the shark alert he was incredulous. "A shark? Here?" he asked. "I don't care anyway. I'm going after that boy."

Stanley dived twice deep into the creek and emerged with the bloodstained body of little Lester in his arms. He struck out for shore and managed to stand up in the water only a few feet from where helping hands were waiting. Then he cried in pain, threw up his arms and was dragged underwater. Courageously he fought off the shark and dragged himself to the bank but died within a few minutes from loss of blood.

SPEEDY RUMOURS

By now word had spread around the creek that a shark was out hunting. Men were preparing to detonate dynamite in the water but the sight of a group of boys in a motor-boat heading for the steamboat pier delayed them. One of those boys was John Dunn, the

last to leave the boat. As he hauled himself onto the pier his left leg dropped back into the water for a few seconds.

It was all the shark needed. Like lightning its lethal jaws closed above John's knee, tearing the flesh away. Clinging desperately to the pier he screamed for help and a dozen townsfolk raced to his side. He was hauled to safety and rushed to a local doctor, Dr H.J.Cooley of Keyport. Dr Cooley tended the terrible wounds as best he could and almost certainly saved John's life. But he could not save the leg.

A few hours later it was amputated by surgeons at the St Peter's Hospital, New Brunswick. John was the shark's last human victim. The hours that followed saw perhaps the biggest fishing expedition in history, with hundreds of sea anglers combing the North Atlantic coast to kill the beast. Many dozens of sharks were killed. One of them, an eight-and-a-half footer caught by taxidermist Michael Schleisser off the New Jersey coast was a great white. Its stomach contained the remains of a number of human victims.

The attacks by this rogue caused such public anxiety in America that the matter was brought before President Wilson and his cabinet. As politicians there was little they could do other than voice their concern.

But 74 years later, an American senator, proved that politicians can be men of action. Congressman Joe Kennedy, son of Robert Kennedy, was sailing with family and friends off Hawaii when he heard a radio distress signal from a yacht nearby.

PROMPT MOVES

He discovered that Mildred Akaka, niece of Hawaii's Democratic senator Daniel Akaka, had been flipped into the sea as she and her passenger tried to haul in a 438lb marlin. Congressman Kennedy located her overturned boat and dived to the rescue with three others in his party. What he didn't know was that a dead 300lb marlin, caught by Mildred earlier, was floating around the capsized vessel.

"I don't know if we got any points for intelligence, it was tiger shark city out there," Kennedy said later. "When I saw the marlin it nearly gave me heart failure.

But it all turned out well. We saved them, the boat and their marlin."

In the southern hemisphere, stretches of the Australian coast are regarded as among the most dangerous in the world for shark attack. Dozens of swimmers have been savaged in the surf by the silent killers.

Only the lucky survive. And in December 1988 one victim, 17-year-old Adam Maguire, was lucky enough to find a friend in circumstances stranger than fiction.

Adam was surfing off a remote stretch of the New South Wales coast when he was hit by a blue shark. Screaming in agony, he watched its jaws grip tightly around his leg. As he waited for what seemed an inevitable death, the vice-like grip of the jaws slackened. Then the huge, muscular body beneath him seemed to lurch in the water as though it had suddenly been transformed from hunter to hunted.

With mounting incredulity, Adam watched as a dolphin butted the shark again and again with its bottle nose. It was still harassing the fish as he swam to the safety of the beach.

"I owe that dolphin my life," he admitted later. "He freed me from the teeth of the shark and then chased it away." At first, many who heard this story found it some-

HE WAS HIT BY A BLUE SHARK. SCREAMING IN AGONY, HE WATCHED ITS JAWS GRIP TIGHTLY AROUND HIS LEG

Below: *For years, dolphins were treated mainly as performing acts for sightseers. Now, scientists suspect their intelligence is second only to that of humankind.*

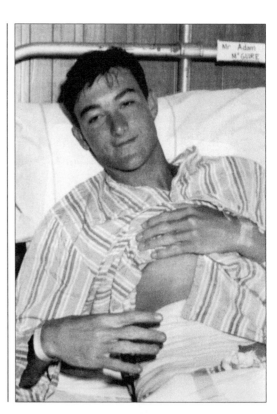

Right: *Adam Maguire, who was rescued from a shark attack by dolphins off the coast of New South Wales, Australia.*

Left: *The British wildlife expert Sir David Attenborough. He says dolphins have a "justifiable reputation" for coming to the rescue of humans.*

Below: *The affinity between dolphins and human beings is extraordinary.*

what difficult to believe. However, there are now at least a dozen well-documented reports of dolphins having come to the rescue of humans in distress. As the highly respected British naturalist Sir David Attenborough puts it: "They have a justifiable reputation for helping man.

"Possibly it is because we are approximately the same size and they feel they are helping others of their own kind."

Sharks may be every seafarer's secret nightmare, but they hardly rank high as the cause of casualties at sea. As anyone who messes about in boats discovers, sooner or later, man's deadliest enemy at sea by far is always the weather.

A TOUGH LADY

Australian lone yachtswoman Anne Lisa Guy lived through just about every malicious whim the winds and sea could hurl at her. In November 1993 she set out from Mooloolaba, Queensland, with the intention of becoming the first woman to circumnavigate Antarctica without stopping. It was a doomed voyage.

Anne, 44, spent more than two months lost at sea without ever seeing or speaking

Above: *President Woodrow Wilson. Such was the terror inspired by the 1916 shark attacks south of New York that the issue was raised at one of his cabinet meetings. Wilson concluded that there was little the government could do.*

"THE WINDS WERE SO BAD THAT I LOCKED MYSELF INSIDE THE BOAT. I WAS THROWN ABOUT, HITTING MY HEAD FOUR TIMES"

---

with another human being. Her 11-metre yacht Wildflower was stripped of its mainsail and lost its automatic steering, long and short wave radios and life raft. Her rescue by the British naval vessel Grey Rover in April 1994 was described as a million-to-one chance. According to a Ministry of Defence spokesman in London: "To say it was a miracle is not an exaggeration."

Anne, a freelance artist with a 23-year-old daughter, later provided a graphic account of her ordeal. "The weather was against me from the start," she said. "I met head winds on the way to New Zealand and, just prior to the Horn on February 20, I had what turned out to be my last radio contact – conversations with a US survey ship and an Australian radio station."

WILD WEATHER

"The winds were so bad that I locked myself inside the boat. I was thrown about, hitting my head four times. The boat did a complete 360 degree roll and I lost my hydrostatic life raft. It was a terrible experience. I was fortunate still to be able to use satellite readings so that I could keep navigating and end up exactly on course at South Georgia.

Above: *John Glennie (left) returns to dry land after surviving for four months on the upturned hull of his trimaran. "We needed a miracle and we got it," he said after being rescued off Great Barrier Island, Auckland.*

ONLY THREE DAYS INTO THE VOYAGE THEIR CRAFT WAS HIT BY A GIANT WAVE AND CAPSIZED. THEY WERE TRAPPED IN AN AIR POCKET

EVERY EXPOSED PART OF HIS BODY WAS BLISTERED FROM THE EFFECTS OF EXTREME SUNBURN

"I had a small spirit stove which I could only make work occasionally. Because my gas cylinders had been damaged, I had no fuel for the galley and had to manage on cold food and drinks."

Anne's plan was to make a landfall in Grytviken Harbour, South Georgia. Twice she tried to sail the few miles to its entrance. Each time strong winds blew her off course. She had to decide whether to try a last-ditch gamble on her paltry outboard motor.

"I was making the decision whether to try to sail in a third time, or risk everything by using what fuel I had left, when I saw the British ship through the high waves," she said. "I thought I had had it. It was a wonderful moment."

The Grey Rover lived up to the best traditions of the Royal Navy's hospitality. An officer was despatched to check on Anne's health and give her some instant sustenance. With the comfortingly large mass of the British ship alongside her confidence was restored. The decision on how to proceed came easily.

"There was the navigation officer on my boat and I was speaking to this nice English gentleman who brought me hot

coffee, sandwiches and orange juice. It reminded me that Norfolk, England, was my home as a child. We started the boat's engine and made it into the harbour."

After a 9,400 mile voyage – equivalent to sailing halfway around the world – Anne knew exactly what she was going to do when her feet touched dry land.

THANKFUL MOMENTS

"I was longing for a hot cup of tea, which I got when we landed on South Georgia," she said. "I insisted on going to the little mission church where I prayed and said thank you for my rescue. And I visited the grave of the explorer Shackleton, who 76 years ago survived here in a small boat after his ship was crushed by pack ice."

Perhaps it is something in the blood of yachtsmen and women that makes them face crisis with fortitude. Certainly the three New Zealanders and an American who survived for four months on the upturned hull of their trimaran needed all the ingenuity they could muster.

The four had set out on a two-week cruise from New Zealand to Tonga. But only three days into the voyage their craft was hit by a giant wave and capsized.

The men were trapped in an air pocket beneath the hull and it took 12 hours for them to cut their way out. By now their radio silence had raised the alarm, and the crew reasoned that it could not be long before they were spotted. But rescue services failed to find them adrift in the Pacific and within a couple of weeks they were given up for dead.

The men organised themselves into rotas – some on watch, some catching fish or seabirds – and managed to retain their sanity. They were eventually picked up by a passing ship on Great Barrier island near Auckland, where the trimaran had been washed up exactly 123 days after beginning its voyage. Skipper John Glennie later told newsmen: "We needed a miracle and we got one. I never doubted we would."

LOST AND ADRIFT

Just as resourceful was pilot Gerry Langford and his three passengers. They were flying back to their homes in Florida from a fishing expedition in the Bahamas when their plane ditched 40 miles off the American coast. They drifted for 42 hours across 100 miles of shark-infested water, clinging to the three life rafts they had managed to salvage.

The men could hear spotter planes above them but failed to attract the attention of the pilots. Then somebody suggested American Express and found the credit card would do nicely to reflect the sun's rays into the cockpit of a circling pilot. Minutes later a rescue was under way.

Coastguard Roger Wethereld said: "I bet they are glad they brought their American Express card. They are lucky to be alive. There are a lot of sharks around."

Student Dirk Steen can afford to blush a little when he re-tells the story of his own bizarre rescue. He threw a lakeside party to celebrate having left a bookshop job. But after the beer flowed he nodded off on his blow-up lilo.

Unfortunately, the lilo then floated out into the middle of Lake Michigan and when Dirk at last woke to realise his predicament it was nightfall. Unwittingly he then began paddling for the far shore of the 73-mile-wide lake.

He wasn't noticed for more than a week. None of his party friends bothered to report him missing because they assumed he had gone home without telling them.

By the time coastguards got to the young German they found him still wearing his T-shirt and cut-off jeans. Every exposed part of his body was blistered from the effects of extreme sunburn.

A LUCKY ESCAPE

"I was on the verge of giving up," he told his rescuers. "The lake is so vast I thought I'd floated into the ocean." Coastguard Robert Tallman said: "It's amazing he's still alive and that he wasn't spotted before now. That area of water is pretty busy."

The highly-trained professionals who man the world's lifeboats and rescue helicopters accept the risk that goes with the job. But just occasionally, a hero emerges who has acted way beyond the call of duty. One such is British lifeboatman Russ Wignall.

In June 1994 Russ, a 34-year-old shrimp fisherman, answered a call to man the Lytham inshore lifeboat near Blackpool, north-west England. There were reports

Above: *The legendary explorer Sir Ernest Shackleton. He survived a shipwreck on South Georgia island in the South Atlantic.*

that a 37ft yacht bound for the Isle of Man, the Gean, was in trouble close to some rocks off Lytham.

On board were two men, Stanley Otley and Paul Edmunds, together with teenager Josephine Martin.

Lytham Lifeboat secretary Frank Kilroy said: "One of our men noticed something a bit funny about about the yacht, which was sitting on the sandbank and was close to the rocks. He called out the lifeboat – then suddenly the wind swung the yacht around and smashed it into rocks. The lifeboat crew arrived in the nick of time."

But the rescue mission wasn't so simple. The craft was so close to the rocks that the inshore boat couldn't risk going alongside. Yet the three occupants were now clinging to the sinking hull. There was only

cued the girl first because she was in so much shock that she couldn't swim. Then I went back twice more and took the two men to the safety of the lifeboat. It was very rough and very cold."

A RELUCTANT HERO

In the best traditions of the Royal National Lifeboat Institution, Russ was very reluctant to be classified as a hero. "I wasn't worried for my own safety," he insisted. "It's all in a day's work."

But his wife Jacqueline, 33, told reporters: "I think he's a hero, even if he doesn't."

Bravery, willpower and luck are the three essential qualities for anyone prepared to risk their lives for others. Eighteen-year-old Gareth Smith from South Wales, seems to be blessed with all three.

In 1992 he and two friends, Simon Roberts, 19, and Stephen Evans, 15, found themselves drifting further and further off the beach near their homes at Ammanford. The boat's engine had spluttered to a standstill and refused to re-start.

After a few hours Simon vowed to swim for help, but just vanished into the sea. Attempts by Gareth and Stephen to attract search helicopters ended in failure.

A BRAVE STRUGGLE

Later Gareth said: "I knew help was there but they couldn't see us, even though I shouted for help from the ship and waved at the helicopter. I could see land for a long time but I couldn't get the boat to it."

Eventually they drifted to within 500 yards of Lundy Island, a three-mile-long precipitous outcrop which lies about 12 miles off the Atlantic coast of North Devon. Gareth hurled himself into the boiling seas, defied the treacherous local currents and then clambered up a 250ft cliff to a lighthouse to raise the alarm.

Exhausted, numbed from the cold and suffering severe sunburn he still managed to give clear instructions on how to reach Stephen, now alone in the drifting boat. Minutes later a coastguard helicopter was winching the youngster to safety. Doctors believe he would have died within the hour.

Racing against time is, of course, the stock in trade of the emergency services. Even so, they had their work cut out one

Above: *Lifeboatman Russ Wignall, who dived into heaving seas three times to rescue three sailors from a sinking yacht.*

one hope and it meant a volunteer lifeboatman swimming out to each of them in turn and shepherding them through the mountainous seas to safety.

Russ Wignall, father of three young children, was that volunteer.

"We only had a few minutes to save them," he said. "We had been searching for them, then suddenly we saw them bobbing about in the waves. The three were hanging on to the side of the boat and would not have lasted much longer. I dived in and res-

chilly April night in 1993 when a liver transplant operation due to take place at the Edinburgh Royal Infirmary, Scotland, was delayed for the most bizarre of reasons.

The patient, an unidentified 25-year-old Scottish woman, had been on the British transplant waiting list for months. Without a new liver, her life would gradually ebb away. Yet the chances of finding a suitable donor, whose organ tissue matched her own, were slim.

The UK Transplant Service (UKTS) does not release details of how its organ donors die. What is known is that this donor came from the Midlands and that late on Friday April 2 the liver was carefully packed in ice, in a sealed container, and rushed under police escort to a 10-seat Cesna 127 plane waiting with its engine running at Birmingham airport.

Captain Simon Wilkinson, 30, and co-pilot Alan Jukes, 42, knew the urgency of their mission. Every second saved now might make the difference between life and death later. They revved up, taxied down the runway and set a course north.

In the early part of the flight all was well. But at around 1am on the Saturday morning the aircraft developed engine trouble. Captain Wilkinson was over rugged country near Musselburgh, six miles east of Edinburgh, and there was no emergency landing area in sight. He had no choice but to ditch in the sea on the Firth of Forth. Miraculously, both he and Alan Jukes survived suffering only from shock.

SAD NEWS

But this presented a new problem for consultant surgeon Hilary Safney and her transplant team. Police were despatched to the Infirmary to tell her: "Sorry, they've lost your liver in the sea." It seemed the operation would have to be postponed.

But UKTS is not an organisation that gives up easily. Within the hour a request for help had gone to the Royal Navy's Scotland and Northern Ireland clearance diving unit. When the divers turned up it was like a rescue services convention. Coastguards and police had sealed off the area, paramedics stood by in case they were needed and the fire brigade trained powerful spotlights on the tip of the plane, just visible above the waves.

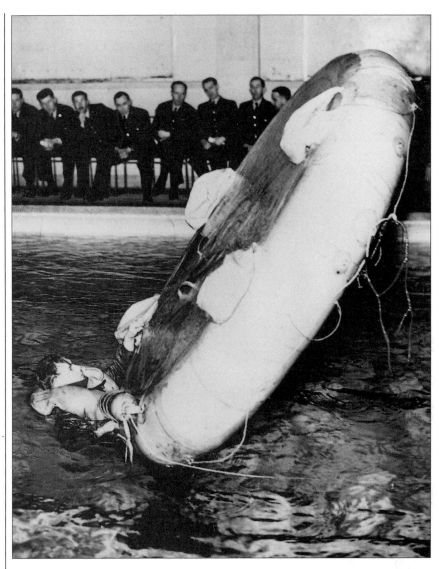

The divers were eventually able to locate the precious cargo and at approximately 3.15am it was delivered to the hospital. After checking that there had been no injuries to the liver, and that all of the seals were intact, the six-hour operation was then successfully completed.

Even in the very midst of gripping life-or-death dramas such as this one, there are moments of humour to be found. The diver who had found the sunken container, Able Seaman John Ravenhall, later admitted that he had only recognised it because he was a keen follower of the BBC TV hospital drama *Casualty*.

"I had a good idea what to look for because I am an avid fan of Casualty," he commented after his heroics. "I got in, saw the box in the fuselage behind the cockpit seat and gave it a big haul.

"You see a lot of these containers on Casualty."

Above: *British RAF pilots demonstrate life-saving techniques for victims of air crashes over open water.*

THEY KNEW THE URGENCY OF THEIR MISSION. EVERY SECOND SAVED NOW MIGHT MAKE THE DIFFERENCE BETWEEN LIFE AND DEATH

TWISTS OF FATE
Modern Miracles

When TV and newspaper editors draw up their daily news schedules they always keep a sharp eye out for a good "miracle" rescue story. Nothing, it seems, appeals to the public more than the triumph of a fellow human being over adversity.

Typical reactions range from open-mouthed wonder ("How on earth did he get out of that?"), to genuine joy ("Thank God he's alive") when a life has been saved. But there are also those who delight in scathing criticism of some "stupid" victim for putting him or herself in a position of danger. The implication is that rescue dramas happen to the reckless. It's not always true.

Being in the wrong place at the wrong time can happen to any of us, at any moment. This chapter is mainly concerned with those unfortunates who, through little or no fault of their own, suddenly fall victim to a twist of fate.

Extremes of weather (another favourite topic of the news man) are the obvious example of this. Advances in meteorology have made forecasts ever more reliable, but even the most committed weatherman would concede that predicting rain or snow for a region is one thing; predicting its severity is quite another.

AN EVENTFUL JOURNEY

James and Jennifer Stolpa, from Paso Robles, Nevada, know all about the vagaries of the American climate. On December 29 1992 they left home with their five-month-old son, Clayton, to attend James' grandmother's funeral in Idaho. It was a 22-hour journey, but not particularly daunting by American standards.

Opposite: *A woman is stretchered to hospital after being stuck upside down in a pothole in Derbyshire, England, for seven hours.*

BEING IN THE WRONG PLACE AT THE WRONG TIME CAN HAPPEN TO ANY OF US, AT ANY MOMENT

Below: *James and Jennifer Stolpa and their five-month-old baby Clayton. They survived blizzards which hit one of North America's most desolate spots.*

"WE'RE NOT DOING
THIS FOR ME, WE'RE
NOT DOING IT FOR YOU —
WE'RE DOING IT FOR
THE BABY"

A few hours into the trip the first of several storms struck, dumping over nine feet of snow across the state. The Stolpa's pickup truck sank into a deep drift 50 miles east of the California-Nevada border, just about the most desolate spot on their entire journey. There were no other paved roads through the mountains and only about 20 homes in an area of 4,000 square miles.

For the first five days the family stayed close together in the truck, huddling together to keep themselves warm and surviving on nothing more than crisps, prenatal tablets and "lots of praying".

Jennifer kept telling her husband: "We're not doing this for me, we're not doing it for you – we're doing it for the baby." But eventually they decided they had to try and find help. They set out in search of another road, taking turns to carry baby Clayton and surviving on rations of biscuits and leftover Christmas cake. Clayton was breastfed and given water from the snow his mother melted in her mouth.

SOLO MISSION

After 12 exhausting miles they stopped to rest and dug a snow cave for shelter. Twenty four hours later James decided he had to take the initiative to save his family and struck out alone across the frozen wastes. The 21-year-old ex-army private waded through snow – often chest deep – for 30 miles in temperatures of minus 20 degrees centigrade. After 22 hours he at last reached the Nevada desert town of Vya where he was spotted by a snow clearing crew.

By then James was rambling and incoherent, but he still managed to impart enough crucial information to identify the spot on Badger Mountain where his family were stranded. Rescuers found them after following footprints from the abandoned truck. Both mother and baby were suffering from

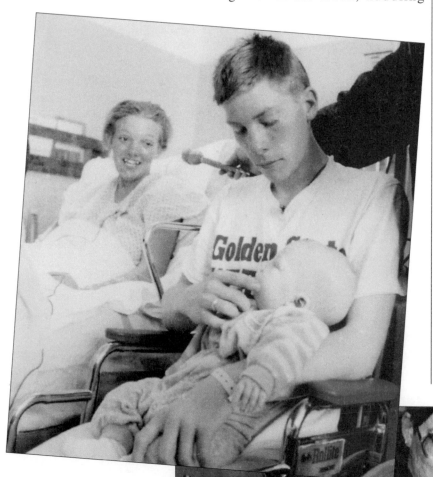

Above: *Jennifer, James and Clayton on the road to recovery. He waded for 30 miles across snow-bound wastes to save his family.*

Right: *Jennifer Stolpa is wheeled into Cedarville Hospital after being rescued from a snow cave on the California-Nevada border.*

dehydration, frostbite and hunger although doctors at Cedarville Hospital described them as being in "remarkable shape".

Jennifer said: "I thought I was going to starve or freeze to death. I thought I was going to die. I have never been so happy to see people in my life. I don't know how we survived. We just kept each other warm and tried to keep our spirits up. I think we both fought to survive for the sake of our son. We had to keep going to keep him alive. I pulled him close to me all the time."

Sheriff Vince Swinney, of Washow County, said: "When we found them the baby was bawling his head off. They either had a guardian angel or they made all the right decisions once they got into trouble."

Severe cold also brought out the best in three-year-old Jolene Daniels. Almost exactly a year after the Stolpas' ordeal she won the hearts of millions of Canadians with a courageous piece of initiative which undoubtably saved her father's life.

A YOUNG HEROINE

Jolene was out for a walk with her father Dale. They were moving through a remote forest several miles from their home in Leoville, Saskatchewan when, suddenly, Dale tripped and fell 30ft, breaking both his legs. Unfazed by her dad's serious predicament, Jolene promised him she would go and get help. And she did!

She ran a mile down snow-covered paths to reach Dale's truck. Then she calmly jumped in and drove for three miles to raise the alarm. The doctors who treated her father said he would have stood little chance of lasting through the bitterly cold night.

Jolene said: "I remembered how my dad did it. I turned on the ignition and switched into gear. I had to stand on the pedals to see."

Even more amazing was the story of little Julius Rosenberg. He was playing with his baby sister Barbara outside their mother's isolated waterside cottage at West Hark Lake, in the Canadian province of Manitoba, when a large black bear appeared. It chased them across a jetty, trapping them with their backs to the cottage. So Julius then persuaded Barbara to jump in the lake with him to escape. Both children were already wearing lifejackets.

It seemed like a good plan... until the bear began swimming after them. It caught three-year-old Barbara by the collar of her life jacket, twisting her round and ducking her under water. But it reckoned without the fury of her big brother.

Julius, five, began pulling his sister away. Then he looked the bear in the eye and growled at it. The animal, slightly non-plussed, let go long enough for the children to get ashore.

They ran to the cottage with the bear still in hot pursuit. But every time it got too close Julius turned and growled at it, stopping it in its tracks.

After failing to get in through a sliding glass window the children at last found an open door and alerted their mother, Denise, who called in the local rangers. The bear was later shot.

Julius told his mother: "There was no place to go, mummy. Each time I growled like this – Arrrgh! – he took one step back and finally scooted off."

Children like Julius are not so rare as we might think. Youngsters confronted with a life-threatening twist of fate often handle it with intelligence and fortitude.

Take three-year-old Charlotte Dabreo from Eccles, Norfolk, England. In March 1992 she was playing quietly at home when her mum Sarah collapsed in front of her.

Above: *Three-year-old Charlotte Dabreo from Norfolk, England, put on her nurse's uniform to help save her mother. When pretend medicine failed, she called for help.*

"I THINK WE BOTH FOUGHT TO SURVIVE FOR THE SAKE OF OUR SON. WE HAD TO KEEP GOING TO KEEP HIM ALIVE"

Charly rushed to her toybox, slipped on her junior nurse's uniform and grabbed her toy medical kit. Then she examined her mother and attempted to administer some pretend medicine.

ADDED COMPLICATIONS

What the little girl could not know was that 22-year-old Sarah was suffering from a serious ear infection which caused her to lose consciousness. When she didn't recover, Charly did what any responsible nurse would do in the circumstances – she called for the doctor. She stood on tip toe to release the bolt on a back door and went to alert a neighbour.

Sarah said: "I just remember waking up and finding Charlotte's medical kit lying around me. She had even got her nurse's uniform out, plastic medicine bottles and her stethoscope. She seemed to know exactly what she had to do when she realised I wasn't playing. She's a very clever little girl."

One of the most intriguing aspects of the human psyche is the way we respond to a crisis, especially where the victim is someone close. There are countless reports of res-

Above: *Tizzy Dawson pictured with British actor John Inman at an awards ceremony in London. She rescued her little sister by lifting a 250lb trailer one-handed.*

___

THE 250LB TRAILER, WHICH HAD BEEN STOWED ON ITS SIDE, COLLAPSED ON TOP OF HER

___

cuers developing "super-human" strength to save a loved one from certain death.

In September 1992 11-year-old Tizzy Dawson was playing in her garden at Macclesfield, Cheshire, England, when she saw sister Lynette clip a camping trailer with her scooter. The 250lb trailer, which had been stowed on its side, collapsed on top of her. From where Tizzy stood it looked like Lynette was being crushed to death.

What happened next was a blur. Tizzy can only remember running forward, then lifting up the trailer with one hand and pulling eight-year-old Lynette clear with the other. Then, as the little girl lay on the ground with her eyes closed, a distraught Tizzy rushed inside, convinced that she had been just too late.

"Mummy, mummy," she cried, "Lynette is dead."

A QUICK RECOVERY

In fact Lynette recovered almost immediately, needing only an overnight stay in hospital. Afterwards the sisters' father Albert said: "I don't know how Tizzy found the strength to lift the trailer by herself, and with just one hand. It's amazing what people can do in times of great stress. It was absolutely incredible.

"Lynette was pinned to the ground. The towbar was pressing against her neck and chest, squeezing the life out of her."

The girls' mother, Christine, 38, said: "Lynette was suffocating and the doctors told us that if Tizzy had not acted so quickly her kidneys would have burst." Tizzy, awarded a medal for heroism by a national newspaper, shrugged off the praise heaped upon her. "I knew I had to do my best to save my sister," she said. "I am just so happy she is alive."

Perhaps the shock of witnessing an imminent death or injury is enough to trigger the mind-over-matter response experienced by Tizzy. It also seems to tap unknown reservoirs of courage.

A MOTHER'S COURAGE

In 1990 Julie Henderson from Castleford, Yorkshire, England, broke her leg in more than 20 places when she hurled herself at the wheels of a 10-ton truck trundling towards her baby's buggy. Julie, 26, used her leg as a brake to slow the lorry. She was dragged screaming down the street but still managed to grab the buggy containing 14-month-old Reece and push it clear. Afterwards she told her mum, Velma: "It wouldn't have bothered me if I'd been killed as long as he was OK."

Betty Gale, a 60-year-old grandmother, is another member of the exclusive super-strength club. In April 1994 she spotted a toddler strapped into the seat of a runaway car and dropped everything to give chase. Although she was only eight stone, Betty managed to cling on to the door handle and bring the vehicle to a halt. She attributed her muscle power to years working as a milk lady in a dairy.

"I noticed there wasn't a driver," she said, "and when I realised there was a kid in there I screamed for help. The car was on the move so I held on as hard as I could. It gradually stopped. Everyone wonders where I got the strength from. I think it was from lifting milk crates for 28 years."

Have-a-go rescuers, by definition, don't stop to weigh the odds on their own safety. Their response to a crisis is instinctive, a kind of internal automatic pilot that ignores warning signals.

Above: *Julie Henderson and baby Reece. She rescued him from a runaway lorry – using her leg as a brake.*

A VICIOUS ATTACK

In May 1992 an English tourist, Susan Kirby, 26, was drawing money from a cashpoint machine in Sydney, Australia when two men mugged her. She struggled to hang on to the notes... until they blasted her with a shotgun at point blank range.

At the sound of the shots security guard Dale Nufer – who worked for Scotland Yard in London before moving to Sydney – looked up to see two men running away. He and a colleague darted after them, though he knew they had a gun.

"My basic training as a policeman took over," said 28-year-old Dale. "There was a right set-to when we caught up with them. We were scrapping on the pavement and I heard one of them shout: 'Shoot them.'

The following day, the Sydney police charged a man with the crimes of attempted murder and armed robbery. Senior officers praised Dale's "astonishing courage" in getting his man.

One of the most dramatic rescues in the history of rail transport happened on the London Underground in March 1990. The hero of the hour emerged as tube driver John Robson. Fate dealt him a dreadful hand, but he played it superbly.

It was a Monday night during the middle of the rush hour. John was waiting at a red light just outside Kings Cross station when he saw a glow getting steadily stronger around the bend ahead. The awful truth dawned that the light belonged to a train. A train on the same line as him. Up to 800 lives were at risk.

FIGHTING ELECTRICITY

John, 42, leant out of his cab and seized two 650-volt power lines serving the oncoming tube train. Mouthing a prayer, he touched them together and felt a slight shock hit his body. It did the trick. The power was cut and the oncoming train slowed gently to a halt.

"I sort of collapsed and rested my head on the controls," said John. "I was just so relieved. Please don't call me a hero. I only did what any other driver would have done." London Underground said: "We have nothing but praise for him."

In May 1991 quick-thinking of a similar kind saved two sisters trapped in the bedroom of their house at Stourbridge, West Midlands, England. A lighted cigarette had set fire to a settee, sparking an inferno across the lower floors. There was no way out. Fortunately the screams of Lucy Ellett, 16, and sister Mandy, 14, were heard by two workmen driving past in a van.

The men, Dave Hannibal, 28, and Chris Cronin, 29, decided there was no time to wait for the fire-brigade. Their works yard – Murphy's Pipe Lines – was nearby and they reckoned a mechanical JCB digger would prove perfect for the rescue. Dave rushed off to alert JCB driver Pat Glavin, 51, while Chris explained to the girls what they were going to do. "I just tried to keep them calm until the others arrived," he said. "Then I climbed into the bucket of the JCB, smashed the glass and carried them out."

Above: *Tube driver John Robson, who grabbed power lines to save his passengers.*

I managed to hold on to my fellow but the other guy got away."

He then dragged the man back to the bank where Susan, who was on a round-the-world trip, lay fighting for her life. She later recovered, despite the fact that two arteries were severed.

Driver Pat added: "We didn't think anything of it at the time but the police seem very pleased. Looking back, those girls would have been gone."

Lucy said: "The lady opposite us heard us and called the fire brigade, but the men got here first. They were marvellous."

AN EDITOR'S DREAM

Rescues such as that one are loved by newspaper editors because they provide a rare opportunity to tell some good, old-fashioned heart-warming news. When a member of the British royal family is involved to boot, the journalists are positively drooling.

In May 1994 the Princess of Wales, still recovering from headlines surrounding her broken marriage to Prince Charles, managed to get her name in the papers for all the right reasons. She had been out running in Regent's Park, central London, when she witnessed a tramp taking a tumble into a canal off York Bridge. She could see that he was unable to swim and she hurriedly raised the emergency services on her mobile phone. Then she rushed to the water's edge to help.

There she was joined by another passer-by, Finnish opera student Kari Kotilla.

He handed the Princess his backpack and his wallet and then plunged in to pull 42-year-old Martin O'Donoghue to the

Above: *The Princess of Wales helped save a tramp in a canal in Regent's Park, London.*

Left: *The scene of the rescue.*

HE HANDED THE PRINCESS HIS BACKPACK AND HIS WALLET AND THEN PLUNGED IN

Right: *Tramp Martin O'Donoghue with the student who helped Princess Diana perform the rescue.*

THE PRINCESS COULD SEE THAT HE WAS UNABLE TO SWIM AND HURRIEDLY RAISED THE EMERGENCY SERVICES

Below: *Lord Snowdon played Good Samaritan to two Canadian tourists.*

bank. Diana helped manoeuvre the tramp into the standard life-saving recovery position while Kari gave him mouth-to-mouth resuscitation and heart massage until some paramedics arrived. Mr O'Donoghue later made a full recovery in the University College Hospital.

DIANA TO THE RESCUE

A Metropolitan Police spokesman later commented: "It is quite clear that had the Princess not been there, Mr O'Donoghue would have been in serious trouble. She helped the rescue and stayed while the man was resuscitated."

Lord Snowdon is another royal who has something of the Good Samaritan about him. In June 1991 he was returning to his car after having a night out in central London when he heard two stranded Canadian tourists debating how they would get back to their hotel. It was 2am and there was not a taxi in sight.

Princess Margaret's ex-husband politely invited Frances Hicks and Olivia Grenkie to join him in his chauffeur-driven limo, whereupon they were whisked round to the Belgravia Hotel in the lap of luxury. Yet neither woman recognised their chivalrous rescuer. It was only when the hotel doorman suddenly snapped to attention that they twigged just how kindly fate had smiled upon them.

A ROYAL TREAT

Mrs Hicks said: "No sooner had we got to our room than the hotel manager rang and asked if we wanted a better one. Next day the hotel made a special breakfast and took us past a queue to get our hair done in the beauty parlour."

In a chapter dedicated largely to innocent victims of fate, it's worth drawing comparison with one man who was anything but. In terms of sheer recklessness, Tom Ngan of Montebello, California, is right up there with the best of them.

In April 1991 21-year-old Tom desperately wanted to patch up a serious rift with his girlfriend, Claudia Leung, 25. He decided on an act which would illustrate his undying love for her. He would climb down the chimney of her house at Cypress and out the fireplace.

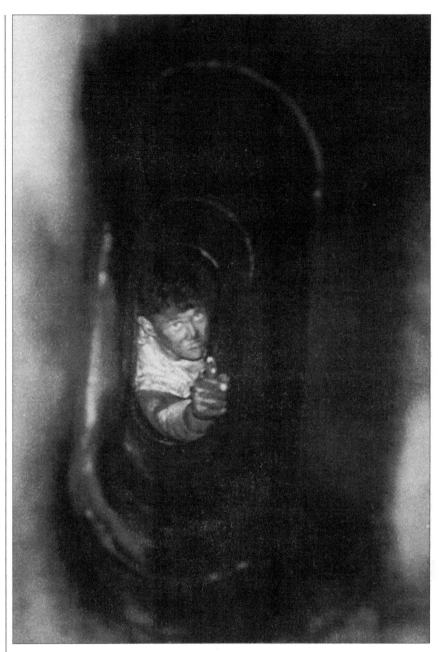

At first all went well. Tom was only 5'7" tall and he found he could wriggle down surprisingly easily. What he didn't know was that the chimney narrowed to just one foot wide at the bottom. At that point his love-conquers-all plan came unstuck. Or rather, it got very stuck.

Unable to move, Tom began yelling to Claudia for help. But she wasn't even at home and in the end it was a neighbour who called for help. After two hours a team of six firemen managed to set him free.

Tom's last hope of a reconciliation with Claudia was to win her sympathy. He failed. "He's pestered me ever since I broke up with him a few weeks ago," she said.

"He's pathetic."

Above: *Tom Ngan looks despairingly up at firefighters as they attempt to extract him from his girlfriend's chimney.*

TRAPPED!
Deadly Struggles

Few situations hold as much terror as being trapped underground. Cut off from clean air and daylight, even the hardiest souls can fall into despair. As with all predicaments, underground rescues have the potential to bring out the very best in people.

Suddenly, to the horror of her friends, 18-month-old Jessica McClure vanished. For a few seconds they stared numbly at the spot where, without warning, the earth had swallowed her up.

Then their screams took on an intensity which brought Jessica's mother Reba racing outside. "What's happened, what's going on?" she cried. Tearfully, the toddlers pointed to where the little girl had disappeared and an awful sense of fear and despair engulfed Reba.

Jessica had plummeted down a disused oil well which, until then, had been thought to be safe. It was impossible to know how far she had fallen but at least she was alive. As Reba screamed frantically down to her baby, she heard a faint answering cry.

Back inside the house, Jessica's aunt was already dialling the emergency services. It was Wednesday, October 14 1988 and for the next 58 hours the whole of America would be gripped by a battle to bring the baby out alive.

DELICATE NEGOTIATIONS

From the start, police and rescue workers realised it would not be possible to simply dig Jessica out from above. With the eight-inch-wide shaft in a grossly unstable state, any excavation could trigger a potentially fatal rockfall inside. Instead, the team decided to dig a parallel shaft some distance away, and then tunnel up to Jessica at an angle of 30 degrees. Soundings suggested she was 22ft below the surface with lumps of rubble perilously piled up above her.

Neighbours now gathered around the house declaring they would not leave until Jessica's fate was known. Many volunteered to dig her out with their bare hands, an offer that had to be politely declined by the rescue team. If she was to survive then she needed to be under the care of professionals.

And there was certainly no shortage of them. Live TV and radio broadcasts had brought offers of assistance flooding in from

Opposite: Firefighter Glenn Millers of Gulfport, Mississippi, pulls 12-year-old Tony Rouse to safety from quicksand on a building site.

AS REBA SCREAMED FRANTICALLY DOWN TO HER BABY, SHE HEARD A FAINT ANSWERING CRY

Below: Rescue workers endure an agonised wait as the operation to free little Jessica McClure continues. One false move could have triggered a rock fall.

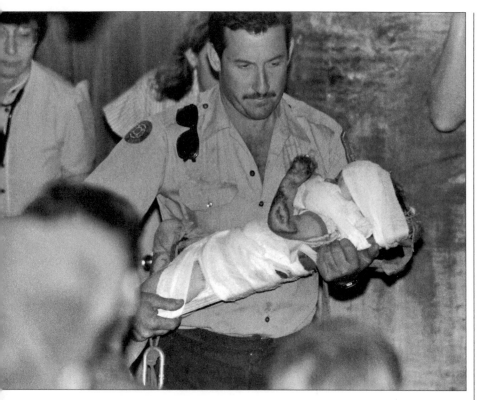

Above: *Dirty, scared… but alive. Jessica McClure is carried to safety in the strong arms of one of her rescuers.*

UNDER THE ARC LIGHTS WHICH BEAMED DOWN, MEN AND WOMEN SWEATED AND TOILED, PRAYING FOR A BREAKTHROUGH

CZECH REPORTED THAT JESSICA WAS ALTERNATING BETWEEN SLEEP, TEARS AND RECITING NURSERY RHYMES

all over the country. Among the leading advisers were local oil industry engineers who knew both the geology of the ground and the design of the well. It was they who recommended digging the parallel shaft.

Once work began it continued non-stop. Under the arc lights which beamed down on the garden, men and women sweated and toiled, praying for a breakthrough. Some, who had shunned sleep, were gently escorted away from the scene and ordered to rest.

The stakes were simply far too high to allow mistakes caused by sleep deprivation. Throughout the slow, deliberate drilling operation, parents Reba, 17, and Chip, 18, talked constantly to their little girl. A special telephone link was lowered into the shaft allowing her to hear their voices clearly. They told her that her favourite teddy bear was waiting to cuddle her when she came up.

They sang songs from her favourite cartoon show *Winnie the Pooh*. When she sobbed they were there to comfort her. And when she pleaded: "Mummy, mummy I'm hungry," Reba gently explained that she would be having a lovely meal just as soon as she was brought out.

Doctors feared that Jessica would not survive more than 36 hours without food and water. But they made the agonising decision not to give her any sustenance in case she

choked. The advice from the drilling team was that they would tunnel through to the trapped girl some time on Friday.

As it turned out the doctors' gamble paid off. Jessica was lying face up on a ledge, her right foot trapped, and unable to move. Had she choked she would almost certainly have died a lonely, terrifying death. The medical team tried to make her as comfortable as possible by pumping down warm air and oxygen.

Throughout Thursday night the tunnelling team, working in shifts, inched its way closer. Many of the men were emotionally drained by their task; conscious that they had to get to the baby before she died but also aware that the vibrations caused by their drills were making her frightened and upset. When the sobbing got too much, a 15-minute halt would be called to allow Jessica's parents or a trained counsellor to reassure her.

One of the rescue team observed. "She has a lot of spirit. She might have been trapped for hours in total darkness 22ft underground but that doesn't stop her getting mad at us from time to time. She's a tough little kid who just wants out. She's crying like a banshee."

SLOW BUT SURE

Police chief Richard Czech summed up the frustration. "She is alive and well and cries when she hears the drill," he said. "We are going slowly for safety. But every time we get close we have a setback and now we have to bring in a new super-powered drill to get all the way through."

The breakthrough came early on Friday morning. A drill bit poked into the cramped passage where Jessica lay and a rescue worker reached out and tickled her leg. She giggled in response.

Back on the surface, rescue supervisors broke the news to TV and radio crews and the hundreds of anxious locals keeping vigil outside. A huge cheer went up. One neighbour said: "It was like everyone's prayers had suddenly been answered."

But the drama wasn't over. Because of her trapped right leg and an awkwardly wedged arm, it was not possible to simply drag the little girl out.

The plan was for a small man to be smeared with vaseline and then inch his way into the well, free her limbs, smother her with vaseline and then ease her into the rescue shaft… and freedom.

Richard Czech reported that Jessica was alternating between sleep, tears and reciting nursery rhymes. He went on: "Jessica is safe. We are with her in the well. We now only have the technical problem of making sure that we do not injure her wedged foot. We are having to be patient. After three days there is no point in rushing matters if it harms this little girl."

HAPPY SCENES

Soon after this statement a crane hauled Jessica to the surface to the cheers and whistles of the rescue team. She was bewildered, tired and dirty but very much alive. Her parents hugged her and held her close, their tears mingling with hers for a few precious seconds. Then she was into an ambulance and away to hospital. As the sirens wailed, the nation breathed a collective sigh of relief.

All three major TV networks had interrupted their schedules to broadcast the rescue live. Among the viewers were President Ronald Reagan and his wife Nancy, who was in hospital awaiting a breast cancer operation. Later, as Jessica recovered, the President actually rang her up to pass on his good wishes.

Although she was in good spirits, the toddler's ordeal had taken its toll. She had lost one fifth of her 21lb body weight and doctors reported that her right foot had become very badly swollen. For a time they thought it might have to be amputated but gradually blood supplies to the foot were restored and the danger passed.

Her only other obvious wound was a deep scraping of the skin above her right eyebrow. Plastic surgeons believed this was operable and would not leave a scar. Dr Carolyn Rhode, of the Midland Memorial Hospital, said: "I think considering the length of time she was in there, and the position she was in, she's a very spunky girl."

At last the townsfolk of Midland could plan their celebration party. Their efforts to

Above: *Happy ending. Jessica toddles out of the Midland Memorial Hospital with her mother, Reba, and father Chip.*

Left: *The Christmas the McClures feared they would never share with Jessica.*

Above: *Jessica meets President George Bush. He was among millions of Americans who prayed for her safe release as the drama unfolded.*

HUGGING HER BABY JESSICA'S MOTHER SAID: "I WANT TO TELL EVERYONE IN THE WORLD. THANK YOU ALL FOR CARING"

---

save Jessica inspired a White House-sponsored community service award and reminded millions of Americans just what can be achieved in a crisis.

As federal mine safety expert Dave Lilly observed: "That's the greatest bunch of people I have ever worked with. Most of the time we had to whip them to get them out of the hole. They were so exhausted they could hardly walk."

At the day-care centre a safety cap was carefully and lovingly fitted over the top of the old well by a welder. It carried the touching words: "For Jessica – with love from all of us."

The little girl's mother was overcome with gratitude. Hugging her baby she said: "I want to tell everyone in the world. Thank you all for caring."

The Jessica McClure rescue is one of the best-known examples of a community uniting around a child's plight. Yet it is by no means unique. Something about the claustrophobic terror of being trapped underground seems to strike a chord with the public.

The rescue of seven-year-old Benny Hooper is a case in point. In 1983 he fell into a 25ft newly-sunk well shaft which his father had dug in the garden of their home at Manorville, New York. Mr Hooper, and two of his neighbours, had been trying to find water. They had just halted work for the evening when the accident happened.

Benny's fall was partially broken by his windcheater jacket, which snagged on rocks on the way down. When he came to rest a few feet above the muddy floor of the shaft one of his arms was trapped in his jacket. But he was conscious and his anxious father could hear him sobbing quietly.

Police, fire and ambulance teams were on the scene in minutes. One detective who called his superiors to brief them of the crisis unwittingly broke the news to the boy's 30-year-old mother, Betty. As a local telephone operator she overheard his report and raced home, close to hysteria.

A VISION OF HORROR

The scene that greeted her must have confirmed her worst fears. Her husband had rallied a team of neighbours who were working frantically with mechanical diggers, picks and spades. Police had rigged up arc lights; medics were pumping oxygen down the shaft. At least they knew Benny was alive. He had managed to grasp a rope lowered to him but with only one free hand had been unable to hold on to it.

By now the professional rescuers had realised the danger of attempting to dig down to Benny. Piped oxygen had dried out the sandy walls of the shaft and sandfalls were occurring with alarming regularity. If Benny was not to be buried alive then there had to be a change of tactics.

Again, the parallel shaft technique was adopted. But even this was fraught with risk. The rescue team were safe enough while they bored down vertically to the required depth. But as soon as they began tunnelling horizontally they started reporting roof falls. Officials in charge ordered them to stop.

They could not put more lives in danger.

Soon 4ft long steel tubing was being lowered into the rescue shaft and then rammed horizontally towards Benny. It was an effective way to shore up the roof but it made for slow progress.

By now the little boy had been trapped for 16 hours and hope was swiftly beginning to fade. A powerful searchlight pointed directly down the well and it showed the extent of the sand-falls. Of Benjamin there was no sign at all. He appeared to have been buried alive.

HOPE EXPIRES

Rescue supervisors called in special sand vacuum pumps from the nearby Brookhaven National Laboratory, an atomic research centre. But their faces betrayed their despondency. This feeling of gloom was transmitted to the scores of neighbours surrounding the Hooper family home. They watched in silence; their mood sombre.

It seemed the effort was too late. The rescuer who broke through to Benny reported: "I have touched him. But he seems to be dead."

Benny was dragged out through the steel tubing and brought to the surface.

Men and women cried as they gazed on what they assumed was the tiny corpse.

Then the corpse moved.

A rescuer yelled: "The boy is opening his eyes." Mr Hooper took up the cry as he raced for the house. "He's alive, he's alive," he shouted. Mrs Hooper, waiting inside for what she assumed would be tragic news, stared at him in disbelief. "It's a miracle," she breathed.

As a doctor pushed a respirator over Benny's face the crowd of several hundred neighbours burst into wild clapping and cheering. Millions watching on TV murmured a silent prayer. Against all the odds, Benny Hooper had made it.

There are countless other examples of youngsters getting themselves trapped on home territory. Domestic building or engineering work, a child's natural curiosity, and distracted parents, can prove a dangerous combination.

Take the case of little Kevin Davis. In September 1990 the 20-month-old baby crawled across the foundations of an extension to his parents' home and promptly plummeted 12ft to the bottom of a narrow,

tapering shaft. He spent 14 hours there as rescuers pumped down oxygen and his mother, 32-year-old Lisa, sang nursery rhymes and told stories to keep him awake.

Later she said: "It was the worst nightmare of my life. One minute he was there playing alongside me and the next he was gone. I thought I would collapse on the spot but then I realised I had to be strong to help him."

As it turned out Kevin, from Denver, Colorado, was unfazed by the rescue operation unfolding around him. As teams of firemen and construction workers dug a parallel shaft next to the foundations he even managed to snooze through the sound of their drills. "He was a proper little hero," said one fireman.

"He didn't make so much as a whimper as we dug towards him."

Kevin was carried to the surface strapped to a stretcher but went on to make a full recovery in hospital. The extension was finished quickly!

Not all such dramas have a happy ending. In 1981 the whole of Italy went into mourning after the death of six-year-old Alfredo Rampi.

Alfredo, who had a heart condition, became trapped almost 200ft down a well in Frascati, 30 miles south of Rome. Rescuers got within a few feet of him, only for him to slip deeper. Less conventional attempts to reach him – by a potholing

Above: *Alfredo Rampi aged six. All Italy mourned his death.*

Below: *A rescuer is lifted out of the 200ft-deep well after failing to reach Alfredo.*

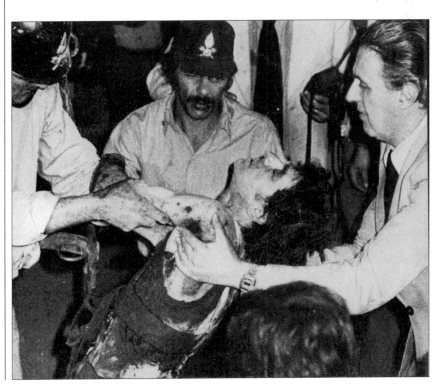

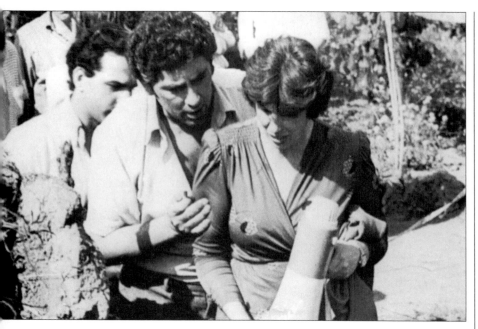

Above: *Alfredo's anguished parents wait to try and reassure their son using a megaphone. Later a phone link was installed in an attempt to maintain his morale.*

ALFREDO DIED BUT HE DID NOT DIE ALONE. ONE FIREMAN IN PARTICULAR, NANDO BROGLIO, BUILT UP A RELATIONSHIP WITH HIM

---

midget and a circus contortionist – both ended in failure.

Alfredo died, but he did not die alone. A microphone and speaker unit had been lowered down to him so that he could communicate directly with those trying to save him. One fireman in particular, Nando Broglio, built up a relationship with the boy over 20 long, painful hours. By the end, Alfredo would talk to no one else.

Nando took over the phone link when Alfredo's mother Franca became too distressed to carry on. His efforts, part of which are transcribed here, moved the world to tears.

MOVING WORDS

Nando: 'Ciao! My name is Nando. I am a fireman. I have come to talk with you and I won't leave you until you are up here with us. I will always stay and I won't sleep so you can keep talking to me as long as you like.'

Alfredo: 'What do you look like?'

Nando: 'Well, I am bearded and I have got four kids and I have heard all about you. Don't worry about the terrible noise which the big drill is making. The worse it is, the better it is for you because we are getting nearer. Imagine a big corkscrew.'

Alfredo: 'Like the one daddy opens his vino with?'

Nando: 'Exactly. But this one is six feet high and three feet wide. It is so big you could easily play helter skelter on it. It is better than the one at Lunar park in Rome.'

Alfredo: 'Would you take me to Lunar Park one day?'

Nando: 'Of course. You will now be my fifth family member and we will all go to the seaside as well.'

Alfredo: 'Will you lift me up and carry me out of here on your shoulders?'

Nando: 'Of course I will. I will give you a big hug and then hand you over to Mummy.'

Nando told the little boy how he had always dreamt of becoming a brave fireman. His dream came true, he said, except that Alfredo was much braver than he was.

CONSTANT REASSURANCE

After 12 hours the conversation lulled and it was assumed Alfredo was sleeping. Nando decided to carry on talking and singing softly so that the boy would hear his voice as soon as he woke.

When Alfredo did stir he immediately let out a blood-curdling yell. Nando waited for him to stop crying then said: "Well that's a relief isn't it. But do I sing so badly that you have to howl like that?"

From the well below came the clear sound of chuckling. Nando told him he could soon choose a pot of his favourite yoghourt – strawberry, cherry or mixed fruit.

The bond between the two seemed to grow stronger by the minute. When one rescue worker broke through to the shaft and yelled down: "My name is Mario, I've come to get you out," Alfredo replied: "Mario? I don't want Mario to take me out of here. I want my Nando to come and carry me out on his shoulders as he promised."

Sadly, Nando never got the chance. Alfredo slipped further down the shaft and became unconscious. Within 24 hours of falling into the well he was dead.

It usually falls to officers from the police, fire and ambulance services to take charge of underground rescues. But, just occasionally, some have-a-go heroes will succeed where the professionals have failed. Seven-year-old Latricia Reese owes her life to just one such team.

In June 1989 pretty, dark-haired Latricia was walking with a cousin outside her home in Houston, Texas. The girls had ventured outside to watch the fury of tropical storm Allison, then at its height. They could not have guessed the danger they were in. Allison was in the process of dumping an astonishing ten inches of rain on the city, setting off flash floods in almost every neighbourhood. One of the floods caught Latricia and swept her down an 18 inch culvert leading down into the sewers. Her chances of survival were put at zero.

Local fire department spokesman Mike Warnke said: "Our people said they could not reach her. The fire department diving team refused to go into the hole where she disappeared because the water was too swift and too dangerous. They said it was moving so fast she would have been swept to the place where the sewer system empties."

Given the extraordinary ferocity of the storm it would be unfair to accuse the divers of failing their duty. The fact that a young life seemed almost certainly to have been lost did not justify putting more lives at risk.

Anyone jumping into the sewer would have been swept along in pitch blackness by underground rapids.

The police certainly expected the inevitable. They placed a watch on the sewer outfall in the hope of spotting Latricia's body as it was churned out.

After 12 hours there was no sign.

But if the emergency services had lost hope, the little girl's mother, Karen, and aunt, April Janish, certainly had not. They knew she had a lot of sense and courage and was strong for her build. As the flood waters began to subside, they begged a gang of local construction workers to search the drain.

It was an inspired move. Swinging a flashlight, the men spotted Latricia clinging to a piece of concrete. She had summoned up hidden reserves to hold herself above the deadly black rapids swirling below. When the rescuers got a rope around her she was still gritting her teeth.

One of the workmen who volunteered to go down the drain, Timothy Gabrysch,

SHE HAD SUMMONED UP HIDDEN RESERVES TO HOLD HERSELF ABOVE THE DEADLY BLACK RAPIDS SWIRLING BELOW

Below: *A successful pothole rescue.*

said: "We used a flashlight and saw a little figure about 30ft under the street. It was pitch dark and she couldn't see anything.

CLINGING TO LIFE

"I have no idea how she stayed there. It was horrible and there was lots of debris swirling about. We began yelling her name and she answered back: 'Who are you?' She seemed reluctant to let go of the concrete she was holding on to because she realised it was her life-line."

Incredibly, Latricia escaped with hardly any ill-effects. Doctors at Houston's Humana Hospital found she had only a few cuts and scratches on her knees and elbows. Although she was in shock, it was a very mild case.

Fire spokesman Warnke said: "It's just a miracle that she could still be alive. She spent the entire night in the city's major sewer system with all that flood water coming down on her." And Latricia herself? "I didn't like it in there," she said. "It was very dirty. I wanted to be out. At first I couldn't breathe but I knew I had to hang on with all my might."

The prospect of being trapped undergound in rising water is the abiding nightmare of many cavers. Even highly experienced expedition leaders, who know all about the dangers in theory, sometimes fail to respond in practice.

In certain cave systems it is nothing short of folly to enter when rain is forecast. Persistent rain is channelled surprisingly quickly through porous rock and within a few hours gentle underground streams can turn into white-water torrents.

In July 1990 a party of five British children aged between 12 and 16 set off with two teachers to explore the Ibbeth Peril cave at Dent on the Yorkshire/Cumbria border. They entered in the early afternoon, crawling along a 15-inch-high passageway which led to a large chamber some 300 yards from the entrance.

The party, from Blackburn, Lancashire, had spotted no sign of a flooding danger. Yet rain had been forecast and as they wriggled and squirmed their way underground it was already beginning to fall. Imperceptibly at first, the Ibbeth Peril river began to rise. By the time the party realised their plight it was too late to act. Their teachers feared that attempting the crawl

back would be suicidal. There was nothing for it but to climb as high as possible in the main chamber and hope for help to arrive.

Fortunately the group had followed standard safety procedures. School colleagues had been informed of the estimated time of return and when this passed, emergency services were alerted.

But getting a team of divers into the cave was impossible. The raging river was now spewing out of the cave entrance with unbelievable power and rescuers could only sit and wait for the rain to stop and the waters inside to fall.

They knew that, for the group inside, every minute was a step closer to death from hypothermia.

To help lift the children's spirits the rescue team poured green, luminous dye into surface streams which fed Ibbeth Peril. Survival, they knew, could be as much about mental fortitude as physical strength.

AN IMPOSSIBLE TASK

David Renshaw, surface controller of the operation, said: "There was no way we could get in. We set watch overnight and monitored the water and weather forecast. When it dropped enough we were able to get two divers and two of the rescue team in. If it had not stopped raining we would have been too late."

First to reach the party was fireman Geoffrey Crossley. He said: "They had managed to keep dry but on the way out the water was rushing at such a rate that some of the young ones were getting washed off

> "THE TWO GIRLS WERE SEMI-CONSCIOUS AND I WOULD SAY ANOTHER FOUR HOURS AND SOME COULD HAVE DIED"

> "IT'S JUST A MIRACLE THAT SHE COULD BE ALIVE. SHE SPENT THE ENTIRE NIGHT IN THE CITY'S SEWAGE SYSTEM"

their feet. We had to put them on a rope."

Others told how close the expedition had been to tragedy. Alan Fawcett, a West Yorkshire accident and emergency officer, said: "The condition of some of them was becoming critical. The two girls were semi-conscious and I would say another four hours and some could have died."

All seven survivors were given emergency treatment at the cave entrance and then rushed to hospital in Lancaster suffering from shock and hypothermia.

They were later allowed home.

As education officials began an inquiry into the incident, local cavers questioned the decision to attempt the cave with the knowledge of the rain forecast. One of them, Jack Pickup explained: "In dry conditions, the cave is no problem at all. But when the river rises the water backs up into the cave and floods the narrow entrance."

"It would be flowing by outside the cave at a quarter of a million gallons a minute."

The Lancashire school party had spent a total of 20 hours underground, bad enough in the circumstances. Yet the rescue of one plucky American cave explorer, New Yorker Emily Mobley, took an agonising four days.

On April 2 1991, Emily and her fellow geographers began a project to map America's largest cave, Lechuguilla in New Mexico's Carlsbad Caverns system. The chamber is more than 54 miles long and 1,563ft deep and some media wags had dubbed her expedition the "journey to the centre of the earth".

Emily was more than two miles into the cave, and 1,000ft below the surface, when

Above: *The expressions on the faces of these mine rescuers tell a story of anxiety and despair. For all the advances in the industry, digging coal remains a dirty, dangerous job.*

IT WAS ALMOST A WEEK BEFORE THE RESCUERS FOUND THEM COLD, HUNGRY AND CONFUSED

---

a rock she'd been gripping gave way and crashed onto her leg. A doctor in the party put a splint on the broken limb and then gave her painkillers to get her through the tortuous journey to the surface.

Inch by inch, she had to drag herself to a central shaft, where colleagues strapped her to a stretcher. From then on it was a nightmare haul up sheer 180ft cliff faces, a labyrinth of cramped crawl-ways and a series of geological "chimneys".

BACK-UP TEAM

Yet at the end of it all her spirit remained completely intact. Pointing at her leg she joked: "There's no way this is going to slow me down at all. I'll be back to carry on the work here."

Emily at least had a full back-up team to see her to safety. Others are not so fortunate.

In 1990, a potholing enthusiast, Gary Lutes, 37, and his sons Gary Jnr, 13, and Tim, nine, made what they had intended would be a brief entry into the New Trout Cave, West Virginia. When their lights failed they were left wandering blind in a maze of passageways.

It was almost a week before rescuers found them cold, hungry and confused.

Even more remarkable is the story of Phillipines mine inspector Roberto Lingaolingao. On July 8 1989 he had the routine duty of looking over a shaft bored by the Atlas Mining Development Company 30 miles north of Cebu.

Roberto was 1,500 feet below the surface when part of the roof caved in. Both his colleagues managed to escape but he was left entombed in a 12ft by 6ft chamber. It took 12 days for a mine rescue crew to get him out. That he survived is due entirely to his willpower and ingenuity.

"There was no way I'd just curl up and accept that this dead end chamber would become the grave of Roberto Lingaolingao," he said. "I spotted a tiny trickle of water seeping down the wall and began collecting it in my hat. A week after the tunnels collapsed I realised I was dying of hunger. I ripped off a piece of my shirt and started unravelling tiny threads. Then I'd roll them into a tight ball, a little bigger than a large pill, and gulp them down with water."

Despite his ordeal Roberto later went back to work, even though he admitted the

"I KNEW IT WAS DANGER-
OUS BUT IT WAS THE
QUICKEST AND MOST
DIRECT WAY"

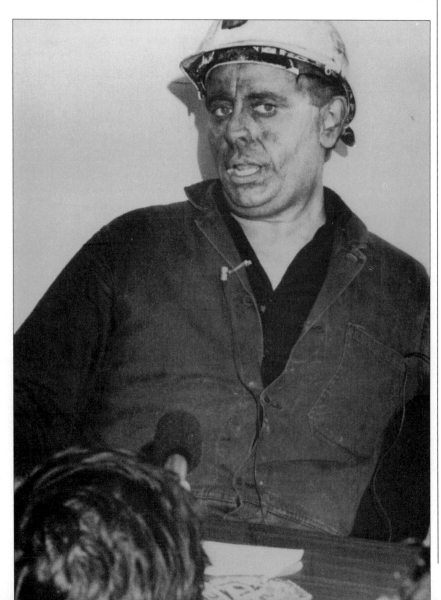

Below: *Ernie Hardy talks to newsmen. One of the men he rescued joked: "I never thought it would feel marvellous to see his face."*

prospect of entering a mine had given him "a few moments of blind terror".

WORKERS' SOLIDARITY

His determination to return to a hard, unforgiving industry is typical of the courage of mineworkers. Their's is not so much a job; more a way of life, and over the centuries the disasters and individual tragedies that beset mining communities seems to bind them ever more tightly together.

There are some who say that modern coal mining is well paid, highly mechanized, technically advanced and far removed from the bad old days of long hours and death-trap pits. That may all be true. But make no mistake, it is still a hard, dirty, dangerous business. One mine accident in 1989 brought this fact home to millions of Britons. It also threw up a reluctant hero! Ernie Hardy, 48, was pit manager at High

Moor colliery near Chesterfield, Derbyshire. On January 13, ten of his men became trapped when 600 tons of rubble collapsed from the roof of a newly-dug 1,000-yard tunnel. The ten, aged between 22 and 47, had no way of knowing whether they would get out alive.

Fortunately for them, on the other side of the rock-fall a minor miracle was taking place. Off-duty miners had heard of the accident and began arriving to volunteer for rescue work. With a professional emergency team they sweated in shifts, clawing at the rock with their bare hands and gradually clearing enough of a passageway to make faint verbal contact.

Yet the voices were not clear enough for officials to know who was still alive. They did not even know whether all the men were in the same place.

It was then that Ernie decided to adopt his own strategy, in breach of all the pit safety rules that are designed to prevent men crawling through unsupported tunnels. Carefully he squirmed 30 yards along a narrow route over the top of the fall, clearing away rubble as he went.

British Coal South Yorkshire director Ted Horton later commented: "We had been shouting backwards and forwards to the men. We had to establish that no one was missing."

SHEER DETERMINATION

"So the colliery manager took it upon himself to crawl through and check the names with those we had been unable to account for. It was a brave action.

"There was always the possibility that he himself could have become trapped."

Speaking after he led his men to freedom, 48-year-old Ernie said: "It was well worth it – especially when I saw their faces and realised they were all safe.

"I was guided by over 30 years' experience in the mining industry. I knew it was dangerous but it was the quickest and most direct way of starting the operation to get the men out."

One of those rescued said later: "Pit managers are a hard lot – and it would be daft to pretend that they are well liked by all of the men.

"I never thought it would feel marvellous to see the face of Ernie Hardy."

VENGEANCE
The law
in their hands

AN UNKIND CUT
Lorena Bobbitt

Lorena Bobbitt was at the centre of the wackiest, weirdest and, some would say, most gruesome court-case to hit America in half a century. In a fit of rage she severed the manhood of her husband John, claiming he had raped her moments before. The trial shone a harsh spotlight on domestic violence.

It arrived in a Ziploc polythene bag looking, as one surgeon would later recall, like a "tatty sausage". It was of average length, cleanly cut, but dirty from lying in a puddle of fetid water – its last resting place after removal from the body of John Bobbitt. This "tatty sausage" was a human penis. Behind its average size and shape lay a story of love, lies, sex, betrayal and brutality on an epic scale.

It was removed from Bobbitt's sleeping body by his wife Lorena – sliced cleanly off with a deft stroke of a steak knife. With that single manouevre the 24-year-old immigrant from Ecuador, who earned her living as a manicurist, propelled herself into the history books of America in a way she had never thought possible. Now, as the fallout from her husband's sensational rape trial has settled – and she has walked free from her own arraignment on malicious wounding charges – the allies on either side of Mr. and Mrs. Bobbitt each remain convinced that the other was the injured party – she, for being trapped in a loveless, violent marriage, he for more obvious reasons. It was rough justice on her part but the kind of justice which a jury of her peers agreed with.

To begin to understand what would drive a wife to sever a man's most sensitive organ from his body – the part of him which defines his very masculinity – entails a journey into the lives of this tormented duo. Many couples, too many, remain trapped in relationships devoid of affection, saturated with violence and anger, yet experts in marital strife are hard pushed to recall an instance where disintegrating love has resulted in such horrifying, excruciating pain. "No more than the pain I endured as a wife who was raped by this monster," said Lorena Bobbitt in her endearing Spanish accent after the incident. She now, by fate's strange quirk, has a future ahead of her rosier than anything that John, whose last job was as a nightclub bouncer, could have provided for her. Hollywood is knocking on her door, her bank account is already swollen with £25,000 paid for celebrity interviews and she has become a St. Joan figure among feminist groups eager to exploit her degradation at the hands of a "rapist" – even though he was never convicted of the crime – for their cause.

THIS "TATTY SAUSAGE" WAS A HUMAN PENIS, LYING IN A PUDDLE OF FETID WATER, ITS LAST RESTING PLACE AFTER REMOVAL

Opposite: *Lorena Bobbitt, who hacked off her husband's penis with a steak knife and threw it from her car window.*

Below: *The penis itself, the removal of which was at the centre of one of America's most sensational court cases.*

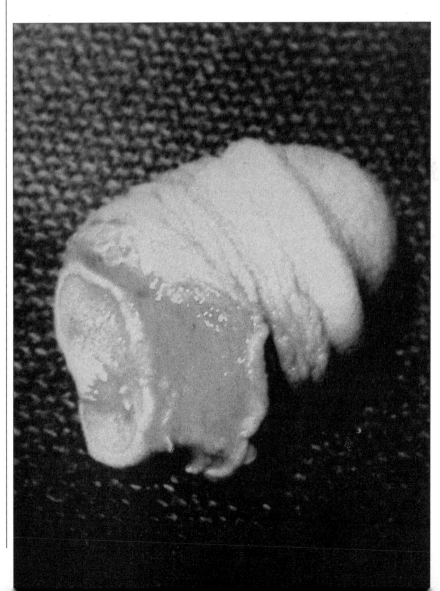

"WHILE I SAW MY PARENTS ARGUE ON OCCASION, I NEVER SAW THEM STRIKE EACH OTHER. THEY WOULD SCREAM, THAT'S ALL"

But can what went on between the two of them ever be as clear cut as the incision that Lorena Bobbitt made on the night of June 23 1993? And will anyone ever really know the truth of just exactly what transpired that fateful night between one man and his wife?

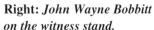

Right: *John Wayne Bobbitt on the witness stand.*

Below: *Outside the court, some of Lorena Bobbitt's supporters let their feelings be known.*

On the face of it, John and Lorena Bobbitt were an unlikely duo from the start. Born in Bucay, Ecuador, her middle class family moved to oil-rich Venezuela when she was a child, settling in the capital Caracas. Her father, a dental technician, was the ideal father and a role model, she says, of what men should be like. "While I saw my parents argue on occasion," she said, "I never saw them strike each other. He certainly would never strike my mother. They would scream, that's all. I wasn't brought up in an abusive atmosphere."

RICH DREAMS

Lorena visited America in 1984 and loved everything about it. It fulfilled all her movie dreams and more. Soon her parents, seeking more prosperity, believed emigration would be good for them all and they arrived in Washington in 1986. But visas were not forthcoming to Venezuelans. There was no criteria, such as political refugee status, which applied to them, so they were ordered home.

Lorena was 17 and determined to stay... whatever the cost. She took English classes and lived illegally with a family friend who had daughters of her age. She got a job as a

nanny with a Latino family before returning to Caracas where she applied, and successfully obtained, a visa from the American Embassy to stay in the States on a student visa. She returned in the late summer of 1986 with her new visa, granting her a six month stay in the country. It was on her return trip that she went to a dance in Stafford, Virginia, near to the Quantico Marine base. There were plenty of attractive, single men seeking out pretty girls as dance – or bed – partners.

One of the men there was John Wayne Bobbitt.

Bobbitt was a Marine rookie, with the trademark stubble haircut and rolling gait that impressed all observers that he was a "hard man" – not one to be easily tangled with. He was also a pretty dim individual who, as a child, suffered from what sociologists now like to call ADD attention deficit disorder. He and his two brothers

Above: *Judge Herman Whisnant sits in silence pondering the trial, which was televised, gripping the nation with its sensational themes of love, betrayal and revenge.*

Left: *Was Lorena Bobbitt's husband a monster of depravity or the victim of her insanity?*

JOHN WAYNE BOBBITT WAS A DIM INDIVIDUAL WHO, AS A CHILD, SUFFERED FROM ATTENTION DEFICIT DISORDER

grew up in Niagara Falls, raised by an aunt and uncle after his father left home in their infancy and his mother suffered a nervous breakdown and was placed in an institution. Growing up he was always in the lowest class at school, placed with the learning-disabled kids. But in the final two years of high school he managed good enough mathematics and reading grades to scrape into a mainstream form.

Bobbitt never excelled at expressing himself and he carried his school nickname with him into the Marines – "Mumbles". He was in trouble for truancy often and bullying once, but there was little to suggest he was violent or sexually perverted. He had a few girlfriends before joining the Marine Corps, none of whom have ever stepped forward to say he behaved brutally towards them.

DELUSIONS OF GRANDEUR

Yet he liked to cultivate a Rambo image, often signing himself as Claude Van Damme, after the movie star, on letters and HP agreements, practicing martial arts by the poolside of his apartment home. "He wasn't simple," said a pal, "but he was perhaps a bit naive. There are some of us who think that this broad may have sunk her hooks into him just as a way to stay in the United States." Lorena knew after her horrendous act of revenge that those were the whispers, but she said emphatically: "No."

They courted after that dance hall meeting, and by 1988 had become engaged. "He was nice," she recalled. "I never really saw any problems there. He used to ask me questions about school and he seemed really interested in me. I had not been out with too many boys before John." She says that it was only a week before their marriage on June 18 1989 that she finally slept with him: "You know, I watch movies, and I always thought that sex, it's like touching, holding, kissing, caressing, and he was never like that. He was never tender. For me, it was rough, I guess. And it never got any better. It was always just in and out."

The relationship degenerated into arguments and petty squabbles almost immediately. At first the rows were over the spartan apartment they were to move into, and John's announcement that his cousin would be living there too.

Above: *Day after day, Lorena Bobbitt had to fight to convince the trial judge that she was mad, not bad. A verdict of acting while she was unbalanced would be the only one that would keep her out of jail.*

Soon, she said, John began drinking heavily and began to be fined on the Marine Base for "lateness" – something which the Corps deny in an official statement. Just six weeks after the wedding, she says, came the first attack. Lorena claimed that after a hair-raising drive home, in which he kept zig-zagging across the road, he attacked her as they walked through the door of the apartment. "He grabbed my hair and slapped me," she said. "He kicked me to the wall. He kept slapping me. A security guard knocked on the door and asked if I was OK. I left that night and slept in my friend's car." Through his lawyer John denied attacking her, claiming instead that she attacked him because he refused to take her to a nightclub that evening. More violence followed, she says. In a fight over whether they should buy a plastic Christmas tree or a real one, she claimed that he used a choke-hold on her "that he learnt in the Marines". He denied it. Despite these rows and the alleged violence, she still wanted his baby and became pregnant the following year – but had the baby aborted when he "went berserk". Through his lawyer John responded: "That is the most ridiculous thing I have ever heard. We mutually decided that the time was not ripe for us to have a child. I was at her side throughout the whole procedure."

MUD FLIES

The whole story of their relationship, played out in court and later in celebrity interviews, was one of point and counterpoint; allegation and counter-allegation – from the number of jobs she said he had (19 to his recollection of six) up to the number of times he beat her. But if it is Lorena who is to be believed, the worst assaults took place when they moved into a house on Pine Street in Manassas, Virginia. In February 1991 she called police saying he had choked her and filed an official complaint. He filed one too, claiming that she had kicked him in the groin. In the end,

---

IN ONE FIGHT, SHE CLAIMED, HE USED A CHOKE-HOLD ON HER "THAT HE LEARNT IN THE MARINES"

Right: *One of Lorena's supporters.*

Below: *Exhibit A – the knife used by Lorena Bobbitt to emasculate her husband.*

both cases were dismissed. It was during the weeks following this, she insists, that he raped her for the first time – setting the tone for the rest of their miserable, worthless marriage. She says he raped her, stole money from her purse to date other women and and beat her up when he came in.

"Absolute lies," said John through his attorney, Greg Murphy. "I never ever hit her except to defend myself. Jeez, she has a

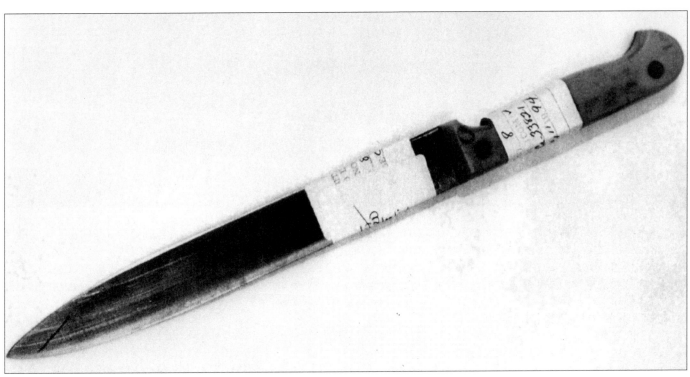

Above: *Lorena gained the sympathy of the nation as she wept on the witness stand, detailing her torment at the hands of her husband.*

temper. I was never unfaithful to her. I was never a rapist. She was never a battered wife." It begs the question why Lorena, who was making around £10,000 a year from the manicure salon, would stay with a man who was so wicked. She replied: "He always made me feel little, that I wouldn't attract anybody else. That I was ugly. I thought: 'Maybe this guy is right. I am not going to have anybody.' I felt like maybe I have to please him."

John left in October 1991, claiming his wife was a liar and thief and, certainly, he was right on the money with the second accusation. Lorena stole dresses from a local boutique and had begun pilfering products from the salon to do nails for a new clientele at her home. She says: "I did it for John, I wasn't getting any money from him." Amazingly, her boss forgave her – as she did when the following month she discovered Lorena had also cooked the books to the tune of £5,000. Instead of going to the police, she insisted she got the money back over time by docking her wages week by week.

Lorena says with repentance: "I just felt like a big desperation. What can I say? I am sorry. I just wanted to look nice for John." The dress store wasn't as understanding as her boss and she ended up with community service orders. A year later, John came home, landing a job at Burger King which he didn't manage to hold down for long. That entailed their move to a cheaper abode... Maplewood Apartments, scene of the unkindest cut of all.

Before the night of June 23 she hatched a plot to secretly tape record one of his "tirades" but he found the recorder and, she says, destroyed it. Afterwards, she claimed he beat, tortured and raped her. Two days

> JOHN WAYNE BOBBITT'S PENIS WAS PACKED IN ICE AND REATTACHED AFTER A MARATHON NINE-HOUR OPERATION

Below: *His image as a wife-beater didn't help John Wayne Bobbitt on the witness stand even though most people were agreed that his wife had taken a terrible revenge on him.*

later, John Wayne Bobbitt's penis was found by policemen sitting in a puddle where Lorena had thrown it. It was packed in ice and re-attached after a marathon nine-hour operation.

It was only during her trial in February 1994 – three months after a jury had cleared him of rape – that the facts emerged about what had happened that night. Lorena, who frequently broke down sobbing during her testimony, claimed that her husband raped her. She remembered going to the kitchen to get a glass of water, staring at the knife, grabbing it in her hand and marching back to the sleeping figure of her husband. She lifted the sheets and with one stroke his manhood was severed. It was, of course, not the way that John remembered the course of events.

Bobbitt, 26, was the first witness on the stand at the trial of his now ex-wife. He told prosecutor Paul Ebert that he had downed five beers and two B52 cocktails – consisting of Baileys Irish Cream, Kahluah

Above: *John Wayne Bobbitt was unconvincing on the witness stand. Public opinion began to swing towards his wife.*

LORENA DROVE IN A BLIND PANIC WITH THE PENIS IN HER HAND BEFORE CASUALLY THROWING IT OUT OF THE CAR WINDOW

and Grand Marnier in a pub crawl the night of the attack. He had had the night off work as a bouncer and had decided to hit the bars of his hometown in Manassas along with his best friend Robbie Johnson, who had come to see him from New York. Bobbitt claimed that he went to bed naked and then fell asleep immediately, only to be woken up by his wife wearing sexy Victoria's Secret silk lingerie.

"I remember responding, caressing her," he said. "But part of me was still asleep, part was not. I don't think I got an erection. I was too exhausted. Then I remember rolling on top of her. But I was really too exhausted to perform. I don't really remember anything else happening. At that point I opened my eyes. She was checking to see if I was able to perform for her. I must have fallen asleep again. Then I felt a couple of jerks on my penis. I felt a lot of pain and thought she had pulled it off. I shot up, real quick, I was bloody and con-

fused, I was hysterical. I caught her out of the corner of my eye. I heard her grunt and then she just ran. I felt dizzy, weird. I knew I had to get some help. I was holding myself with both hands. I woke up Robbie and he took me to hospital."

BLIND RAGE

Lorena for her part drove in a blind panic with the penis in her hand before casually tossed it out of her car window, the offending object of all her hatred ending up in a puddle of water near a motorway entrance ramp.

Surgeon James Sehn, who led the team of surgeons in a nine-hour operation to re-attach it – it was recovered by police officers an hour later after Lorena turned herself in – said: "It was a successful re-attachment. There have been less than 100 of these operations ever carried out. It is a man's worst nightmare, but if things go well he should regain use of it for his sex life, although it was quite badly damaged."

Lorena's testimony during her trial certainly had a profound effect outside the courtroom on those jurors who had acquitted her husband of rape in November. Four of them said they would convict him "in a shot" if they were trying him now. An avalanche of testimony from Lorena and his friends about his brutal behaviour convinced them – as it did much of America – that Bobbitt got his just desserts. The problem during his trial was that the jury was restricted to evidence on the night that his penis was severed. Lorena was able to call witnesses about past behaviour because her defence hinged on convincing the jurors that she was driven to the desperate act due to years and years of abuse. Juror William Dogt said: "I would convict him now with what I know. He sounds a sonofabitch. It makes me very angry. I am sorry that I wasn't able to see all of this evidence." Juror Belinda Gibson agreed, adding: "If this was allowed at his trial he would still be cooling his heels in jail now. We could only go on what was in front of us at the time – and that sucked."

Below: *The trial was an enormous strain on Lorena Bobbitt.*

Bobbitt appeared as casually arrogant after the attack as he was before – confident that he will regain full sexual use of his re-attached organ, joking with his neighbours and reporters at his wife's trial about his new nickname of "Stubby" and boasting to some about how much money he will make from talk shows and Hollywood "when all this is over". But he remained all too aware that, in a complex and murky case, she became a symbol of suffering womanhood exalted by feminists eager to further the cause of "wimmin" tak-

Above: *Flowers for the victor: in the end jurors decided she had acted in a moment of madness.*

ing revenge on brutal men. Even Christine Sehn, wife of surgeon Sehn who, with colleagues, re-attached the penis, became an object of hate for these crusaders. "I get shouted at in the street and threatened," said Christine. "I have heard women say that they wish my husband had put his organ down the waste disposal system."

Technically, Lorena Bobbitt's act was one of revenge in the eyes of the law, not self-defence. The rape she claims occurred happened before she picked up the knife, not afterwards. "It is immensely difficult to know who is guilty and innocent in this whole mess," said legal expert Paul Schaeffer in Washington, before the trial began. "Did he deserve this even if he was abusive? Shouldn't she have left before? Or should she be praised for striking out, ensuring he wouldn't rape again? Marital rape is very murky territory. I fear it won't become much clearer due to this case."

But, as rough as her justice was on him, the jury was finally with her at the end of her two week trial with a verdict that essentially judged her "mad not bad". They found that Lorena acted on an "irresistible impulse" in a moment of temporary insanity and that therefore she was not guilty of maliciously wounding her husband. But she was led away to a mental hospital for a 45

> THE VERDICT OPENED THE DOOR TO RICHES IN THE SHAPE OF FILM OFFERS, TV DEALS AND LUCRATIVE TALK SHOW FEES

Below: *Bobbitt stands outside the courtroom with his mother Marilyn Biro after his acquittal the year before on charges of rape. But his image took a further battering at Lorena's trial.*

day stay where she underwent tests to gauge when she should be returned to society. In the end she stayed less than 45 days and is now free, pursuing the American dream.

The verdict spared her from a potential 20-year jail term – and instead has ultimately opened the door to riches in the shape of film offers, TV deals and lucrative talk show fees. There were cheers outside the courthouse when the verdict came down, the roars of approval from a contingent of Latino women who had made it a shrine to her during the two weeks that she was on trial. John Wayne Bobbitt said he was "amazed" at the verdict. Yet many believe that the couple – who prosecutor Paul Ebert claimed "were not playing with a full deck" in the game of life – both got their just desserts.

ADOLF EICHMANN
Israel's Solution

As the architect of the Final Solution, Adolf Eichmann killed six million people. Yet when he was caught he seemed as banal as a bank clerk or store salesman. His kidnapping and trial was a message to fugitive Nazis everywhere that there is no hiding place and that their crimes will never be forgotten.

Nations live by laws – codes of conduct to maintain civility, decency and respect for all others. Yet in 1960 the state of Israel carried out one of the most sensational and audacious kidnappings of all time in complete contravention of its own – and international – laws. A special squad of commandos from the Mossad, led by the organisation's head himself, plucked from obscurity a little-known factory worker called Ricardo Klement from a slum outside the Argentine capital of Buenos Aires and flew him to Israel where he stood trial under his real name – Adolf Eichmann.

As Eichmann he was no factory worker but the architect of Adolf Hitler's "Final Solution of the Jewish Question" – the systematic, brutal and efficient extermination of the "lesser races" that Hitler's Nazi creed determined had no place in his society or on this earth.

THE STATE OF ISRAEL CARRIED OUT ONE OF THE MOST SENSATIONAL AND AUDACIOUS KIDNAPPINGS OF ALL TIME

Opposite: *The Death's Head cap and superior sneer of Adolf Eichmann, the fanatical Nazi responsible for the 'Final Solution to the Jewish Question'.*

Below: *A concentration camp in Austria, liberated by the US Army. These scenes resulted from Adolf Hitler and his henchman, Eichmann's, 'philosophy'.*

Justice took years to catch up with Adolf Eichmann – even if it had arrived by the most unjust and unorthodox fashion – but there are few on this planet who could ever weep for him when it was finally delivered.

The Holocaust he engineered stands as the most monumental crime in history – the systematic extermination of six million Jews and the murders of a further six million Russians, Poles, gypsies, homosexuals and other inferiors who threatened Hitler's warped vision of a racially-pure world dominated by his cruel stormtroopers. It took a mind of unfathomable coldness, of deeply twisted logic devoid of human emotions like love and kindness, to pluck the entire, maniacal Holocaust theory out of the Nazi's perverted philosophy and put it into practice. Such a mind belonged to Adolf Eichmann.

Eichmann shares a place in hell with the truly evil criminals who have scorched history. For although his uniform was never spattered with an innocent's blood, although he never pulled a trigger in anger or kicked a Jew being dragged from his home at midnight, it is accurate to say that he is the biggest mass murderer of them all.

THE HOLOCAUST, WHICH EICHMANN ENGINEERED, STANDS AS THE MOST MONUMENTAL CRIME IN HISTORY

Right: *St. Stephen's Cathedral in Vienna, a city corrupted by Eichmann, who made it his base of operations.*

Below: *Another city that Adolf Eichmann would come to know in his last years of exile – the Avenida de Mayo in Buenos Aires, Argentina.*

Eichmann made the trains – the awful trains, shunting through darkened Europe at night with their wretched human cargoes crammed into cattle wagons – run on time to the infernos of the death camps. He organised the round-ups, the timetables and garnered the manpower and hardware necessary to make the whole diabolical scheme possible. At war's end he was the top fugitive Nazi with a conscience that did not even prick him over the deeds he had done.

A SAD INDIVIDUAL

Adolf Eichmann was a lieutenant colonel in the dreaded SS. A mediocrity for all of his life, the silver lightning SS flashes and the fear which his uniform inspired in people were well suited to his disciplined, subordinate character. Born in Solingen, Germany – a town famous for its high-grade steel which was used to make knives and surgical instruments – he grew up in Austria when his father's job

Below: *After his life of privelege with the Nazis, Eichmann was reduced to poverty on the run.*

as an accountant took him to Linz. Karl Eichmann ran a loveless household which nurtured respect for thrift and order – qualities deeply imbued into his first-born son Adolf and his other four children. As a teenager he was a poor student who preferred to spend his time daydreaming, talk-

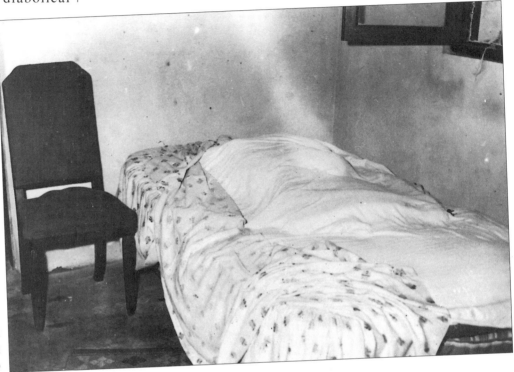

ing with the men who had served in the Kaiser's army at the front in the Great War, drinking in their tales of glory and sharing their disgust that the politicians, not the soldiers, had lost Germany the war. As Nazism began to thrive in both Germany and Austria he drifted towards the flags and the rhetoric which blamed an international Jewish conspiracy for the defeat. He relished the mad speeches made by Dr. Leopold Poetsch, the rabid Austrian anti-semite, who railed against anything and everything Jewish for all of Germany's ills.

By 1939, after spells as a junior member in the SS, his career had rocketed along with the fortunes of the Nazis and as the world stood poised on the brink of total war, he found himself under the direct control of Reinhard Heydrich or Hangman Heydrich as he was later to be known by

Above: *Klaus Eichmann, son of the man who engineered the deaths of six million people, makes a futile attempt, in a Buenos Aires restaurant, to declare his father 'innocent'.*

HE DRIFTED TOWARDS THE RHETORIC THAT BLAMED AN INTERNATIONAL JEWISH CONSPIRACY FOR THE DEFEAT

HE RELISHED THE MAD SPEECHES MADE BY DR.LEOPOLD POETSCH, THE RABID AUSTRIAN ANTI-SEMITE

Right: *Eichmann, stripped of his menacing SS uniform, looks like a harmless railway clerk.*

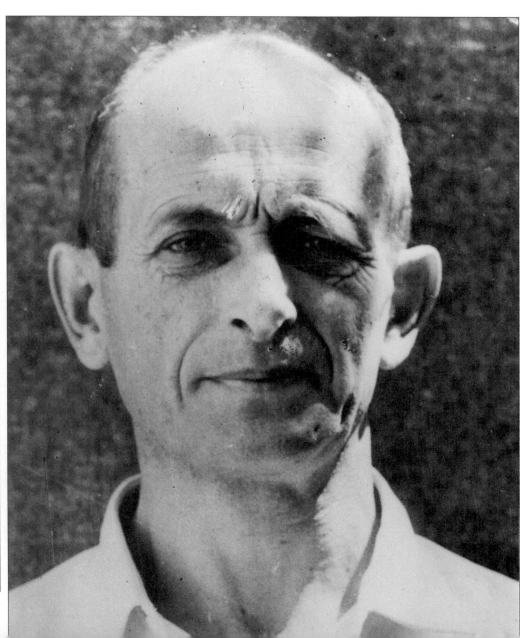

the souls he tormented – and was promoted to captain. Heydrich was tipped as the successor to the Fuehrer and charged with selecting hardened SS men for the great tasks which lay ahead in "cleansing" Europe of her Jews and other undesirables. With his recommendation to Himmler for his promotion, Heydrich wrote that Eichmann "should direct the entire Jewish emigration question". Eichmann created his own file for it.

He called it the Final Solution.

There were to be factories created for the specific purpose of killing human beings by the hundred thousand. Under a new department headed by Eichmann called ID IV – but known within the SS ranks simply as The Eichmann Authority – he ordered the construction of ghettoes in major Polish cities like Warsaw and Lodz where the Jews

Left: *A doctor inspects Eichmann shortly before the trial begins.*

Bottom Left: *A quiet moment of relaxation for the man with the murder of millions on his mind.*

Below: *Eichmann wades through mountains of books and paperwork in his bid to try to defend the indefensible in court.*

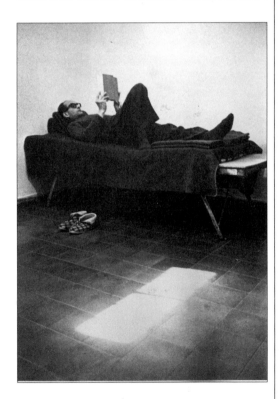

were penned into leper-like communities that had vanished in the Middle Ages. He planned for disease and hunger to take its toll among the Jews so that valuable Reich ammunition would not be wasted on them.

He authorised the experiments with mobile gas vans – where Jews were crammed into sealed trucks and killed by the carbon monoxide gas from the engine exhaust – and he drew up the plans for Auschwitz-Birkenau, in the south of the country close to the ancient medieval city

Right: *Before the trial of the Nazi monster, Israeli post office personnel are given a course in teleprinting so that the day's proceedings can be flashed to newsmen around the world.*

THE GREAT PLAINS OF RUSSIA WERE TO BECOME HIS PERSONAL KILLING FIELDS FOR THE 'INFERIOR RACES'

Below: *The heavily fortified courtroom where the trial was conducted.*

of Krakow, to become the Armaggeddon for Jews.

As, one by one, the nations of western Europe fell to Hitler's blitzkrieg, Eichmann organised the round-ups at the railheads for transportation to the east. In 1941, when Hitler launched Operation Barbarossa, his invasion of the USSR, Eichmann was a lieutenant colonel and the great plains of Russia were to become his personal killing fields for the 'inferior races'.

The gas vans had proved themselves to be ineffective and the mass shootings of Jews and Slavs across Russia were time-consuming, costly and traumatic – even for hardened SS men. They had to drink bottles of brandy to get through an afternoon of murder, and even then the

corpses were merely buried, not burned. In his office in Berlin Eichmann pressed for more efficient killing methods where every part of a body – hair, gold teeth, body fat – could be utilised after death for

the greater good of the Reich. He pushed for the use of Zyklon B gas in the chambers at Auschwitz – colossal rooms masquerading as bath-houses that could "process" 10,000 human beings every 24 hours – and he neatly tabulated the numbers of the dead alongside figures of looted wealth. He also kept count on how many bars of soap were made from the rendered fat of the victims and how many mattresses were stuffed with the hair of the nameless dead.

In 1942, at a villa formerly owned by a prominent Jewish family in the pleasant Berlin suburb of Wannsee, the Nazis made their full and final pact with the devil. Eichmann was there for the conference hosted by his boss Heydrich. There was only one subject on the agenda: "The final solution of the Jewish question in Europe." Here the euphemisms of re-settlement, processing and re-location were dropped. The Third Reich was embarking on the biggest single crusade of mass murder in history and behind it all, oiling the machinery of genocide, stood Adolf Eichmann.

Eichmann became a kind of witch-finder general with complete and utter authority over who was to live and who was to die. He ruled, for instance, that the offspring of mixed Aryan and Jewish marriages were to be sent to the concentration camps. He decreed that the Krimchak people of the Crimea – which was arguably an Aryan tribe – were "racially unsound" and he had them exterminated. Not since medieval warlords ruled Europe has such evil power been vested in one man.

Even when the tide of war began to turn and the SS hierarchy began to look for ways to make their parts in the holocaust look better, or to bury their past completely, Eichmann pushed ahead with new energy and vigour. More pragmatic SS men argued that the extermination of the Jews was secondary to winning the war. Not to Eichmann. He relentlessly continued to press for more freight trucks to transport his victims, more manpower to staff the camps, more gas for the chambers and more diesel fuel for the crematoriums.

In 1944, with the allies snapping at the gates of Germany, he set off for Hungary where, by dint of the nation's status as a German ally and the independence of her

Above: *Eichmann's wife, perhaps the only woman in the world who was to mourn his passing.*

ruler Miklos Horthy, the nation's 800,000 Jews had remained largely free from persecution. Eichmann took this as a personal affront and arrived in Budapest to organise their departure to the death camps. From mid-May until July, 437,000 Jews were entrained and executed. It was, he said, one of the more gratifying periods in his life.

The unique characteristic of Eichmann was that he believed wholeheartedly in the righteousness of his mission. He saw himself as a subservient disciple of the religion of Nazism and, like a monk in a monastic order, deprived himself in his zeal to complete his mission. By this time the heady grandeur of his earlier times in Vienna, when he swanned around the city in Rothschild's limousine terrifying hapless Rabbis, had evaporated. Instead, he was gaunt, tired and thinner, but his eyes burned with the fire of the zealot. He despised those who tried to cover up what had been done in the name of National

HE SAW HIMSELF AS A SUBSERVIENT DISCIPLE OF THE RELIGION OF NAZISM AND DEPRIVED HIMSELF IN HIS ZEAL FOR HIS MISSION

Below: *In his bulletproof dock, Eichmann tried day after day to portray himself as a victim of the regime he served.*

Socialism. He could not understand why the virtues of the extermination programme were not broadcast to all.

But the end he refused to see was coming at a lightning pace. Allied saturation bombing cut most major rail junctions in Europe, the death camps in Poland had been liberated or destroyed by their masters and the ghettos were in flames. In October 1944 he left Budapest on a forced march with hundreds of thousands of civilians as hostages. As he made his way back to a burning, beleaguered Berlin he was able to report to Himmler that, by his reckonings, four million Jews had died in the death camps and a further two million had been executed by the Einzatgruppen – execution squads – which roamed Russia. He was, in part, contented that so much had been achieved, but concerned that so much of his work was left undone. While others had committed the heinous crimes his fervent belief in the cause and devoted work had

lent intellectual credibility to the whole berserk scheme. He had, as one historian memorably remarked of him, drenched his soul in blood.

In the chaos of the final days of the Reich, as the Russians pounded what was once the cleanest city in Europe into brick-dust, Eichmann escaped. In April 1945 he made his way with a fellow band of fanatics to the Austrian Tyrol where he hoped to forge a "Werewolf" unit – a guerilla group committed to fighting the occupying allies until Germany was once again free.

Almost immediately after entering the mountains his comrades ordered him to leave. His reputation had preceded him and, loyal Germans though they were, they did not want to be tarred with the same brush as Eichmann. He wandered down a lonely mountain path with some ammunition and light provisions and set out to lose himself in the chaos engulfing his homeland in the days immediately following Germany's collapse.

A HUNTED MAN

Everywhere there was a price on his head. Survivors from all over Europe put him at the top of their most-wanted Nazi list and a ten-man commando unit was formed from death camp survivors in Poland with the specific task of bringing him to justice. Together with his adjutant, Rudolf Jaenisch, he made his way through Bavaria wearing the uniform of a Luftwaffe corporal.

He was captured twice by American troops – the first time he escaped to Munich after being put in charge of the holding camp's motor pool – and upon recapture claimed he was a lieutenant in the Waffen, or fighting, SS. At the Oberdachstetten camp in Silesia he led a relatively untroubled existence. But he heard reports coming through from the war crimes tribunal being assembled in Nuremberg reports which were frequently laced with the words Eichmann, monster, and mass murder.

Figuring that it would only be time before his true identity was revealed, he set about making plans for a third escape. He got away in January 1946 after escaping from a roadmending crew. Using the alias Otto Heniger in the Celle district, he lived there for the next four years as a lumber-

*Above: **Eichmann stands before the judges shortly before he is condemned to death.***

THERE WAS A PRICE ON HIS HEAD. SURVIVORS FROM ALL OVER EUROPE PUT HIM AT THE TOP OF THEIR MOST-WANTED NAZI LIST

jack, raising chickens on the side to supplement his meagre wages.

He knew that he could not stay in Germany. By 1950 the name Eichmann and the extermination of the Jews were inseparable. Using the aid of ODESSA – the sinister Nazi network of former SS men – he obtained a set of false papers and headed for South America where he vanished, protected by the old comrades and nurtured by a government that had as much regard for human rights as the one he once served. Vera Eichmann and the couple's two sons arrived on false papers in Argentina in 1952 and his life in exile seemed complete.

There was no remorse for what had been done during the madness of the Third Reich. He told Dutch Nazi journalist Willem Sassen, in tape-recorded interviews: "I have to conclude in my own defence that I was neither a murderer nor a mass murderer. I carried out with a clear conscience and faithful heart the duty

imposed upon me. I was always a good German, I am today a good German, and I shall always be a good German!"

Good was not the word that Nazi hunters around the world would use to describe him. He was the vilest of them all, but his escape had been so thorough that it seemed if he had got clean away. It wasn't until 1957 when a blind Jew named Lothar Hermann, living in a suburb of Buenos Aires, had his curiosity aroused about the children of a man called Ricardo Klement. His daughter had been seeing a young man who called himself Nicholas Eichmann and he stupidly boasted to her that Klement was not his real name, but Adolf – Adolf Eichmann. It meant nothing to her, but to her old father it meant everything.

SWIFT ACTION

The old man contacted a friend in the German police in Bonn who in turn passed on his intelligence to Fritz Bauer, the public prosecutor of the German province of Hesse. Bauer believed there was something to the old man's story and sent all the information to Isser Harel, the legendary head of Mossad. It was David Ben Gurion, premier of the fledgling Israeli state, who uttered two words to Harel when he came to him seeking permission to kidnap the killer of so many Jewish people. Those words were: "Do it."

Isser Harel – Isser the Little, founding father of Mossad, the ultra-daring Israeli secret service – began to assemble a team

Above: *SS Chief Heinrich Himmler walks with Nazi bigwigs in a quarry adjacent to a concentration camp.*

HE WAS THE VILEST OF THEM ALL, BUT HIS ESCAPE HAD BEEN SO THOROUGH THAT IT SEEMED AS IF HE HAD GOT CLEAN AWAY

THE ISRAELI PREMIER UTTERED TWO WORDS WHEN HARLE ASKED PERMISSION TO KIDNAP EICHMANN: "DO IT"

for the mission. Harel knew that he could not rely on any benevolence from the government of Argentina. Many Nazis had been granted refuge there in the years following the defeat of Nazi Germany; a request for extradition would have been declined and the prey they sought – Eichmann – would vanish once more. There was only one way to get him to answer before God and the law – and that meant breaking laws in the process. But there was no other way.

THE TRAIL GOES COLD

A hand-picked team of Mossad agents arrived in Buenos Aires on a reconnaissance mission early in 1958 but the house at 4621 Chacabuco Street was deserted. The family Klement – the name meant nothing to Harel and his men at the time – had left there with no forwarding address just two months earlier. Isser Harel felt that the old Nazi must have had a sixth sense. The trail went cold.

It was not until December 1959 that it was picked up again when a Mossad agent discovered that Nicholas Eichmann worked in a motorcycle repair shop in the city. Harel had been on the brink of cancelling the operation – then as now, large expenditures could only be justified if there was the firm likelihood of results. But they got a break from a disaffected member of the German community in Buenos Aires who told them where Eichmann's son worked. An agent trailed him to the dismal city suburb of San Fernando where mangy dogs roamed in the streets and the houses were bare, cheap affairs with primitive sewage and electricity supplies that often went out. A surveillance team was quickly assembled to stake out the home of Ricardo Klement. For many days the team watched the balding, bespectacled clerk at the local Mercedes Benz plant return home, but they were uncertain it was him. Few photos of the monster existed and the years had gone by. It wasn't until he appeared on March 21 1960 clutching a big bouquet of flowers that the team were satisfied they had him. A quick check in the Eichmann dossier confirmed that it was his wife's birthday and, like any dutiful husband, he was congratulating her with flowers.

From Solingen, to Linz, to Rothschild's

home in Vienna which he seized, to Dachau and Auschwitz and Berlin, the world's foulest tormentor had ended his days in a crumbling house on Garibaldi Street, Buenos Aires. Peter Malkin, one of the Mossad agents assigned to the team, who had lost numerous relatives in the Holocaust he managed, was aghast when he first laid eyes on him.

In his book Eichmann In My Hands, he described how he saw Eichmann sitting with his son on his lap, staring out at a railway embankment. "The boy sat at the man's lap, both of them gazing out. They stayed that way, both of them staring out, for a long time, seeming to daydream in unison. Then, off to my right, there came a rumbling noise.

"Slowly it began to grow louder. Now the man stirred and pointed. A moment later a freight train appeared, roaring on the tracks almost below me. All at once I was hit by an almost indescribable sense of revulsion. The father was smiling slightly, and his lips were moving. Finger extended,

THE WORLD'S FOULEST TORMENTOR HAD ENDED HIS DAYS IN A CRUMBLING HOUSE ON GARIBALDI STREET, BUENOS AIRES

Below: *A plaque erected by the liberating British soldiers who came upon the human abattoir of Belsen in their drive across Germany.*

he was helping the child count.

"'You bastard,' I thought. 'Still with the trains!'"

Events moved rapidly after the positive identification. A travel agency was set up in a major European city – still secret to this day – which processed the travel permits and documents necessary for the team to travel to Argentina. Safe houses were rented all over the city, including a villa with shutters on the window where the beast would be held before he could be smuggled from the country. On May 11 1960 it was decided to snatch Eichmann.

On that night the agents positioned themselves on the streets near his home and in the safe houses. All of them had lost numerous relatives in the war and all would have had ample personal scores to settle. But there was no gratuitous violence on the agents' part – they were professionals trained to subjugate their own feelings. But it wasn't easy. As they waited, three buses – any one of which Eichmann could have been on – pulled up and sped off without

been gazing at the engine, together with the accomplice in the back, bundled him into the vehicle.

With a pistol to his head Adolf Eichmann was told: "Make one sound and you are dead." He was covered with a blanket and driven to a safe house. There his armpit was checked for the tell-tale SS number which every member of the "superman" elite had tattooed on him. It was missing, in it's place a crude scar. But there was no pretence on Ricardo Klement's part. He looked calmly at his captors and said in perfect German: "Ich bin Adolf Eichmann" – I am Adolf Eichmann.

With these words many of the Mossad agents broke down. Here was the man who had assigned their families to the gas chambers and crematoria of Europe; a man who was so drenched in the blood of innocents that no sentence could ever atone for what he did. Yet for the next ten days they lived in close proximity with him as he remained shackled to a bed, astounding and disgusting his captors with his knowledge of Hebrew and the Talmud.

Getting him out of Argentina was far more dangerous than the simple kidnapping and finally Harel risked all on a simple ploy. He drugged Eichmann, dressed him in the uniform of an El Al pilot and

Above: *Eichmann listens to the German translation of the testimony against him.*

Right: *A picture of the young Eichmann as he begins his climb up the SS ladder.*

WITH A PISTOL TO HIS HEAD ADOLF EICHMANN WAS FIRMLY TOLD: "MAKE ONE SOUND AND YOU ARE DEAD"

disgorging the single passenger the Eichmann team wanted. The agents prayed that he had not been tipped off by an old Nazi network and already fled.

But at 8.00pm another bus turned up and Ricardo Klement stepped off, wandering with nonchalance towards the door of his home. He passed a car with the bonnet up and two men intently studying the engine. He didn't know that a third man was lying on the floor of the vehicle or that the car parked on the opposite side of the road was positioned to shine its lights directly into his eyes. As he passed the "broken" vehicle the men who had

arranged for a jet of the national airline to be at the city's airport. He drove through security with the drugged prey sandwiched between two agents, similarly dressed, convincing the airport guards that their friend had imbibed too much of the local Argentine hospitality the night before.

HISTORICAL SCENES

Twenty four hours later they were back in Israel. The Israeli parliament, the Knesset, has never witnessed such scenes before or since as the time Ben Gurion rose and said: "I have to announce that a short time ago one of the greatest of Nazi criminals was found by the Israeli secret service. Adolf Eichmann, who was responsible, together with the Nazi leaders, for what they called the 'Final Solution of the Jewish problem,' – that is, the extermination of six million Jews of Europe. Adolf Eichmann is already under arrest in Israel and he will be brought to trial in Israel."

If the world expected a fanged monster in the dock it was sadly disappointed. The banality of evil was exemplified in the bald, shrivelled man in the glass-covered stand who dressed in a sober suit and looked like a faceless commuter late home from the office. In his trial which lasted from April 11 to August 14 1961, there was no repentance, no hatred, no remorse and no bitterness, save that he did not understand why the Jewish people hated him because he had merely obeyed orders and surely that was a trait that was worthy of admiration in any man? Justification for the Holocaust belonged to somebody else – he was merely a cog in the great corrupt wheel of Nazism.

On December 1 1961 Adolf Eichmann was sentenced to die and on May 31 the following year he rejected an appeal by a Protestant minister that he repent as he was led into the death chamber.

Refusing a hood as he mounted the scaffold at Ramle Prison, he said: "Long live Germany. Long live Argentina. Long live Austria. These are the countries with which I have been most closely associated and I shall not forget them. I greet my wife, family and friends. I had to obey the rules of war and my flag. I am ready."

His remains were cremated and scattered at sea. No prayers were said for him and few wept for him. Justice had been done and perhaps there was some small crumb of comfort in the verdict for the survivors of so many murdered innocents.

Above: *Liberation came too late for these victims of Eichmann and his henchmen, murdered in the name of Nazism in the Buchenwald concentration camp in Germany.*

THE BANALITY OF EVIL WAS EXEMPLIFIED IN THE BALD, SHRIVELLED MAN IN THE GLASS-COVERED STAND DRESSED IN A SOBER SUIT

AS HE MOUNTED THE SCAFFOLD HE SAID… "LONG LIVE GERMANY. LONG LIVE ARGENTINA. LONG LIVE AUSTRIA"

THE DUTTON BOYS
Innocent Killers

There was no sunshine, no magic in the Dutton Boys' childhood – only pain at the hands of their father. They suffered immeasurably in the filthy shack they called home. The law called them murderers but in the end they had snapped and taken justice into their tiny hands the only way they knew how.

Rush Springs in Oklahoma is an unlikely setting for Satanic rites, child rape and murder. It is a small town where, the saying goes: "People know about it when you're born and care about it when you die." But they didn't care about Lonnie Dutton, the town bully who was shot dead with a deer-hunting rifle by his two tormented sons as he slept. There were no tears shed for the man they called Lucifer, no cries for justice. Instead the entire focus of a nation where 23,000 people die a year by guns turned to his killers as a campaign mounted for them to be allowed to get away with murder. Only since Lucifer was despatched to hell has the nightmare world he created for his children on earth been fully revealed.

In a caravan park that was home to Herman Dutton, 15, brother Druie, 12, brother Jake, eight, and sister Alicia, ten, all of the innocence and magic of childhood was stolen away by Lucifer. He worshipped the devil after his drunken bourbon binges, decorating the floor of his filthy home with pentangles constructed from salt and a skull with spent gun cartridges for eyes. He regularly raped Alicia, forcing the boys to watch. He also raped them. "Affection" was limited to birthday cards which he signed: "Happy birthday s**theads, love daddy."

They are children who never cried. Lucifer had beaten into them at an early age to equate fresh tears with fresh pain. There was no running water, no electricity, no telephone in their twilight world which the creaking American welfare system had let fall through the bureaucratic cracks. Lucifer never allowed any children to visit his own – not that they would have wanted to stay long anyway with the pungent odour of goats, chickens, turkeys and pigeons, which he kept inside, stinking the place up. The children suffered in silence at the hands of this brute until they could bear

Above: *Herman (top) and Druie (bottom) Dutton.*

Opposite: *The shack that became a living hell.*

Above: *This was the filthy, stinking shack that the boys knew as home.*

ONE NIGHT THE TWO DUTTON BOYS DECIDED THAT THEY WOULD HAVE TO BLOW THEIR DADDY'S HEAD OFF

no more. One night the boys, who had forged an incredible bond of love and companionship between themselves because there was none coming their way from any other quarter, decided they would have to blow their daddy's head off.

On a hot July afternoon in 1993 the boys worked in the garden, tending to a few scrawny vegetables that struggled to survive beneath the blistering sun. As they raked the weeds and tended to the stalks of the tomato plants, there suddenly came a cry from Alicia inside the filthy shack they called home. Suddenly the door, supported on a couple of loose-nail hinges, flew open and their sister burst into the garden, her face flushed and her clothes in disarray. "He's been messing with me again," she sobbed. "Daddy's been messing with me again." The boys turned to look at each other. Something telepathic passed between them. No words were spoken although both knew what was going to happen, what must happen. They were going to kill their daddy.

Taking the rifle that he used to stalk deer in the nearby woods, Herman placed the barrel against his father's head and Druie pulled the trigger. Herman was originally supposed to be the "triggerman" but he chickened out at the last moment. So he held the barrel while Druie positioned the gun. A single shot that would echo all across America, finally up to the bronze-and-oak doors of the Supreme Court in Washington itself, was fired. Four days short of his 40th birthday Lonnie Dutton died, unloved and unmourned.

POWERFUL SUPPORT

Killing is a black and white affair in this rural community plumb in the centre of a state where murderers still fry in the electric chair. It provokes shock and righteous rage. But the slaughter of Lonnie Dutton provoked another kind of rage – the rage of people turning out in their thousands to support the boys. It began with the telephone lines burning up. Fourteen-year-old Haylee Golden called her schoolpals. "Can you believe it?" she said. "I was in the same class as Herman. He was so quiet, so shy. He never said nuthin' unless he was asked first. He was only ever in trouble once the whole time I was at school with him – and only then for throwing a basketball in the aisle of the school bus. If he were violent I would have seen it. But he was just there, filling a place at a desk and saying and doin' nuthin'. God, it just hit everybody so hard."

The dead father was an unemployed roofer who people knew was a drinker and a loudmouth. All that townsfolk knew was that the boys' mother had been gone for years and that he ruled his home with a fist of iron. Or did they know more? Did they really know what he was doing to those unfortunate children, day in, day out? Did they know yet keep silent – out of fear of him or of fear of confronting those taboos in society which loom out of the dark side of man's soul to torment us all?

Little things once ignored by all now swelled to immense importance. What seemed like a black eye on one of the children months ago now became a piece of the puzzle. A bruise on the head another piece. Slowly it dawned on those who had lived with these boys, among these boys, in the close-knit town that they had allowed – by their silence, by their inaction – terrible things to occur. "I remember one time," said John Clifton, a pal of Herman's at school, "that he had an enormous bruise on his head. He said a goat kicked him. Now I guess the poor guy was lying to cover up for his father. Maybe that's what everyone did in this town for a long time – cover up for a really bad dude."

Children in town regarded Mr. Dutton as a cross between the bogeyman and the town drunk. Amy Worthington, another school friend of the boys, said: "Just his appearance – he was scary looking. But no-one thought he was doing these things to his kids. I mean, at least, no-one talked about it. I sure didn't know." Yet the facts

THE DEAD FATHER WAS AN UNEMPLOYED ROOFER WHO PEOPLE KNEW WAS A DRINKER AND A LOUDMOUTH

Below: *It was upon this sofa that Lonnie Dutton breathed his last, the victim of a shot to the head four days before his 40th birthday.*

blue sash around the tree in front or a poster in the window that read: "We support you!" At weekends convoys of 500 vehicles rolled the 18 miles to court hearings for the boys. And at a meeting of the town's citizens – 1,000 of the 1,100 residents – they unanimously voted to press for their freedom all the way to the Supreme Court.

At that meeting one Linda Munn stood up and told the assembled crowd, a seething sea of blue ribbons: "He was a bad man, a man I was afraid of too as much as you." Linda Munn's words meant a lot, because she is the sister of the dead bully. "These children learned never to cry because to cry meant to get hurt," she said, wiping away tears. "We can't let them be hurt anymore."

As the townspeople campaigned for the murder charges against the boys to be dropped a collective feeling of guilt has also settled like a dark fog on their shoulders "You see, we KNEW what was happenin' but we did NUTHIN'" said Becky Fitzgerald, a teacher who had known the hulking bully all her life. "What could we do? The welfare people went there six times, and each time said they could discern no evidence of abuse. If they couldn't help, who could?" After the killing the boys went to a public telephone and called for an ambulance, saying that a burglar had shot him. But they both burst into tears within minutes of making the call, and

circulated pretty damn quick, first in the town, then the state, then across the country. The appalling way he had treated his children turned a clear-cut case of juvenile delinquent murder into something approaching a people's crusade for justice – justice for THEM, not the dead man. Across the state and in neighbouring towns and cities blue ribbons began flying for the Dutton boys. Soon there wasn't a house or a shack in Rush Springs that didn't have a

Above: *Lonnie Dutton's grave, still without a headstone. No one wants to buy one for him after what he did to the children.*

when cops arrived blurted out the whole rotten story of their miserable existence and how they decided to end it.

Cops still have trouble to this day comprehending the filth and squalor they lived in. There was a recipe for making moonshine whiskey pinned by the door and ammunition for the 9mm. pistol he always carried in his blue overalls scattered over the floor. One policeman vomited at the scene not at the sight of his shattered head and blood seeping over the filthy sofa, but from the stench. There were dishes with rotting food piled high on the stove and rat trails leading to a rodent nest trailed across the floor. One officer said: "We knew that he wasn't an ornery critter but God, nothing prepared us for what we found in his house. I was expecting to want to horse-whip his sons after what they done. Instead, I wanted to scoop them up in my arms, take them home to my wife and tell them that not all adults were bad, that there are decent, loving folks in the world." Lonnie Dutton's abuse of his children had begun at an early age – he even made them beat their mother, Rose Marie, before she fled in fear of her life in 1989. The children would later recount how they used to creep up to their mother and apologise to her afterwards, while their drunken tormentor slept off his latest bender.

THERE WERE DISHES PILED HIGH ON THE STOVE AND RAT TRAILS LEADING TO A RODENT NEST TRAILED ACROSS THE FLOOR

Below: *Everywhere across town the signs of support for the boys went up after the killing.*

Luther Dutton, father of Lonnie and grandpa to the boys who killed him, says he has trouble fathoming how things got so bad for so long. But he now says: "I guess I have to take their side and say that, really, he tortured those children into doing what they did. They killed him, but maybe he really killed himself."

Those sentiments echoed around the town, from the lowest farmhands to the teachers at the school. Herman's maths teacher Fred Fitzgerald said: "No-one condones what was done but if you were young and undernourished and you had been abused all your life, and you have had to stand by and watch your little sister being sexually abused and you are in a corner and you don't have any way out, then what are you going to do?"

Fitzgerald and his teacher wife Becky formed a committee to support Herman and

Above: *Lonnie Dutton's sister Linda Munn. "These children learned never to cry because to cry meant to get hurt," she said, wiping away tears. "We can't let them be hurt anymore."*

WELFARE OFFICIALS WERE
PLACED UNDER POLICE
PROTECTION IN THE
AFTERMATH OF
THE SLAYING

Druie while authorities pondered over what to do with them. Townsfolk, many of whom are on welfare themselves and who could hardly be described as affluent, swarmed to their home with donations of clothing, money and antiques – anything which they thought might be sold to raise cash for a legal defence fund.

Most townspeople didn't want the boys to be tried at all, but the prospect of city-slicker lawyers making them stand trial in an adult court on juvenile charges seemed to loom on the horizon.

"After that it became imperative that we tried to get them in court as juveniles," said Fitzgerald. "There is no way they should have been tried as adults." Of course, some law and order officials believed that many other disenchanted children with parents perhaps not quite so demonic as Lucifer might be tempted to solve their adolescent

woes with a bullet. "That is exactly our concern," said Gene Christian, the attorney handling the Dutton boys case. "For our part we wanted to make sure that the message wasn't sent out that the proper way to deal with problems is to kill someone and become a local hero."

Grandpa Dutton sniffed at the high-mindedness of the DA and recounted what Herman had said to police when he was arrested and told he might be in an awful lot of trouble. He said: "He looked up at the cop and then looked down at the ground and said: 'There ain't nothin' that you can do to me that I ain't already gone through.' That's the God's honest truth to it, right there."

Welfare officials in Rush Springs were placed under police protection in the aftermath of the slaying. Feelings ran high against the social workers who never once tried to remove the boys from the clutches of someone who everyone knew – or suspected, or had a good hunch – was a monster. Mary Smith, whose 21-month-old grandaughter was Lucifer's great niece, told of how "everyone knew" him as a most wicked sadist. She said: "He was crude and evil. I saw him with my grandaughter once, flicking his middle finger against her skull in a game he called 'plinky'. He did it until she cried and was then satisfied. "He was a bastard through and through. I think that's the best word anyone can think to say of him."

A GLIMPSE OF NORMALITY

The cops say the boys are warm hearted, intelligent and fiercely protective of one another and their other siblings. On the way from the scene of the crime to the police station they stopped and bought the boys a hamburger from McDonalds. The boys were astonished at such a place. They had never seen one before.

A police spokesman said in the wake of the murder: "All he basically allowed them to do was go to school and come straight home. They had a dog's life. Their mother left years ago and he got custody. We feel for these children but the law is the law."

Rush Springs describes itself as the Watermelon Capital of the World, and boasts that during wartime Sir Winston Churchill, on a visit to President Roosevelt in Washington, once dined on their fabled produce. Now it has earned a new name and new fame for itself, in a way that no-one could possibly foresee or want.

"It'll go all the way to the White House," said Mrs. Munn, their aunt. "They can't prosecute little boys who suffered like this if enough people say they were driven to it. What they need now is healing, not punishment – and this town is ready to give 'em that, because it's what they deserved all along."

Mrs. Munn was proved right in the end. A trial found there was no case to answer, after the judge took advice from the Supreme Court in Washington. The boys had gotten away with murder – a particularly rough form of justice, but a fitting one in this case. Now psychologists and mind experts are working with all the Dutton children to try to give them back some of

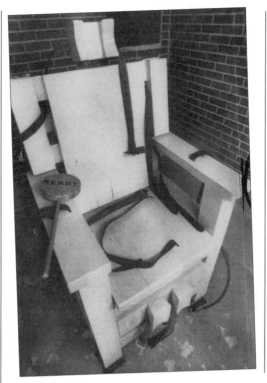

"I SAW HIM WITH MY GRANDAUGHTER ONCE, FLICKING HIS MIDDLE FINGER AGAINST HER SKULL... UNTIL SHE CRIED"

Left: *The electric chair – where the Dutton Boys could have been headed had they been older and the nation less sympathetic towards them.*

the childhood they lost. Dr. Alex Buziskin, a child expert in Washington, said: "They suffered immensely but they found a decency and a love between themselves that all the hatred emanating from their cruel father could not destroy. There is every hope that they can become loving and responsible adults who will be able to put this terrible ordeal behind them."

Above: *The Supreme Court in Washington, final arbiter of justice in America, was consulted over the Dutton case.*

FAWAZ YOUNIS
No Hiding Place

The capture of Fawaz Younis was Ronald Reagan's message to terrorists everywhere that retribution for their crimes could come at any time and in any place. It was a daring plan that brought the Arab to America and left the world open-mouthed at the sheer scale and audacity of the action.

In the latter half of this century a new crime needing new solutions has been the bane of western democracies: terrorism . Whether home-grown like the Basque separatists in Spain or the IRA in Northern Ireland, or exported abroad by fundamentalist fanatics from the Middle East, the laws by which nations tick have often been powerless in the face of this onslaught.

WPC Yvonne Fletcher, for instance, perished in a London street outside the Libyan embassy in 1984 and her killers were set free for diplomatic reasons to return to their homeland. And how many of the masterminds of such outrages as the Birmingham pub bombing or the Hyde Park slaughter of army bandsmen and their horses have been brought to book? Fighting terrorism is a complex and frustrating occupation that often involves breaching the laws that a nation sets. No single act of overriding the written rules in pursuit of justice tops the capture of Fawaz Younis.

NO SINGLE ACT OF OVERRIDING THE WRITTEN RULES IN PURSUIT OF JUSTICE TOPS THE CAPTURE OF YOUNIS

Opposite: *The face of the captured terrorist stares directly ahead, pondering the kind of justice that awaits him.*

Below: *Fawaz Younis at Beirut Airport, reading a statement about his 'glorious' hijacking of a plane that was to be blown to bits moments later.*

For sheer audacity, skill, nerves and execution it stands as a symbol – and a warning to terrorists all over the globe – that the fury of a democracy can be fierce and that complacency is something that they simply cannot afford.

It was Ronald Reagan, during his presidency of America, who sanctioned the taking of Fawaz Younis. Reagan breathed a new patriotism into his country and banished the shame and anguish of Vietnam from the public psyche. At home he bolstered the crime fighting agencies in major cities and took on the druglords to try to regain neighbourhoods for families. Yet on the international stage terrorism seemed to mock him from every corner of the globe.

In 1985 a TWA flight from Athens was hijacked after take-off and US Navy diver Robert Stethem was brutally tortured to death. In October of the same year the Achille Lauro ship was hijacked at sea by Arab fanatics which resulted in the murder

Above: Younis never had much time for justice but in America he was forced to stand trial by jury in the time-honoured fashion.

REAGAN FELT IMPOTENT IN THE FACE OF THIS FURIOUS ASSAULT ON HIS PEOPLE AND THOSE OF OTHER FREE NATIONS

of American citizen Leon Klinghofer killed by being pushed into the sea in his wheelchair to drown. In December a wanton attack at Rome airport killed 15 people while on the same day at Vienna airport a simultaneous massacre carried out by disciples of terror chief Abu Nidal killed three and wounded 42. Four more American citizens were killed in April 1986 when a bomb exploded aboard a jetliner as it approached Athens airport and Americans were being held hostage in God-knows-what kind of conditions in hell-hole jails beneath the ruins of Beirut.

HUGE RESOURCES

It was no wonder that President Reagan, who commanded the mightiest arsenal of weaponry on earth, the largest spy services, the largest fleets and air forces, felt impotent in the face of this furious assault on his people and those of other free nations. But he decided on one glorious counter stroke, an escapade of stunning originality that was designed to send a message loud and clear to the terrorists: "You can run – but you can never hide." Consulting with his CIA, FBI and Pentagon chiefs, Ronald Reagan sanctioned the kidnapping of a terrorist chieftain from the battle-scarred terrorist enclave of Beirut. "Do it," he ordered, "for mankind."

The target for this international kidnapping was to be Fawaz Younis, a terrorist who had emerged as a power-player in the bloody and dangerous battleground of the Middle East. He was identified in CIA files after the hi-jacking of a Royal Jordanian Airlines jet, an operation which he commanded. For 53 hours the eight guards aboard the plane were systematically beaten to within an inch of their lives on his specific orders. The plane was then landed

THE FLAMES OF THE BURNING AIRCRAFT WERE REFLECTED IN THE HATE-FILLED EYES OF YOUNIS AS HE JUMPED FOR JOY

Below: *Hooded and menacing, the hijackers of the TWA plane that Younis commandeered read a statement after the release of their American captives.*

at Beirut airport, the guards and other hostages released and the fuselage of the plane was raked with gunfire. One hundred and twenty million pounds of aircraft burned on the tarmac, the flames reflected in the hate-filled eyes of Fawaz Younis as he jumped for joy and was caught on camera by a western journalist.

Younis, further CIA enquiries determined, was also aboard the hi-jacked TWA flight on which Robert Stethem was beaten to death. He was aligned with a dangerously fanatical terrorist group in Beirut that had links to Iran. His terrorist pedigree made him a perfect choice for a lesson in rough justice. But there was one other aspect that made him stand out – he was careless. In a world where most of the major players stay in the background, Younis was cocky and brash, preferring to flaunt his evil trade openly in Beirut and

boasting about it to anyone who would listen. His "visibility" made him all the more tempting for the grandiose scheme that the joint intelligence and military chiefs were planning.

In October 1986 President Reagan was presented with the plans for Operation Goldenrod, the code-name for the plot to kidnap Fawaz Younis and bring him to trial in America. He signed it in the knowledge that, at last, the west was hitting back.

There were certain ground rules that Reagan laid down from the start to the CIA, the FBI and the Drug Enforcement Administration, which was also in on the operation. He did not want America charged with international piracy over a kidnapping from a sovereign state, so he suggested that Younis be kidnapped somewhere neutral, preferably somewhere at sea. He also wanted him brought back to America with the utmost haste. FBI assistant director Oliver Revell told his team: "This is going to be one of the most important counter-terrorist operations ever staged by the US government. The risks are enor-mous – the prestige and the credibility of freedom-loving democracies are on the line. These are high stakes for which we are playing, gentlemen, and failure is not an option."

THE KEY DEFECTOR

A key to the eventual capture of Younis was the "turning" early on, by DEA officials in Cyprus seeking to stem the flow of cheap marijuana into America from the Middle East, of a drug dealer who knew him. Jamal Hamdan was an Arab with connections in the drug trade, the illegal weapons market and myriad other nefarious practices.

With the promise of immunity from prosecution and easy money he revealed everything he knew about guerilla bosses in Lebanon. And one of those very bosses, whom he served as a driver and right-hand man, was Fawaz Younis. Recruiting Hamdan was one of those strokes of great good luck that every daring enterprises needs to succeed.

THE RISKS ARE ENORMOUS – THE PRESTIGE AND THE CREDIBILITY OF FREEDOM-LOVING DEMOCRACIES ARE ON THE LINE

Below: **A fanatic holds a gun to a TWA pilot's head at Beirut Airport in 1985. Scenes like this made America's President Reagan determined to bring the guilty to justice.**

He was to be the bait in Operation Goldenrod. An elaborate sting operation was set in place. Hamdan would contact Younis in Beirut, clearly richer and more successful than when he had left it. He would make contact with his old friend and mentor, lure the greedy Younis by promising to let him into the secret of his wealth and arrange the rendezvous from which he could be taken in chains to America.

CARELESS WORDS

Younis had no idea that his former friend had become a CIA "spook" when he received a telephone call from him in Cyprus in 1987. The line was bugged but Younis didn't know that and he spoke with wild abandon about a variety of things, including his mistress, his two children and his involvement with fanatical and deadly terrorism. It was to be the first of many calls in which Younis spilled the beans on his involvement in the death of Stethem, the Royal Jordanian hi-jack and the structure of guerilla cells in Beirut, including their leaders.

In one taped extract which the FBI has since released, Younis boasted of the brutality he meted out to the people aboard the Royal Jordanian jet. He said: "I got inside and locked the plane's captain in the cockpit. The people were on the floor, their

hands on their heads. Everyone, no exceptions. I got a stewardess and asked her about the security men. There were eight. I took their neckties and tied their hands behind their backs. We started beating them. We took four machine guns and eight pistols from them. We kept them tied for 48 hours. We stayed 53 hours flying."

Hamdan, in return, talked about a life of riches on Cyprus, of how he had gotten into several deals that he was willing to let his old Beirut friend in on. In August 1987 he came to Cyprus and the two went on a five-day drinking binge at clubs the length and breadth of the island. Younis complained at this meeting that he was short of money. "No problem," announced Hamdan, handing him $4,000 from a special slush fund set up by his CIA handlers.

"There is more of this too. You want in?" Younis, his revolutionary zeal blunted by greed, said he certainly did. Hamdan, in a carefully rehearsed speech, told him about a man named Joseph who was willing to pay big bucks for a courier who was willing to export his illegal merchandise. Dabbling in illegality had been a trademark of Younis all his life.

He wanted in on the deal since his second-hand dealing business and off-hours taxi-driving in Beirut was bringing him in a pittance which was barely enough to support his wife and two children.

THE LINE WAS BUGGED BUT YOUNIS DIDN'T KNOW THAT AS HE SPOKE WITH WILD ABANDON OF HIS TERRORIST ACTIVITIES

Left: *Marilyn and Leon Kilnghofer were aboard the cruise liner Achille Lauro when fanatics hijacked it and pushed wheelchair-bound Mr Klinghofer overboard.*

Below: *The Achille Lauro, the cruise liner whose name became famous as a target of death-dealing terrorism.*

On September 7 1987, the attorney general of America, Edwin Meese, was presented with an arrest warrant for Fawaz Younis together with the final details of the plan to capture him. Meese signed it, fully aware of the implications for American prestige abroad for either success or failure of the plan.

On September 10 Younis returned to Cyprus on a ticket bought with CIA cash for the appointment with the mysterious Joseph. To keep up the free-spending, wealthy appearance, Hamdan was given even more cash to lavish on his old friend. He took him on a tour of the most expensive nightclubs, bought him trinkets of western decadence, including a pricey watch and designer shoes. This was a slice

Above: *The FBI headquarters in Washington, one of the nerve centres from which the hunt for Fawaz Younis was co-ordinated.*

THIS WAS A SLICE OF THE WESTERN LIFESTYLE WHICH YOUNIS AS AN URBAN GUERILLA HAD SWORN TO DESTROY

of the western lifestyle which Younis as an urban guerilla had sworn to destroy. "When are we going to meet Joseph?" asked Younis in a conversation picked up by the numerous listening devices in Hamdan's apartment. "I am in a hurry to get moving." Hamdan informed him that they were to meet him on the luxury yacht that he used to transport his merchandise around the Mediterranean. On the night of September 12, at the Sheraton Hotel in Limassol, Younis slept for the last time in clean sheets and as a free man. His capture was set for the next day.

Waiting to take him back to America was a US Air Force pilot, Commander Philip Voss, who was destined to go into the record books for his mission. Voss is one of the most experienced pilots in the US forces, having clocked 3,000 hours flying time alone on the S-3 Lockheed Viking aircraft. He is one of only 20 pilots in the world with such experience – experience that marked him down as the courier of the very special cargo of Fawaz Younis. He was aboard the USS Saratoga, an aircraft carrier, and was awaiting delivery of his special passenger. A week earlier he had been asked to draw up plans for a flight from his mother vessel that would take him back to America without stopping. He had to arrange the logistics of re-fuelling and routing. It was a challenge, but one he was perfectly capable of meeting.

Unlucky September 13 dawned bright and sunny, the wave tips beneath the hotel room where Younis had slept sparkling in the light. After breakfast Hamdan introduced Younis to a man he claimed was his brother – in reality, an operative of Arabic descent. He had bought a small launch which was waiting to take them to an 80-foot long yacht waiting off the shoreline. The boat looked impressive to Younis, like a millionaire's toy. He was very much looking forward to meeting the owner of such a splendid vessel – Mr. Fixit himself, the redoubtable Joseph.

A SITTING TARGET

The trip to the boat took 90 minutes, with Younis remaining in blissful ignorance of what awaited him once he set foot on the planking of the deck. He had dressed as if he was headed out to a party – beige shorts, green shirt, sandals, expensive gold watch and numerous pieces of gold jewellery. A CIA man remarked: "It seemed as if he had got the idea from a magazine about how people dressed for such parties. Clearly he had forgotten about his terrorism and was now hungry for a slice of the action."

Hamdan had warned him he would be searched by Joseph's "bodyguards" when he boarded the yacht, and two CIA men gave him a thorough frisking before he was handed a beer and told to go to the stern while Joseph was alerted in his cabin. As Younis gazed back on the shoreline two men approached him and, nodding together in unison, kicked his legs from under him. He hit the deck with such force he broke both his wrists.

Below: *Ronald Reagan, the Great Communicator and fighter of terrorism worldwide, in a wistful pose.*

As he was handcuffed from behind FBI special agent Dimitry Droujinski told him in Arabic: "You are under arrest by the government of the United States of America. Anything you say may be taken down and used in evidence against you. You are wanted for crimes of international terrorism, including kidnapping, murder and arson." Droujinski later said: "He said nothing. But the look of utter disbelief spoke volumes. He had long considered himself superior intellectually and physically to anyone in the west. Now he had let himself be conned and you could see that he hated himself for it."

Above: *An AWACS radar plane which helped guide the plane carrying its terrorist cargo to refuelling points and eventually to Washington.*

Below Right: *The Viking sub-killer plane which was deployed for the record-breaking flight that brought Younis from the Mediterranean to Washington DC.*

YOUNIS WAS QUIZZED EN-ROUTE BY CIA OPERATIVES AND ADMITTED HIS CRIMES FRANKLY AND FULLY

VOSS, HIS TANKS FULL, BANKED HARD, SIGNALLED THAT THE MISSION WAS ON AND SPED OFF AT FULL SPEED FOR AMERICA

Once he was bound and blindfolded, the yacht – another CIA purchase in an operation that would ultimately end up costing over £10,000,000 – steamed full ahead for its pre-destined rendezvous with the USS Butte, an ammunition ship an hour away. Once Younis was safely on board, the Butte headed for the Balearic Islands, four days' sailing away for a second rendezvous with the Saratoga and commander Voss'

Lockheed plane. Younis was quizzed en-route by CIA operatives and admitted his crimes frankly and fully.

Aboard the Saratoga he was immediately strapped into the aircraft which sped off the flight deck at 135 miles an hour. Overhead flew a re-fuelling tanker which immediately replaced the fuel he burned off during take-off. Voss, his tanks full, banked hard and signalled that the mission was on and sped off at full speed for America. Halfway across the Atlantic he again re-fuelled in mid-air.

AN UNEXPECTED ARRIVAL

Thirteen hours and ten minutes later he radioed into the Andrews Air Force Base that he was coming in to land. Security for the mission had been so tight that the civilian air traffic controllers had not even been told to expect his plane! Luckily military officials broke into the conversation between ground control and Voss and he was given immediate clearance to land – bringing home the prize in a solo-flight that became the longest such flight from a carrier-launched plane in history.

Younis was still stunned and dazed when he stepped on to the tarmac at the base to be whisked away by waiting FBI cars. The agencies that had captured him broadcast the fact to the news media instantly. They wanted every mad mullah, every fundamentalist despot or nationalist fanatic everywhere who wanted to change the world with the bomb and the bullet to know that the arm of American justice was long and swift. It was a searing message and one Reagan was proud ton deliver.

Younis was tried and sentenced to 20 years in jail. But his sentence was not important in the grand scheme of things. What WAS important was that western nations,

long perceived by their enemies to be weak and corrupt, proved that they could fight just as dirty as their enemies when it came to enforcing the rules to keep civilised society intact and functioning.

Above: *A once unthinkable scene is made into reality outside the White House as former Middle Eastern terrorist Yasser Arafat pledges peace with Israeli prime minister Yitzhak Rabin.*

Left: *The White House, from where Ronald Reagan issued the command to get Younis into an American court… by any means necessary.*

END OF THE TSAR
The USSR's Shame

It was one of the most unimaginable events in history: the Russian royal family being wiped out in a single night. Even the Bolsheviks, the revolutionaries who had founded the new communist Soviet Union, realised they should try to keep that bloody act secret from the outside world.

They lived in a splendour that mere mortals can only imagine. There were palaces too numerous to count, balls too numerous to attend, country estates so vast that it could take a week to travel across them… and even then they would not have covered all the land. They ate and drank of the finest that the world produced and cared little, even nought, for the suffering of the people who lived under them.

They were the last of the Romanovs, the Imperial Russian dynasty who had ruled that great and massive land for generations – always in the same fashion, always adamant that dark words like "progress" and "democracy" should not sully their magnificent empire. But they were living in a world of false dreams by the time the 20th Century dawned. The hurricane forces of change would snuff them out like a candle. And, because of their indifference to the suffering of the masses during the glory days, they would eventually die like cattle,

THERE WERE PALACES TOO NUMEROUS TO COUNT, BALLS TOO NUMEROUS TO ATTEND, VAST COUNTRY ESTATES

Opposite: *Tsar Nicholas of Russia, supreme autocrat of a vast nation that stretched from the borders of western Europe to the depths of Siberia.*

Below: *The Tsar with his daughters, a picture taken by the men who would form the killing squad.*

Above: *The doomed Romanov children.*

justice meted out to them by the revolutionaries who despised their rule. It was an ignominious end, but a predictable one for rulers who lost touch with their subjects.

Tsar Nicholas, the son of Alexander III, was a charming man, but an autocratic, sensitive and weak leader, always out of step with the great social and political changes sweeping the world – including those that would soon envelop his own backward land. He had been brought up to revere the divine right of kings – like himself – to believe that he was God's missionary, born to look after the great mass of peoples that made up Holy Russia. He was living in a fool's paradise. His rule started in 1894 with a pronouncement that he would reign as his forebears had – with total and utter autonomy. He continued the

---

IT WAS AN IGNOMINIOUS END, BUT A PREDICTABLE ONE FOR RULERS WHO HAD LOST TOUCH WITH THEIR SUBJECTS

---

suppression of opposing political forces, the persecution of religious minorities and the "Russification" of the borderlands, creating widespread hatred even outside his motherland's frontiers. He paid no heed to the growing dissatisfaction within his country, the great revolutionary movement that was growing daily, even though his secret police force, the Okhrana, warned him of the danger of Marxism and Leninism seeping into the political thought and blood of the ever-more militant peasantry.

In St. Petersburg in 1905 the first revolution occurred in Russia. Workers, hungry for bread, starving in the system which bound them as feudal serfs to landowners, marched on the grand Winter Palace. Dozens of them were cut down by gunfire outside the gates by loyal cossacks and police, the snow turned red with their blood as they tried peacefully to present a petition demanding change to their ruler. The martyred dead would not be forgotten by those manipulating the seething, angry masses on the road to irreversible reform. Unmoved by the losses the Tsar said afterwards: "Under no circumstances will I ever agree to a representative form of government, for I consider it harmful to the trust of God." At least 130 died – probably a conservative estimate – and at least three times that number were wounded, many of them seriously. The slashing sabres of the mounted cossacks had done much of the grim work.

Nicholas was striving to preserve an old order that guaranteed poverty and misery for the masses and splendour and indulgence for the aristocracy. In doing so he was signing his own death warrant, that of his family and that of Imperial Russia – but the ink would not be dry until 1917. The Great War, which began in 1914, only served to hasten his demise. Russia was bleeding itself to death on the battlefield against the Czar's cousin Kaiser Wilhelm. Russian manpower alone was not enough to staunch the losses which were running at a phenomenal rate. The situation was so dire that the Czar heeded pleas from his generals and left St. Petersburg for the front to assume command.

THE MAD MONK

The haughty Tsarina Alexandra was left behind to become the supreme power over the internal running of the country – a country broke, starving and sliding inexorably into chaos that would eventually lead to a second, successful revolution. But although she was the acting head of state, it was the debauched monk with the hypnotic gaze – Rasputin – who became the real ruler of Russia. This conman with mesmeric eyes had wormed his way into the Imperial court with questionable healing powers which he exercised upon the royal offspring and heir, the Tsarevitch Alexis. Alexandra was strong-willed and the true power behind the Romanov throne. Nicholas often confided to the Kaiser of Germany before the war that he felt ruling "such a burden". He would much rather retreat to his country estates to hunt and drink from his vast wine cellar.

Above: *Alexandra in happier times, dressed in full imperial finery as the Tsarina of Russia.*

By now utterly under his influence, the Tsarina was Rasputin's puppet who did his bidding completely. His influence ranged from the appointment of church officials to the selection of cabinet ministers. He chose incompetent opportunists over dignified and hard working civil servants, the ignorant over the intelligent and the weak over

Above: Tsar Nicholas reviews troops of the Imperial Guard in St. Petersburg before the revolution that shook Russian society.

THE GLORY OF HUNDREDS OF YEARS UNRAVELLED IN A MATTER OF WEEKS WITH MOMENTOUS LOSSES IN BATTLE

the strong. He strengthened the grip of the Romanov autocracy on the nation – at a time when it desperately needed loosening and issued harsh penalties for civil disturbances. History's epitaph for Rasputin was best summed up by moderate revolutionary Alexander Kerensky who said: "If there had been no Rasputin, there would have been no Lenin."

The glory of hundreds of years unravelled in a matter of weeks when 1917 saw momentous battle losses with no hope of improvement. In March of that year, with the army bleeding white in the snow, the peasants of the great cities starving – the war had taken 15 million men off of the land – the inhabitants of the city of St. Petersburg rioted.

And this time the Cossacks refused to cut them down.

A new government was proclaimed by the revolutionaries, even as Tsar Nicholas at the front despatched regiments of elite guards to crush the uprising. Concession was not a word in his vocabulary – he either ruled supreme or he did not. Finally, he could not.

All his ministers and dukes, grand marshalls and generals, persuaded him that the hour to abdicate had come. Nicholas thought he was merely passing on the throne to his brother when he signed the paper of abdication on March 15 1917, but in reality he was signing the execution warrant for the entire Romanov dynasty.

On March 22 America became the first foreign power to recognise the provisional government, which gave more credence for the revolutionaries to do with the last of the Romanovs as they pleased.

At first it pleased them to take him and the Imperial children to the royal palace at Tsarkoe Seloe, the "fantastic village" 15 miles away from the capital that had been a vacation retreat for the Romanovs for 300 years. Here he and his wife were taunted by brutish guards who refused to let them even walk in the spacious grounds.

Mail was censored, the aristocracy that had been the friends and relations of the family were imprisoned, exiled or butchered and the hoped-for rescue of the family by an alliance of other European crowned heads seemed more remote with each passing day.

A HATE FIGURE

Robert Massie, in his book *Nicholas and Alexandra*, which chronicled their reign and downfall, said: "In the weeks after the abdication feelings mounted against all the Romanovs. The focus of popular hatred was the Tsar and his family at Tsarkoe Selo. From the moment of abdication, rumours spread that 'Citizen Romanov' and his wife 'Alexandra the German' were working secretly to betray the country to the Germans and with their help restore the autocracy…

"It was at this point, with public opinion aroused and the Soviet demanding that Nicholas be thrown into the fortress that the Provisional Government placed

FROM THE MOMENT OF ABDICATION, RUMOURS SPREAD THAT THE TSAR AND TSARINA WERE ABOUT TO BETRAY THEIR COUNTRY

Below: *This was the real face of the Russia of Tsar Nicholas – a vast wilderness of grinding poverty where people were still serfs.*

responsibility for the safety of the Imperial family entirely on Kerensky's shoulders."

Alexander Kerensky, who was justice minister of the government in the turbulent first days after the overthrow, was at a loss to decide what to do with the Romanovs. He visited them and gave stirring speeches to the former servants that they were now free, began an investigation in to the ex-Tsarina's "pro-German activities" and generally put the fear of the growing totalitarian machine of the Soviet into everyone. In reality, he had little idea – as did anyone – about what to do with the symbols of the ancien regime now that the workers had assumed control of the country. As the weeks went by it became plain that the governments of the allied powers did not want to risk Russian withdrawal from the war by offering sanctuary to them and the Soviets, at first, were reluctant to try them

Opposite Top: *The appalling social conditions in Russia created the circumstances for bloody revolution.*

Opposite Below: *Lenin speaks to the masses with his ally Leon Trotsky to his right, March 1917.*

Right and Below: *The 'Mad Monk', Rasputin, who wielded incredible power over Czarina Alexandra and Russian high society.*

for fear of arousing new support for an old order. In the end, on April 17 1917, after ten years away from Russia, Vladimir Illyich Ulyanov – better known under his revolutionary name of Lenin – returned to the new Russia and their fate was sealed.

UNCERTAIN TIMES

There was turbulence to come for months in Russia with Lenin having to abscond over the border to Finland in July for the more moderate Kerensky to become premier. But he never doubted for a moment on two things – that he would return shortly as supreme leader and that the entire family of the Tsar had to be wiped out before Russia could properly begin a new chapter in her history. Fearful for the deposed Tsar, the new leader Kerensky ordered him and his family in August to prepare for a long journey.

The Provisional Government had decided to remove them to Tobolsk in Siberia. For four days the entire ex-royal family and its retinue of servants and devotees trundled eastwards, the vastness of the Russian landscape passing by with increasing monotony from their train windows. At the stations in the wildernesses there were no

Above and Right: *The Great War was the catalyst for the revolution that would destroy Nicholas Romanov as ill-equipped Russian soldiers died in their millions. Kaiser Wilhelm was a cousin of the Tsar and a fervent believer in the divine right of kings. Yet the Great War he instigated did for Nicholas – and eventually for him.*

THE TSAR AND HIS FAMILY WERE PLACED ON SOLDIERS' RATIONS... THE SERVANTS WERE DISMISSED

people to wave to a Tsar vanishing from the pages of history – the red guards were posted at every single one to keep the proletariat away. Finally the train arrived in the dreary provincial town where the Romanov tribe were to be held for eight more months.

In October, as the former Tsar cut wood during the day and his wife attended mass and did needlepoint in the governor's mansion that was now their prison, the second cataclysmic revolution shook Russia. This time the moderate Kerensky was ousted and the hardliner Lenin was placed in power. The screws began to be tightened little by little on them. First they were placed on soldier's rations – no more quails' eggs, caviar, haunches of venison and beef, but black bread, jam and bacon. Most of the servants were dismissed. Money, which had been allowed the Czar to buy luxuries, was cut to a minimum. While Nicholas and Alexandra prayed that they – along

with the royal children Alexis, 13, and the Grand Duchesses Olga, 22, Tatiana, 20, Marie, 18, Anastasia, 15 – would be saved by a European monarchy, hope seemed to fade with each passing day.

THE HOUSE OF FEAR

The family were moved to Ekaterinburg in the Urals in April 1918 to a mansion with an ominous title: "The House of Special Purpose". Formerly the home of a successful merchant, the house sat on a hill and Bolshevik soldiers built a high fence around it to prevent the curious from gawking at the prize captives and the Romanovs from entertaining any ideas about escape. Initially just Nicholas and Alexandra were taken but the following month the royal children arrived.

In Moscow there was heated debate going on about what to do with them. Lenin had long favoured execution for them – a silent, swift execution that no one would talk about with no details of a grave that could become a shrine – a touchstone of faith to those that clinged to the ideals of the old order. Yet it was a fine line he walked; he wanted international recognition for the new Union of Soviet Socialist

Above: *The Tsarina Alexandra in a wheelchair at Ekaterinburg. A few weeks after this picture was taken she was assassinated along with the rest of her family.*

Left: *Granduchess Anastasia works at Ekaterinburg just a few days before she was murdered.*

LENIN HAD LONG FAVOURED EXECUTION FOR THEM — A SILENT, SWIFT EXECUTION THAT NO ONE WOULD TALK ABOUT

Above: *The Romanovs who have never ruled. Granduchess Leonida Georgievna and husband Grand Duke Georgi, to her right, return to their homeland after the collapse of communism.*

Republics and did not want their deaths to be the pretext for foreign intervention in the revolution. But that matter was to be decided for him by foreign powers anyway – and would seal the fate of the family.

Bolshevism's feeble grip on Russia was challenged early in 1918 by foreign powers, including British soldiers and American marines, who landed in a bid to aid loyalist Tsarist forces fighting the Bolsheviks. The allies wanted the Tsar on the throne so he would rescind the Bolshevik-inspired peace treaty with Germany and get Russia back into the war before the hundreds of Prussian divisions that had fought on the eastern front could be hurled into the trenches of the western one. The Ural Soviet sent a delegation to Moscow in July to ask what should be done with the prisoners in "The House of Special Purpose" now that the foreigners were on the soil of the motherland, possibly contemplating the release of the Romanovs.

The reply was: kill them.

The final details were worked out by a secret revolutionary court that convened on July 12 in Ekaterinburg. Isiah Goloshchekin, the local soviet leader and committed revolutionary, presided over what must have been the first secret trial in a nation that, years later, would use them under Stalin to murder millions. He said that they must be killed in case the loyalist White armies overran Ekaterinburg and attempted a rescue. "There must be no bodies, no evidence," he said. "The Romanovs must vanish from the face of the earth."

Jacob Yurovksy, a leader of the local secret police, the Cheka, arranged the details. On July 16 he ordered the kitchen boy sent away from the house. At 7.00 p.m. he summoned ten Cheka men to collect the heavy military revolvers from the guards outside. He told them: "Tonight we shoot the whole family, everybody. Notify the guards outside not to be alarmed if they hear shots." The family went to sleep at 10.30 p.m. that night, unaware that it was to be their last.

At midnight Yurovsky woke them, telling them that the White Army was on the march and that they were to be moved. They were led into a basement room, unsuspecting that this was to be the execution chamber. Massie, in *Nicholas and Alexandra*, described the final moments:

"Behind their mother stood the four girls and Dr. Botkin, the valet Trupp, the cook Kharitonov and Demidova, the empress's parlourmaid. Demidova carried two pillows, one of which she placed in the chair behind the empress's back. The other pillow she clutched tightly. Inside, sewed deep into the feathers, was a box containing a collection of the Imperial jewels.

THE END ARRIVES

"When all were assembled, Yurovsky re-entered the room, followed by his entire Cheka squad carrying revolvers. He stepped forward and declared quickly: 'Your relations have tried to save you. They have failed and now we must now shoot you.'

"Nicholas, his arm still around Alexis, began to rise from his chair to protect his wife and son. He just had time to say 'What...?' before Yurovsky pointed his revolver directly at the Tsar's head and fired. Nicholas died instantly. At this signal, the entire squad of executioners began to shoot. Alexandra had time only to raise her hand and make the sign of the cross before she too was killed by a single bullet. Olga, Tatiana and Marie, standing behind their mother, were hit and died quickly. Botkin, Kharitonov and Trupp also fell in the hail of bullets.

Demidova, the maid, survived the first volley and, rather than reload, the executioners took rifles from the next room and pursued her, stabbing her with bayonets... at last she fell, pierced by bayonets more than 30 times." Alexis was alive – he was executed with two shots in the ear. Anastasia was also bayoneted to death.

The bodies were burned with reserves of gasoline stored in the grounds of the house. For three days the bonfires raged, and in between the burnings the bones were taken out by the Cheka assassins and beaten into

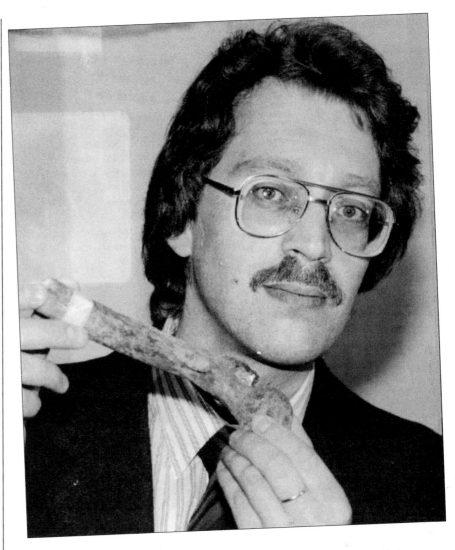

dust. Acid was poured over the larger remains, the clothing was burned and the bloodstains from the walls of the cellar were wiped down to erase traces of the appalling massacre that had taken place.

In Moscow the machinery of lies was whirring within hours of the murders. A declaration was issued on July 20 stating that only Nicholas had been executed "for his numerous crimes against the people". The rest of the Romanovs, lied the new rulers of his land, were transferred to a secret place of safety. A year later the government admitted that all were dead, but still wouldn't take responsibility for it. Instead, Lenin ordered the arrest of 28 "counter revolutionaries" who he said had ordered the murder of the Tsar's family to discredit his own Bolshevik party. There was a show trial and five of the hapless 28 were executed.

A new order settled on Russia in which countless millions more would die to ensure the survival of the totalitarian state.

Above: *The grisly evidence that the Tsar and his family were murdered is displayed by Dr Pavel Ivanov after the execution site was exhumed in July 1993. He holds up a bone belonging to Nicholas, the last Tsar of all the Russias.*

"YOUR RELATIONS HAVE TRIED TO SAVE YOU. THEY HAVE FAILED AND NOW WE MUST SHOOT YOU"

BERNARD GOETZ
The Subway Vigilante

Riding on a New York subway train, Bernie Goetz, a normally mild-mannered electrical store employee pulled out a handgun and shot a clutch of black youths trying to mug him. The case polarised the city and sharply mirrored Charles Bronson's vengeance movie Death Wish.

New York cinema audiences had never seen anything quite like Charles Bronson's starring role in *Death Wish*. When the film was first released in the mid 1970s – just as the word mugging was entering the English language – residents of the bad Big Apple were at the forefront of the losing fight against street crime. Day after day violence was entering their lives – on the subways, in the streets, even in the home. There was a growing sense of despair, of hopelessness as the have nots took what they wanted from the haves.

That is why *Death Wish* – the story of an average man who becomes an avenger after his wife and daughter are raped by three thugs in the city – opened to such rapturous applause among usually cynical moviegoers. Here was a real celluloid hero to cheer for – a 20th Century Mr. Normal who snaps when crime touches the things he cherishes most. Night after night the violent picture

DAY AFTER DAY VIOLENCE WAS ENTERING THEIR LIVES – ON THE SUBWAYS, IN THE STREETS, EVEN IN THE HOME

Opposite: *Bernie Goetz, the good citizen who snapped.*

Below: *Fame, or infamy, brought certain rewards to Goetz, including a regular spot on a radio show.*

Above: *Charles Bronson plays the vigilante in the 1974 movie* **Death Wish** *– a film which had obvious parallels with the Goetz case.*

received standing ovations from the audiences who identified more than anybody else with the frustration shown by Bronson's character. They cheered when he shot, beat and otherwise wounded the bad guys in an explosion of emotional release.

REAL-LIFE DRAMA

Yet just years later the bullets would be real when another Mr. Average, this time not a figment of a director's imagination, was confronted by would-be muggers on an underground train in the city. The shots that Bernie Goetz fired into the young men who were intent on robbing him reverberate to this day. To many he was a saint – to others a sinner, his actions motivated by racism and intolerance.

But Bernie Goetz, even after a spell in prison for his actions, remains defiant – and his brand of DIY rough justice remains admired by millions in a country where thousands die each year in violent crimes.

It was December 22 1984 when Goetz committed the act that would propel him

THE SHOTS THAT BERNIE GOETZ FIRED INTO THE YOUNG MEN WHO WERE INTENT ON ROBBING HIM REVERBERATE TO THIS DAY

Left: *Bronson in* **Death Wish,** *an ordinary white guy hitting back at the urban terrorists who were making New Yorkers' lives a misery.*

Below: *Blowing bad guys away, Charles Bronson in* **Death Wish 3.**

forever into history. It was a cold night and the city was preparing itself for the Christmas festivities. Goetz, a white, middle class electrical engineer, was on his way home from his downtown workplace on an underground train when his eye was caught by four black youths fooling around in the same car. That was nothing new on the subway system in New York: freaks, beggars, robbers, botherers – they all rode the subway system home because it was cheap and it was fast. But for years the

Above: *Subway sentinels The Guardian Angels were among those community groups who embraced Goetz for what he did on the train.*

Opposite Top: *Under arrest: Bernie Goetz, Mr Normal.*
Opposite Below: *Goetz's lawyer, Barry Slotnick, at a reconstruction of the scene of the crime.*

incidences of violent crime aboard subway trains had been rising in the city and every passenger was alert to the dangers real and imagined. Goetz was no different when it came to being aware, but he differed very, very radically from the majority of New Yorkers – he carried a gun.

Although New York has a high murder rate and other incidences of violence, the citizens for the most part are not armed. Strict gun controls have been in place for years and only a few permits are granted

each year to those applicants with the most compelling reasons for needing one. Goetz's gun was a silver .38 revolver, the kind used by police, and it was illegal, purchased by him in Florida, where gun controls are much more lax, and transported illegally across state lines to New York. He had bought the gun for protection and had never used it in anger. But tonight was different – tonight the mild-mannered electrical engineer would write his name in blood and plunge a usually unshockable city into emotional chaos.

DANGEROUS GAMES

As Goetz, 34 at the time of the shootings and unmarried, would later recall, he saw the four black youths "fooling around" and kept a watch on them from the corner of his

Above: *New York governor Mario Cuomo struggled to appeal to the population of the city to regard Goetz as a common criminal.*

ing sharpened screwdrivers. Goetz, who said that he saw "a gleam in the eye" of one of the thugs, pulled out his revolver and began blasting away.

"I believed then and I believe now," he told detectives later, "that they were about to beat me and to rob me. I had been mugged twice before. I was not prepared to become another statistic of violent crime in this city. I defended myself with reasonable force in the only way I knew how."

SWIFT ACTION

Wheeling around, Goetz turned on the four young men and opened fire, sending others in the railcar diving for the floor. His four victims never had a chance as the man who later became known all over the world as The Subway Vigilante picked them off one by one. Troy Canty, the youth in whose eye Goetz detected the gleam of robbery, was the first to be hit.

Canty, 18, was slightly wounded in the arm and played dead on the floor of the carriage. He later told one of the first officers on the scene: "We were going to rob him but the white guy shot us first." James Ramseur, 18, was a petty hood with a string of convictions for burglary and robbery. He too was only slightly wounded. Barry Allen, 18, took bullets in the leg and arm, but his injuries too were superficial. It was Darrell Cabey, a 19-year-old hoodlum, who suffered the most. Even by his own account Goetz walked over to him after he was hit once and said: "You don't look too bad. Here's another." With that he pumped another slug into him – a bullet that left his spinal cord shattered.

The gunfire had sent passengers cowering for their lives and they stayed that way while the gunsmoke cleared. The train, a Seventh Avenue express, jerked to a halt just short of a station after someone in another car had pulled the emergency cord. A conductor approached the gunman, who was breathing heavily, and said: "Hey, you OK buddy? You a cop?" Goetz put his revolver away and said: "No. They just tried to rip me off." Then he jumped from between the cars on to the tracks and vanished into the labyrinthine tunnels. New York, a city where ethnic tensions simmer just beneath the surface of everyday life, was about to be thrown into turmoil.

eye. His gun was in his chest pocket, loaded with copper-cased ammunition – for greater penetration. The bullets were also snub-nosed, which spelled greater penetration and more capability of causing massive wounds. Goetz didn't think he would have to use it. He later told cops that he just "felt safer" having it on him.

On that graffiti-stained train, rattling through the dark tunnel, the four youths sauntered up to Goetz as he sat reading a book, his peripheral vision sending out alarm bells to him that trouble was on the way. One of the toughs demanded $5 from him – about £2.50 then – and Goetz refused. He would later tell police that he knew something was "going down". But no guns were pulled on him, no weapons brandished – although three of them were carry-

The calls that flooded police hotlines after the shooting were the worst news of all for city officials attempting to portray the gunman as a criminal after the incident. The phone lines were intended to collect information pointing to the suspect so he could be arrested. Instead, thousands telephoned in to express their admiration for the shooter. The genie of the Bronson *Death Wish* film was out of the bottle as the more sane voices in the city pleaded for calm. New York Mayor Ed Koch branded the shootings "animal behaviour". Swimming against the tide of popular opinion he added: "Undoubtedly, those who called the police lines were those who had their macabre anti-crime fantasies lived out. But it is wrong. If you allow instant

Above: *Mayor Ed Koch of New York City had to calm racial tensions in the city following the shootings.*

self-meted-out justice, we would have crimes committed against innocent people. That is the difference between civilised society and the wild west."

Mario Cuomo, governor of the entire state of New York, and a passionate opponent of the death penalty, joined Koch in condemning the shootings. He said: "If this man was defending himself against attack with reasonable force he could be legally, if not morally, justified. But the available facts indicate otherwise. And if we're talking about vindication, or impatience with using the judicial system, we're talking about attempted execution. The people hollering their support for this guy should think of it that way. Unilateral execution without trial – does that really sound so appealing? Anyone who cares about the subways and the city should look at the larger issues involved here. We are living in a time when there is increasing disre-

Above: Shooting victim James Ramseur lashes out at a TV cameraman.

"WE MUST TURN THAT PASSION DOWN," SAID THE GOVERNOR OF NEW YORK. "DO WE REALLY WANT GUNLAW LIKE THIS?"

spect for the subtle wisdom of the law. Throughout history, we have seen people whipped up by the inability of the system to work for them. That doesn't mean we must junk the system. People have supported the killing of millions of Jews, the imprisoning of the Japanese during WW2 – and thought they were right at the moment when their passion was turned up too high. We must turn that passion down. Do we really want gunlaw like this?"

Unfortunately for the governor and the mayor, the answer from the war-weary citizens in the front line trenches of the crime war seemed to be a resounding: "Yes." Transit policemen, the armed, uniformed guards who patrolled the subway system were increasingly accosted by commuters who told them not to look too hard for the gunman. WABC talk show host Bob Grant had to install 30 extra lines to deal with the mammoth shock-wave of support. He said:

"The callers are overwhelmingly sympathetic to the shooter. They are saying that maybe he struck a blow for them and now perhaps they might not become the victims of muggers because they in turn will think twice." In one particularly stark reflection of the mood lingering over the city a halo was drawn over the police wanted sketch of the suspect at a west side subway station where it was posted.

A PUBLIC HERO

Newspapers made The Subway Vigilante the most famous man in America. There were offers for him to turn himself in laced with cash incentives; one eccentric millionaire even offered to fly him any place, anywhere in the world, aboard a private jet because he was so proud of what he did. The virtual canonisation of the gunman was severely displeasing to the district

Above: *The youths in the Goetz case were soon back on the street, indulging in more petty crime.*

GOETZ LOOKED INWARD TO HIMSELF AND DECIDED HE HAD TO GIVE HIMSELF UP TO THE POLICE, WHATEVER THE CONSEQUENCES

attorney's office which knew that any prosecution, if he was caught, would be highly unlikely to be successful in such a climate of public applause for the crime.

Goetz, a man of above average intelligence, knew that what he had done was wrong in the eyes of the law, even though he perceived his actions to be right, and that the authorities would be out to punish him severely. While pondering whether or not to turn himself in he was intrigued by the way press and public had held him up as a symbol of rightousness fighting back instead of as an attempted killer. "The people are looking for an easy answer," he told a friend. "They are looking for a good guy defending himself or a Clint Eastwood. But there are no easy answers." Goetz looked inward to himself and decided he had to give himself up to police, whatever the consequences might be. Almost a month after the shootings he turned himself in –

and was soon under arrest on attempted murder and wounding charges.

AN ACTION HERO

For some he was a vicious vigilante, motivated partly by racial prejudice and partly by an uncontrollable rage; for others he was a hero who had finally acted for the man in the street who felt himself powerless in the face of the unending violence. Whatever he was, Goetz aroused strong feelings. There was no-one neutral to be found in New York city, let alone in America. It was to be another two years before the case came to trial – a time during which some of the men he shot at least showed consistency in pursuit of their criminal careers.

FOR SOME HE WAS A VICIOUS VIGILANTE, MOTIVATED BY RACIAL PREJUDICE AND UNCONTROLLABLE RAGE

Below: *Guardian Angel allies shield Goetz as he arrives at court while jurors debate his fate.*

Canty was arrested for stealing from video arcades and drugs. Ramseur was sentenced from ten to 25 years for rape, sodomy and robbery.

Barry Allen was sentenced for one to four years for robbery. Only Cabey was incapable of either going straight or continuing in his tough Bronx neighbourhood on a pathway of crime – he was paralysed from the waist down and unable to move. Of all of the victims, he naturally engendered the most sympathy.

When Goetz eventually came to trial he argued vociferously that his actions were entirely in self-defence. William Kunstler, the lawyer for Cabey, said: "It is a clear-cut case of right and wrong. Do we want gun-law in our streets, justice meted out by people who think they can become judge, jury

and executioner or as a civilisation will we place our faith in the institutions of law and order, that is the police and the courts? To acquit Goetz is a vote for the basest in man."

But the jury who judged Goetz were his peers. They lived every day with the same kind of fears about crime that he did. They came down on his side and declared him innocent of all charges except one; they had to convict him of illegal possession of a gun because it was clear that he had broken many laws in acquiring it.

"This is an indictment of the liberal prescriptions that have had a great deal to do with New York's social disorders," said the prominent and influential Wall Street Journal. Journalist George Hackett noted in Newsweek: "The Goetz case crossed class

Above: *The trial polarised the city – those for and against what Goetz did. Here the opposing points of view are argued by the man in the street outside the court.*

IN JAIL HE WAS BOMBARDED BY LETTERS OF SUPPORT AND OFFERS OF JOBS AND VACATIONS WHEN HE MADE IT OUT

---

and colour lines and spoke to a collective fantasy: as we become a nation of crime victims, who amongst us hasn't taken imagined revenge? And anyone with a television had the grist to reach a verdict."

Under a New York statute that set penalties for illegal possession of a handgun Goetz had to be sent to prison for a minimum of a year. Legal manoeuvring postponed the sentence but in January 1989 he became prisoner No. 78900316 at the Brooklyn House of Detention. He was bombarded by letters of support and offers of jobs and vacations when he made it out.

When he came out in September 1989, he faced civil lawsuits totalling £38 million. But his deed, and his lack of repentance for it, remains. "Would I do the same again?" he said. "The answer is yes."

A FATHER'S REVENGE
Justified Violence

Steven Owen was a respecter of the law and of people. But when a man killed his son with a piece of reckless driving and showed no remorse it was too much for Steven to take. After a harrowing court case, a jury's verdict let him walk free after he had been charged with shooting his tormentor.

Criminal actions were something that mild-mannered Steven Owen had never contemplated. He enjoyed a happy life with his wife Marilyn, sons Terry, 18 and Darren, 12, who was the apple of his eye. At 36, he was that rare creature in modern times – a happily married man who was contented with his lot. In rural Sheppey, Kent, he was known as a mild-mannered man – so gentle, in fact, that his wife once called him "milder than Fairy Liquid".

Yet a terrible rage was planted in the mind of Steven Owen the day that his son was killed – a rage that would lead him to commit a crime of terrible violence. Because the killer of his son never apologised for what happened, because he laughed in his face, because he was free after just a short time in jail, to return to society, Steven Owen took the law into his own hands and gunned him down at point blank range.

A TERRIBLE RAGE WAS PLANTED IN THE MIND OF STEVEN OWEN ON THE DAY THAT HIS SON WAS KILLED

Opposite: *Total victory for Steven and Marilyn Owen when he walked free from court after a jury had decided he should not be imprisoned for the shooting of the man who killed his son.*

Below: *Steven Owen, who took his own form of revenge for his son's death.*

Above: *Marilyn Owen stood by her husband throughout his trial.*

would never bring his son back, but it exorcised his own demons and proved that British justice can have compassion and common sense at times when it often seems that both commodities are sadly lacking.

The Owen family world fell apart on Friday October 13 1989. On that day their son Darren, a bright, cheery boy with a cycling proficiency certificate testifying to his skill on two wheels, was knocked beneath a 20-ton lorry driven by a man who should never have been behind the wheel. Kevin Taylor, 32, had one eye, had never held a full heavy goods vehicle licence and was a man with a supreme sense of selfishness and self-preservation. Taylor had been driving recklessly when his lorry clipped Darren on his bike and dragged him beneath the wheels. Instead of stopping, to aid the stricken boy or call the police, he slammed his truck into a lower gear and sped away, leaving the life to ebb out of the little boy at the side of the road.

A NARROW ESCAPE

As he sped away in his tipper truck, he may well have claimed a second victim of his appalling negligence and irresponsibility. Motorist Rosemary Blake was forced to brake hard to avoid Taylor as he sped

He pleaded not guilty to the crime, fully aware that he could expect little mercy for such a cold and calculating mission. But mercy was exactly what he got. Just as the police were reluctant to prosecute him, so a jury of his peers was even more reluctant to find him guilty. What Steven Owen did

away, intent on leaving the scene as quickly as possible. But Mrs Taylor was three months pregnant at the time and the seatbelt cut hard into her as she swerved into an emergency stop. Later her baby daughter Emily suffered numerous health problems with her eyes, ears and heart. She

said: "This truck was coming towards us and I thought we were going to die. My other two children were in the car as well and I thought we were all done for.

"But it is Emily who has suffered the most. Doctors have said that everything that has happened to her could have been caused by that seatbelt tightening across me as I came to a stop."

It didn't take police long to catch up with Kevin Taylor – a man with a past when it came to such hit-and-runs. He had been questioned by police officers in 1978 over the hit-and-run death of another little boy called Warren Kent. Warren was killed by a truck regularly driven by Taylor that was later found burned out. There was nothing else to link him to the death and so no-one was ever charged for the crime. But in this one they had him "bang to rights". Log sheets for his lorry put him in the area at the time and place of Darren Owen's death. He was arrested, charged and finally came before court where he was sentenced to 18 months in jail. For Steven Owen, it was a pathetically small sentence for a man who had taken away the life of his son.

Because of the legal system, because of time off for good behaviour, Taylor – who had never passed a driving test – was out of

Above: *A terrible rage was planted in the mind of Steven Owen the day that his son was killed.*

IT DIDN'T TAKE LONG FOR
POLICE TO CATCH UP WITH
KEVIN TAYLOR – A MAN
WITH A PAST WHEN IT
CAME TO HIT-AND-RUNS

jail in 12 months. Thoughts of revenge began to weigh heavily on Steven Owen's mind – and they were thoughts shared by his friends and neighbours on the Isle of Sheppey who figured he had had a pretty raw deal when all was considered.

As Owen began thinking of some kind of revenge the offers to aid him began flooding into his home. By his own account

Above and Opposite: *What upset Steven and Marilyn most was the callousness of their son's killer.*

Opposite Below: *A locket with Darren's picture and memories were all that were left for Darren's mother.*

there were "20 or so" offers of a gun. Others offered him an alibi if he did want to take the law into his own hands. Still more telephoned and wrote offering him their sincere sympathy.

What upset Owen and his family the most was the callousness displayed by Taylor. He never once apologised for what happened, never offered a kind word of comfort or paid a visit to say he regretted what had happened. When Steven Owen began tailing his son's killer to pubs he was repelled by what he saw.

He witnessed the killer drunkenly leave, watched the smile on his face that seemed to mock him. "I first set eyes on him a couple of weeks after Darren died, before he had gone to jail. Marilyn and I had been outside the pub about half-an-hour when he came out with his girlfriend. He was staggering and laughing and I was sick with rage. I didn't do anything because I didn't know what to do. All I knew was that I couldn't stand by and do nothing. I had to do something for Darren."

A SENSE OF RAGE

Steven Owen would later describe the feeling that came over him as one of a "pounding sense of failure". So he decided to tail his quarry without really having any sense

of what he would do if he were to catch him unawares. He had a 12-bore shotgun which he used for clay pigeon shooting, but it never occurred to him to use that.

Yet one morning, after Taylor was out of jail, Owen went to his doorstep and discovered a white plastic carrier bag there with a sawn-off double barrelled shotgun inside… and two cartridges. Someone as appalled as he was by what had happened had placed it there during the night. It was a lethal gift that he stored in his garden shed for use at a later date.

Four months later, as Taylor walked to his local pub with his common-law wife Alison Barratt, Owen drove up out of the shadows with the gun on the front seat of his car. Immediately thinking of himself, Taylor grabbed her to use as a human shield, shouting: "Don't shoot! Don't shoot!" The sight sickened Owen, proving to him once more how cowardly his son's killer was. "He was grabbing her so tightly I could see the whites of his knuckles," said Owen later. "That memory will stay with me for the rest of my life." At one point,

Taylor lashed out at him with his arm then, spinning his common-law-wife around, he turned on his heels and began to run. That was when Steven Owen opened fire, hitting both of them. Owen added: "I remember shouting out to him: 'Leave her alone, leave her alone – it's you I want to deal with.' I intended to hurt him but not to kill him. I wanted to make him feel the hurt I and my family had been feeling."

A SERIOUS ATTACK

Alison was only slightly grazed but Taylor was severely wounded in the back. He was in hospital for weeks as his attacker languished in jail without bail. Soon word began to spread of the motive for his attack and it was judge Sir Peter Webster who showed the first humanitarian instinct in the sad case. The attack had come shortly before Christmas 1990 and he granted him bail at Maidstone Crown Court to spend it with his family. As he emerged from the cells, pending his trial on attempted murder charges and wounding with intent, he said: "This marvellous judge has restored my confidence in British justice. I am ready to

Above: It didn't take police long to catch up with Kevin Taylor, a man with a history of hit-and-runs.

Right and Opposite Top: The strain shows on the Owens' faces as the trial continues.

face the judge and jury after I have spent some time with my family."

The trial was eagerly anticipated by press, public and legal experts. Jonathan Crawford, a legal expert, said: "For the jury the case was clear-cut. There was no doubt that he had shot the man in question and no doubt that it was pre-meditated. It should have been as simple as night following day that he would be found guilty and imprisoned. But it was his performance in court, when the sheer raw emotion of what he had suffered came through, that won the day for him. He made those jurors FEEL his pain, understand his anguish to the point they could accept his brand of rough justice for his nemesis.

Rarely in a British court has someone's evidence been so powerful and so truthful. He was clearly guilty of something, but the jury ruled that he was only guilty of loving his son too much. And under the circumstances I think the whole legal community was overwhelmed with joy at the verdict, along with the general public."

"THE SHEER RAW EMOTION OF WHAT HE HAD SUFFERED CAME THROUGH, AND WON THE DAY FOR HIM"

Below: *When Steven Owen saw Taylor getting drunk in pubs the smile on his face seemed to be there simply to mock the distraught, grieving father.*

When it came time for Steven Owen to give testimony in the court the silence was deafening. Two of the nine women on the jury sobbed as he told of the moment when he came to avenge his son's death. He wept himself as he summoned up his last reserves of sanity and strength to give an account of what happened that day. He told the court: "It was as though my soul and spirit were not there. I was looking down upon the shell of me that was there. At that point I was as close to insanity as anyone

Above: *Alone with her grief and the brief solace of victory, only time and the goodwill of a nation will heal Marilyn Owen's wounds.*

Opposite: *Relief for Steven and Marilyn Owen when he walked free from court.*

could be. I shot him twice with a sawn-off shotgun because I wanted to hurt him. He never showed any remorse – in fact, quite the contrary. He insulted my family and the memory of my dead son Darren. He showed contempt for the law of life. I wanted him to admit that he had caused Darren's death in an absolutely horrific, callous and cowardly way." In a letter that he wrote to the court he told of how he saw his son in hospital. With poignance and pain he wrote: "It must have all been a terrible mistake, but no, his head was distorted and blue. He had dried blood over parts of him and there was no breath. I asked to be left alone with him and held his hand. It was cold and still. Our son, who we had given life to and raised from a baby until now, had had the life crushed out of him by a callous criminal."

Afterwards he spoke fully of what had gone through his mind when he pulled the trigger on the man who claimed his son's life. His voice breaking with emotion he said: "I cannot summon up regret for what I did, nor remorse. My family has suffered too much for that. Every time I go to sleep I have a nightmare. I see the wheels go over Darren's smiling, innocent face. That is what so much of this has been about.

"Immediately after I had done it I felt relieved. After two years of going up blind alleys, banging my head against a brick wall, feeling useless and pathetic, I had finally done something for Darren. But, no, it hasn't taken the pain away and I think I know that nothing will.

NO APOLOGIES

"With the trial, I wanted to hear Taylor say what he had done to our son. He has never so much as apologised to us for Darren's death. I was prepared to go to jail just to hear the bastard say sorry. But he couldn't even do it in front of the judge and jury trying me. That must show what a bastard he is.

"I can remember the day it all happened so well. I can remember over the police radio news coming through that the driver hadn't stopped – that he had crashed into a car in his dash to get away. So much was happening then. You can't take it in. But when it is all over the callousness of it haunts you. It will haunt me forever."

Later police gave him back his treasured 12-bore shotgun which they had seized for the duration of his trial. He denied he was a menace, some avenger who would go in search of other prey. There would be no more targets for Steven Owen, not after the one man who altered his life so radically had been in his sights. He added: "I trust myself fully – I believe I am more responsible than many licence holders. I am not an evil gunman – it is not as if I am going to go out and shoot someone else. What happened with Taylor was something

*Above: **For the Owens, the end of the trial signalled the begining of their attempt to rebuild their lives.***

entirely different and it is not going to happen again. I am now considering selling the gun, which is worth around £400-£500. It's all over now."

But he confessed that he could not be sure it was over as far as Taylor was concerned. He moved away to Essex, fearful that the man he stalked would want to take revenge on him. He said: "I am frightened my family will be hurt again by this man. Moving away from the area where it all happened could be the start of a new life. All I have done since Darren was killed is live and breathe that man Taylor. Getting this court case over is the first step on the road to recovery."

"The jury got it wrong," pronounced Alison Barrat, who, along with Taylor, is probably the only person to think of the verdict in such a way. "We don't want to talk about it anymore." The case is now closed on the shooting tragedy – but the landmark decision by the jury stands as testimony that justice is capable of latitude and interpretation when applied with common sense and compassion.

INDELIBLE
EVIDENCE

LAB DETECTION
Scientific Evidence

From Henry Faulds' original pioneering ideas on fingerprinting to the ultra-modern process of DNA testing was a quantum leap that was accomplished in little more than a century. It is a leap that has spelled nothing but bad news for society's villains, now unable to rely on a good alibi.

No-one on earth laments the passing of the "good old days" more than the professional criminal. For as time has gone by, so the arm of the law has grown ever longer thanks to the miracles of forensic science. Applying chemistry, physics, biology and pathology to sleuthing has combined to give us space-age methods of divining criminal acts and, thereby, bringing the perpetrators of them to justice. Just as the safebreaker in early-Victorian times would scoff at the very idea that a single fingerprint could lead him to swing from the gallows, so the murderer of the 1970s didn't realise that within a decade a single drop of blood would give sleuths his very genetic make-up in the process now known as DNA.

Before science was applied to crime the catching of society's miscreants was pretty much a hit-and-miss affair. Unless a murder weapon or stolen property was found upon the culprit – or he was marked by the signs of struggle with his victim – there was every likelihood that he would get clean away with his misdeed. One of the earliest and most significant crime-fighting techniques to be taken on board by police authorities all over the world must, of course, be the process of fingerprinting. In 1864 in India a servant of Her Majesty's empire named William Herschel noted that

no two fingerprints are ever alike and began using the system to pay pensioned Indian Army soldiers who could not read and write; the presence of their right index finger print each payday testified to their identity. His system was improved upon some years later by a dour Scotsman named Henry Faulds, who in 1880 wrote to Nature magazine suggesting that this might be a way of identifying "society's criminal elements". There followed a certain amount of acrimonious squabbling between the two gentlemen as to who had rights to the aforementioned "discovery" but, nonetheless, between them they had discovered the system of logging criminals that is still in place today.

It was a third individual, Sir Francis Galton, who took the "dab" out of the realms of the possible into the practical. In 1892 he published a book called simply *Fingerprints* which proved conclusively that no two were ever alike. That same year the first murder ever to be solved by fingerprinting was committed in Necochea, Argentina. A woman named Francesca Rojas ran into the hut of her neighbour screaming that her two children aged four and six had been murdered. She put the blame on a man named Velasquez who she said had been pressuring her to marry, say-

THE ARM OF THE LAW HAS GROWN EVER LONGER THANKS TO THE MIRACLES OF FORENSIC SCIENCE

WILLIAM HERSCHEL NOTED THAT NO TWO FINGERPRINTS ARE EVER ALIKE AND BEGAN USING THE SYSTEM

Below: *A celebrated case in which 'dabs' found at the crime scene proved the undoing of kidnap-killer Arthur Hosein.*

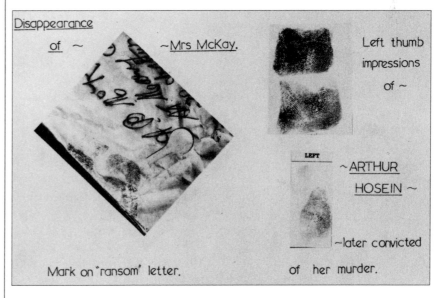

Disappearance of ~ ~Mrs McKay.

Mark on 'ransom' letter.

Left thumb impressions of ~

LEFT ~ARTHUR HOSEIN ~

~later convicted of her murder.

ing that she had returned home from work and found the children dead in bed. Velasquez was tortured by the local police but he maintained his innocence. Colin Wilson, Author of *The Mammoth Book of True Crime*, takes up the story: "A police

Opposite: *Henry Faulds, founding father of modern detection.*

Above: *Dusting a bottle for fingerprints – the film left behind clearly shows the imprint.*

broke down and confessed – she had murdered her two children because she wanted to marry a young lover who objected to them. This Argentine Lady Macbeth, who tried to rid herself of illegitimate children and an unwanted lover with one blow, obviously deserves to stand very high on a list of the world's worst women."

Nowadays the FBI in America is the repository of the most fingerprints on earth, over 200 million of them that can all be accessed by the major law enforcement agencies in the country within minutes. The FBI handles 30,000 fingerprint enquiries each day using laser beams to scan 80 fingerprints a second to find a match. In Britain there are some two-and-a-half million fingerprints on file on the police national computer in Hendon.

SOPHISTICATED DETECTION

While the collating and keeping of fingerprints has grown more technical, so has their retrieval from crime scenes. Iodine fumes and niohydrin spray can be used to lift prints from porous surfaces. Even lip-prints can be classified and there is a case of a hit-and-run driver in America where the lip-prints of the victim were taken from the bumper of the suspect's vehicle. But only two per-cent of crimes are solved by fingerprints today, even though their importance cannot be underestimated.

A single print was enough to trap John Cannan in Britain in 1987 for the abduction and sex murder of newlywed Shirley Banks. Cannan, 25, was caught driving the woman's car but claimed to have purchased it at an auction. He insisted he had never met the woman – she was missing, presumed dead – and police were still on the hunt for clues. A police search of his flat in Bristol turned up a dossier from a private detective Cannan had hired – and on it was a single fingerprint. This was matched from prints that were taken from the dead woman's home and office. Paul Jobbins, a senior fingerprint officer with Avon police, was gratified to see his work lead to Cannan being sentenced to life imprisonment for murder and rape.

After the evolution of fingerprinting came blood as the next weapon in the arsenal of law and order. Its unique properties, which enabled scientists to develop serums

inspector named Alvarez went out to investigate from La Plata. And he knew something about the work of a Dalmatian named Juan Vucetich, head of the Statistical Bureau of Police in Buenos Aires who had developed his own fingerprint system after reading an article by Galton. Alvarez went into the woman's hut and searched for clues. All he could find was a bloody thumb-print on a door. Alvarez sawed off the portion of the door and took it back to headquarters. Then he sent for Rojas and made her give a thumb-print. Alvarez knew very little about classification, but it was quite obvious that the two prints were identical. When he showed the woman the two prints through a magnifying glass, she

against diptheria and snake bites, could be used to identify the perpetrators of crime using simple laboratory tests. Initially the process merely told investigators whether blood was human or animal – as in the case of a French murderer who was sent to the guillotine in 1902 after a test showed that the blood he was covered with was not from a rabbit as claimed but from a human being – and soon blood was classified into three separate groupings thanks to the research of the Austrian-born scientist Dr. Karl Landsteiner. Landsteiner, who emigrated to America, received the Nobel prize in 1930 for his work in classifying blood – a boon to doctors, hospitals and patients, but no less a landmark discovery for sleuths. His OAB system categorised humans as having type O, type A or type B blood groups, all classified according to their immunological properties.

Twenty years before this, in 1910 in England, came the first British murder trial at which blood was to play a crucial role. Isabella Wilson, a 70-year-old junkshop keeper, was found brutalised and strangled to death in the back of her premises in Slough. A shifty character named William Broome, who had designs upon acquiring the shabby store, was a chief suspect in the murder but had moved away on the day she was found dead. Police later tracked him down to Harlesden in North London where a prostitute friend gave him an alibi that he had been with her when the old lady was being killed. But Dr. William Wilcox, the chief expert on bloodstains at the Home Office, found traces of blood under the victim's fingernails – traces which he matched to scratches on Broome's face. Broome probably did not derive any satisfaction from the fact that, as he mounted the gallows to be hanged for the murder, he had gone into the criminal history books as the first villain to be brought to book by blood.

MISSING EVIDENCE

Another famous murder case was once solved because of the *lack* of bloodstains. A famous French criminologist named Alexandre Lacassagne plotted the correlation between blood spots at a crime scene and the position of the victim at the time of death. For instance: blood dropped vertically from a stationary object makes a circular spot with ragged edges. The greater the distance the blood has to drop, the greater the crenellations. If blood moves from a moving object it leaves spots resembling exclamation marks indicating the direction the victim was heading in. Thanks to Professor Lacassagne, police forces were able to draw up charts for crime scene detectives to reconstruct what had happened to murder victims.

Such a chart came in useful for the examination of 43-year-old Catherine McCluskey, found lying in the middle of the road in Glasgow on July 29 1950. At first appearances the corpse seemed to have been dragged along the road by a car or lorry, a long trail of blood marking her path along the tarmac.

Professor Andrew Alison, the pathologist working on the case, examined the body and he concluded that her injuries were not consistent with having been knocked down by a hit-and-run driver. He surmised that she had either been bludgeoned and dragged to make it look like an accident or that she had been deliberately run over – murdered. The victim was a woman with numerous boyfriends, all of

A FRENCH MURDERER WENT TO THE GUILLOTINE AFTER A TEST SHOWED THE BLOOD COVERING HIM WAS NOT FROM A RABBIT

Below: *In 1864 in India, a servant of Her Majesty's empire, William Herschel, noted that no two fingerprints were ever alike and began using the system to pay off pensioned Indian Army soldiers.*

considerable amounts of blood on his trousers if he had indeed tried to free her. There was not a speck. So, too, another killer went to the gallows because of blood – this time because of the lack of it.

As the ways to kill a human being became more sophisticated it became necessary for police forces to equip themselves with the technology to catch murderers. The greatest challenges for lab experts have come from firearms, where the study known as ballistics has become an art unto itself. It was in Paris in May 1912, at the Congress of Legal Medicine, that ballistics was accepted as a new branch of forensic science in its own right.

The necessity for this had been the advancements in firearms, particularly cheap ones like those made by Colt in America, which took guns out of the hands of the ruling class and put them into the grip of a great mass of seething, discontented people – the proletariat. Ballistics works in much the same way as fingerprinting. Every gun has a unique signature which leaves its mark upon bullets fired into a victim. Tracing the gun is usually the first step in solving the crime.

At the Paris conference in 1912 Professor Victor Balthazard, an eminent expert, spoke of a case in which a man named Guillotin had been shot dead. Upon

whom were tracked down by police. One of them even turned out to be a policeman, James Robertson, who soon became the main suspect in her death. His home was searched and a large quantity of stolen property was found. Although an indication of his dishonesty, it didn't pin a deliberate murder on him.

But he broke under questioning and said that he accidentally knocked her over after dropping her off at home and that he moved the car "backwards and forwards in an attempt to free her". When this failed, he claimed, he at first tried to pull the woman free but then panicked and left the body there.

This "confession" was unmasked as the fallacy it was by the fact that the victim had no injuries to her legs. Professor John Glaister, an expert in Lacassagne's methods, had said that there would have been

examination, his body was found to contain several bullets. When the main suspect in the case, a man called Houssard, was brought into custody, Professor Balthazard was brought in to examine his weapon. Local firearms experts in the south of France were unable to detect whether or not the bullets had been fired from his gun, but Balthazard was able to point out no less than 86 similarities between his gun barrel and marks on the bullets. Houssard was guillotined and Balthazard's methods of comparing marks on projectiles to the metal tubes that expelled them laid the foundations for ballistic science.

A member of the New York State prosecutor's office called Charles Waite refined that science into the art it has become. He devoted his life to firearms investigation, spurred on by a trial in America in which a man's life was spared because of proof that a bullet which killed a man had come from a gun other than his own. For ten years, with the aid of gun manufacturers across

Above: *The crime at Katyn Wood. Forensic evidence showed that the mass slaughter was by Stalin's killers.*

Opposite Top: *James Robertson – a lack of bloodstains at the scene of Catherine McCluskey's demise pinned her murder on him.*

Opposite Below: *The body of his victim, which he had despatched by running over her in a car.*

America, he catalogued every type of weapon together with the signature that it left upon bullets. Next he began chronicling European imports and then, to refine the system even further, approached the Bausch and Lomb Optical Company to make him a microscope for comparing bullets. A man named Philip Gravelle then proceeded to invent the "comparison microscope" which could place a test bullet next to a murder scene bullet for instant comparison. A physicist called John H. Fischer then made a device called a helixometer, a slender, lighted probe for the study of gun barrels. Armed, as it were, with all this new information, Waite and Calvin Goddard, a friend and former army doctor, set up the Bureau of Forensic Ballistics in New York in 1923.

Ballistic knowledge was vigorously pursued all over the world. The greatest mass-exhumation of bodies for forensic study of the bullets that put them in the ground was carried out by Nazi Germany.

Above: *Dr Hawley Harvey Crippen. Poisons found in the stomach of his wife caught the sinsister but clever physician.*

GENERALS AND
LIEUTENANTS WERE BOUND
AND SHOT IN THE BACK OF
THE HEAD AND BURIED IN
MASSIVE LIME PITS

In 1940, some 4,000 Polish officers, from generals to lieutenants, were bound and shot in the back of the head and buried in massive lime pits shrouded by the towering fir trees that made up the forest of Katyn, near Smolensk in Western Russia. The corpses were discovered during Germany's invasion of Russia in 1943 and immediate propaganda was made of it – the Germans said that they had been murdered by the NKVD, Stalin's dreaded butchers. All the victims had their hands tied to a macabre noose around their necks which tightened if they struggled, all bore the same single-entry head wound testifying to their methodical execution.

It was later learned the liquidations at the Katyn Forest began on April 3 1941 and did not end until May 13, five weeks later. In the previous week the prisoners

were rounded up in their respective camps at Kozelsk, Starobelsk and Ostashkov and taken in batches of 50 to 500 to railheads to board cattlewagons for unknown destinations. It was the 4,400 prisoners of the Kozelsk camp whose final halt was to be the forest at Katyn.

Dr. Gerhard Buhtz, a professor of forensic medicine from a leading German university, was put in charge of the exhumation and examination of the grave pits which were re-opened in early March 1943. For ten weeks the stink of rotten flesh and Egyptian tobacco – the Germans smoked it to mask the smell of the dead – mingled with the scents of moss and pine sap as the murdered men were disinterred and laid out. Three separate commissions were invited by the Germans into Katyn. The first was entirely German, the second composed of scientists and forensic experts from Switzerland, Belgium, Hungary and Bulgaria and the third entirely Polish. The evidence was mightily in favour of the German viewpoint. Although the ammunition was German, records from the manufacturing plants showed it to be batches sold to Lithuania before the war which was later seized by NKVD police units. Buhtz used the tests pioneered by Waite to test the bullets and the guns from which they came – there was no doubt that the Soviets were to blame for the massacre.

THE APPLIANCE OF SCIENCE

For close to five decades the crime at Katyn Wood remained the single biggest whodunnit of World War Two. The Germans claimed that the Russians had done it, the Russians that the Germans were the perpetrators. But simple scientific facts proved that it was a Soviet crime. Stalin was able to do many things as dictator, but altering indisputable scientific facts was not one of them.

It is far from Europe and Russia, in America, where the need for ballistic science remains greatest. Among the population there are 75 million guns – and rising. Sixty three people die each day from firearms while in Britain and other European countries, firearms deaths are still minimal. Each day the FBI ballistics unit increases its knowledge to take on board details of the latest killing weapons, like machine guns and pump-action shot-guns being used by the drug gangs and the mobsters. When it comes to ballistics, the Americans lead the world.

But it is probably fair to say that when it comes to stone cold corpses, Britain must take much credit for criminal pathology. In this century great criminal pathologists like Bernard Spilsbury, Francis Camps and Keith Simpson have helped to solve some of the most baffling murder cases. British medicine has always enjoyed an enviable reputation around the globe – it followed that the application of that to crime detection produced some of the most brilliant medico-legal brains of all time. What do they look for when first presented with that mass of cold flesh that was once a living, breathing human being? And how can they tell what the cause of death was when often all they are presented with is a pile of decomposing or burned flesh wrapped around a few skeletal bones?

SUREFIRE CLUES

Of course, that is their trade and what may seem the medical equivalent of looking for a needle in a haystack is often elementary. No smoke on lung tissue on a charred corpse means death before the fire – there was no inhalation. Similarly, no water in the lungs of a "drowning" victim means they were dead before they hit the water. Broken bones in the throat of a corpse found by an empty bottle of pills means the tablets were forced down instead of being swallowed voluntarily.

And what layman could have found in over 400lbs of human "sludge" – rendered down by the acid of notorious killer John George Haigh – a single gallstone and single hairpin? Professor Keith Simpson found them and they were the clues which sent Haigh to the gallows as one of the most notorious killers in British history.

Identifying a corpse from just a few particles of flesh and bone is, of course, the hardest task facing forensic pathologists, but it is one which they invariably rise to the occasion to meet. Sir Bernard Spilsbury, who became as famous as a pop star might be nowadays because of his awesome presence in court and unmatched knowledge of crime, cut his teeth on some of the most infamous murders in British

history – including one that bears the name of a man known from the jungles of the Amazon to the ice floes of the Arctic: Dr. Crippen. Sir Bernard was 33 and unknight-ed when he became involved in the Crippen case in 1910, but his success in that most chilling of cases only served to propel him into forensic fame.

Dr. Hawley Crippen was an American-born physician working in London whose attentions wandered from his wife Belle – dominant, overbearing, cool towards the bespectacled doctor – towards a mistress called Ethel Neave, who took the fancy name Ethel LeNeve because she thought it made her more sophisticated. Although he divorced his wife she hovered on the periphery of Crippen's life with Ethel, casting a long shadow over his new, younger lover. He decided that shadow could only be lifted with her death, which he duly

WHEN IT COMES TO STONE COLD CORPSES, BRITAIN MUST TAKE MUCH CREDIT FOR CRIMINAL PATHOLOGY

Below: *Ethel LeNeve, mistress of the wicked Dr Crippen.*

dispensed by poisoning her, dismembering her and covering what remained of the corpse with quicklime and fleeing to America to begin life afresh in the New World. Chief Inspector Walter Drew of Scotland Yard sent the famous telegraphic warning that served as the first Marconi message to arrest a murderer.

It was left to Spilsbury to examine what was left to determine what had killed her and if her death could be pinned on Crippen. Firstly, Spilsbury was able to prove the traces of hyoscine poison in her stomach – a poison which the good doctor had purchased shortly before she vanished. Brian Marriner, the respected author of *On Death's Bloody Trail*, a work on forensic science, wrote: "Then the next most important clue was a piece of flesh from the abdomen which bore an operation scar – as had Mrs. Crippen. Defence experts claimed it was just a piece of flesh from the thigh, and the scar was just a fold in the skin. Spilsbury, in his calm and patient manner, showed that it came from the abdomen, pointing out that part of the rectus muscle of the abdominal wall was still attached to the specimen in question. He had shamed his elders with superior knowledge." Spilsbury won that case and many hundreds more before his own loneliness and demons drove him to take his own life.

SILENT TESTIMONY

Forensic pathologists are also invaluable for those crimes to which there have been no witnesses. When Juliet Marion Hulme and Pauline Yvonne Parker were brought before the Crown in Christchurch, New Zealand, in 1954, the case received worldwide attention because of its morbid themes. Like the case of the Chicago thrill killers Loeb and Leopold – a couple of intellectuals who killed a small boy in the mistaken belief that they could get away with the perfect murder – psychologists were at pains to try to explain the fusion of two normal, caring minds into a single unit bent on misery and death. For that is what Juliet and Pauline descended to when they feared that their parents were bent on breaking up their friendship.

In a bid to forestall or prevent the break-up they believed was coming they plotted, and carried out, the murder of Mrs. Honora

Below: *The wicked duo Juliet Marion Hulme and Pauline Parker after their arrest for the murder of Pauline's mother.*

Mary Parker. Mrs. Parker, 45, Pauline's mother, was bludgeoned repeatedly to death by the vile duo who tried to cover their tracks by claiming she had fallen. It was on June 22 1954 that two hysterical girls, covered in blood, shattered the tranquility of the afternoon tea ritual at a sedate Christchurch restaurant when they burst through the doors. "Mummy's been hurt," blurted out Pauline. "She's hurt, covered with blood." Tearfully they begged the manageress of the restaurant to phone for police while they gulped down sugared tea in an apparent attempt to ease their shock.

Some of the customers went with the police and the girls to a beauty spot in a nearby park that was close to a small bridge over a stream. Lying in a pool of blood, with her face unrecognisable, was Mrs. Parker. She was quite dead.

There were no witnesses to what had happened and immediate sympathy was with the hysterical girls. They explained she had fallen on a rocky path and that she had banged her head and died.

It wasn't until the pathologist examined the corpse and said there was bruising around the throat consistent with her having been held down as blow after blow – he speculated as many as 49 – was rained down on her head. The girls were sent away for long periods.

POISONOUS INDIVIDUALS

Another speciality of the forensic boffins is venom. Poison has always been a form of murder that British killers have been particularly fond of. One of them, Graham Young, was of that breed who thought himself cleverer than the experts pitted against him. But he too would go down in the record books – not only for his victims, but because he was trapped due to the miracles of forensic science.

From his earliest days the boy who would grow up to become immortalised as The Broadmoor Poisoner was spellbound by potions which slowly squeezed the life out of his helpless victims. A thrill killer, it was the sensation of power which fuelled his manic desires and his intelligence which masked his wicked games.

When he was finally caught for poisoning his aunt, his father and his school chum – luckily they didn't die although he had at 14 murdered his stepmother and got away with it – he spent nine years in Broadmoor, only to be released from incarceration to murder twice more.

In April 1971, after he had been released, came the job advertisement in a local paper which would seal his fate – and that of several of his workmates. He saw an offer of employment with the John Hadland company of Bovingdon, in Hertfordshire, for a storeman's position. Hadland's was an old established family firm that manufactured high grade optical and photographic equipment.

Above: *One of the most famous pathologists Britain has ever produced – Professor Keith Simpson.*

POISON HAS ALWAYS BEEN A FORM OF MURDER THAT BRITISH KILLERS HAVE BEEN PARTICULARLY FOND OF

He impressed managing director Godfrey Foster at his interview, and explained that his long time away from regular employment was due to a nervous breakdown he had suffered. Foster checked up with the training centre and also Broadmoor, but received such glowing references as to the young man's abilities and recovery that he offered him the job.

On Monday May 10 1971 Graham Young arrived at Hadlands. The company thought that they were getting a storeman. In reality they had hired an angel of death. With his £24-per-week wages he rented a £4-per-week bedsitter which in short order became his own little shop of horrors.

He lined his cupboards and shelves with an increasing collection of poisons, among them the antimony tartrate with which he had begun his fledgling career as a poisoner.

Above: *Computers like these are now used by Scotland Yard and major crimefighting agencies around the world to store information on criminals.*

THEY WERE BEING SLOWLY POISONED BY THALLIUM, A SEVERELY RESTRICTED POISON THAT IS USED TO KILL RATS

At work he was regarded, in turns, as a quiet, often distant young man or a belligerent, persistent speaker if he touched on the subjects of politics or chemistry. His best friend at work was 41-year-old Ron Hewitt, whose job he was taking. Ron stayed on to show the new man the ropes and introduced him to the other hands in the plant. Many showed great kindness to Young, lending him money and giving him cigarettes when he had none. Young repaid their affection and warmth by being the first one at the tea trolley when it trundled in during morning breaks.

The terror had begun.

On Thursday June 3, less than a month after he started there, Bob Egle, 59, who worked as storeroom boss, was taken ill with diarrhoea, cramps and nausea. Next, Ron Hewitt fell violently ill, suffering the

same symptoms accompanied by acute stomach pains and burning sensations at the back of his throat. Workers at Hadlands called the mystery pains "the bug". In fact they were being slowly poisoned by thallium, a severely restricted poison used to kill rats that is so toxic it can cause death merely by being handled. Young bought the poison from chemists in London and was putting the tasteless, odourless chemical into his workmates' teas. On Wednesday July 7 Bob Egle died. His was a horrible, painful death, caused by a paralysis which spread throughout his body before it caused his heart to fail. There was no inquest on his body because doctors misinterpreted his illness as being bronchial-pneumonia linked to polyneuritis.

In September, after a relatively quiet summer, in which Young was often away, the nightmare continued. Fred Biggs, a part-time worker, was the next target. After 20 days of agonising cramps and pains he died. Four other workers were poisoned, two of them ending up in hospital with all their hair gone and with severe cases of depression brought on by the poison that they had ingested through the tainted tea.

It wasn't until Hadlands brought in a local doctor, Iain Anderson, to talk to staff and try to track down what was poisoning the workforce, that the noose began closing around Young's neck. Anderson said he had run down numerous checks but was unable to determine the source of the "bug". Young, unable to suppress his own ego over his knowledge of poisons, soon took the meeting over.

He reeled off mind-numbing statistics about poison and its effects – so much so that Anderson became suspicious. After consulting with the company management, Scotland Yard was called in. They ran a background check on all company employees – a move that was guaranteed to shine the light on the unsavoury past activities of Graham Young.

A COLD-HEARTED KILLER

Forensic scientists from the government research station at Aldermaston were called in and it was believed that thallium had caused the deaths and the illnesses. Thallium is a metal-based poison that has no smell, is colourless and tasteless. Young was arrested at his father's house, making himself an egg sandwich. As he was being led away he said to police: "Which ones are they doing me for, then?" The authorities were concerned that they did not have enough evidence on Young, and as both the bodies of his victims had been burned they feared he would, quite literally, get away with murder once again.

But in a forensic first the ashes of one of the cremated corpses showed traces of thallium in them. A process that is called "atomic absorption spectrometry" was deployed in which five micrograms of Thallium per gram of ash were found. On December 3 he was charged with murdering Egle. Now he wanted maximum publicity – the notoriety of Crippen and others that he now felt he had rightly earned. So he pleaded not guilty.

Later he was also charged with the murder of Fred Biggs and the attempted murders of two others and of further administering poison to two others. He went into the history books and captivity at St. Albans Court in 1972.

Now the world of the forensic expert is shifting away from blood and bone, hair and tissue, into the realm of sci-fi where lasers and electron microscopes are at the forefront of the war on crime.

The forensic science laboratory of Scotland Yard is now one of the most highly advanced criminal investigation labs on earth, where great emphasis and faith is being placed on laser technology. Graham Jackson, the Met's laser expert, likes to joke that he can literally make "clues glow in the dark" with his technology. He cites the case, for instance, of an Essex policeman who had been asked to look out for a truck involved in a hit-and-run case.

IN A FORENSIC FIRST THE ASHES OF ONE OF THE CREMATED CORPSES SHOWED TRACES OF THALLIUM

Below: *Graham Young, the Broadmoor poisoner, who sent so many innocents to their deaths.*

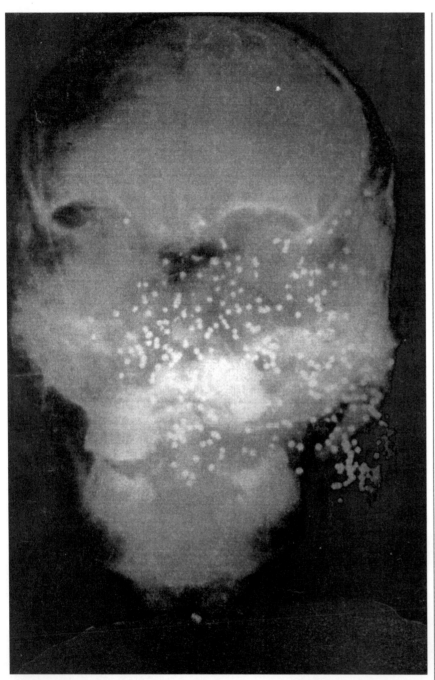

Above: *A head x-ray showing a pattern of shotgun pellets on the victim's left side.*

forensic lab. According to Dr. Ray Williams, the lab's director, the number showed up on his hand after it was subjected to laser-light! "He was not so much astonished by the technology but relieved that his hand was still in one piece," said Dr. Williams.

Laser technology is now also coming into its own in the field of fingerprinting. Until recently, the standard method of gleaning fingerprints from a crime scene was to dust aluminium powder over everything and hope that it stuck. For various reasons it may not – and in the old days that would have been the end of it.

But thanks to lasers many acids found in the ordinary human fingerprint fluoresce under laser light. In a darkened room the display can be spectacular – hundreds of "dabs" showing up where ordinary aluminium powder failed to detect them. The lights can also read underneath the correction fluid pasted over a word to reveal the word that was corrected.

Jackson said: "It has improved previous methods of detection considerably. Things like shoeprints, fingerprints, fibres, marks on bodies, stains and so on. It has proved possible to recover these types of evidence on occasions when often they cannot be seen at all by the human eye."

A METICULOUS MICROSCOPE

The scanning electron microscope is another high-tech tool worth its weight in gold. This uses electron beams instead of rays of light to identify fingerprints in circunstances which, on the surface, may seem impossible. For example, gunmen often carry firearms in rolled-up newspapers, the surface of which no-one believed a fingerprint could be retrieved from. A fingerprint on a picture, for example, is made up of thousands of tiny dots which would interfere with a laser scan. But the electron microscope can get around the problem. Firstly, the forensic scientist paints the page with a liquid containing a suspension of silver. When it comes into contact with the fingerprint the silver separates. When the page is then scanned the fingerprint stands out because the heavy silver atoms bounce back the electrons fired at them by the microscope while the lighter carbon atoms of the paper and ink do not.

The officer in question thought he had spotted the offending lorry while out on his beat, wrote the registration number down on his hand and ran to the nearest telephone box to call it in to check with the station. It was the wrong number and the marks on his hand were erased later that night in the officer's bathtub. The next day a telex came into the station where he was based from police in the north of England seeking a hijacked vehicle.

Feeling that the number of the lorry he had written down might be that of the hijacked truck he tried to recall the digits, without luck. Then he was sent to the

Dr. Williams cites the case of the assasination attempt upon the Israeli ambassador to Britain in 1982 as one of those which would never have led to a conviction if it had not been for the great strides forward in forensic technology. When the accused, Hussein Said, stood in the witness box in February 1983 he was confident of an acquittal. The man he had shot, Shlomo Argov, was too ill from his wounds to give evidence, the police had discharged their own firearms at the scene and Said had said nothing under interrogation to incriminate himself. Traces of gunpowder and gun oil found on Said after the attempt could, said his lawyers, just as easily have come from the police weapons.

A TRICKY SITUATION

Dr. Williams called it a "classic forensic conundrum. We had the problem of associating this arrested man first of all with the discarded weapon used to shoot the ambassador and with the ambassador himself. And we had to somehow discard all possibility that the evidence found on the accused had come from the police guns."

When a gun is fired what happens is that the firing pin strikes the primer at the base of the cartridge, detonating it by percussion and setting off the main propellant. The gases given off condense and particles of solid material settle on the person firing the gun. They are of a very particular type, containing a combination of three elements – lead, barium and antimony. This combination is found, and found only, in particles left behind from gunfire. Dr. Williams set the Met's scanning electron microscope to work to solve the puzzle.

"Analysis of the guns, ammunition and residue samples taken from the suspect, the police and the victim told a remarkable story," said Dr. Williams, who described the whole sleuthing process for this puzzle as "elegant". The particle analysis showed traces of mercury on the discarded weapon, the one the prosecution said had been used to shoot the ambassador. Mercury also showed up on the suspect and on the flesh and clothing of the ambassador. The combination of residue particles, it turned out, was characteristic of ammunition fromIron Curtain countries, China and the Middle East. Europe and America hadn't used mercury in ordnance for 30 years. Analysis of police weapons and clothing showed only the trinity of barium, antimony and lead.

"None of these were found on the assailant or on the gun that had been fired," said Dr. Williams. "So we eliminated the possibility that the police, in their arresting of the man, had passed on firearms residue from their own weapons. So there was a clear-cut link, and a very elegant link, between assailant, victim and weapon." The jury returned a verdict of guilty on Said – another victory that was due to the leaps and bounds made by forensic boffins.

MERCURY SHOWED UP ON THE DISCARDED WEAPON, THE SUSPECT AND ON THE FLESH AND CLOTHING OF THE AMBASSADOR

"THERE WAS A CLEAR-CUT LINK, AND A VERY ELEGANT LINK, BETWEEN ASSAILANT, VICTIM AND WEAPON," SAID DR WILLIAMS

Below: *A slow-motion picture of a shotgun cartridge spewing out its lethal contents. Such minute details aid police in determining from what distance victims were shot.*

WILLIAM HEIRENS
The Mama's Boy

William Heirens pitted his evil wits against the best that law enforcement could throw at him after committing crimes against defenceless victims. He lost his perverse battle with the law, thanks to the advancements in forensic science that pinned him to his crimes like a butterfly to a board.

It was a balmy day in Chicago on June 3 1945, the breeze coming from Lake Michigan affording little relief to the residents of the huge metropolis. Many sought shelter on that afternoon in movie theatres – one of the few places, aside from the huge slaughterhouses which gave the city its nickname "Hog Town" – that had air conditioning. Attractive widow Josephine Alice Ross was thinking of going to the cinema that day too, but instead stayed at home... a decision that was to cost her her life. The nude body of the 43-year-old woman was found later on her bed, her skirt and a nylon stocking tied around her throat. But she hadn't died from strangulation – huge knife wounds covered her face and neck and it was later determined that she bled to death. The most peculiar aspect of the crime scene to detectives was the blood-soaked towels and her own pyjamas lying in a tub of water in the bathroom. Captain Frank Reynolds of the Chicago police department glanced at his men and said: "The killer washed the blood from the body. This is a new one on me."

The body of the dead woman was found at lunchtime that day by her 17-year-old daughter who had left the apartment shortly before 9.00am, so she had been murdered in a four-hour time period. There was no sexual assualt on the body, no money was missing, no valuables taken. It all pointed to a frenzied, motiveless murder. The killer, police learned, would have had no trouble entering the apartment as she never kept

THE NUDE BODY OF THE WOMAN WAS FOUND LATER ON HER BED, HER SKIRT AND A NYLON STOCKING TIED AROUND HER THROAT

Opposite: *The face of pure evil stares through the bars of a cell. There was to be no escape for William Heirens.*

Below: *Josephine Ross (left) and Frances Brown (right), two of Heirens' victims.*

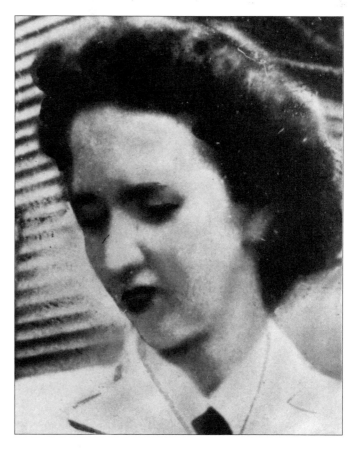

Above: *A monster's victim, six-year-old Suzanne Degnan (left), seen here with her sister Elizabeth.*

SCRAWLED ON A WALL WAS A MESSAGE: "FOR HEAVEN'S SAKE CATCH ME BEFORE I KILL MORE. I CANNOT CONTROL MYSELF"

the door locked. And he was a methodical man – he had wiped the place clean of all fingerprints. He was so thorough the forensic experts didn't even find a print of her daughter or her sister who also lived there.

Yet on that first day they questioned two eyewitnesses, a janitor and a neighbour, who swore that they had seen a hatless young man walking into the building wearing a white sweater and dark trousers with his hair brushed back in a pompadour. One saw him enter, the other saw him leaving around two hours later – the delay was probably the result of his obsessive cleaning of the apartment.

Months went by and no suspect was turned up. The initial police theory that the man was a lover of Mrs. Ross who had lost his head in an argument could not be substantiated. Every man who knew the widow was questioned and eliminated from the investigation. But as time went on several more apparently meaningless, equally brutal attacks were made on women in the city.

On October 1 Veronica Hudzinski, 19, was shot with a revolver and barely lived.

Four days later Army nurse Evelyn Peterson was beaten unconscious in her home and was in the process of being strangled with electrical flex when the man suddenly stopped and asked if he could get her a doctor. He walked calmly from the apartment as she clung to life... but not before he wiped the place clean of dabs. A second unexplained shooting happened on December 5, and again the victim managed to escape with just minor injuries.

But five days later the body of 30-year-old Frances Brown was found draped over a washtub at the residential Pine Crest Hotel. Near the body, scrawled on a wall in her bright red lipstick, was a message: "For Heaven's Sake Catch Me Before I Kill More. I Cannot Control Myself." The victim had been shot, strangled, and her face mutliated with deep knife wounds. And her body had been washed of blood and the room wiped down meticulously to remove all fingerprints. She too had not been sexually molested.

A VITAL MISTAKE

Yet this time the killer made one slight slip. He had indeed been methodical in removing the fingerprints, but not methodical enough. On the left jamb of the bathroom door was a print of one finger. It was a seemingly hopeless task matching this one print to an individual as the Chicago police department filed and classified fingerprints according to the dominant characteristics of all five fingers. Nevertheless a police sergeant named Thomas Laffey was assigned the mindbending task of sorting through 1,250,000 sets of prints. If nothing else, public opinion needed to be satisfied that everything was being done.

But four weeks later the horror of the murders and woundings receded in the public consciousness with the kidnapping of six-year-old Suzanne Degnan. Suzanne had gone to bed on the evening of January 7 1946 in her parents' home a mile from the Ross murder site – and the next morning her father James, going into her bedroom, found the window was open and the bed empty.

Two policemen cruising the area in a patrol car were there within a minute, one of them finding on the floor of her room a note that read: "Get $20,000 Ready & Wait For Word. Do Not Notify FBI or Police. Bills in 5's and 10's." On the reverse side of the note in capitals was the threat: "BURN THIS FOR HER SAFETY."

With police help, her father made a desperate and heart-rending appeal on the city radio station to return the little girl. The police didn't initially tell him, but the clues at the crime scene pointed to the fact that her abductor could be the same maniac responsible for the murders and woundings. There was a single print on the note that didn't correspond to the print found at the last murder… but did correspond with a fragment of fingerprint that a second search of the first murder scene had thrown up! Police were downcast and certain that a man of such a psychotic nature might already have murdered the little girl.

Later that night, as her father's wireless appeal was repeated over the city airwaves, two detectives lifted the lid of a storm drain. Floating in the sewer water beneath was the head of Suzanne. The rest of her body was missing.

During the next four hours Mayor Kelly had to repeatedly go on the air to assure Chicagoans of their safety. In the same period the other parts of little Suzanne's body were found in various sewers across the city. Something approaching panic gripped the usually stoical citizens of Chicago, many of whom protested outside the police department headquarters. Yet some progress was already being made in the hunt for the killer even as they shouted threats of violence.

EYES OF TRUTH

A witness was found who could have seen the murderer; a former Marine had been parked in his car near the Degnan home talking to his girlfriend when he saw a young man walk by with a shopping bag. The shopping bag was later found containing parts of the little girl's dismembered body. An intensive search of the region

---

FLOATING IN THE SEWER BENEATH WAS THE HEAD OF SUZANNE. THE REST OF HER BODY WAS MISSING

Below: *Mr and Mrs James Degnan, the strain showing in their tired eyes, wait for news of their little girl.*

turned up a small piece of twisted wire on which were found three head hairs that matched Suzanne's. A handkerchief was wrapped round one end of the wire – a hanky bearing the initials 3168-S. Sherman. It was customary for soldiers at the time to mark their possessions with the last four digits of their serial numbers. A search was launched to find the owner.

THE EXPERTS' ESTIMATE

As the hunt was on, forensic experts determined that Suzanne had died between 12.30 and 1.00am, strangled with the piece of wire that was found with the handkerchief. There were traces of coal dust on her feet and in her hair roots. Other than that, various parts of the body appeared to have been washed after they had been cut away. But the clue of the coal was later to prove significant in catching the killer.

Detectives believed that the coal dust indicated the girl had been dissected in a

Above: *Bones sifted from the ashes of an incinerator in Chicago – the incinerator that Heirens used as his DIY crematorium for his victims.*

DETECTIVES BELIEVED THAT THE COAL DUST INDICATED THE GIRL HAD BEEN DISSECTED IN A CELLAR

---

cellar. The next morning police began house-to-house searches of all cellars in the neighbourhood of Suzanne's home. In the afternoon they appeared to strike gold. In the basement of a four-storey house on Winthrop Avenue, just a block from her home, detectives found faint smears of blood in the basement and in a drain trap discovered bits of flesh and blonde hairs.

A woman tenant in the apartment directly above said she had been disturbed at 2.30am by someone in the laundry room running water. A new shipment of coal had come that morning and when detectives moved it they discovered bloodstains from the bin on the floor.

A locker belonging to one of the tenants had been forced open. Inside it had been the shopping bag which was eventually found floating in the sewer with parts of Suzanne's body inside. The man didn't live in the building as a door was found forced. Later police would find out that the handkerchief belonged to an innocent sailor called Sherman whose home had been burgled. They now believed they were looking for a thief who had been transformed into an unstoppable, murderous beast.

Harry Gold, a man who had been on holiday in Florida when the Suzanne murder occurred, returned home to find his apartment – one that overlooked the dead girl's home – ransacked. They believed the culprit had gone to the apartment on a burglary and on an impulse had seen the little girl and decided to enter the apartment for another moneymaking scheme – except that his own berserk impulses were unable to stop him ultimately from killing her.

The guilty man's arrest, despite one of the largest police efforts in Chicago history, finally came through pure chance – even though it wasn't for some hours that they realised that the man they had could be the maniac they were seeking. A youthful burglar was caught after being chased by police. The sprightly thief was fleet-footed and gave a long chase, turning to fire on his pursuer. But an off duty police officer final-

---

THEY WERE LOOKING FOR A THIEF WHO HAD BEEN TRANSFORMED INTO AN UNSTOPPABLE, MURDEROUS BEAST

Below: *A telegram from the FBI showing that Heirens' palm prints matched those on the ransom note in the Degnan child case.*

ly hurled three flowerpots on to his head and he offered no more resistance. Papers on the youth identified him as William Heirens, a 17-year-old student at the Chicago University.

PREVIOUS FORM

A check on police records showed that he had been arrested in 1942, when he was 13, for carrying a pistol. Other arrests were for a string of burglaries – six homes which he torched after looting. Heirens was taken to a prison hospital for wounds sustained during his arrest. While he recovered, police seized a large arsenal of weapons at the house where he lived with his parents in a city suburb. These included a rifle, a .25 calibre pistol, two .38 revolvers and four more pistols and a rifle hidden under tarpaulin on the roof.

This seemed encouraging enough, but Heirens lay in a coma in hospital. As he remained unconscious a search of his room on the university campus turned up stolen

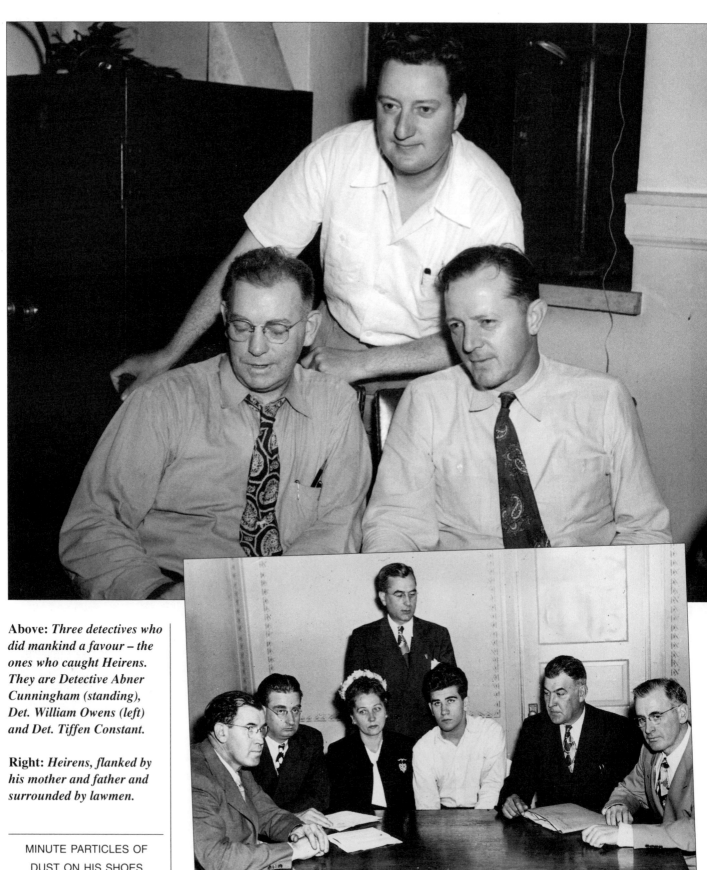

Above: *Three detectives who did mankind a favour – the ones who caught Heirens. They are Detective Abner Cunningham (standing), Det. William Owens (left) and Det. Tiffen Constant.*

Right: *Heirens, flanked by his mother and father and surrounded by lawmen.*

MINUTE PARTICLES OF DUST ON HIS SHOES MATCHED THE DUST IN THE CELLAR WHERE THE LITTLE GIRL WAS CUT UP

property from dozens of burglaries – including items taken from the Gold home opposite the murdered girl's house. But it didn't link him directly with the murders – not until a dirty pair of shoes was handed to the forensic department that had collated scenes-of-crime clues. An examination of minute particles of dust on the soles of his shoes matched exactly the coal dust found in the cellar where the little girl was cut up.

A police department expert, Brian Connolly, said: "There are hundreds of grades of coal, thousands of sub-grades. But using a chemical solution and a machine which span the dust particles from the shoes and the cellar we were able to determine, without question, that they had come from the same source. Whatever else he did or didn't do, those shoes and the person in them had been in that cellar. And the samples were all taken while he was unaware. There was more. Underneath the killer's fingernails were minute quantities of soap. These were removed as he slept and placed through similar testing at a laboratory which determined that it was exact-

Above: *Carried from his hospital bed by detectives, Heirens is pictured en route to his appointment with a lie detector machine.*

ly the same kind of soap which he had used to wash the chopped-up corpse with."

For three days more, police kept this information from him, preferring a confession to relying solely on forensic evidence. Too often before it had been thrown out of court by laymen jurors who were medieval in their outlook when it came to "new fangled" devices such as acid tests, solutions and spectrographs.

When he finally came around from his "coma" – a feigned state which police think was a device to bide him some thinking time – he rambled on about another man called George Murman being responsible for the crimes. He agreed to go under sodium pentathol – truth serum – an experiment that backfired badly for the police.

AN INTERESTING DRUG

The injection of sodium pentathol induces the patient to a state of narcosynthesis, blotting out the active mind, freeing the subconscious state to answer questions. Most times the person who receives the drug cannot help himself in telling the truth. But Heirens spoke of the mystery man George with such clarity and conviction that the police and FBI thought they had blown it. The stenographic record of the polygraph machine linked up to him seemed to suggest that every answer he gave, however implausible, was the truth. Only the undisputed forensic evidence gave the police hope of proceeding with the prosecution. Detective Chief Storms said: "We could have nailed him on burglary charges no problem, but the truth test stymied us. We needed that forensic badly."

An extensive search across America, utilising police files, FBI data, servicemen's records, missing persons' records and social security numbers failed to find any record of a George Murman, the mystery man that Heirens said he befriended in a hotel in Chicago shortly before the little girl was murdered.

Police were willing to risk a prosecution on the strength of the forensic evidence alone when Heirens was forced to undergo a psychiatric examination. Mind doctors believed that Heirens had managed to sink into a deep psychotic state in which he possessed an alter ego – George – that had carried out the killings.

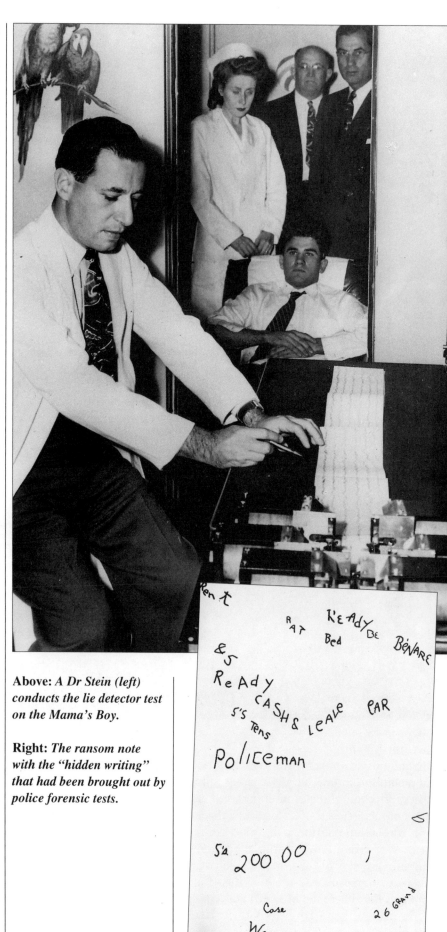

Above: *A Dr Stein (left) conducts the lie detector test on the Mama's Boy.*

Right: *The ransom note with the "hidden writing" that had been brought out by police forensic tests.*

He was indicted on a total of 27 burglaries and four woundings as a means of holding him in jail while enquiries continued. There was still no proof of linking him with the murders unless he confessed. There seemed little chance of a direct confession and so the case was to hinge on the soap and coal dust.

Yet on August 6 the same impulses that had snapped to change him from a burglar to murder, snapped to turn him from innocent to guilty. He admitted killing the two women and the child, saying he derived sexual satisfaction from the deaths even though he didn't rape them or otherwise sexually molest them. "I got a real thrill," he said. "It was more the breaking in than the murders. I just lost it. But I never touched them in that way." He could not say why he had lingered for two hours each time over the deaths of his victims, nor why he had washed them.

REAL FANTASY

And he finally admitted that George was a figment of his own imagination. "To me he's very real," said Heirens. "He exists. You can accept George as being me but, well, it's hard to explain. A couple of times I had talks with him. I suppose I was really talking to myself. I wrote lots of notes to him which I kept."

It was during his confession that psychiatrists noted continued references to his mother, about how he always wanted to please her throughout his life and how he always seemed to fail to do so. Hence the nickname "Mama's Boy" which stuck with him through the trial and the rest of his days behind bars.

On September 7 1946 he pleaded guilty to the murders and was ordered to be held for life without any possibility of parole. Shortly after entering the Illinois State Penitentiary he became an unruly, troublesome prisoner who was often in trouble for fighting and infracting other prison rules. He was again examined by psychiatrists who deemed him insane and he was transferred to a mental institution similar to Britain's Broadmoor.

William Heirens tore up the rule book for serial killers. Men who kill mature women don't go after children. Burglars don't become serial killers. Burglars don't

HE ADMITTED KILLING THE TWO WOMEN AND THE CHILD, SAYING HE DERIVED SEXUAL SATISFACTION FROM THE DEATHS

Below: *Smiling and casual, this portrait of Heirens was snapped just after his attempted suicide.*

become snipers who shoot women. The only thread running through his crimes was the strange washing-up afterwards of the bodies which brings the police to an ironic postscript to his evil reign. For forensic scientist David Steinman said: "Had he washed the bodies in warm water instead of cold – and wiped his shoes with warm water instead of cold – he would have removed the forensic evidence. That in turn would have made police loathe to charge him and in turn he would have served some time for burglary and been on the streets of Chicago within a decade. We are lucky he didn't have warm water."

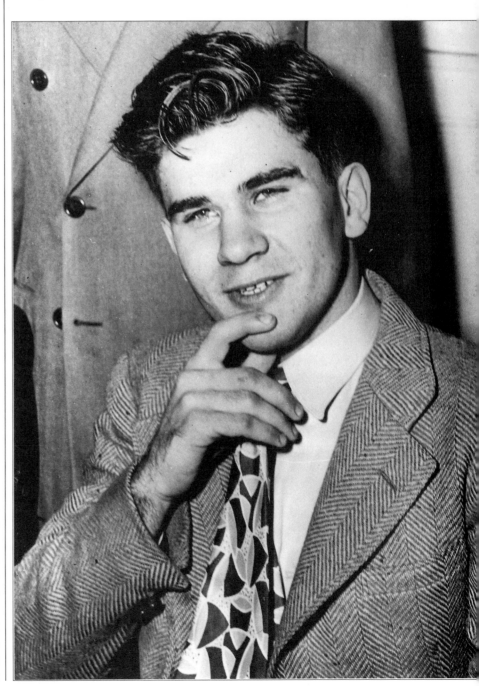

KAREN PRICE
Face Value

The case of Karen Price stands unmatched in British criminal history. It was a work of such intensive labour, painstaking forensic investigation, brilliant deduction and awesome teamwork that it deserves to stand apart from all other cases in this or any other century.

Thanks to the brilliance shown by the team in identifying murder victim Karen Price from nothing more than her fleshless skull her killers were caught and imprisoned. One prominent academic said that the case "significantly advanced forensic science in this country by 20 years". More than that, it enabled justice to be done and for the family of the missing girl to finally – more than ten years after she disappeared – place her remains in a grave where she could rest in peace and they could mourn her with respect.

Karen Price was murdered a decade earlier but the corpse of the woman who was to become so valuable in the forensic fight against crime was actually discovered on the afternoon of December 7 1989. Workmen Keith Lloyd, Syd Williams, Billy David and Paul Bodenham had been gutting a house in Fitzhamon Embankment, Cardiff, an address bordering a seedy red light area of the city. Number 29, a gothic three-storey building, was being converted into flats as was the custom with many turn-of-the-century homes in this bedsit area of the Welsh capital. On this afternoon, as dusk was falling, it became apparent to the men that the trench they had been digging in the garden for a new wastepipe was not going to be deep enough. Lloyd jumped into the excavation to dig another

six inches down – but his pickaxe head hit a soft object. Closer inspection revealed it to be a carpet tied with electrical flex. When the cigar-shaped object was removed and the flex untied a human skeleton was revealed as the contents.

Within an hour the area had been sealed off as a murder site. Forensic experts collected soil samples while a police pathologist examined the remains. Most of the flesh had gone but rotting particles of clothing still draped off some of the bones. Blonde curls were visible around the skull and a pair of gilt earrings were found nearby. It became clear from the most senior officer present to the most junior rookie that identifying such a body would be a mammoth task. Detective Chief Superintendent John Williams, head of South Wales CID, viewed the body the day

WHEN THE CIGAR-SHAPED OBJECT WAS REMOVED AND THE FLEX UNTIED A HUMAN SKELETON WAS REVEALED

Opposite: *Karen Price's body was found a decade after she went missing.*

Below: *It was when renovations were being carried out at this house that the Woman Without a Face was discovered.*

*Above: **Richard Neave, a man who has built reconstructions of numerous historical figures.***

DET. CHF. SUPT. WILLIAMS
PLEDGED "TO CALL IN
EVERY 'OLOGIST IN THE
BOOK TO SOLVE
THE CRIME"

---

it was found and said: "I didn't think it was possible to reconstruct a face from what I saw." In fact the medical and forensic experts set out to accomplish nothing less than the total reconstruction of a long-dead body. It was to be an extraordinary alliance of pathology, odontology – the study of teeth – forensic tests on the clothing, anthropology, entomology – the study of insects – a brilliant medical illustrator and geneticists. Each of them deserves a slice of the credit in bringing the murderers of this young girl to book.

The first stage in the investigation was the police decision to treat her death as murder. Det. Chf. Supt. Williams said he was satisfied, even before hearing from the pathologist, that a body being buried in a garden was clearly due to foul play and pledged to "call in every 'ologist in the book the solve the crime". On the evening of the day that the corpse was discovered it was laid out in the morgue at the Cardiff Royal Infirmary for inspection by Dr. Bernard Knight, professor of pathology at the Welsh Institute of Forensic Medicine. He determined that the skeleton was of a young white woman, about 5ft. 4ins. tall. The doctor said analysis of the bones suggested a girl in her mid-teens but he had not determined the cause of death.

While the pathological team examined the corpse the soil that it had lain in was coming under the intense scrutiny of Nicholas Coles, a Welsh archaeological expert. Unfortunately, his examination of the grave site was fruitless because much of the soil had already been removed by workmen before they had jumped into the ditch to deepen it.

A MACABRE INVESTIGATION

The next cog in the machinery of identification was the Home Office forensic laboratory at Chepstow, Gwent. Most of the material had rotted, but the clay in which she had lain had preserved some remnants. Working from the material which survived the scientists were able to determine that her bra was a size 36B and had been manufactured by the Shadowline company in Liverpool and sold in Cardiff through a company called Mrs. Knickers. This was an important piece of the puzzle – as police liaised with missing persons' bureaux over the number of missing teenaged girls in Britain it seemed likely that she was local and had purchased the items there. Her sweatshirt was size 18, manufactured by the American firm Levi for the British market and sold around 1980 – placing her death at some time in the last decade.

The skull was delivered to the Natural History Museum in London where anthropologists Dr. Christopher Stringer and Theya Molleson examined it from every angle, measured it and fed the data into a computer programme used to identify 2,500 different skull types from around the world. They determined the girl's skull was from a caucasian female.

Further examination of the teeth and jaw made them speculate that she was probably not an indigenous Briton – widening the net to immigrants and visitors to the

Left: *In an American case, a girl's identity was discovered using the same techniques as those employed in the Karen Price case.*

Below: *Every minute detail of the skull was examined time and time again.*

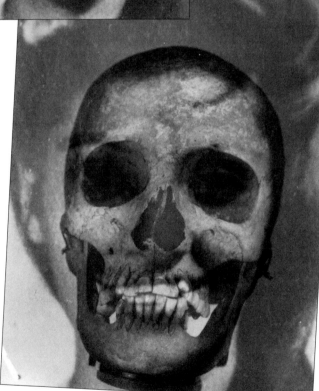

country. The skull became the focus of the inquiry – it was undamaged and from it much more could be gleaned than from any other part of the skeleton.

Dr. David Whittaker, the forensic dental adviser to the Home Office, used a tried and trusted method to try to gauge her age from the teeth. He took a cross section of one tooth and, rather like determining the age of a tree by counting the rings of a sawed trunk, speculated "80 per-cent" certain that she was 15-and-a-half when she

HE MEASURED HOW LONG THE CADAVER HAD LAIN IN THE GROUND BY EXAMINING DEAD INSECT TISSUE FOUND WITH HER

died. He also found traces of blood in capillaries in the skull. These tiny veins are usually empty at death, except in cases of violent death; he speculated that she had met her end at the hands of a strangler. He also remarked that the poor quality of the dental work indicated that she had spent time under the care of a foreign dentist, but he couldn't pin down a country.

HUMAN COMPLICATIONS

A 70-strong police team meanwhile embarked on all the routine, necessary enquiries related to such a murder. It was estimated by Williams that some 700 people had lived in the house and the adjoining one during the decade, many of them drifters who stayed for only a short while. But no-one quizzed seemed to remember a fair-haired teenager. Williams began to sense that as the case progressed he was going to have to rely more and more on the "boffins" who were methodically trying to find out who Miss X was.

The next person to be called in provided some of the most fascinating clues. In December 1989 and January the following year the skull, soil samples, skeletal remains and clothing particles were examined by Dr. Zakeria Erzincliogu, a brilliant Cambridge University professor specialising in entomology – the lives of insects.

He was able to measure how long the cadaver had lain in the ground by examining the dead insect tissue found with her. Woodlice, phorid flies – tissue-eating insects – and bluebottle larvae, the eggs of flies. The first two indicated that the girl had been buried in the ground for five years at least, placing her death before 1984, which corresponded with the clothing found on her.

More importantly, the bluebottle eggs could only have been laid on the corpse when it was exposed to air and in this he estimated that her body had been unburied for two days after her murder.

It was all leading somewhere but no-one knew quite where. That is when one of the police officers recalled reading about a renowned artist who had been helping to build a plaster-cast of a victim of the 1987 Kings Cross Underground fire who had remained unidentified since then. Williams thought it was worth contacting Richard

Neave, a 54-year-old medical illustrator who was based at Manchester University. Neave's skill came in re-constructing human faces based just on the shape, size and contours of their skulls. He started on the face of Miss X by making a plastercast of the skull and gradually built up features using modelling clay.

He was the first to admit that putting the features on a skull is the part "where art and science meet" and that mistakes can occur. But probably there is no-one in the world with his skill or attention to detail. During a lengthy career he has put the faces on long-dead Egyptian mummies, a murder victim whose killers were caught thanks to his efforts and the ancient ruler Phillip of Macedon.

He gained his expertise in human anatomy by watching surgical procedures and dissections at medical universities across Britain and has honed his skills to a finer-than-fine art. He saw the task of re-creating Miss X as a great forensic challenge and the skull was placed in a cardboard box and driven to him by police.

PAINSTAKING CONSTRUCTION

Neave received the skull on December 18 and set to work. He used anatomical sketchbooks while he started to "build" the face, muscle by muscle, feeling with his fingers where the flesh, bone, muscle and sinew would have been on every square centimetre of her face. He uses exact measurements on muscle depth and skin type based on figures of real people and applies them to whatever age he is working to.

It is very methodical work that has to be done carefully piece by piece because, he says, "I am not a sculptor making a piece of art-work – it is a scientific construction." In the case of Miss X he said: "I used all the information that was gathered from experts. You have to remember that she was only 15-and-a-half, healthy, lots of elasticity in her face. Life won't have driven a truck over her face."

Nose and lips could be done first because the skull doesn't dictate their size or thickness. Then he continued his moulding of the eyebrows, forehead, cheeks, chin and ears until, in two days, he was satisfied with what he had in front of him.

On January 8 1990 Det. Chf. Supt. Williams called a press conference in Cardiff during which photographs of the reconstruction were handed out to representatives of TV and newspapers. The photo-

Below: *All the efforts of the investigators were to prove worthwhile for the comfort they brought to Karen's family. They also made British crime history.*

graph was also made into a "have you seen this girl?" poster which was issued to police stations all over Britain for distribution at social halls, railway and bus stations and other places where crowds congregate.

The face was of a young girl with slightly flared nose and straggly hair. But it was a complete face, a complete human being, not a shadowy artist's impression which have often proved worse than useless in tracking down criminals and missing persons.

The speed with which the girl's identity came after that press conference was truly astonishing. Forty eight hours after the nationwide appeals went out two social workers in Cardiff contacted police to say they believed the girl looked like a young runaway called Karen Price, aged 15.

She had been in care when she went missing in 1981, said the informants, and were emphatic it was her. Other names of missing girls were offered up too, but they were all traced.

FINAL CONFIRMATION

It then fell on police to find Karen Price's dental records, which turned up in a Cardiff dentist's storeroom in late January 1990 and were sent to the expert Whittaker for analysis. He said there was no doubt that the dead girl was Karen Price. Further confirmation came when Dr. Peter Vanezis, a senior lecturer in forensic medicine at the London Hospital, was sent a photo of Karen. Using the latest video-computer technology he electronically superimposed the photograph of Karen on to her skull and got an almost perfect match.

The corpse had a name and she had a family who would now be able to mourn for her properly.

Between January and July 1990, as police efforts concentrated on finding her killers, further forensic work was carried out. Police were determined to get a DNA match through genetic fingerprinting – which would prove scientifically it was her. This was obtaned by sending a bone sample from Karen's femur to Dr. Erik Hagelberg of the Institute of Molecular Medicine at Oxford University.

Her test involved chilling the bone with liquid nitrogen, then crushing it to extract the DNA. Professor Alec Jeffreys, of the department of genetics at Leicester University – the man who invented DNA fingerprinting – compared the DNA with blood samples taken from Karen's parents, who had been traced in the intervening time. Despite being used on bones of such an age and subject to decay, he was able to say better than "99.9 per-cent that these are the remains of Karen Price".

The life of Karen Price was, police discovered, an unhappy one. Her father Michael and her mother Anita Nicholaidis were divorced when she was a child and she went into the care of the Glamorgan social services when she was 10. Her mother's Greek-Cypriot roots accounted for Karen's teeth appearing "foreign". Not long before her 16th birthday she was moved to an assessment centre for troublesome children where decisions were to be made about her future. But she absconded on July 8 1981, joining the legions of missing children who make up a lost army in Britain.

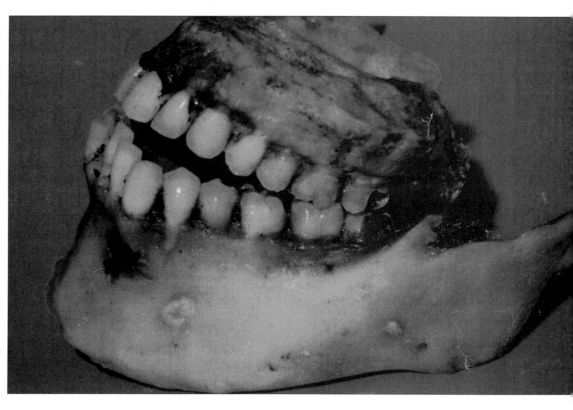

Above: *The teeth of Karen Price – although it would take far more than her dentures to identify her.*

THE CORPSE HAD A NAME AND SHE HAD A FAMILY WHO WOULD NOW BE ABLE TO MOURN FOR HER PROPERLY

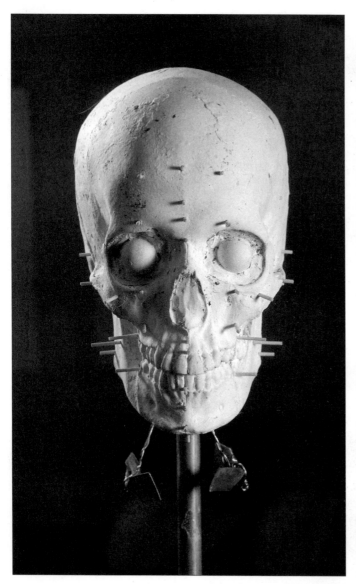

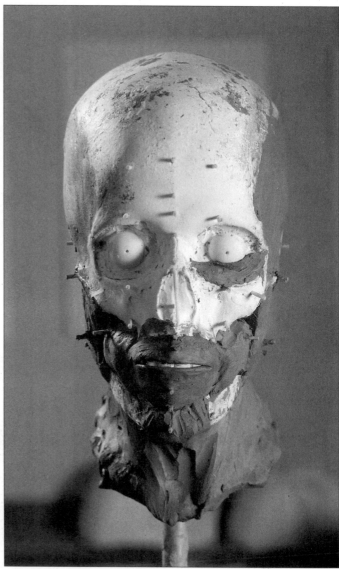

There was no police hunt for her and, apparently, no-one to weep for her. She simply became just another statistic in an ever-lengthening book.

The police issued further appeals, concentrating once more on people who had one time been resident of the house where the body was buried. Sifting through records they found that an Alan Charlton had once been resident in the bottom flat – the flat from which the off-cut of carpet came that was used to wrap Karen's body. Charlton lived in Bridgewater, Somerset, and had recently been released from a jail sentence for attempting to rape a 55-year-old woman. It was interesting to the police, but inconclusive.

But soon after he was interviewed a TV appeal went out for more information and a young girl who had been at school with Karen came forward. She said a a man

Above: *The model of the skull begins to take shape with wooden skewers inserted to determine the correct depth of flesh and skin. It was a laborious process but one that was to pay enormous dividends.*

caled Idris Ali had boasted that he knew Karen. He was eventually interviewed and, unexpectedly during what the police considered a routine suspect-elimination session, he broke down and confessed: "I killed her. I am sorry."

Ali fingered an accomplice – the attempted rapist Charlton who had been seen by lawmen previously. He also implicated another girl, whose identity was withheld at their subsequent trial, who knew about the killing but escaped prosecution because of what she knew. She was to prove a star witness at the trial of the two men. It turned out that Ali had persuaded Karen to become a prostitute while the two were together at a school for disadvantaged children. Ali became her pimp and pimp to the other girl, simply known as Miss X at the trial. Charlton came into the scene when he said he could organise porno

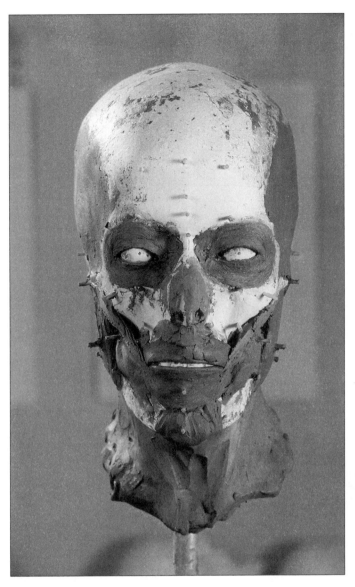

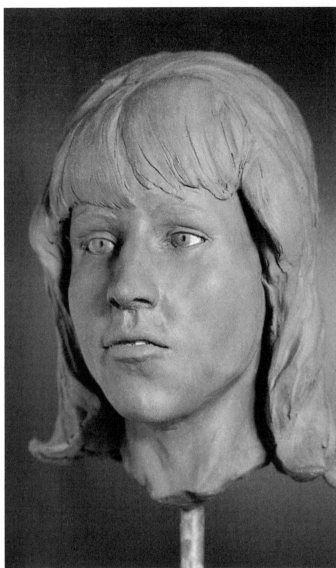

movies and drugs in his basement flat at… Fitzhamon Embankment. The girls would procure the clients and they would all share in the profits.

But something went wrong. Miss X testified that Karen refused to be photographed naked. She quarrelled with the men and Charlton exploded, beating her to death in the basement. Her body was left exposed for four days – hence the bluebottle larvae found on the skeleton – and she was later interred by Ali and Charlton in the back garden. After so many years they figured their secret was safe.

But in a five week trial which ended at Cardiff Crown Court on February 26 1991 justice finally caught up with them when they were jailed for life. After Mr. Justice Hose had sentenced the prisoners he paid special compliments to the unique alliance of law enforcement, forensic and scientific

Above: *Slowly but surely the model began to resemble less a Hallowe'en caricature and more the face of a beautiful girl whose life was brutally and cruelly snuffed out. Finally, this sculpture was unveiled to the world, and the girl who had no dignity in death was finally accorded the full rights of a Christian burial.*

people who had collaborated so unselfishly in the process of finding out the identity of the corpse. Det. Chf. Supt. Williams, who has since left the force, paid particular tribute to Neave, whose masterful reconstruction of Karen's face was, in his opinion, integral in finding out who she was. He said: "I don't know whether we would have done it without him.

"It was of the utmost importance that the identity of the girl was corroborated beyond doubt. That was the first objective. It was a bonus that we were able to charge two people with murder. Co-operation between the police and the forensic experts reached new heights and in my 33 years as a police officer this case was unique."

Karen Price was given a decent, Christian burial. It was, perhaps, one of the few times in her short, sad life that she was truly recognised by society.

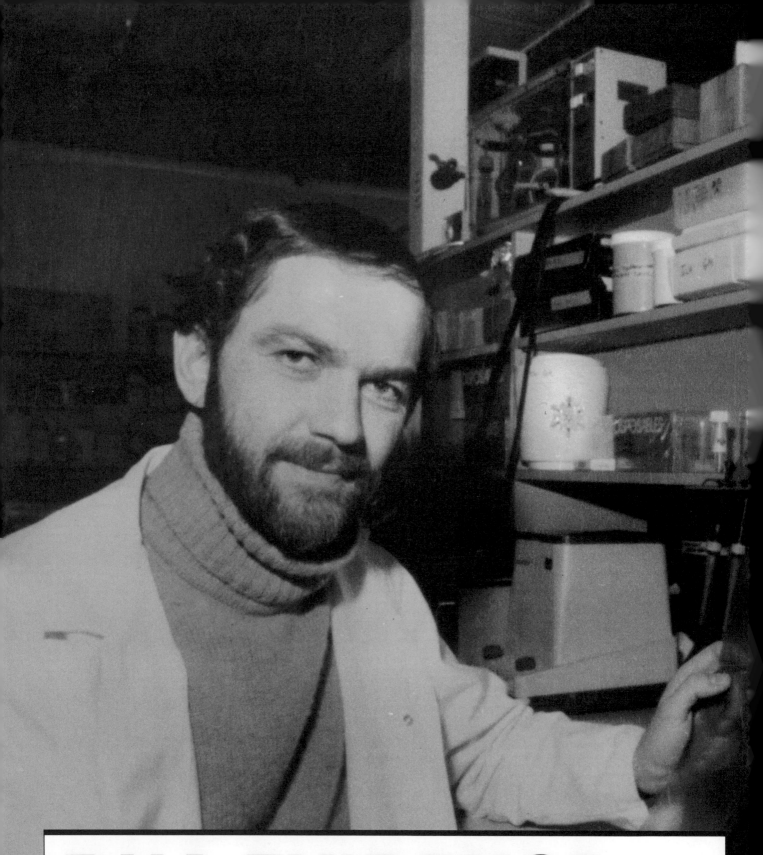

DNA EVIDENCE
Fingering Criminals

Professor Sir Alec Jeffreys of the University of Leicester stumbled upon the miracle of DNA fingerprinting while he was researching another subject. His brilliance has taken away all hiding places for criminals and advanced the detection of crime more than any other single discovery.

It was a revolutionary request that sparked an enormous amount of controversy. It came when police hunting the maniacal killer of two young girls stepped forward to say they would be "fingerprinting" 2,000 men of a single village in a bid to trap their man. But it wasn't fingerprinting in the normal sense, an ink pad and roller to take the dabs of every male over a certain age in the community. This was "genetic fingerprinting", the technique devised by a brilliant university professor that would compare the living tissue of a person with tissue samples found on the two dead schoolgirls.

The human DNA cannot lie and if the police had a match they also had their killer. There were complaints about civil liberty violations, wrangling from a major chemical company which laid claim to the licensing rights on the process and scepticism from certain old-fashioned lawmen who doubted whether such a new-fangled system could ever replace the old tried and

THE HUMAN DNA CANNOT LIE AND IF THE POLICE HAD A MATCH THEY ALSO HAD THEIR KILLER

Opposite: *Professor Sir Alec Jeffreys, discoverer of DNA.*

Below: *Taking a blood sample is all that is needed to begin DNA analysis.*

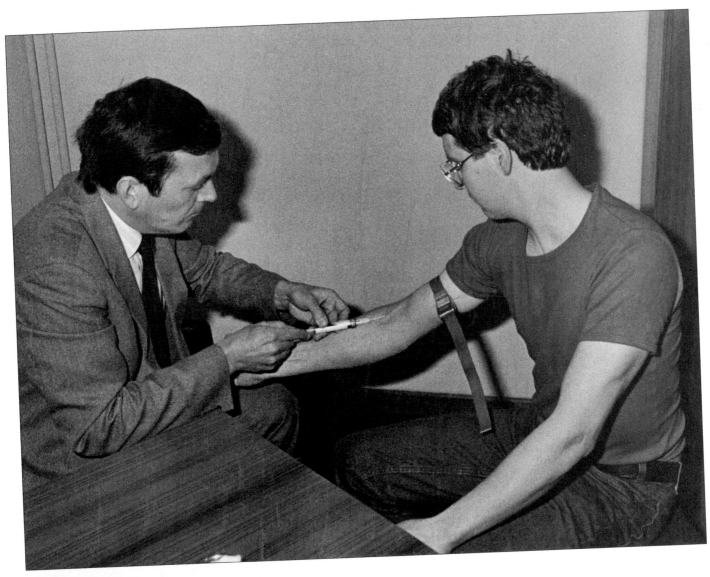

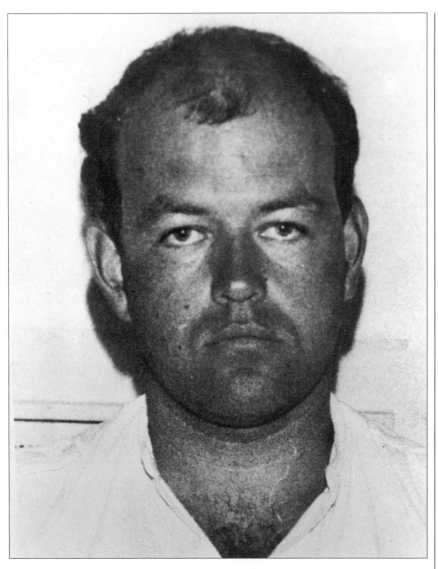

Above: *Colin Pitchfork, the brutal sex killer who sent a man in his place to give blood when he feared that the DNA test would find him out.*

Right: *Dawn Ashworth, one of Pitchfork's victims.*

THE MURDERS WERE OF
SUCH DEPRAVITY THAT
THEY MENTALLY SCARRED
THE INHABITANTS OF THE
REGION FOR YEARS

---

checks through the nationwide police computer to locate sex offenders and child murderers who had been released from jail near to the time of the killing. The enquiry dragged on for months with numerous CID officers manning an emergency incident room, desperately waiting for the one phone call or lead that would set them on the killer's trail. Eventually the investigation, although never closed, was forced to wind down as police manpower was needed for everyday crimefighting.

Three years later came the second brutal killing that bore many of the hallmarks of the first. Dawn Ashworth, also 15, was walking from a friend's home in Enderby to her own on July 31 1986 when she too failed to show up. Her body was found partially covered by hay three days later, near a footpath linking Enderby and Narborough. She too had been raped, but her physical injuries were worse than Lynda's; this time the killer had inflicted much more suffering in his attack.

A post-mortem examination disclosed horrifying injuries to her face, head and private parts. Senior officers at the scene of the crime were certain that the two attacks were linked – that somewhere in their quiet community was dwelling a monster who had urges that could not be controlled.

trusted policing methods. But the test worked 100 per-cent – sending the guilty man to prison for life and ensuring a place for DNA fingerprinting in criminal detection for decades to come.

The murders of the two girls came three years apart in Leicestershire, murders of such brutality and depravity that they mentally scarred the inhabitants of the region for years. Lynda Mann, 15, was the first to die. She set off from her home in Narborough, Leics., to see a friend in the nearby village of Enderby. It was the evening of November 21 1983 and the girls were going to spend an evening playing records and going over their schoolwork. But Lynda never arrived – her body was found the next morning near a footpath, raped and strangled with her own scarf, tied, police said, with "maniacal ferocity". There was a massive police hunt, nationwide appeals for help and the usual cross-

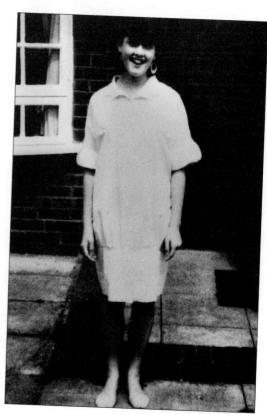

There was another huge manhunt, another mass appeal, anything that could home in on the killer who, the police were certain, was local. His knowledge of the footpaths around the village, near the M1 motorway and just five miles south-west of Leicester, led them to believe he could not be a stranger. Yet he had left no discernible clues at the crime scene... or had he? For in the years that spanned the murders a professor called Alec Jeffreys – later Sir Alec – had literally stumbled upon an astonishing new technique that would have profound consequences for crime and its detection all over the world.

AN ACCIDENTAL MIRACLE

Professor Jeffreys of the University of Leicester stumbled upon DNA fingerprinting while he was researching something else. DNA stands for deoxyribonucleic acid, found in the nuclei of all human body cells. Later Professor Jeffreys would say with characteristic understatement: "Like all good scientific breakthroughs, it was made while searching for something else and shows how important good basic university science is for Britain."

He was working on haemoglobin genes when he discovered that human DNA – the gossamer chemical strands of genetic material that determine individual body characteristics – are unique from person to person. Just as there are no two fingerprints alike, so there are no two specimens of human DNA alike. The possibilities for his discovery became limitless – in learning about the very building blocks of life, in the study of pregnancies and in the application of forensic science. By analysing these sections of DNA, called mini-satellites, a clear genetic fingerprint of a human being can be built up. "From a single drop of blood," said Dr. Jeffreys, "a bar code, unique to an individual, can be made.

"The test is highly accurate and is generally much better than present blood and other tests which often produce inconclusive results." The chiefs of police throughout Britain were not slow in recognising the fantastic potential of his discovery.

Detective Inspector Derek Pearse, leading the investigation into the two murders, first made use of Dr. Jeffrey's remarkable

technique to clear a suspect. Richard Buckland, a 17-year-old youth, was wrongly accused and charged with murdering Dawn. He had been seen hanging around the murder scene and was unable to explain his whereabouts on the night to the satisfaction of police officers. He was dramatically freed when DNA tests failed to link him to the murder because the DNA found on both bodies was the same – and he didn't possess it. It led the police toput into effect plans for the biggest DNA testing ever – across three villages in the area involving 2,000 men. So convinced were they that the killer was local they believed he was bound to be flushed out. Police emphasised that the tests were "purely voluntary" – but it was clear that the finger of suspicion would hover unerringly over those individuals who did not step forward.

Thousands of letters were sent out and testing sites arranged for this unique exper-

Above: Police at the scene of the Lynda Mann murder. It would take an operation unprecedented in the history of crime detection to finally nail her killer.

HE HAD STUMBLED UPON A TECHNIQUE THAT WOULD HAVE PROFOUND CONSEQUENCES FOR CRIME

iment in the science of crime fighting. But before it got off the ground there were problems. The chemical giant ICI claimed it owned the exclusive rights to the test and clearly felt it had expertise to offer.

In a statement in January 1987 the company said: "We know nothing about police plans to use our test. We are very concerned about this. We are the only people who have the right and capacity to carry out wide-scale testing using genetic fingerprinting but Leicester police haven't approached us at all."

ICI had indeed bought the copyright from Professor Jeffreys. There were also disquieting rumbles from some civil liberties quarters who felt personal rights could be trampled on in the mass test. But in time the problems were smoothed over and the government labs at Aldermaston were made ready to receive the tests.

Police wrote to men in the three villages between the ages of 17 and 33. Det. Insp. Pearse said: "The public response has so

Above: *The grieving parents of Dawn Ashworth, with Det. Chf. Supt. David Baker at their side, made a plea for the killer to give himself up.*

Right: *A policewoman dressed in clothes similar to Dawn's strolls near to where her body was found in a bid to jog the memories of potential witnesses.*

THOUSANDS OF LETTERS WERE SENT OUT AND TESTING SITES ARRANGED FOR A UNIQUE EXPERIMENT IN CRIME FIGHTING

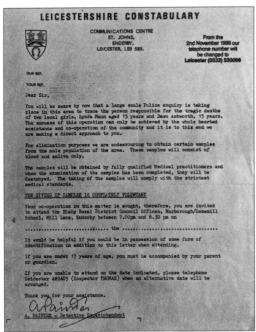

LEICESTERSHIRE CONSTABULARY

COMMUNICATIONS CENTRE
ST. JOHNS,
ENDERBY,
LEICESTER, LE9 5BX.

From the
2nd November 1986 our
telephone number will
be changed to
Leicester (0533) 530066

OUR REF.

YOUR REF.

Dear Sir,

You will be aware by now that a large scale Police enquiry is taking
place in this area to trace the person responsible for the tragic deaths
of two local girls, Lynda Mann aged 15 years and Dawn Ashworth, 15 years.
The success of this operation can only be achieved by the whole hearted
assistance and co-operation of the community and it is to this end we
are making a direct approach to you.

For elimination purposes we are endeavouring to obtain certain samples
from the male population of the area. These samples will consist of
blood and saliva only.

The samples will be obtained by fully qualified Medical practitioners and
when the examination of the samples has been completed, they will be
destroyed. The taking of the samples will comply with the strictest
medical standards.

THE GIVING OF SAMPLES IS COMPLETELY VOLUNTARY

Your co-operation in this matter is sought, therefore, you are invited
to attend the Blaby Rural District Council Offices, Narborough/Danemill
School, Mill Lane, Enderby between 7.00pm and 8.30 pm on

.... the ....

It would be helpful if you could be in possession of some form of
identification in addition to this letter when attending.

If you are under 17 years of age, you must be accompanied by your parent
or guardian.

If you are unable to attend on the date indicated, please telephone
Leicester 482405 (Inspector THOMAS) when an alternative date will be
arranged.

Thank you for your assistance.

A. PAINTER - Detective Superintendent

Left: *The letter sent to the male population in the area around the murder site.*

Below: *Ian Kelly, who had his blood tested in Colin Pitchfork's place.*

far been overwhelming. Hundreds of people have phoned the murder incident room to book a test, including students and servicemen. We haven't had one refusal so far." For some men, the tests were a great weight off their minds – they had become the target of suspicion and innuendo in a small community where neighbour was being turned against neighbour in the witch-hunt hysteria that surrounded the search for the killer. Groups of youths were among those volunteering together, so it could be seen that they were volunteering.

LIVING IN FEAR

But one man who had no intention of volunteering for anything was Colin Pitchfork. Pitchfork, of Littlethorpe – one of the villages earmarked for the test – had much to be afraid of, for it was he who had murdered the innocent schoolgirls to satisfy his perverted lust. A 27-year-old misfit with a history of exposing himself to women, he had been careful at the crimesites not to leave behind any items of clothing or other clues which might possibly lead detectives to his door. Yet he had read the newspapers; he knew that he could not possibly hope to beat the DNA test.

At the bakery where he worked Pitchfork told workmates he had previous convictions for indecent exposure before he married in 1981. He laughed them off, attributing them to high-spiritedness after

drinking, saying he wasn't "a pervert" but merely someone the police were out to get for what he considered a minor crime.

Using that as his theme he began to pester his workmates to step forward in his place. He tried to persuade them that the police would never know that he was at home if they went and gave their sample. "They want to fit me up for what happened before," he told them. "I would be a prime target for the police hoping to pin this on someone." The power of the DNA test was clearly great, even though it had not been performed on him. He offered one young man £50 to go in his place, then another £200. Finally, he persuaded a workmate named Ian Kelly, 23, to go instead and even coached him after hours at the bakery in how to forge his signature and memorise

"extraordinary lengths" to evade justice, but that in the end his partner in the deception had had second thoughts about it.

Judge Mr. Justice Otton had special praise for Dr. Jeffreys' breakthrough, saying: "In this case it not only led to the apprehension of the correct murderer, but also ensured that suspicion was removed from an innocent man.

"Had it not been for genetic fingerprinting, Colin Pitchfork might still be at liberty and that is too terrible a thing to contemplate." Kelly, of Leicester, admitting providing blood and saliva samples to police while pretending to be Pitchfork. He admitted conspiracy and was jailed for 18 months, suspended for two years. Pitchfork had told police that he never intended to murder the two girls – merely to achieve a sexual thrill by exposing himself to them.

certain details of his family life. On January 22 1986 Kelly stepped forward at the incident room pretending to be Colin Pitchfork. His blood sample was taken and the name of Colin Pitchfork was removed from suspects in due course when it was found that his DNA did not match that found at the murder scene.

But Kelly, essentially a decent young man who was cajoled and pressurised into taking the test, began to have his doubts. He talked it over among workmates who also thought that Pitchfork's reluctance might be based on more than a mere suspicion that the police were after him for previous convictions of exposing himself.

One of these workmates went to police and told them of the deception. A police squad swooped that night and both men were arrested. As he was being taken into custody it dawned on police that only Pitchfork and one other man, excused from giving a sample for medical reasons, were the only ones who did not respond to their appeal for help. And when a sample of Pitchfork's blood and hair was sent off for analysis it linked him to both murders, murders which he could no longer deny.

He appeared at Leicester Crown Court a year later where he was sentenced to two terms of life imprisonment and concurrent terms for the sexual assaults on the girls, plus conspiracy to pervert the course of justice. Mr. Brian Escott-Cox, QC, prosecuting, told the court that he had gone to

Both were random attacks that went wrong. He became highly aroused, raped them then killed them to prevent identification.

After Pitchfork's conviction, the potential for genetic fingerprinting leaped onwards. Police may soon have genetic "photofits" at their disposal, predicting the sex, race, hair and eye colour of suspects from forensic samples. Dr. Jeffreys said that rapid advances in molecular genetics means that semen, blood or even tiny traces of saliva from the scene of a crime could reveal their owner's characteristics. DNA profiles are anonymous at present – it is impossible to tell if samples are from a teenager or a 50-year-old.

AN IMPERFECT SOLUTION

But Dr. Jeffreys said that "decoding" a person's genetic make-up would lead to even more clues. He said: "Criminal investigations where DNA evidence is available will frequently flounder due to the lack of a suspect. The sex of an individual can already be determined by a simple method of DNA analysis, but that is about it.

"Some of the difficulties scientists face include height, which is partly due to genetic make-up but also partly due to environment. It's not as simple as saying: 'Here's a band on the DNA fingerprint so their nose will be a certain number of centimetres long.' There might be a case for keeping the profiles of previous offenders. In the end it will come down to assessing whether such a database would be cost effective." Soon, very soon, what Dr. Jeffreys calls "fantastically small" amounts of DNA could lead to full genetic profiles. It means a kidnapper who licks the stamp for his ransom demand could be caught by the minute spittle left on it. Such is the power of the discovery that Dr. Jeffreys stumbled on by accident!

Now both the Home Office and the FBI in America are considering a DNA database that would span both countries. A database of all previous sex offenders – given that a high proportion of them re-offend after release from jail – might be the logical course to pursue. Dr. Jeffreys makes the point that had there been one in effect when Pitchfork was around, "we would have caught him, the Yorkshire Ripper and every rapist and murderer when there is

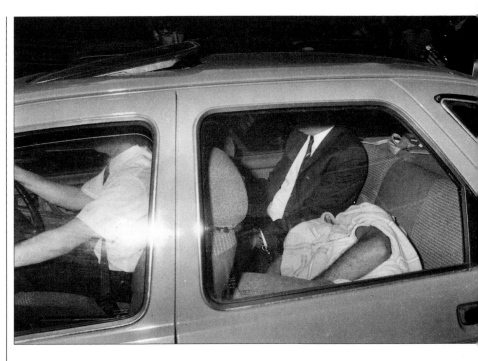

Above: *Colin Pitchfork, his head hidden under a blanket, is driven away from a court hearing. He was eventually sentenced to life.*

Opposite Top: *Yorkshire Ripper, Peter Sutcliffe (extreme right), might have been caught more quickly if DNA had been in existence when he was on the loose in the 1970s.*

Opposite Below: *A smiling killer in a morning suit – Colin Pitchfork on his wedding day in 1981.*

GIVEN THE POTENTIAL OF DNA TESTING, THE ONLY CRUCIAL QUESTION IS HOW FAR HUMAN CURIOSITY WISHES TO GO

---

plenty of biological evidence but no suspect". The civil liberties arguments against such a database appear groundless when it is considered that the genetic code reveals absolutely nothing about a person.

"There is no way a bureaucrat could divine anything about you other than the fact that the material came from you – the anonymous nature of these patterns is vital," said Dr. Jeffreys.

Since the success in the murders case the number of applications for DNA tests have multiplied; in the first 18 months following the case he was besieged by immigrant families imploring him to DNA-test their families to establish relationship. "Settling immigration cases has been wonderful," said the professor. "It is wonderfully worthwhile." It has also been used to determine paternity of a baby in a number of lawsuits, which, he says, "just reveal what squalid and complicated lives some people have".

Given the untold potential of the testing, the only crucial question is how far human curiousity wishes to go. Tests can determine if a person is carrying a defective gene which at 20 could lead to the onset of a fatal disease at 40 or 50. "Do people really want to know about these time bombs inside them?" he asked.

Yet whatever the future applications, Leicestershire police and the people of that county have cause to be eternally grateful to him for putting behind bars a man who deserved no place in decent society.

SILENT WITNESSES
The Maggot Murder

A bleached skull and some rotting bones… nothing to give a clue to detectives with regard to who might have killed the victim whose gravesite they were now gathered around. But an honest army of silent witnesses, in the shape of loathsome, writhing maggots, would finally capture the killer.

A pathologist must have a strong stomach as well as steady nerves when it comes to carrying out his or her extraordinary duties. Corpses are rarely in a pristine state – decomposition makes them stink to high-heaven, as well as providing a feeding ground for insects of every kind. This very "unpleasantness" is used now in certain crime-prevention programmes in America. In Columbus, Georgia, for example, first-time drug offenders have to sit through full-blown criminal autopsies. Many of them can cope with the dissection of the body – the removal of the heart, liver, brain for examination – but those who faint invariably do so because of the stench of decomposition, or at the sight of creepy-crawlies that have wormed their way into the cadaver.

But to trained experts these parasites seeking food and refuge in a corpse are sometimes a welcome sight. Their very presence can render up a wealth of clues as

TO TRAINED EXPERTS, PARASITES SEEKING FOOD AND REFUGE IN A CORPSE ARE SOMETIMES A WELCOME SIGHT

Opposite: *Maggots feasting on a human skull.*

Below: *Police search Bracknell Woods for clues to the corpse in The Maggot Murder.*

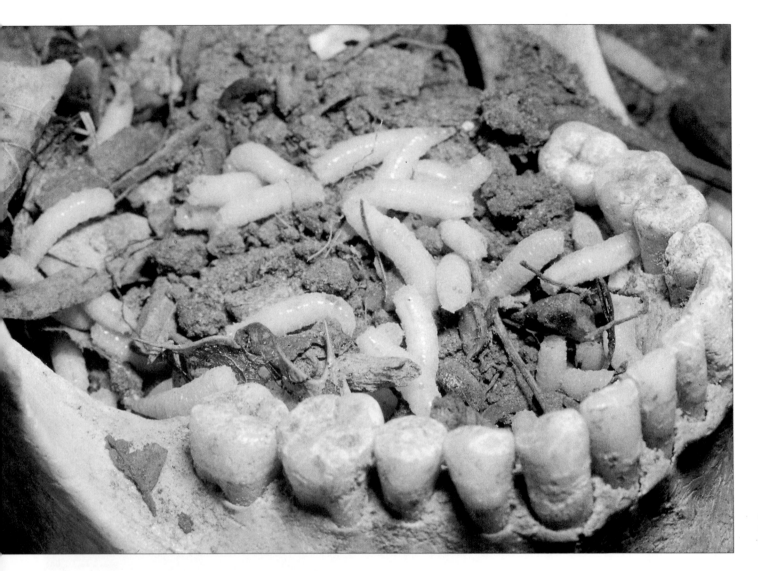

Above: *Maggots writhe between the teeth of the victim's skull. They would hold the key to solving the otherwise baffling case.*

THOSE WRIGGLING, WHITE, FAT BODIES LIVING WITHIN THE CORPSE WOULD PROVIDE THE KEY TO THE KILLER

to when the person died, how long they had been exposed to air before death and even provide clues as to where the murder may have taken place. In June 1964 Britain's foremost Home Office pathologist Professor Keith Simpson began his examination of a maggot-infested corpse. The stench was terrible, the state of the body lamentable. But never was an expert more glad to see those wriggling, white, fat bodies living within the corpse... visitors who would provide the key to the killer.

Two 13-year-old boys out for a day's fishing near Bracknell Woods in Berkshire on June 28 of that year paused before going to the riverbank to look for a small, dead animal that might be maggot-infested. Paul Fay and Tony King had done this countless times before, seeking out a pigeon or a rabbit, maybe a starling, that had been long dead and ripe for larvae. As they cut through the dry undergrowth they saw an unusual sight – maggots writhing on a mound of grass when usually they had to sweep aside leaves or undergrowth to get to the object which they fed off.

It was quite a find and would save the boys plenty of time in their quest for live bait. Yet as they started to collect the maggots, they pulled away the turf to reveal a semi-rotted human arm with a hand still attached to it that suddenly flopped out of the hole. Running out of fear and shock the boys bolted to the nearest police station. Their fishing trip abandoned, the maggot site became a murder investigation within 30 minutes.

Detective Chief Superintendent Arthur Lawson was disturbed at his home shortly after his Sunday lunch that day. The chief of the Berkshire CID, he supervised the careful removal of the corpse from its shallow grave. The body was that of a fully-grown man, fully clothed, lying on his back, the head wrapped in towelling. Scenes-of-crime officers – SOCOS in police parlance – were unable to garner much evidence from the actual gravesite. There were no tyre tracks visible through the vegetation on the soft earth to indicate how the body was brought there; no weapons, glasses or other pieces of clothing that might have belonged to the unfortunate victim's murderer were found either.

Lawson speculated from the state of the body that it might have been several weeks old, but Professor Simpson – who had also been disturbed from a post-lunch snooze in his garden – surprised him by deducing that the body was no more than 12 days old at the most. "It is astonishing how quickly maggots will eat up the flesh," he said. "I have seen a body reduced to this state in as little as ten days."

THE EXPERT'S VIEW

It became clear that the forensic evidence offered up by the cadaver would be of supreme importance – both in identification and in any prosection of the perpetrator of the crime. Professor Simpson described the maggots in his autobiography *Forty Years of Murder*.

"I thought it safe to assume the maggots were larvae of the bluebottle Calliphora erythocephalus, but I preserved samples because the maggots of other flies of the calliphorine type, with slightly different hatching times, are not dissimilar to the naked eye. The ordinary life history of the bluebottle is quite simple: the eggs are laid in daylight, usually sunlight, and in warm weather they hatch on the first day.

"The tiny 'first instar' maggot sheds its skin after eight to 14 hours, and the second instar after a further two to three days. The third instar, the fisherman's maggot, feeds voraciously for five or six days before going into a pupa case. The larvae I was looking at were mature, indeed elderly, fat, indolent, third-stage maggots, but they were not in pupa cases. Therefore I estimated that the eggs had been laid nine or ten days earlier. Adding a little more time to allow for the bluebottles getting to the dead body, I reckon death had occurred on the 16th or the 17th of June.' The maggots were to play a vital role in the case.

Due to the extreme fragility of the corpse, Professor Simpson decided to do some of his autopsy at the site, fearing that the body might break up in transit. Tell-tale small pools of blood either side of the head and a similar pool inside the voice box – coupled with the detection of crushed bones in the larynx – told him that the man had died with a vicious blow to the windpipe, perhaps more than one.

Back in the laboratory the remains yielded other data: he had broken his left arm when he was young and the fracture had not set properly and the skeleton measured 5ft 3ins. Now it was a question of matching the remains to a person – which was where Professor Simpson left off and the police came into their own again.

Below: *The decomposing body of Peter Thomas, a man who found justice through the maggots which feasted on his remains.*

Above: *The bluebottle fly, whose larvae hatched on the body of Thomas, thereby providing the forensic expert with invaluable clues as to his death.*

Opposite Top: *Dr Keith Simpson, the undisputed genius of British forensic science. His expertise would crack the mystery of The Maggot Murder.*

Opposite Bottom: *Dr Simpson in his usual pose, crouching down at a crime scene – this one is the infamous Haigh 'acid bath' murders.*

As with all murders the immediate checks are with missing persons. Chief Supt. Lawson checked with the central office for such information – then, as now, Scotland Yard. The missing persons bureau highlighted the fact that a Peter Thomas had vanished from his home in Lydney, Gloucestershire, on June 16.

A Scotland Yard "heavyweight" detective, Superintendent Horace Faber, had been down to the countryside at the request of the local constabulary to help out on the disappearance. When he learned that there might be a link between the missing person and the corpse that had turned up in the woods 100 miles away he attached himself to the crime squad.

Thomas matched the characteristics of the corpse. He was listed as being the same height as the cadaver, he had broken his left arm in childhood and, more importantly, he had a criminal record. Simpson was telegraphed to take fngerprints off of the decaying flesh of the corpse. They established beyond doubt that the corpse which had become a feast for maggots was indeed that of the man from Lydney. The police now had identity and cause of death – it was time to concentrate on the killer and the motive for the violent end.

Enquiries soon discovered that Thomas had been living a life on the edge of poverty in a wooden bungalow. The scene at his home was one of bachelor untidiness writ large – half-eaten meals, uncleaned plates, empty soup tins everywhere. He was receiving unemployment benefit, although a police search of the unkempt property revealed that, some years earlier, he had been in receipt of the not-insubstantial sum of £5,000 in an inheritance, left to him by his father in his will when he died three years earlier. The money was loaned to a Thomas Brittle, a heating-radiator salesman of Hook, Hampshire.

More significantly, paperwork revealed that "this debt shall be repaid no later than the 30th of June 1964". The instinct of hardened policemen was aroused by the coincidence that the due date of the loan repayment fell in the same month that the man was murdered. Suspicion fell upon the Thomas Brittle to whom the money had been loaned – loaned, it later turned out, against the advice of Thomas' lawyer who said it was a "bad prospect".

Detectives learned that Brittle had advertised in a newspaper seeking investors for an agricultural project – namely that he would pay 12-and-a-half per-cent for six months to anyone willing to offer up the cash. Thomas did – and it was to cost him his life. Brittle was questioned, cautioned, and arrested for the murder – despite the lack of evidence against him.

LIES AND ALIBIS

In custody he admitted that he had gone to Lydney on June 16 – the day of the dead man's disappearance. He said that he had repaid the money – although, of course, it was not to be found in Thomas' modest bungalow, nor at the crime scene. He said he had won the repayment cash on the horses at Epsom, although could not give to police the names of the winning steeds. There was no forensic on his clothes, on his car or on any of his possessions to link him to the murder. And he produced a hitch-hiker to swear that he had picked him up en route to pay back the money. "I ask you, would I have given a lift to someone if I was on my way to kill him?" he asked police with a look of wide-eyed innocence.

Police had expected to find at least a trace of evidence in the car. Crimes of violence are always about an exchange

between parties, whether of bodily fluids, blood or tissue. The criminal and the victim tend to leave traces – however microscopic – of their presence. Yet on Thomas' body there was nothing connected to Brittle. The case dragged on for months – then there came a break. A Dennis Roberts, who lived in Gloucester, stepped forward to say he had seen Thomas at Gloucester bus station on June 20 – a date he was certain of because he was on strike for the first time in his life from the fabrics factory where he worked. This information seemed to clear Brittle – he had the testimony of the hitch-hiker to back him up that he had been going to see him four days previously. If he was still alive four days later, how could he be the culprit?

In the end, it came down to the workings of the maggots – those silent but ravenous guardians of the corpse – which would determine guilt or innocence.

Professor Simpson was working in his laboratory when Faber of the Yard came to see him about the testimony of Roberts. "Is it possible he was killed on the 20th and was only dead for eight days?" Faber asked Simpson. "No it isn't," answered the expert. "And I am ready to stand up to severe cross-examination on the point if it comes to trial."

To back up his verbal assurance Professor Simpson attached a note to the Director of Public Prosecutions, on whom the decision rested as to whether to bring Brittle to trial. It read: "I have today been shown a copy of a statement by Dennis John Roberts to the effect that on Saturday, 20th June, he saw a man whom he recognised as Peter Thomas at a bus station.

"The condition of the body when examined in the wood suggested in the first instance, while still at the scene – 'some nine or ten days, possibly more' – was a minimum period. Nothing in the post-mortem state of the body suggested any special conditions likely to have accelerated the ordinary process of maggot infestation and disintegration of the body. I have had considerable experience in the timing of death and would regard Dennis Roberts' statement as being wholly inconsistent with my findings." Professor Simpson was prepared to swear on the writhing larvae of the bluebottle fly against the word of a defence witness.

The DPP passed on the prosecution – he felt there was not enough evidence to convict Brittle. However, a jury at the inquest returned an extraordinary verdict – "that Thomas had been murdered by a person around about the 17th of June". And in a rider they named that person as Brittle. The Coroner then had no choice but to commit Brittle into custody while a reluctant DPP pressed ahead with his prosecution – a prosecution in which he hoped writhing maggots would make the star witnesses!

The counsel for the defence in the case was the redoubtable Quintin Hogg, later to become Lord Hailsham, the Lord Chancellor. Professor Simpson knew he

PROFESSOR SIMPSON WAS PREPARED TO SWEAR ON THE WRITHING LARVAE OF THE BLUEBOTTLE FLY

IN THE END THE JURY DECIDED THAT THE MAGGOTS WERE MORE RELIABLE THAN THE DEFENCE WITNESS

"NOTHING IN THE STATE OF THE BODY SUGGESTED CONDITIONS LIKELY TO HAVE ACCELERATED MAGGOT INFESTATION"

to hatch, and the three stages of maggot instar to develop before pupation.

I added up the times and in court said, as deliberately and as purposefully as I knew how: 'I had no doubt that this man had been dead some ten days.' Nine or ten was a minimum." He also supplied expert testimony on the blow or blows which killed the dead man – in his opinion karate-chop type strikes to the throat, such as might be administered by someone who was an expert in unarmed combat. And the defendant, it turned out, had taken Commando training in the British Army and had learned such manoeuvres...

Professor Simpson was too much of an expert to doubt – even for Quintin Hogg, who asked no further questions of him. He tried to shake the prosecution evidence about the maggots from Professor McKenny-Hughes, a specialist in insects. He hoped this eminent entomologist would be able to refute the testimony about the maggots, but he only reinforced the pathologist's opinion. When asked if the flies might have been laying their eggs at midnight rather than midday the academic replied: "Oh dear me no. No self-respecting bluebottle lays eggs at midnight. At midday, perhaps, but not at midnight."

The trial took place nine months after Brittle was arrested. The prosecution made much of the fact that time had blurred the memory of the man who had allegedly seen the dead man at the bus stop. But Dennis Roberts was not to be dissauded from his initial testimony and the jury, after a five day trial, had to decide upon the unreliable sighting or the expert testimony of Professor Simpson. They decided the maggots were more reliable and Brittle was given a life sentence for murder.

Professor Simpson said: "The case was particularly satisfying to me. My insistence on the timing of death has become pretty well known, to the police, to the Director of Public Prosecutions, the lawyers – and the Press, who would have scented a public disgrace for me if I had been wrong."

Legal expert James Staniford added this postscript: "It was an extraordinary victory for forensic expertise, indeed a landmark case, presented in such a way so as not to baffle the jury and allow them to come to the right conclusion about a particularly cold-blooded murderer."

would be given a hard time in the witness box by this courtroom expert, but he was convinced that the maggots had to have been there before the time Roberts swore he saw the victim alive at the bus station.

CLEAR EVIDENCE

In his autobiography he recounted: "When I was examined by the crown counsel, Ralph Cusack, I set out as clearly and as briefly as I could the nature of the fat, third instar maggot, not yet pupated, yet plainly having passed the growing-up stages from the day the eggs hatched. I further set out the several periods of time that it took eggs

Above: The counsel for the defence in the case was the redoubtable Quintin Hogg, later to become Lord Hailsham, the Lord Chancellor.

GORDON HAY
Marks of Death

From the horrifying condition of her dead body, it was obvious that 15-year-old schoolgirl Linda Peacock had fallen prey to a savage beast. There were few clues left at the murder scene to aid police… but, thanks to teethmarks that had been left on the corpse, justice was eventually done.

They found the girl in a cemetery, her violated body lying between two graves and beneath the shadow of a fully grown yew tree. The little town of Biggar, midway between Edinburgh and Glasgow, was not used to such depraved murder. The girl, later identified as 15-year-old Linda Peacock, had not been raped during the frenzied assault on her on the night of August 6 1967, but her clothing was pushed up to expose her breasts. When police were called to the murder scene the next morning they began the usual hunt for clues – the search for minutiae which even the cleverest criminal must leave behind at the site of a crime.

There was little to make the scene of crime officer and the pathologist happy about the possibility of finding who had done this to the poor victim. But then a veteran police sergeant noticed the strange bruising around the right breast and took photographs of it. Detective Sgt. John Paton had attended dozens of murder scenes, arsons, rapes and break-ins during his 20 years on the force. There was something about the bruising which made him convinced that it was a human bite, although it did not have the usual teeth outline. It was he alone who had grasped the significance of the wound – and a good job he did. For in doing so the case of Linda Peacock went into the criminal history books because her killer was the first ever to be caught by his teeth.

Criminal odontology – the study of teeth in relation to crimes and criminals – was a relatively murky area to British experts in the 1950s. The Scandinavians seemed to lead the world in research and the application of the new science in relation to crime solving. Teeth, it was learned, largely thanks to the expertise of Swedish expert Gosta Gustavson – have many of the properties of fingerprints when it comes to individual characteristics. Together with his wife Anna Greta he had also discovered it was possible to divine the age of a corpse by careful microscopic investigation of molars. Yet there had never been a conviction in a British court based solely on teeth identification the way there had been with

SOMETHING ABOUT THE BRUISING CONVINCED DETECTIVE SGT. JOHN PATON THAT IT WAS A HUMAN BITE

Opposite: *Linda Peacock's body, covered by tarpaulin in the graveyard where it was discovered.*

Below: *Bitemarks would lead to the killer of innocent schoolgirl Linda.*

Above: *Police at the Peacock murder scene undertaking the usual hunt for clues. But clues were in short supply in this case.*

WHEN LINDA PEACOCK'S BITEMARKS WERE ANALYSED FURTHER IT SET IN MOTION A BRILLIANT CRIMINAL INVESTIGATION

Right: *Twenty years before the Hay case, a vampire killer had spread terror across London, claiming five victims.*

Daily Mirror — FRI MAR. 4 1949 — ONE PENNY — No. 14,098 — Registered at G.P.O. as a Newspaper

FORWARD WITH THE PEOPLE

VAMPIRE— A MAN HELD

THE Vampire Killer will never strike again. He is safely behind bars, powerless to lure victims to a hideous death.

This is the assurance which the *Daily Mirror* can give today. It is the considered conclusion of the finest detective brains in the country.

The full tally of the Vampire's crimes is still not known.

It may take squads of police many weeks yet to piece together full details of the murderer and his ghastly practices. So far five murders are attributed to him. They are:—

Dr. Archibald Henderson;

Mrs. Rosalie Mercy Henderson, his wife;

Mr. Donald McSwan;

Mrs. Amy McSwan, his wife; and

Mr. Donald John McSwan, their son.

The police believe that Donald McSwan, junior, was the first of the Vampire's victims—in 1945—followed two months later by his parents.

Dr. and Mrs. Henderson are known to have disappeared in February of last year.

Genteel

Hour after hour, before relays of detectives and shorthand writers crowded into the buff-painted interrogation room of a London police station the Vampire has been questioned.

Drinking mug after mug of strong police tea—but never forgetting to crook his little finger genteelly away from the coarse china —the Vampire has shown himself a most ... easy mannered.

He wears a quiet suit, of immaculate cut, with a discreet tie. His hair is sleekly brushed, his nails well-kept.

From the interrogation room he has now gone back ...

No. 79—room of horror

In tins, bags and little parcels, detectives bring specimens from the back-basement of 79, Gloucester-road, London, S.W., in which the McSwans are believed to have been slain. Police digging found false teeth in the floor.

Held captive for a month?

Made to sign alibi notes, says brother

AFTER killing Dr. Henderson, the Vampire is believed to have kept Mrs. Henderson alive for at least a month writing letters—and signing typewritten letters—to relatives and friends.

When the Vampire thought himself safe, Rosalie Mercy Henderson followed her husband to a ghastly death.

This theory is held by her brother, Mr. Arnold Henry Burlin, 35, hotelier, of Arnfield-road, Withington, Manchester.

"I am convinced," he told the *Daily Mirror* last night, "that my sister was kept under duress for at least a month before she was shot and her body disposed of.

"During that time I believe she was forced to sign typewritten letters posted in different parts of the country to allay any suspicions of mine."

Dr. and Mrs. Archibald Henderson disappeared in February 16, 1948.

But on February 27 Mr. Burlin received a letter from his sister, saying they were going to Glasgow.

He continued to receive letters until March 21.

A letter followed every phone call Mr. Burlin made to one of his sister's friends, asking for news and talking about ...

Mrs. Rosalie Henderson

fingerprints and blood groups. When Linda Peacock's bitemarks were analysed further it set in motion a brilliant criminal investigation which would change that.

Dr. Warren Harvey, Scotland's leading expert in forensic odontology and lecturer to the Scottish Detective Training School, was the first to inspect Sgt. Paton's photographs. He concurred that the marks on her breast were indeed of teeth and human ones at that. Yet there was a troublesome aspect to their location; it seemed from examination of the corpse – she had been strangled and the bite was inflicted just moments after death – that the bite had come from behind. It would have taken an act of some considerable contortion, but was not impossible. The only formidable task was finding a man whose teeth matched the indentations of the bite.

INITIAL SUSPICIONS

Chief Superintendent William Muncie of the Lanarkshire CID handled the police investigation while Dr. Harvey enlisted specialist help from further afield. The crime bore all the classic hallmarks of an attempted sexual assault that had gone wrong. He believed that the girl had been approached for sex, she had resisted and in doing so had sealed her fate. Such crimes are in the category of "opportunist" and are rarely planned; Muncie was certain, therefore, that he was looking for a local man with a knowledge of the area and, obviously, the girl. He and his officers spent ten days interviewing all 3,000 men in the locality and, to a man, they all had alibis and were eliminated from the enquiry.

The only place he hadn't been to was a nearby borstal for young offenders where 29 apprentices-in-crime were

undergoing incarceration and training in the hope that they would go straight. Dr. Harvey said to Muncie: "It seems as if your enquiries are now winding down in regards to local males on the outside – perhaps it would be prudent for me to ask you to check the teeth of those inside. I think that dental casts should be made of all the inmates." Each boy inside signed a form which read: "I have been told that this is in relation to the investigation into the death

Below: *Police chiefs William Muncie (left) and Det. Insp. Weir pore over maps of the murder area in their hunt for the killer.*

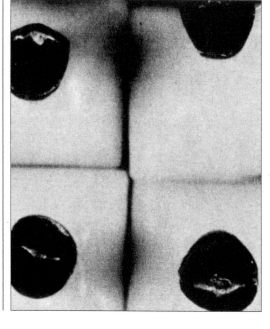

Left: *Professor Keith Simpson, Britain's most eminent criminal pathologist, played a key role in the investigation.*

Right: *Copper plate models of Gordon Hay's teeth, clearly illustrating the pits which would trap him.*

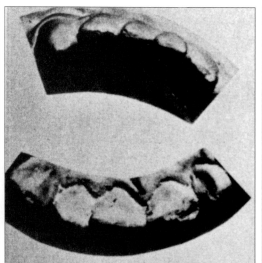

Left: *Casts of Hay's upper and lower teeth, vital links in the chain of evidence that led to him being fingered as the girl's killer.*

of Linda Peacock. It has been made clear to me that I can refuse to comply with the test. It has also been made clear to me that should my dental impressions be linked with other evidence in the case they may be produced as evidence."

The boys in the borstal, aged between 14 and 17 – none of whom possessed a particularly high IQ – all volunteered for the project which, if nothing else, gave them a day out from their drab surroundings. At Glasgow's Dental Hospital, plaster casts were made of each one's teeth. Experiments then began trying to match individual teeth to the marks found on the girl's breast. The largest mark was a very dark oval, about 13mm by 7mm, and there were four smaller ones.

Dr. Harvey later said: "I examined the casts with Detective Inspector Osborne Butler of the Identification Bureau of Glasgow Police. Several were instantly recognisable as being useless to the case because they possessed no jagged teeth capable of inflicting the marks. I decided to call in the aid of another expert."

The expert he called upon was Britain's most eminent criminal pathologist and forensic expert – Professor Keith Simpson – who listed the notorious Haigh acid bath

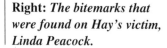

EXPERIMENTS THEN BEGAN, TRYING TO MATCH INDIVIDUAL TEETH TO THE MARKS FOUND ON THE GIRL'S BREAST

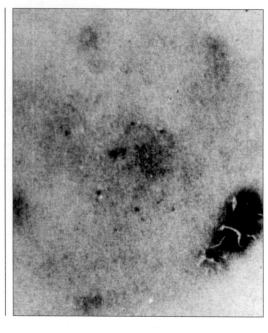

Right: *The bitemarks that were found on Hay's victim, Linda Peacock.*

murders as one of his celebrated cases. Increasingly, Professor Simpson had been at the forefront of advancing the scientific application of forensic odontology into crime solving. He was a great friend of the Swedish expert Gustavson and had given evidence on the importance of teeth and their value as a source of clues at a number of trials and inquests.

At his base in Guys Hospital, London, Professor Simpson and Dr. Harvey made new casts of resin, which were tougher, and whittled the 29 boys down to five major suspects. From the resin casts they made models capable of "occlusal" movements – that is, capable of biting in much the same way as a living human. A female body was brought from the morgue and tests were begun. Initially, Simpson had concurred

Above: *Guys Hospital, London, where expert analysis led to the teeth which belonged to the killer of Linda Peacock.*

LEFT ON THE PROFESSOR'S NAIL WERE MARKS IDENTICAL TO THOSE THAT HAD BEEN FOUND ON THE DEAD GIRL

with Harvey that one particular cast labelled No.14 – the experts were not provided with names – was the prime suspect, but tests ruled him out completely. Starting from the beginning again, all 29 casts were examined under the most stringent scientific conditions. Attention focussed on two curiously shaped abrasions – abrasions which no-one believed could have been made by teeth; there was certainly no such mention of them in Gustavson's "Bible" *Forensic Odontology*.

But later, re-examination of the teeth of suspect No.11 turned up something definite. Dr. Harvey pressed the upper and lower right canines of the cast into his thumbnail for several seconds and with considerable pressure; when he released them, left on the base of the nail were

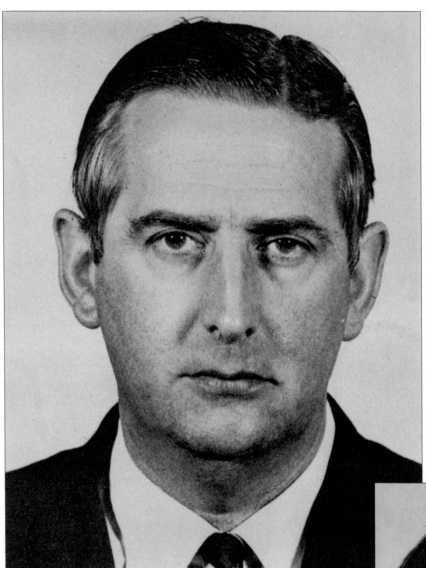

was not so far fetched as it might seem. The mark of the ligature round her neck was most pronounced in the front and least at the back, showing she had been strangled from behind. Blood in front of her left ear, from one of her head wounds, had clotted while she was vertical. Her left wrist had been tied with a piece of string – burned off after death, leaving a scorch-mark and a blister – and her arm had probably been held behind her. And, although Harvey and Butler did not yet know it, mud had been observed on the knees of No.11's jeans that night, suggesting he had been kneeling on the ground."

It was five weeks after the murder by the time the final tests had been done and all three members of the scientific team were convinced that Number 11 was their suspect. That coincided with Chf. Supt. Muncie's theories too because he had spent time interviewing the boys and the only one whose alibi he didn't feel comfortable with was his. No. 11 was a callow 17-year-old called Gordon Hay, a hardened petty thief, car stealer and general bad boy who had been in trouble with the law since he

Above: *Det. Supt. Osborne Butler of the identification bureau of the Glasgow police co-operated closely with odontologists on the case.*

Right: *Gordon Hay's teeth-marks condemned him as the killer.*

"THE MAN WHO HAD KILLED HER HAD COME OVER THE GIRL'S SHOULDER WHILE SHE WAS SITTING... HE HAD EXTREME DEXTERITY"

marks identical to those that were found on the dead girl.

Harvey was still concerned about the angle at which the bite marks appeared to have been made. Later, in a scientific paper about the case, he wrote: "Since, to put it mildly, this orientation seemed strange a further attempt was made with the other four models. But apart from the already-discredited No.14, none of the others fitted at all. It was my opinion that the attacker, the man who had killed her, had come over the girl's right shoulder while she was sitting and that he had extreme dexterity."

Professor Simpson, writing of the case years later, said: "The medical evidence showed this

was nine. He was also a compulsive liar, coupled with a feral cunning which alerted him when danger was around. There were no clues to link him to the murder other than the statement of one other boy and Muncie's own hunch. As far as the authorities were concerned, all the boys were tucked up in their beds in the barrack-style dorms when Linda Peacock met her untimely and violent end.

KEY EVIDENCE

The other lad in the dormitory, who remained anonymous due to his age, told Muncie: "On August 6 one of our masters saw Hay in the dining room at about 10.00pm and another one saw him at 10.30pm lying in bed in his pyjamas. But I saw him come through the window. His hair was blown about and he was dirty and sweaty and out of breath. We had heard some screaming from the direction of the cemetery and I couldn't help thinking that he had had something to do with it. The day before he had been allowed out on a good conduct pass and had gone to a local fair where he met a girl. He couldn't stop bragging about her when he came back – said she was a 'nice bit of stuff' and that he would like to have sex with her."

Above and Left: *Linda Peacock – a life of promise lay ahead until she was brutally murdered by a deranged borstal boy. Linda was a gentle soul who loved animals as much as she loved people.*

Above: *Linda's pretty home, a home from which she went missing forever on that fateful night in 1967.*

"CIRCUMSTANTIAL EVIDENCE WAS CLEARLY INSUFFICIENT AND, THEREFORE, THE DENTAL EVIDENCE WAS CRUCIAL"

Muncie's detectives interviewed Hay again but kept back from him the evidence of the youth who had seen him come in the window. He even volunteered to them that he had indeed met the dead girl, but that he was sound asleep when she was killed. There was no hard evidence, just circumstantial, to link him to the crime. Police even made a healthy P.C. run from the crime scene to the borstal to see if it could be done in a couple of minutes; it could.

DISMAL RUMOURS

Yet there was consternation among senior officers, shared by the Procurator Fiscal, that a prosecution would fail without more tangible evidence. Professor Simpson said: "Circumstantial evidence was clearly insufficient and, therefore, the dental evidence was crucial. Harvey and Butler came back to London and showed me the latest results of their work. I encouraged them to make a

more detailed study of Hay's teeth and to prepare scaled 'overlay' transparencies. They fitted the scale bitemark print perfectly – of that there was no doubt."

Dr. Harvey researched deeper and found that minute pits on Hay's teeth could have been caused by drinking water without fluoride added when he was a child. This was significant because in previous criminal cases abroad, bitemark identifications had usually required the identification of five teeth – the team had identified just two. But an examination of government records in Scotland showed that no-one else had more than one pitted-tooth. Professor Simpson felt that all the evidence of his teeth put together would be enough to gain a conviction, adding: "A jury should have no difficulty in understanding this evidence and appreciating its simple strength. It is akin to tool-marking evidence or fingerprints."

The Procurator Fiscal decided to let the prosecution proceed. Hay was arrested and charged with murder and pleaded not guilty when he came before Lord Justice Grant at the High Court of Justice in Edinburgh. His trial lasted nine days, during which Hay vehemently denied having anything to do with the crime. The evidence – medical evidence on the teeth alone amounting to 400 pages of manuscript – would have to speak for itself with the aid of testimony from Dr. Harvey and Professor Simpson.

COOL DEFENCE

It was Professor Simpson who would face the cool, challenging questions from Hay's defence counsel William Stewart, Q.C., who attempted to call up the expertise of Gustavson in defending his client – a case of trying to rescue him by using the evidence of those who would seek to damn him. Professor Simpson later wrote in his autobiography: "When I was in the witness box the defence counsel, as I had expected, quoted from the Swedish expert Gustavson's book, to which I had written a foreword published in an English translation. 'Do you agree with the view expressed inside the book'," asked Stewart, "'that at least four or five teeth, and they say they are adjacent teeth, should correspond exactly before a positive identification can be made?'

"'I think it is a sound view,' I answered, 'but I think probably a better attitude is a general one; that is to say that the more points of comparison that can be pointed to, the more points of proof and the fewer the less certain.'"

Hay sat impassive throughout his trial, paying no heed to the massive press attention or the sketch artists who drew him while he was in the dock. He understood that, on the surface, everything rested on those tooth marks and whether or not a jury would accept such evidence to condemn him to imprisonment. The trial lasted nine days and at the end of it observers thought that the accused man had a singularly smug look on his face, as if he expected to be out that evening.

After deliberating less than three hours the jury returned a verdict of guilty. Hay was attempting to shout at the judge when he was hurried to the cells to begin his detention "at Her Majesty's pleasure". Police commented later that friends of Linda had told them of the borstal boy she had met at the fair, but that she had not been attracted to him. Hay, for his part, was inflamed with lust, particularly at the sight of her well-developed breasts. She had resisted him. In his frenzy and with his agile body, he had lunged at her from behind to leave the signature that would commit him to jail for years.

As part of his summing up, Lord Justice Grant paid special praise to the work of the forensic experts. "Forensic odontology," he said, "as it is called, is a relatively new science. But of course there must be a first time for everything."

Because of Hay's insatiable lust, a lassie had died… and a young man who was supposed to be salvaged from crime had gone into the record books.

IN HIS FRENZY HE HAD LUNGED AT HER TO LEAVE THE SIGNATURE THAT WOULD COMMIT HIM TO JAIL FOR YEARS

Below: *William Muncie, Chief Superintendent of the Lanarkshire CID, handled the police investigation. It was of great comfort to him and Linda's family to know that justice had been done.*

EMMETT-DUNNE
A Deadly Affair

Frederick Emmett-Dunne brought shame upon his British Army uniform. He dallied with the wife of another soldier and when his passion was inflamed, killed his rival. It was almost the perfect murder, but forensic science was to unearth the evil sergeant and ensure a long prison sentence for him.

Post-war Germany for British Army garrison troops was a dismal billet. Rationing was still enforced, the local population was often resentful and the bombed-out towns and cities offered little in the way of entertaining diversions. Life, for the most part, centred on the base itself where the wives of married men became as bored as their husbands in the tiresome duty of policing a defeated nation.

The boredom of one such wife, and the interest shown in her by a sergeant named Frederick Emmett-Dunne, was to lead to murder… a murder the sergeant nearly got clean away with. But 15 months after the lid was closed on the coffin of his rival the body still yielded vital clues – clues a second forensic expert would detect… and finally send Emmett-Dunne to jail for life.

It was early in the morning of December 1 1953 that the body of Sgt. Ernie Watters was found hanging in a barrack block at the Glamorgan Barracks in Duisberg, "discovered" by Sgt. Emmett-Dunne and another man. It seemed from the scene that it was a suicide; on the ground was a bucket which had been turned on its side, indicating that the dead man had stood on it as a makeshift gallows and kicked it aside to allow the rope to tighten around his neck.

There was an Army enquiry followed by an Army inquest which judged that the unfortunate sergeant had taken his own life due to depression – even though all who knew him testified that he was a cheerful man with seemingly little to worry about. He had no money problems, no skeletons in his closet and was an efficient and well-liked soldier.

But Dr. Alan Womack, the pathologist who carried out the post-mortem, added his expert testimony to ensure that a suicide verdict was recorded. Dr. Womack testified that death had come from hanging because of the broken cricoid bone – a bone in the throat just below the thyroid – in his neck. He was wrong, and because of it a murderer walked scot-free.

NO SECRETS

Sgt. Emmett-Dunne had killed him, and even before the ink was dry on the inquest report the rumours began circulating about him. Emmett-Dunne had taken a fancy to Watters' German-born wife Mia some time before and his attentions had not been unrequited. There were snatched brief encounters while her husband was on duty and he was not; excursions to the local cinema and picnics in the rolling countryside.

At dances and other social functions the other members of this insular community tut-tutted at the apparent closeness with which they danced, the glances that lingered too long over the mess table. None of this was presented at the inquest, of course, but six months after the body of Sgt. Watters

Above: *Sergeant Reginald Ernie Watters and his German bride Mia. She later found solace in the arms of another sergeant.*

Opposite: *Military police escort Frederick Emmett-Dunne (centre), as he faces charges of murdering a fellow soldier.*

AN ARMY INQUIRY FOLLOWED BY AN ARMY INQUEST JUDGED THAT THE UNFORTUNATE SERGEANT HAD TAKEN HIS OWN LIFE

Above and Below: *The killer and his black widow – Sergeant Emmett-Dunne acts as escort to the former Mrs Mia Watters.*

had been laid to rest Sgt. Emmett-Dunne married the widow. There were stage whispers of "I told you so" sweeping the camp, and soon they were to come to the ears of the top brass.

The Army decided that perhaps the inquest first time around had been too hasty. Anonymous letters were sent to them informing on the marriage between the widow and Emmett-Dunne. After consultations with the War Office and the Home Office, the Army was informed that it had no choice but to call in Scotland Yard.

By the time Dr. Francis Camps, a distinguished Home Office pathologist arrived in Germany accompanied by two detectives from Scotland Yard, Emmett-Dunne and his new bride were back in Britain, the murder now having happened a full 15 months previously.

Of course, what the police needed was evidence of murder – no rumour in the world would stand up to scrutiny in a court of law, be it martial or civilian, without the foundations of truth to underpin it.

FURTHER INVESTIGATIONS

As the body was disinterred in Germany, Emmett–Dunne was questioned at his new home in Somerset, England, about his relationship with Mrs. Watters before she married him. He sensed the direction the conversation was going in and stormed: "My only crime was marrying before the proper lapse of time prescribed by Victorian morality!" Indeed, there was little the police could do without hard evidence – it was his word against a lot of people who smelled something fishy, but could offer nothing by way of hard fact.

The task facing Dr. Camps from the decomposing remains of Watters was to find evidence of murder. Dr. Womack, who had carried out the first post mortem was a skilled and dedicated pathologist, but it turned out that he was mistaken in deciding that the cause of death was strangulation. Dr. Camps laboured intensively in the Army morgue until he came up with the real cause of Watters' demise.

Where the unfortunate man's voice box had been remained evidence of blood. The small bones of the larynx were crushed and he was able to pick them out one by one like small chicken bones. Such bones would not be broken by a rope's pressure but by the sudden, swift, blow of a hand or blunt object. Perhaps, and most probably, surmised the eminent forensic expert, by a man trained in unarmed combat, like a

commando or other armed forces specialist. Bleeding in the windpipe had caused death within minutes. John Rowland, who made a study of the case in his 1958 book *More Criminal Files*, said: "Mr. Mervyn Griffith-Jones was the prosecutor at Emmett-Dunne's trial. He pointed out that Dr. Womack, though his post-mortem had been carefully and meticulously carried out, had been a comparatively inexperienced pathologist, and had made an error in his interpretation of the facts.

Dr. Camps, who had superintended the exhumation of the body, and had carried out a further and more detailed examination of the remains, was satisfied that death was not due to strangulation followed upon hanging, but to a sudden and severe blow, delivered by the hand of a murderer on the front of Watters' throat."

In April 1955 the police felt they had enough – thanks to the forensic examination of the corpse – to charge Emmett-Dunne with murder, and build a case in which the circumstantial evidence was interwoven with the undeniable expert testimony of Dr. Camps, then probably the most eminent man in his field. Emmett-Dunne was flown back to Germany and charged there on April 15 by a military court. The trial even-

tually opened in Dusseldorf on June 27 with Mr. Griffith Jones outlining the affair which led to murder. He said that the trysting between the two had started at the end of 1952 and had carried on right up until the time of Watters' death.

He centred his case on the behaviour of the accused towards Mrs. Watters while she was still married; how he stayed on the base while Watters took part in an exercise

Above: *Witnesses arrive at Emmett-Dunne's court martial in Dusseldorf to give evidence of his infatuation with Mrs Watters.*

"DEATH WAS DUE TO A SUDDEN, SEVERE BLOW, DELIVERED BY THE HAND OF A MURDERER ON THE FRONT OF WATTERS' THROAT"

Left: *Mr Griffith-Jones, who led the prosecution against Emmett-Dunne, leaves the courtroom in Germany after the suspect was found guilty of murder.*

Emmett-Dunne, said: "I quite understand your theory.' Dr. Camps shot back at him, rather curtly: "It is not a theory; it is straightforward mechanics."

His description of how the blow had been delivered, how he had discovered it due to the exhumation of the body, made it impossible for Emmett-Dunne to plead innocence any longer. Instead of just "finding" the body he now said that he had killed him only after Watters had threatened him with a revolver.

Mr. Curtis-Brown told the court: "Watters had threatened the accused with a .38 pistol, saying: 'You are too big and too cocky in barracks.' Emmett-Dunne, thinking that Watters was about to shoot, had struck the blow that killed him. Then he had panicked and faked the suicide."

Three days into the court martial trial – it was held under Army regulations – 34-year-old Emmett-Dunne took the stand. He said: "Watters had accused me of living with his wife in Cologne when he had been absent on military exercises. I told him that he was talking out of the side of his hat. There was no love affair between me and Mia – that happened later when we met in England.

that he should have been on; how he had enjoyed picnics with her in the countryside; how telephone records at the base showed numerous phone calls to her married quarters whenever duty rosters showed that her husband was away on duty elsewhere. "Shortly before Watters' death," Mr. Griffith-Jones said, "Emmett-Dunne had said to Sergeant Browne that there was a certain person in the barracks who would be committing suicide if his wife did not learn to behave herself. The court might feel that this statement was made to pave the way for the faked suicide which Emmett-Dunne was already planning."

DEMONSTRATIVE EVIDENCE

Dr. Camps called into court several officers trained in the use of unarmed combat, the kind of combat that taught men how to kill with their bare hands. Dr. Camps said: "It is my contention that he actually killed Watters as he was sitting beside him, perhaps in a chair, perhaps in a car." After the soldiers had presented this in court Mr. Derek Curtis-Brown, Q.C., defending

Above: *The beautiful Mia Watters, later to become Mrs Emmett-Dunne.*

"EMMETT-DUNNE SAID... THERE WAS A CERTAIN PERSON IN THE BARRACKS WHO WOULD BE COMMITTING SUICIDE"

Right: *Emmett-Dunne maintained throughout that he was innocent but overwhelming forensic testimony sealed his fate.*

We had been good friends who liked to dance together, that is all.

"There is not a word of truth to what the prosecution has had to say."

But he had not reckoned on the damning testimony of a half-brother, Ronald Emmett, who was living in another part of the barracks. He came forward at the last minute to say that the accused had sent for him at 8.00pm on the night of the murder to say that he had killed a man in an argument. He wanted Emmett to give him an alibi, to say that they had been together all evening. He then led his half-brother over to the entrance to the barrack block where he showed him the corpse of Sgt. Watters hidden under a cape. "He said if we could lift him up," said Ronald Emmett in court, "we could make it look like suicide.

"I refused. I went to bed, but I didn't tell anybody, not until now." Ronald Emmett said he had come forward because of the expertise of the Home Office pathologist. "Once he said that it was a blow to throat," he said, "and not some kind of accident, like the fellow had hit his head like I was led to believe, then I felt I had no choice but to speak up." Emmett-Dunne was indeed back home living in Cheshire when the story of the exhumation and discovery was carried out. He added: "In view of the way events moved I knew I had to come forward with the whole story."

The Army tribunal found Frederick Emmett-Dunne guilty in Germany – which was just as well for him. The death penalty

Above and Below: *Scenes outside the court martial in Dusseldorf where Emmett-Dunne was found guilty of murder.*

was still in force in Britain, but not there. He was therefore sentenced to life imprisonment. Immediately after sentencing he was sent back to Britain to serve time in a maximum security jail among other murderers, robbers and rapists. Mia stood by him, claiming she believed in his innocence and that she was certain he had been in a fight that had gone wrong. But there was too much evidence in the trial for her not to be left with some nagging doubts.

FRUITLESS PLEAS

Back home in England he tried his best to get his sentence altered with petitions to the government of the day and even the Queen. All decided that it was best for him to remain behind bars. The case itself is something of a textbook one for criminal pathologists and forensic experts. Crime writer George Crossen said: "If they had been more discreet in their affair the body of the dead man would never have been dug up. If he had not been dug up Dr. Camps would never have detected the clues of the single killing blow.

"If he had not detected the evidence of the single killing blow Emmett-Dunne would have gotten away with that rare thing – the perfect murder. In the end, he was defeated by a medical science that was far, far more precise than him."

GEORGI MARKOV
Murder by Umbrella

Bulgarian writer Georgi Markov's sensitivites could not cope with the brutal Bulgarian regime he and his countrymen had to endure under communism. He escaped to Britain, to voice his protests to greater effect. But his life was to end in one of the modern era's most notorious assassinations.

Georgi Markov's murder in London is probably the most intriguing and original assassination of this century. Individuals have certainly been killed in numerous and monstrous ways down the years of this turbulent century – shot, stabbed, garroted, hanged, drowned and poisoned – but none reached the heights of Ian Fleming-esque originality and cunning as the fate which befell Bulgarian defector Markov. He was poisoned as he walked down a London street in broad daylight, his fate sealed by a small poisoned capsule delivered into his leg by – an umbrella! The story of his diabolical end is one that continues to fascinate and mesmerise, long after the communist chieftans who plotted his end have themselves passed into history.

A STRIDENT VOICE

Markov, 49 when he died, was a dissident from the orthodox communist regime in Bulgaria who had managed to defect to the West and settle in London. An educated, urbane individual, he had first angered the totalitarian rulers of his homeland in the late 1960s when he still lived there. Before then, he had towed the party line, written the saccharine-sweet prose that praised the glories of communism.

For his efforts he was rewarded with a BMW car, an opulent home and an account with foreign currency that allowed him to buy the best in luxuries that his countrymen could only dream of. Yet Markov was a sensitive, caring individual who eventually woke up to the blind injustices of the regime and decided to take a stand against them. Then he penned a play about a plot to

Opposite: Georgi Markov, victim of one of the most cunning assassinations of the Cold War.

NO ASSASSINATION REACHED THE HEIGHTS OF IAN FLEMING-ESQUE ORIGINALITY AS THAT WHICH BEFELL MARKOV

HE WAS A SENSITIVE, CARING INDIVIDUAL WHO EVENTUALLY WOKE UP TO THE BLIND INJUSTICES OF THE REGIME

Below: London, where Markov began a new life in the early 1970s.

murder a general – a work clearly anti-government and perceived by the dictator-in-residence, Todor Zhivkov, as an incitement to civil unrest.

VICIOUS PERSECUTION

Markov suffered the usual state harassment – loss of privileges, surveillance, warnings – before he escaped to Italy and from there to London, where he was granted political asylum. But if Zhivkov and his minions thought they had heard the last of him they were very much mistaken. Markov got a job with the Bulgarian section of the BBC foreign service. From his office at Bush House in the Aldwych, he transmitted messages back to his enslaved homeland that riled the communist chieftains even more. Soon Markov became the magnificent obsession for Zhivkov, who was determined to silence him… one way or another.

On the morning of September 7 1978, Markov drove from his home in Clapham to

MARKOV BECAME THE MAGNIFICENT OBSESSION OF ZHIVKOV WHO WAS DETERMINED TO SILENCE HIM… ONE WAY OR ANOTHER

Below: *Bush House, where Georgi Markov found employment with the BBC in the 1970s.*

Bush House, but the London traffic was appalling. Markov could not get his car parked anywhere near his office and so ended up putting it in a vacant spot near Waterloo Bridge. He walked to his office, completed a day's work and went back around 6.00pm to retrieve his vehicle to move it nearer to Bush House. After parking it near the Strand he once more set off back towards his office when he felt a sharp stab of pain in the back of his right thigh. He thought it had come from the accidental prod of an umbrella, the wielder of the offending instrument being a man in a bus queue. When Markov turned to face the man he mumbled profuse apologies in a thick, Eastern European accent, and then slipped out of the bus queue to jump into a cab.

Just four days later Georgi Markov would be dead.

Upon getting back to the office his leg had already begun to stiffen up. He showed a colleague what had happened and said: "Look at that! Some fool stabbed me with

an umbrella!" He showed off a wound like a pimple, with purple and red widening out from the centre to the flesh around. But Markov had been mistaken in believing he had been stabbed by the umbrella tip itself. In fact, the brolly contained a highly sophisticated spring-loaded device in the tip which actually shot poison into his leg, like a silent dart gun. Markov stayed on at the BBC to read news and current affairs bulletins at 11.00pm, but he felt increasingly feverish – a condition he put down to flu. But he was too ill to work the following day and his wife Annabella drove him to St. James Hospital in Balham when his temperature soared over 100 degrees.

A STRANGE INJURY

Doctors were puzzled by the puncture wound on his thigh – too big to have come from either a hypodermic syringe or an insect bite – but they did not at first perceive its true significance. His condition continued to worsen as the hours wore on. By the third day he was given massive antibiotic injections to try to counter an alarming rise in the white corpuscle count in his bloodstream. Doctors who registered his white corpuscle count upon entry to the hospital listed it as 10,600. Soon it raced to an "unbelievable" 26,300. But Markov still failed to respond to treatment and on the fourth day he died of a massive heart attack.

It was only because of the suddenness and mysteriousness of his death that a postmortem was needed to determine what had actually killed him. When traces of the poison ricin were discovered the telephones rang in Whitehall's corridors of power. Forensic scientist Dr. Robert Keeley found the tiny metal ball in Markov's leg which had been used to deliver the poison while Dr. David Gaul, of the top secret Chemical Defence Establishment at Porton Down, provided all the information on poisons and antidotes. Scotland Yard's Anti-Terrorist Squad and MI5 were also informed of the findings of the autopsy.

Dr. Keeley found the tiny metal ball only after X-rays had been taken around the area of the puncture wound on the deceased's right thigh. It measured 1.52mm in diameter and was made from an alloy of platinum and iridium, a compound noted for its resistance to corrosion and one which can

Above: *President Zhivkov, Bulgarian ruler at the time of the markov killing.*

THE BROLLY CONTAINED A HIGHLY SOPHISTICATED SPRING-LOADED DEVICE IN THE TIP WHICH ACTUALLY SHOT POISON INTO HIS LEG

only be worked in a high-temperature furnace. The minute sphere was drilled through with two holes that met in a centre well where the poison rested. Dr. Keeley had examined a similar ball sent from Paris once the European intelligence agencies of NATO began co-operating over the disturbing death of Markov. This ball too had been recovered from the body of a Bulgarian defector, Vladimir Kostov, but he had been lucky enough to survive the experience.

A RECIPE FOR DEATH

Dr. Gaul later testified at Markov's inquest in London in January 1979 about the ricin poison. Dr. Gaul said: "Tests have ruled out that he died from any other kind of venom, be it from snakes, scorpions, spiders or marine life. Ricin tests were carried out on a live pig and the symptoms it developed before death were almost identical to those suffered by Mr. Markov before his death."

The ricin poison, he told the inquest, came from the seeds of the castor oil plant which, incidentally, grows in abundance in Bulgaria. "There is no legitimate use for ricin," said Dr. Gaul. "And there is no known antidote."

Mrs. Markov said at the inquest that it was her strong belief that her husband had died at the hands of a foreign assassin

Right: *The assassin's "umberella" contained a sophisticated weapon which was used to inject the poison.*

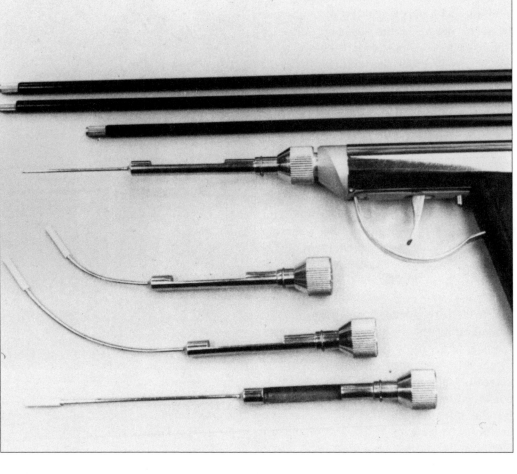

IT STOKED UP THE OLD FEARS OF THE SOVIET COLOSSUS WAITING BEYOND THE HORIZON TO CRUSH ALL OPPONENTS

WHEN THE TRUTH DID COME OUT IT WAS EVERY BIT AS FANTASTIC AS THE THEORIES WOVEN AT THE TIME

working on the orders of the Bulgarian secret police. But Cold War or not, diplomatic niceties had to be maintained. Besides, the operation had been so swift and so well carried out that there was nothing to connect the government of a sovereign country with the murder of a single defector. Whatever Whitehall and MI5 spy-catchers privately thought, in public there was little that could be said or done and, consequently, Markov was recorded by West London Coroner Dr. Gavin Thurston as having been "unlawfully killed".

The papers, however, had a field day. No-one could recall such an audacious murder of an exile in a Western capital. It stoked up the old fears of the Soviet collossus waiting beyond the horizon to crush all opponents and provided endless fodder for polticians, spy writers and right-wingers who spoke menacingly of the Soviet bear waiting to devour us all. Yet it would be many years before the real truth of what happened to Georgi Markov was made public. It would take the collapse of communism in Russia and her satellite states itself. But when the truth did come out it was every bit as fantas-

tic as the theories woven at the time. The mission to eliminate Markov was sanctioned by the head of the KGB himself in Moscow after a request from the paranoid dictator Zhivkov and involved tests on animals and a condemned man.

Details of the assassination were finally revealed by Oleg Kalugin, a Major General in the KGB who was given the task of preparing it by the KGB chairman Yuri Andropov himself. Kalugin, once head of the KGB's counter intelligence branch, was a devoted disciple of the Soviet state. He says he found the task onerous, but that duty meant it was Markov's life… or his.

PRESIDENTIAL HATRED

Kalugin said: "The problem with Markov was raised by the Bulgarians in 1977. Members of their security organisation visited Moscow and told us they had difficulties. Markov was greatly disliked by the Bulgarian president Zhivkov. The president wanted to get rid of him because he was upset by Markov's broadcasts on the BBC's foreign service. They were vehemently anti-communist and anti-Zhivkov. The president felt that Markov's activities were undermining the very foundations of his regime.

"My counterpart in Bulgaria was Vladid Todorov, who regularly came to Moscow to discuss many problems, but he would always end up touching on Markov. At that stage we just listened politely and he went away. But then one day in the spring of 1978 I attended one of our regular meetings with the KGB chairman Yuri Andropov in his office in Moscow. Also there was Vladimir Kyryuchkov, then chief of the intelligence service and later the boss of the KGB, and Vice Admiral Usatov, another senior intelligence official. As the meeting was about to end Kryuchkov said on his own initiative: "We have a request from the Bulgarian interior minister Stoyanov to physically eliminate one of their dissidents, a Mr. Markov. They want us to help them."

A STUNNING REQUEST

"I recall vividly that Andropov was somewhat taken aback. He did not answer straight away. He sat pensively for a while, then he got up and started walking up and down. Then he said: 'You know what? I am against political assassinations. This is not the way to solve our political problems. Let the Bulgarians do it themselves if they wish to. Why should we be involved?' Still walking up and down he ended emphatically: 'I am against it.'

"Kryuchkov, clearly surprised by this negative answer, started cajoling the chairman. 'Mr. Andropov, it is Mr. Zhivkov's request. If we decline to co-operate with the Bulgarians then Mr. Zhivkov might think the Bulgarians are out of favour with the KGB or maybe Mr. Zhivkov is out of favour with the Soviet leadership.

"It is a political problem and we must face it. We cannot simply turn down the Bulgarians' request.'

"Comrade Andropov, who later became president of the USSR, continued walking up and down saying: 'I'm against it.' But he was obviously convinced by the political expediency, and finally he said: 'OK, OK, but I want no direct participation. You provide the weapons, whatever is needed, and give the Bulgarians all the instructions. But then to hell with them. Let them do the final

Left: *Yuri Andropov, head of the KGB, gave the order for Markov's assassination to go ahead.*

THE PRESIDENT FELT
THAT MARKOV WAS
UNDERMINING THE VERY
FOUNDATIONS OF
THE REGIME

job themselves.' Since I was present and my role covered dealing with the problems of primarily Soviet traitors I was called on to handle this, even though a Bulgarian was involved. I was given the job of preparing the ground for the execution of the man.

Below: *Dr Bernard Riley arrives to give evidence at the inquest into the defector's death.*

Right: *The dissident's proud widow Annabella has tears still glistening in her eyes as she arrives to give evidence at the inquest into his death.*

THREE TYPES OF POISON, AND THE MEANS OF DELIVERING IT INTO MARKOV'S BODY, WERE DISCUSSED

"IT PROPELLED A SMALL PELLET FILLED WITH POISON WHICH PENETRATED THE SKIN AND DISSOLVED QUICKLY"

Chairman Andropov told me: 'Kalugin, you take charge of this. You do it.'"

Kalugin summoned Colonel Sergei Golobev, who ran "wet" operations for the KGB – wet being the in-house term for assassinations – and told him to report to the agency's Directorate of Science and Technology which dealt with everything from wiretaps to chemical weapons. Three types of poison, and the means of delivering it into Markov's body, were discussed before it was settled that the umbrella would be used.

He went on: "The Bulgarians had designed a small gadget like a fountain pen, about five inches long, which could be fired from a distance of a metre-and-a-half.

It propelled a small pellet filled with poison which penetrated the skin and dissolved quickly, leaving no trace. The device was fitted into an umbrella and operated from the handle. But the Bulgarians, wary of earlier failures and the fury of Zhivkov, insisted on testing it first. They tested it on a horse and the horse died within hours. They then tested it on a man who was under sentence of death."

AN INHUMAN TEST

"The man was taken out of his condemned cell for a walk and the guards shot at him with this pellet from the distance of about a metre. The man was startled as he felt the pain in the back of his knee, and started shouting and crying. He thought the moment of execution had arrived without anyone telling him. Then he calmed down, recovered and actually survived the attack. Moscow was informed and the scientists started working again to try to enhance the poison. In the end they came up with more effective pellets.

"After Markov was executed I was given a small token of the Bulgarians' appreciation – a Browning hunting rifle with a bronze plaque inscribed by their interior minister. I did not feel happy about such things but I was a loyal servant of the state myself. I had to obey orders too, orders given to me by Mr. Andropov. To refuse the chairman of the KGB would have been suicide for me."

Later, as a result of this interview, which he gave to a British newspaper, Kalugin was arrested by Scotland Yard and held for 24 hours while the Director of Public Prosecutions pondered his case. He decided that there was not enough evidence to proceed on a charge of conspiracy to commit murder. After his brush with British justice Kalugin said: "My participation in his death was precisely zero."

THE MYSTERY ASSASSIN

As to the assassin and the poisoned umbrella – they have vanished into history along with the regime that made them. Books since published in post-communist Sofia suggest that the assassin may be a retired Bulgarian diplomat living in his nation's capital, but Markov's friends dismiss this. Scotland Yard enquiries in his country as well as exhaustive checks in Britain after the attack have failed to turn up a culprit.

The death of Markov has gone unavenged long after the dictator who ordered his demise has himself fallen. The file on his death disappeared from Bulgarian secret service offices just after the collapse of the regime in 1990 and there is little hope now of anyone being brought to book for the murder.

His widow Annabella took some solace from a visit to Bulgaria after the fall of communism when she stood in a crowd of 100,000 people in freezing temperatures and heard them reel off the names of those murdered under Zhivkov's regime – with

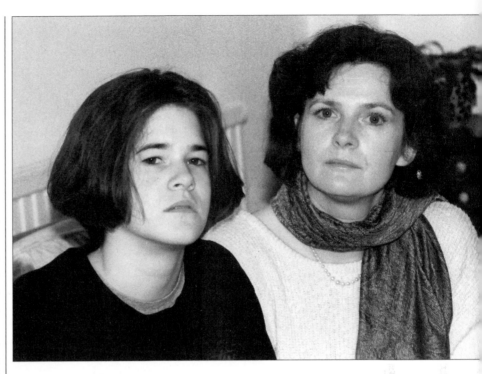

the cry of "killer!" to Zhivkov after every name. When it came to the name of Georgi Markov there was the biggest cheer of them all. He was loved by the Bulgarian people because he managed to make them laugh at their rulers – and there is nothing that a dictator fears quite so much as being laughed at; it means he is no longer feared.

But perhaps there is one epitaph to his memory that the writer – a humanitarian figure who believed in the ultimate good of man – would be pleased with. Early tests of a "magic bullet" treatment for cancer, based on the poison used to kill him, have shown remarkable results. Professor Philip Thorpe of the University of Texas South West Medical Centre says the first trials on patients have been "uncommonly good".

The therapy uses a monoclonal antibody linked to ricin. The ricin antibody recognises molecules exclusive to a certain type of blood cell. Once it finds them it sticks and delivers the fatal ricin to the cell. Fifteen patients with a cancer called B-Cell lymphoma, or non-Hodgkin's lymphoma, which causes more than 3,000 deaths each year in Britain, took part in the trial in 1993. Professor Thorpe reported that six of them had the size of their tumour reduced by more than half within a week of therapy.

If nothing else came from his death, Markov would surely smile at such lifesaving progress coming from the very venom that killed him.

Above: A grown-up Sasha, Markov's daughter, poses with her widowed mother in London in 1991, two years after the hated communist regime that killed a loving husband and father had been consigned to the scrapheap of history.

THE ASSASSIN AND THE POISONED UMBRELLA HAVE VANISHED INTO HISTORY ALONG WITH THE REGIME THAT MADE THEM

WHEN IT CAME TO THE NAME OF MARKOV THERE WAS THE BIGGEST CHEER OF ALL. HE WAS LOVED BY THE BULGARIAN PEOPLE

JOHN LIST
The Murderous Dad

It was a horrific case but, at the same time, it should have been an easy one for the police to solve. A family had been wiped out except for the father, who automatically became the chief suspect. Yet it was to be two decades before the forces of law and order caught up with killer and arch-hypocrite John List.

John Emil List was a modest man with much to be modest about. He looked like the humdrum, churchgoing accountant that he was. He neither smoked nor drank, had no interest in women or gambling and rarely took a vacation. He was parsimonious to the nth degree – turning the heat in the family's rambling mansion home so low in winter that all were forced to wear boiler suits to stay warm. German was the language spoken in the home in New Jersey, even though the furthest List had gotten to the land of his forefathers was a brochure from a travel agency. It was a miserable life for his wife Helen, their three children and his elderly mother – made more miserable by his dire financial straits and insistence on Bible-bashing at every given opportunity.

List, a man troubled by demons we can only guess at, decided to end what he saw as his family's "suffering" in this world. On a cold, foggy night in November 1971 – plagued by his children's apparent ungodliness, distraught at the looming spectre of financial ruin clouding his ordered life – John List took two handguns and wiped out his wife, three children and mother. The Friday before the massacre his daughter Patricia, 16, had told her high school drama teacher in the bucolic town of Westfield, New Jersey, that she was afraid her father was going to kill her – acting, in his eyes, was akin to prostitution. The teacher thought her prophesy nothing more than teenaged histrionics although she had told him: "He called us around the table and said he would have to kill us because he could no longer support us. He said he could not look after us the way he wanted to."

Her drama teacher never acted on her pleas and on Tuesday, November 9 1971, John List set about his macabre plan. He cancelled newspaper, milk and mail deliveries, informed the schools his children attended that the family would be visiting a sick relative out of town and told his bosses at a local bank that he was taking the day off sick.

LIST, A MAN TROUBLED BY DEMONS WE CAN ONLY GUESS AT, DECIDED TO END WHAT HE SAW AS HIS FAMILY'S "SUFFERING"

Opposite: *The seemingly timid John List murdered his family.*

Below: *John List after a brilliant piece of forensic modelling had led to his capture.*

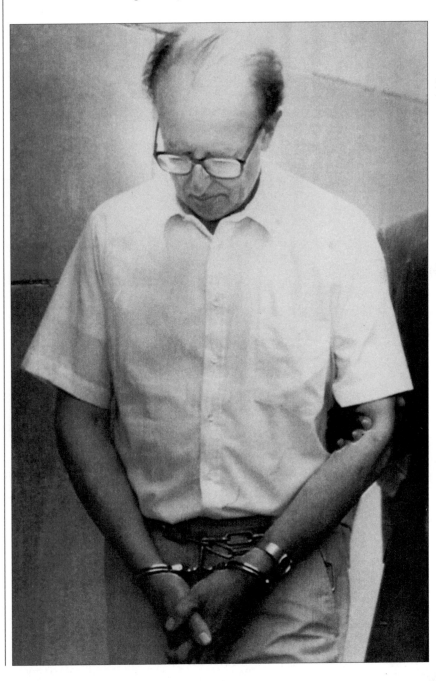

Behind the locked doors of the rambling, run-down mansion that was the unhappy family home, List executed his loved ones one by one. It was not until a month later, the house still brightly lit, that police broke into 431 Hillside Avenue with Edward Illiano, the drama teacher who had heard Patricia's fears first hand. Inside they saw a vision of hell. Laid out on the floor of the mansion's old ballroom were Helen List, aged 46, next to children John Frederick, 15, Frederick Michael, 13, and Patricia. John's body alone was riddled with ten bullets, although autopsies showed that death was brought about for all of them with a single bullet in the back of the head.

List's 84-year-old mother Alma was found on the third floor underneath a sloping roof near a bathub. List had attemped to drag her body downstairs but was unable to do so. Police found a filing cabinet in the house with the murder weapons along with five letters – one to his employer, one to his wife's mother, one to his mother's sister, one to his wife's sister and one to his local

pastor – a rambling five page self-justification in which List tried to explain what led him to such a gruesome act. He wrote: "I know that what has been done is wrong from all that I have been taught and that any reasons I might give will not make it right. But you will at least possibly understand why I felt I had to do this."

DESPERATE TIMES

"I wasn't earning anywhere near enough to support us. Everything I tried seemed to fall to pieces. True, we could have gone bankrupt and maybe gone on welfare. But... knowing the type of location that one would have to live in, plus the environment for the children, plus the effect on them knowing they were on welfare was just more than I thought they could or should endure...

"With Pat being so determined to get into acting I was also fearful about what that might do to her continuing to be a Christian. Also with Helen, not going to

---

DEATH WAS BROUGHT ABOUT FOR ALL OF LIST'S FAMILY WITH A SINGLE BULLET IN THE BACK OF THE HEAD

Below: *John List pictured with the family he massacred. Daughter Patricia stands behind, next to him is his wife Helen and sons John and Frederick.*

church. The whole family seems to be slipping from Christianity. I knew this would harm the family eventually. At least I am certain all have gone to heaven now. If this had gone on who knows if this would be the case. I am sure many will say 'How could anyone do such a horrible thing?' My only answer is it isn't easy…

"It may seem cowardly to have always shot from behind but I didn't want any of them to know even at the last second that I had to do this… I am only concerned with making my peace with God and of this I am assured because of Christ dying even for me. P.S. Mother is in the hallway in the attic, 3rd floor. She was too heavy to move." He also said he had got down on his hands and knees and prayed after every killing – comfort for his soul that did little good for his innocent victims.

A QUICK GETAWAY

John Emil List, however, had vanished by the time police trawled trough the scene of indescribable horror. List, 46, left behind everything that identified him – his wallet, his driver's licence, his college class ring, even his overcoat and boots. He had methodically wiped up the blood from the executions with a towel – and eerily left classical music playing on an intercom system that stretched throughout the rambling 19-room mansion – before vanishing into the great expanse of North America. His first trip was to a bank where he withdrew $2,100 in bonds belonging to his mother. Then he drove to New York's Kennedy Airport where his Chevy car was found by authorities two days after the discovery of the bodies on December 7. James Moran, the Westfield Police Chief who was among the first of the lawmen to witness the rotting bodies in that room, made a vow to himself to track List down until the day he died. In the end he didn't succeed – but he did nevertheless live to see justice done.

For the next 18 years John List lived as a phantom in America. James Moran knew he was alive, knew he had adopted a new identity somewhere, but every lead drew a blank. In the first days and weeks after the discovery of the bodies the publicity was intense; America, brutalised as it is by violent crime, was sickened to its core by a man capable of such a monstrous act.

Tip-off lines to the FBI and police burned with information – policemen logged thousands of man hours following up leads that proved to be false. The insignificant List, who served as a private in World War Two and a reservist in the Korean War, had vanished off the face of the earth.

In Westfield in the weeks following the murder the List house became a kind of gruesome tourist attraction with people driving by to stare at the turn-of-the-century structure. Local children nicknamed it the "Norman Bates Motel" after the grisly murder site in the Hitchcock thriller *Psycho*. The attraction lasted little more than a year – it was mysteriously destroyed by fire in 1972. By then, a full 12 months after the killings, the trail had gone colder than an Arctic night. While frustrated FBI agents trawled across America, South America and Europe, John Emil List was living in a small town near Denver, Colorado. And for his new life he had taken out a new name – Robert P. Clark. The insignificant accountant with an obsession for orderliness and religion was working at his profession and attending the same kind of Lutheran church that he had left behind in New Jersey.

Above: *Robert Clark, otherwise known as John List, arrives at court to answer for his savage murders.*

HE SAID HE HAD GOT DOWN ON HIS HANDS AND KNEES AND PRAYED AFTER EVERY KILLING – COMFORT FOR HIS SOUL

On November 22 1971, 12 days after the killings, he had applied for a new Social Security number – in America the key to a new identity. Anyone under 50 can get a number without question and his was taken out in the name of Robert Peter Clark, residing at Motel Deville, 650 W. Paltax St., Denver, Colorado.

On the application he listed his parents as dead and his year of birth as being 1931. He did what so many on the run from justice failed to do – camouflaged himself by hiding in plain sight. His first job was as a night cook in a roadside diner, but he soon plucked up enough courage to list himself in the phone book as an accountant. He was back at his old trade… and he had managed to get away with murder.

Above: *FBI posters cry out for information on List.* **Below:** *Finally List is caught.*

In 1977, so confident of life in his new identity, he courted a divorcee called Delores Miller whom he had met through a church singles group. Delores had many of the qualities of his murdered wife – before she strayed from the path of righteousness – and soon they were a couple in all but marriage. He put that right in 1985 when she became the second Mrs. List – and, in many respects, the sixth victim of the unfeeling monster.

A WILD GOOSE CHASE

Throughout these years the hunt continued for him without success. The only things that brought it into the public mind were occasional newspaper articles about the murders on anniversary dates. "Police Still Pursue Mass Killer", "14 Years And No List", "Police Still Baffled", they screamed with monotonous regularity. List lived a life of monotony and regularity, scrupulously avoiding any trouble, anything that might lay a trail to his new life in a new town 2,000 miles from the murders. Chief Moran laboured ceaselessly, checking out the leads and calls that flooded in each time a newspaper resurrected the murders, but each time there was no luck. Moran, however, remained optimistic, saying: "So he was careful, so he was keeping a low profile. So he was a nondescript kind of guy, so he never did one single thing to draw attention to himself. Nonetheless, I knew that one day he would make a mistake and that someone would be waiting to snap the cuffs on him. I hoped so much it would be me."

In the latter half of the 1980s List moved with his wife to Richmond, Virginia – now less than 500 miles from the murder scene. Still wimpy, still churchgoing, he nevertheless enjoyed watching TV on a regular basis and one of his favourite programme was *America's Most Wanted*, a weekly expose of the killers, conmen, rapists, robbers and bad guys who were wanted by the FBI. It was the programme that would eventually lead to his capture.

America's Most Wanted was approached by an officer on the murder squad and

JOHN EMIL LIST

asked if it could broadcast an appeal about List. Margaret Roberts, the show's managing editor, was keen to help, but hampered by the lack of recent photos of him. Michael Lindner, an executive producer of the show which had an impressive track record of catching fugitives, thought he could solve the problem with the aid of a 47-year-old commercial photographer and forensic sculptor called Frank Bender. Bender had specialised in recent years in creating busts of fugitives for law enforcement authorities across America. In the case of List, all he had to work with was a 1971 photo, a computerised update on his image and a police description. "It was a challenge," said Bender, adding: "But I think I had worked on harder projects."

Bender's journey into forensic sculpture had begun in 1977 by accident. Accompanying a friend on a tour of the

THE FORENSIC SCULPTOR TACKED UP ENLARGED PHOTOS OF LIST IN THE KITCHEN OF HIS HOME AND STUDIED THEM INTENSELY

Left: *Commercial photographer and forensic sculptor Frank Bender specialised in creating busts of fugitives for law enforcement authorities across America.*

Below: *All Bender had to work on to create the bust of List was a 1971 photo, a computerised update on his image and a police description. "It was a challenge," said Bender. "But I think I had worked on harder projects."*

Philadelphia morgue he had been shown the corpse of a woman shot three times through the head at point-blank range. Because of wounds and advanced decomposition, identification of the body was impossible. As an artistic experiment he rebuilt her face – and the woman was identified two days after he completed the cast in clay. Since then his work as a "physiognomic reconstructionist" had continued unabated and he was regarded as the foremost expert in the field.

A PSYCHOLOGICAL PROFILE

Bender turned to a friend, criminal psychologist Richard Walter from Michigan, for help in fleshing out details about List and what made him tick. Walter speculated that he would be the kind of guy who wouldn't be a health freak, that he was a worrier whose age would show. He would probably wear the same kind of eyeglasses, show the same nervous strain in his face, that his hair would have receded further, leaving a very high forehead and a partially bald cranium. He would have sagging jowls and a downturned, saddened look. Bender was convinced the psychological profile was right and set to work making the clay bust of the fugitive.

Day after day he moulded the face. He tacked up enlarged photos of List in the kitchen of his home and studied them intensely. He glued rubber erases to a fibreglass skull to attain the right thickness and then filled in the gaps with the clay. He kept reminding himself of what Walter had

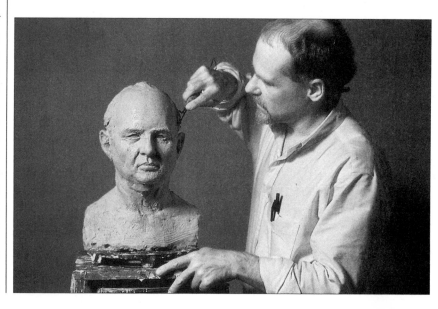

Above: *On May 1 1990, John List was sentenced to life imprisonment without the possibility of parole.*

"HIS ACTS STAND AS A PERMANENT, PATHETIC AND PROFANE EXAMPLE OF MAN'S INHUMANITY TO MAN"

said about him ageing, about how he would look aged 63 and not 46. Finally, satisfied with what he saw, he made a plaster mould that he then filled in with fibreglass. Afterwards he painted the model with flesh tones and handed it over to the producers of *America's Most Wanted*.

On Sunday May 21 1989 the show aired… and luck was on the side of justice. Robert Clark, nee John List, had travelled to a church social and so missed his favourite show, one that chronicled in depth his crimes, culminating with the sculpture and description of him as a pen-pusher, quiet, a nonentity. Afterwards there were 300 phone calls within minutes, all from people who claimed to know the wherabouts and new identity of John List. But only one of them proved to be correct and that came from Wanda Flannery, a friend of his wife Dolores back in Denver. "That's Bob!" she screamed when the image of the bust played on her TV screen. She rang the hotline and gave the operator the name, address and phone number of Bob Clark in Virginia.

Tracing down the hundreds of leads took time, but on June 1 1989, at 10.00 am, FBI agent Kevin August from Richmond, together with three colleagues, knocked at the door of the Clark home in Midlothian, near Richmond. Delores answered the door and mumbled the address of the small-town law firm where her husband was working. There, a little over one hour later, August confronted the fugitive and asked him: "Are you John List?" "No I am not," he lied, but August was convinced.

Three agents pinned him to the wall while August read him his rights. "My name is Robert Clark," said List, trying to bluff it out. But two hours later a fingerprint test proved him to be John List – fingerprints on file at the police station where he had applied for a firearms permit for the weapons to slaughter his family. The game was up after 18 years.

Former police chief Moran was one of the first to hear the news. "It's him?" was his first reaction, stunned that he had been caught by a clever model of his features when every method of modern detection had failed to find him in close to two decades of searching. "Then I said it was the best thing that had ever happened to me. That bum should never get away with what he did." List was charged with five counts of murder and caged pending a trial – the outcome of which was a foregone conclusion, even though at his arraignment on July 10 he pleaded not guilty, and insisted he was Robert Clark, not John Emil List.

A SENSIBLE PLEA

In February 1990 his attorney made him see sense and admit to being the fugitive, yet he pleaded not guilty to first degree murder at his full trial in April, claiming he had acted out of love for his family and that it was not a premeditated massacre. Clearly, with the letters left behind and his escape route planned, this was a nonsense. List's confessions to a psychiatrist were read out which showed him to be the ultimate, sneering criminal who believed himself above both God's law and that of man. In the end the jury, nine days after the trial began, found him guilty of all five counts of wilful murder. John List had been brought to book by a lump of clay fashioned by the skilful hands of a man who had never ever seen him.

When he was sentenced on May 1 1990 to life imprisonment without the possibility of parole, John List told the court: "I wish to inform the court that I remain truly sorry for the tragedy which happened in 1971. I feel that due to my mental state at the time I was unaccountable for what happened. I ask all those who were affected by this for their forgiveness, their understanding and their prayers. Thank You."

Judge Wertheimer lashed him from the bench: "His acts stand as a permanent, pathetic and profane example to the potential of man's inhumanity to man. They will not be soon or easily forgotten, and the name of John Emil List will be eternally synonymous with the concepts of selfishness, horror and evil."

John List rots in jail – and finally his family can rest in peace.

BEYOND REASONABLE DOUBT

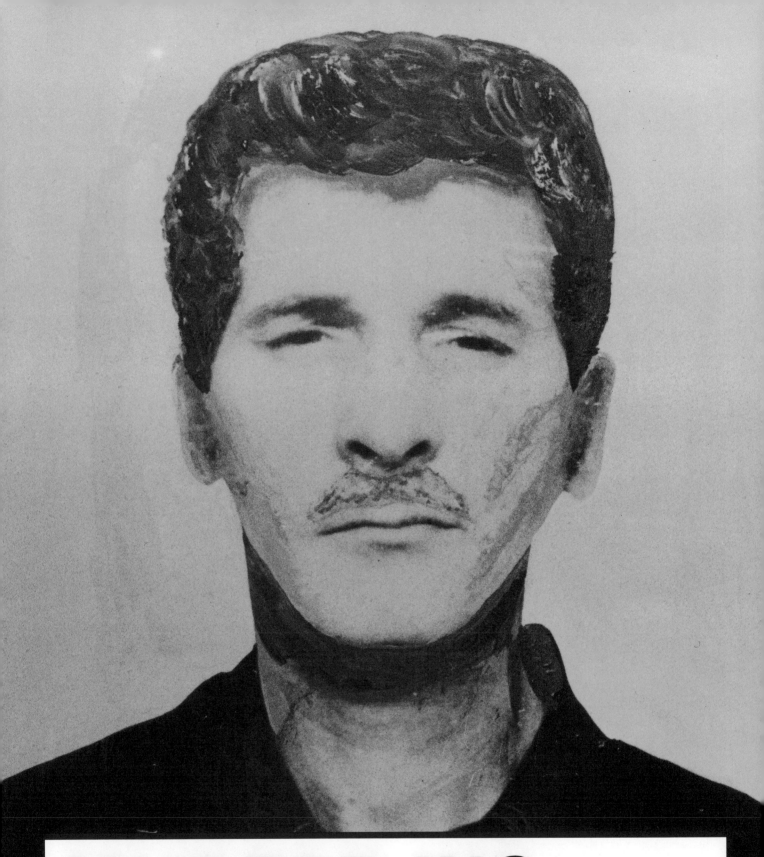

MURDER INC.
Cheapskate Killers

An innocuous block of flats in East London hid behind its walls scenes of medieval horror. There, the killing company known as Murder Inc. burned their victims in a tiny grate, later sprinkling their ashes from car windows. If ever criminals deserved to be found guilty, it was the perpetrators of these crimes.

He was one of the most formidable figures ever to stand in the dock of Number One Court at the Old Bailey; a small space that has seen some of history's most infamous individuals grace its confines. He made no speeches during his time in court, preferring that the prosecution did all the talking while he left his "not guilty" plea to speak for him. Harry "Big H" MacKenny hoped that the jury would believe the unbelievable – that he was not a mass murderer, but a lifesaver who had been framed.

At the end of his trial he leapt to his feet and screamed abuse and invective as the jury returned, beyond reasonable doubt, with guilty verdicts. Listening to the appalling catalogue of evidence stacked against him, it is inconceivable to believe that MacKenny could have conned himself into thinking that it could have gone any other way for him.

HE LEAPT TO HIS FEET AND SCREAMED ABUSE AND INVECTIVE AS THE JURY RETURNED GUILTY VERDICTS

Opposite: *John Henry Childs, the killer who cracked and turned Queen's Evidence against the comrades in crime.*

Below: *The flat where victims were turned from corpses to ashes.*

DOLPHIN HOUSE

The macabre story began in a small fireplace in a small flat in a grimy part of East London, barely enough for more than one or two logs at a time. Outside, washing strung on the walkway of the flats fluttered in the breeze while dirty kids kicked a ball and tin cans around in the concrete play area outside the entrances. Inside flat 13 in Dolphin House, High Street, Poplar, the coals burned down to red hot embers. John Childs, the tenant of the overheated apartment, slugged whisky straight from a bottle. He handed it to Harry "Big H" MacKenny, who drank a deep draught, savouring the hot liquid as it burned on the way down before spreading a warm, mellow feeling throughout him. It was not a social drink. The men needed this liquor to steel themselves for the night's work ahead.

The fire, which was boosted with a gas burner to increase the heat, cast flickering, ominous shadows over the paraphernalia on the walls. Four knives, a pump-action shotgun, a shield, four axes, a crossbow, a

pump-action air rifle, a compressed-air spear gun, Chinese flails and a fencing mask testified that the resident of this flat was a man who clearly dabbled in violence and violent things.

Childs, dressed in a weird black outfit that made him resemble a Victorian undertaker, put more smokeless fuel on to the grate as Big H went out to the back room. There Childs had installed an industrial mincing machine – bought for £25 from a wholesale butcher who advertised in Exchange and Mart magazine – a butcher's block, knives and hooks.

Hanging from the hooks were various human body parts. They had been dismembered earlier by Childs as he waited for Big H to come around and help him with the disposal of the corpse.

CALLOUS KILLERS

Piece by piece, as if carting home a joint for Sunday lunch, Big H carried through the human remains to Childs in the sitting room. The fire reached maximum heat and, for the next eighteen hours, the flames were fed with flesh and bone, fat drained off, the bones broken with mallets, the ash put into plastic bags to be finally scattered to the four winds by MacKenny as Childs drove them along the Barking by-pass in East London. The whisky blotted out the awful reality of what they were doing... the contract killings they specialised in for £25 down payment and easy instalments for the balance. They called themselves Murder Inc., and before they were caught half-a-dozen people were murdered for the paltry sum of a few thousand pounds.

Murder Inc. actually went on to become a triumvirate of misfits, although it was Childs and MacKenny who did all the killing. The third villain, who would eventually join Big H and Childs in the dock at the Old Bailey, in November 1980, was Terence Pinfold, a petty criminal and failed bank robber. An outsider in the terrible alliance of MacKenny and Childs, he was a hypocritical, weak man with the failing of most paranoid power lovers; he thought himself a cut above the other two and would become enraged if he thought they were laughing at him behind his back. Together they killed, for discount prices, using guns, a swordstick and an axe, dis-

Above: *A Teddy Bear of the sort manufactured by Terence Eve.*

Opposite top: *The unprepossessing base where Murder Inc. committed their crimes.*

Opposite bottom: *The farm that was once owned by George Brett before he and 10-year-old son Terry were sten-gunned to death by Big H.*

membering the corpses at Childs' flat or at a disused factory in Chadwell Heath, Essex, that had once been used for manufacturing teddy bears.

The founding of this vile business came about when Pinfold and MacKenny became friends in the early 1970s. In 1972, at a factory in Chadwell Heath, they began making teddy bears with another man, Terence 'Teddy Bear' Eve. A secondary line at the factory was lifejackets. Although MacKenny was a psychotic killer, he was also an enigma, a talented, self-taught man who was a first class diver and qualified pilot. He once invented a unique diver's valve that was hailed in the trade press as a breakthrough and a life-jacket which incorporated the best points of six other types of

Above: *The interior of the Teddy Bear factory where George Brett and his 10-year-old son Terry were murdered.*

A SEEDY, SMALL-TIME CROOK, PINFOLD BUNGLED EVERYTHING HE DID, FROM BURGLARY TO ARMED ROBBERY

---

life preserver. He drastically cut the weight of the existing systems by converting the diver's oxygen cylinder so that it would also inflate the life-jacket. The old method used a separate cylinder for the job.

At the factory the men grandly called themselves 'directors' and dressed in snazzy suits. But MacKenny was extremely lazy, refusing to rise much before midday each day, and soon the life-jacket business began, slowly but surely, to slide. The stuffed toys business, however, under the direction of Eve, continued to thrive with orders from all over the country. It was his success which would eventually lead him to becoming a victim.

It's clear at which point MacKenny turned the corner from legitimate business-man to murderer; it occurred in 1974 with the release from jail of John Childs.

Childs had known MacKenny in East London for several years, and had been friendly in the late 1960s in prison with Pinfold who was serving time for a rob-bery. A seedy, small-time crook, he had been in court on no less than 17 occasions and had served three jail sentences. From burglary to armed robbery, he bungled everything he did, but he always har-boured the ambition to become a kingpin of crime in the East End, just like the Kray twins Reg and Ron whose reputation he admired so much. He also pulled a bank robbery once with Pinfold in south Woodford, Essex, saving Pinfold from capture when he was attacked by two bank staff after he failed to draw out his Walther .38 automatic in time to threaten them. They fled empty handed from that botched affair.

Childs was not even his real name. He was born Martin Jones, but took on the pseudonym when he rented the £6 per-week flat which he planned to turn into the human abattoir. A deeply unhinged psychopath, he liked to pull his own toenails out with a pair of pliers when dark moods overcame him. His greatest fantasy was – and still is, by all accounts – to have a waxwork model of himself repose in Madame Tussaud's in Baker Street.

The two of them formed their macabre new business. Each had contacts in the underworld on both sides of the Thames; each knew that they were all capable of going ahead. For discount prices – £25 to £50 down and easy repayments on the balance – they would take human life. Pinfold, reluctantly, was drawn in.

Before the first contract killing, Childs murdered Terence Eve, the man whose soft toy business was thriving. Early in 1975 he shot him dead with an automatic pistol, took MacKenny with him to the Poplar flat, and spent 14 hours burning Eve's corpse in a grate as the pair of them drank a litre of whisky. Pinfold, who never murdered, was later found guilty at the Old Bailey of ordering the killing and jailed for life. The jury were convinced that his greed harnessed Childs' macabre talents for the job.

SMALL-FRY

In February of that same year they received their first contract for £1,800 – a pathetically small sum compared to the fees charged by international, professional hitmen. The target was George Brett, a haulage contractor who lived on a farm in Upminster, Essex. Brett was on the fringes of the underworld – a dodgy deal here, a suspect load there – but was not a big-time criminal. But somewhere along the line, George Brett had crossed the line when his enemies learned that he had started 'grassing' them up to police as a paid informer. He was marked for death and the bargain-basement killing team were the perfect instrument to use.

Childs, a man obsessed with weapons and with a theatrical air about him, donned a wig, heavy eyebrows and dyed his straggly beard with black boot polish when he went to meet Brett to propose a lucrative business deal. Within a mile of his farmhouse he parked his car, stripped down to a

tracksuit and ran along the roadside, pretending to be a jogger. When he "accidentally" bumped into Mrs. Brett, he got chatting and told her he was a engineer whose firm needed transport. She arranged a meeting with her husband who was "just the man you're looking for".

A killing zone was arranged at the factory. Tarpaulin sheets lined with plastic, to collect blood, were laid out in an area at the back of the site. Childs went back to the farm the following day dressed as a city gent to bring Brett to the factory. At the very last minute, just as he was manoeuvring his car out of the yard, Brett's young son Terence, aged 10, ran across. "Dad, can I come along for the ride?" he said, pleadingly. The boy climbed into the car for the last journey of his short life.

A DEEPLY UNHINGED PSYCHOPATH, HE LIKED TO PULL HIS OWN TOENAILS OUT WITH A PAIR OF PLIERS IN HIS DARK MOODS

Below: *The police hunt at Beredens Farm for George and Terry Brett.*

Above: *At Beredens Farm a large section of the farmyard was dug up as police looked for the bodies.*

AT THE FACTORY THE BOY
WAS HELD BY CHILDS
WHILE WATCHING HIS
FATHER'S HEAD BEING
BLOWN OFF

MACKENNY TOOK ONE OF
GEORGE BRETT'S EYES
FROM HIS CORPSE WITH
THE INTENTION OF
PRESERVING IT IN VINEGAR

At the factory he was held by Childs while watching his father's head blown off with a silenced Sten gun by Big H. Then the boy was cut in half by bullets fired from the same gun. As he looked at the boy's corpse MacKenny said: "It don't matter – he's only a grass's son." They were cut up, taken in plastic bin liners to Child's flat and burned. Then their ashes were thrown from the moving car. They had simply vanished from the face of the earth. Except for one of 35-year-old George Brett's eyes... MacKenny took it from his corpse with the intention of preserving it in vinegar.

The rubicon had been crossed. Killing for cash, they thought, was this simple.

The next to die was Frederick Sherwood, proprietor of a nursing home in Herne Bay, Kent. Sherwood, 48, was wanted out of the way by a business rival keen on muscling in on his lucrative enterprise. MacKenny discovered his car was for sale and lured him there on the pretext of being interested in buying it for £480. When Sherwood arrived the same killing zone had been prepared and he was shot through the head by MacKenny at the same time as Childs smashed a sledge-hammer over him. At the factory his legs were sawn off, the body complete with dismembered limbs taken to Childs' flat where it was sawed and hacked

into smaller pieces and once again burned in the 18-inch-wide grate. It is still now known how much they charged for that particular contract killing.

A chilling insight into the menace they generated was provided by Mike Fielder, a veteran crime reporter for The Sun, who visited the death factory for a story about the disappearance of Eve. He said: "I came face to face with the killers in their factory of death. Pinfold told me that Eve had vanished with £600 in takings and had got 'a bit of woman trouble'.

"As we talked both MacKenny, 6 ft 5 ins tall and an unmistakeable figure, and Childs hovered nearby without joining in the conversation.

"Pinfold stonewalled every question. I got a guided tour of the factory from Pinfold.

"He showed me the teddy bear production line and how the toys were stuffed with foam rubber. Then he cheekily asked for my help in trying to prove that he had been 'framed' by the police on a £20,000 bank raid charge. At the time he said he had just been granted bail while awaiting trial. I said I would make a few enquiries on his behalf. But I felt in my bones that Pinfold was an evil and dangerous man. I never returned to the factory. And if I had known then what the world knows now, I would not have slept easy in my bed that night. A prying newspaperman would have made a tempting target for murder."

ANOTHER BRUTAL KILLING

Robert Brown, 36, an escaped prisoner who ended up working at the factory, was the next victim. He was killed with an axe by Childs because he "irritated him", and, like the others, disposed of in the grate.

While they touted for murders, MacKenny and Childs also drew up a lurid "shopping list" among the underworld of the kind of "services" that their organisation was offering. For £50 they would break someone's nose. For £500 they would blow kneecaps off with a shotgun. And for two grand – £2,000 – they would kill. They offered to help slum landlords deal with bothersome tenants by slipping diseased rats through letterboxes and they touted their talents to the right-wing National Front party – promising to deal with "troublesome Pakis" if they so wished. They even hit on the hare-brained idea that Lord Lucan, the runaway peer wanted for the murder of his nanny in Belgravia, was still alive, so they offered his relatives bargain-basement contracts on anyone who showed "malevolence" towards the Earl! The offer was never taken seriously. Another person they approached was the self-confessed racialist Robert Relf, the 56-year-old white supremacist who had gone to jail in Leamington for refusing to take down a sign which offered his house for sale to a white person only. Relf would later tell police: "MacKenny thought I would be a good customer. They thought I had a lot of black enemies that I wanted to dispose of. MacKenny put it to me that if I had any bother with coloureds he would get them 'seen to'. He said they could either get rid of them altogether or just frighten them off like break their arms and legs – for a price. I told him I wasn't interested. I know I'm a racialist but I'm not going for things like that – not with any violence."

A VICIOUS FRIEND

The next, and last, victim was Ronald Andrews – a man killed over MacKenny's lust for his wife. Andrews, 35, a roofing contractor, was MacKenny's best friend, a man he had known since his childhood days in Camberwell. But twice-married MacKenny, always a lady's man, did not let friendship stand in the way of what he wanted. He had been carrying on an affair for some time with his wife, Gwen, deciding, with the aid of Childs to murder him in the autumn of 1978.

MacKenny lured him to the DIY crematorium in Poplar on the pretext of introducing him to a private detective who alleged-

> THEY SLIPPED DISEASED RATS THROUGH LETTERBOXES AND OFFERED THEIR SERVICES TO THE NATIONAL FRONT

Below: *The farm was pulled apart as the police conducted the most thorough of searches.*

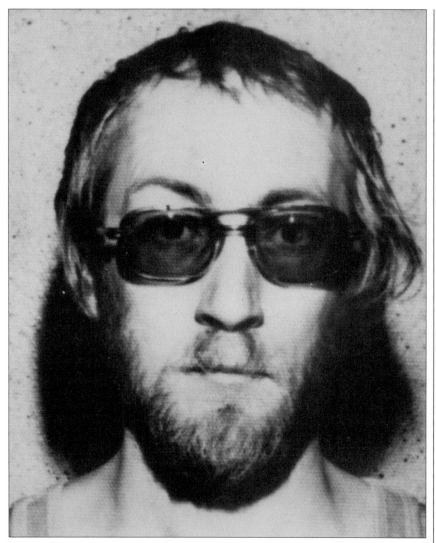

Andrews' car to the River Nene and dumped it in the black waters. Wearing frogman's gear, he waited until the car completely filled up with water before breaking out and swimming to the surface. He hoped that police would think that the body had been swept away by the current. Days later, when Ron Andrews was already ashes, MacKenny stood with Gwendoline on the banks of the river and comforted her as the car was dragged up from the depths.

PAYING THE PRICE FOR EVIL

By this time, Childs' nerves were almost completely shot. He had grown sleepless, wracked by nightmares about the terrible things he had done. He was now drinking at least one bottle, sometimes two, of whisky each night, merely to blot out the memories to get some sleep. He would later tell police that he had, in his paranoia, become convinced that MacKenny was out to kill him. He wanted to get the first shot in and began practising with pictures of MacKenny tied to a tree in Epping Forest that he took pot-shots at with a crossbow.

MacKenny, too, began to question some of the murders, particularly the killing of Andrews. In one moment of remorse he

ly had information on affairs his wife was having with other men. The private detective turned out to be Childs. Andrews was lulled into a false sense of security, being offered tea by MacKenny who then went out into the kitchen, pretending to have a conversation with "Mrs. Childs", although in reality there was no-one else there.

Concealing a .38 revolver under a tea-towel he came back in, ripped the towel away, and shot him point blank through the back of the skull. Then his body was sawed up into log-size pieces, parts of it grated down in the industrial mincer and the flesh burned in the grate. Childs had to drink two bottles of whisky… his nerves were close to cracking.

To cover up the killing Childs had got his ex-wife to write a loving postcard to "Dear Ron", which was posted from Wisbech, Cambridgeshire, to his wife – MacKenny wanted it to appear to her that her husband was the cheat. He drove

*Above: **The defendants were desperate men.***

*Right: **Henry 'Big H' MacKenny, one of the vilest killers ever to stand trial for multiple murder.***

HIS BODY WAS SAWED INTO LOG-SIZE PIECES, PARTS OF IT GRATED DOWN IN THE INDUSTRIAL MINCER. FLESH BURNED IN THE GRATE

murder squad incident room. With information from a further two informers, a 20-strong task force called Cater's Company began the task of seeking hard evidence to back up the uncorroborated statements of criminals.

CRIMINAL LINKS

Childs was arrested for questioning over a £500,000 security van robbery in Hertfordshire in the summer of 1979. But he soon realised he had been offered up by a "squealer" for something far more damaging than mere armed robberies or grievous bodily harm. With his nerve completely broken, he turned supergrass, confessing to six killings, detailing every single gruesome episode. The hardened detectives could simply not believe that human beings could be so thoroughly disposed of in an 18-inch-grate in a council flat. So to test the theory two officers were assigned the task of burning an 11-and-a-half-stone pig in the flat. They had reduced the animal to ashes in 13 hours, pulverised its bones and disposed of the ashes from a car on the Barking by-pass – just like Childs and MacKenny had done. Childs hoped that his full confession would be enough to earn him a pardon. He was sadly mistaken.

With detectives sent to interview all the associates of the missing people, tracking down the places where they drank and where they placed their bets, forensic evi-

said to Childs: "I shouldn't have done that. He was my best mate." But he was nowhere near as close-to-the-edge as his partner... although time was rapidly running out for them both.

Police had been probing the disappearances of all the victims, but had nothing to tie them in – until the end of 1978 when a suspect wanted for a string of armed robberies in the home counties began talking of an underworld hit team. Villains all over knew of the gruesome speciality of Childs and MacKenny, but true to their criminal code, they stayed silent.

This particular suspect named Childs and MacKenny, although to police it seemed almost impossible to prove. For if what the crook was saying, there would be no bodies, no forensic evidence, to ever link them with the crimes.

The squad assigned to cracking the case was led by Det. Chief Supt. Frank Cater, later Commander Cater, a lawman with an outstanding record of success against organised crime in the capital. His second-in-command was Det. Insp. Geoffrey Foxall, responsible for co-ordinating operations and all relevant information in the

Above: *The Volkswagen which led police on a high-speed chase and the capture of Big H.*
Below: *The Barking by-pass, resting place for many of Big H's murder victims.*

Above: *The blue Mercedes which George Brett and his son Terry drove in their appointment with brutal murder.*

They came to trial at the Old Bailey in October 1980 – the largest mass murder case ever to be brought where no victims had ever been discovered. For close to two months the jury listened to what judge Mr. Justice May called "a story I have seldom heard even in these violent times."

MacKenny and Pinfold were in the dock, their erstwhile business partner and cohort in crime John Childs paraded before them as their chief prosecution witness. Childs left nothing out. He detailed every gory move that he and MacKenny had made. Pinfold was made to look weak and pathetic; even though he wanted Terence Eve dead, Childs had to confess that he did not take part in the killing. He told the court: "I live in fear of my life now. I was a professional criminal and I have broken the code."

For their part, the police revealed how two detectives who were on the squad which cracked the case were under constant fear of their lives from another underworld contract, put out on them by acquaintances of MacKenny while they delved into their murders.

Big H, defiant to the end, insisted he was a life-saver, the inventor of the life-jacket and breathing apparatus at the factory, not a cold-blooded killer. But John Childs' description of his callous remark over the dead body of 10-year-old Terry Brett virtually froze the courtroom.

He was convicted of murdering the Bretts, Eve and Frederick Sherwood and jailed for four life terms, concurrently, with Mr. Justice May recommending that he serve not less than 25 years. The pitiful Pinfold, the outsider in the drama who just got greedy over wanting the teddy bear factory for himself, was sentenced to life imprisonment for ordering Eve's murder.

dence proved more difficult. A search of the teddy bear factory showed only an area where large amounts of concentrated acid had been poured to remove bloodstains. But there was one mark in the floor which corresponded to the tip of a bullet that had been disguised with the aid of polish and wax. It was the first small, but significant clue, that would eventually lead to the downfall of Murder Inc.

THE BIG SEARCH

In July 1979 a massive dragnet was set up by police to find MacKenny. But he too had his underworld contacts. He realised that he had been sold out by Childs and had gone to ground, and managed to elude capture despite a massive poster campaign combined with radio and TV appeals. He was eventually found to be staying at a house in Morse Close, Plaistow, East London, the home of his friends William and Pauline Woodcraft.

A large team of armed officers, wearing bullet-proof vests, ringed the house, evacuating some neighbours while telling others to keep quiet and stay indoors. Shortly after 1.00 a.m. on September 21, police telephoned the house, spoke to Mrs. Woodcraft, and told her that the place was surrounded. MacKenny, realising the hopelessness of the situation, came out without a shot being fired.

> THE TRIAL AT THE OLD BAILEY WAS THE LARGEST MASS MURDER CASE WHERE NO VICTIMS HAD EVER BEEN DISCOVERED

> TWO DETECTIVES ON THE SQUAD WERE UNDER CONSTANT FEAR OF THEIR LIVES FROM ANOTHER UNDERWORLD CONTRACT

DRAMATIC SCENES

There were scenes of high drama in the heavily guarded courtroom on Friday November 28 1980 as the judge came to sentence MacKenny. He told him: "The public needs to be protected from your criminal and totally unjustified activities." MacKenny, tall, greying, dressed in a cream suit, shouted back: "Straight people need to be protected from you." The judge, ignoring this outburst as prison officers restrained him, said: "This is one of the most macabre cases ever heard, even in this famous building." Again MacKenny interrupted: "I think you are a hypocrite. Bring this farce to a close. Do your worst. I killed nobody. I have saved lives!" The Judge said, as he was surrounded in the dock by yet more prison officers: "You have killed for no reason whatever – two for gain and one your best friend because you wanted his wife." Big H then began a torrent of abuse and swear words, his invective echoing all the way down to the cells as he was led away to begin his 25 years locked away from civilised society.

Psychopath Childs was sentenced to life with little hope of ever seeing the world

> BIG H BEGAN A TORRENT OF ABUSE AND SWEAR WORDS, HIS INVECTIVE ECHOING ALL THE WAY DOWN TO THE CELLS

Below: *The Old Bailey, where a jury decided, beyond reasonable doubt, that the killers who made up Murder Inc. needed to be put away from society.*

outside of an institution ever again. But even from behind bars the hot breath of his menace can still be felt. In August 1983 he attempted, from his cell at Hull maximum security prison, to write the memoirs of Murder Inc. On prison notepaper he wrote to Redbridge council, the local authority which gave planning permission for the teddy bear factory. He asked for the council to send him the plans of the factory for one of his chapters. The council had to treat the request "like any other". But an official said: "We feel like telling him to get lost. He certainly has a nerve."

The Home Office had the final say. Institution rules forbid inmates of Her Majesty's Prisons from profiting from such ventures and he will never be allowed to have his grisly memoirs published while he languishes inside. Instead, he can console himself that he might, indeed, one day end up immortalised in the chamber of horrors at Madame Tussaud's.

ROOM 606
A Race Case

Mike Tyson, the man with the meanest fists on the planet, became a number in the system when he was found guilty of rape and sentenced to time in a tough jail. It was the worst setback for world-class boxing in years, a tragedy for his victim, and a blow to the black community in America who idolised him.

The bathing-suit belles giggled nervously in their skimpy suits, wobbling on their high heels as their hero hove into view. Mike Tyson, ex-heavyweight boxing champion of the world, was even more awesome close-up than he was on the screen punching his opponents to kingdom come. Tyson, a born-again bachelor since his highly publicised divorce from actress Robin Givens two years before, moved at ease among the beauties, aware of both his physical appeal and his incredible stature among the black communities of America. And these girls were all his "own" – black girls competing in an all-black beauty pageant at an exposition in the midwestern city of Indianapolis in 1991.

"How ya doin baby?" grinned Tyson to one girl after another. Sometimes the comments were much lewder, much cruder, but some of these girls were from the ghetto like Tyson – they both understood and spoke the language of the streets. Few were

THESE GIRLS WERE ALL HIS "OWN"… "HOW YA DOIN' BABY?" GRINNED MIKE TYSON AT ONE GIRL AFTER ANOTHER

Opposite: *Mike Tyson, a champion humbled.*

Below: *Before Tyson's problems with Desiree Washington began, his shattered marriage to actress Robin Givens was played out in public – much to his discomfort.*

Above: *Mike Tyson and his flamboyant manager Don King, on top of the world after winning a world title fight in Las Vegas in 1987.*

IT BECAME CLEAR TO A WATCHING WORLD THAT HE WAS A BRUTISH MAN WHO TOOK WHAT HE WANTED WHEN HE WANTED IT

offended by the boxer's purple language and sexist remarks.

One 18-year-old among the contestants that day was particularly overawed at being in the presence of boxing's maestro. Desiree Washington, a vivacious beauty, a scholar, a girl from a nice middle-class home, didn't hear the risque banter; she just hoped with baited breath that the man idolised by her entire family would stop to speak with her. He did – and their separate worlds ended. For Mike Tyson, champ, became Mike Tyson, rapist. For the next few years he was destined to languish in a maximum security American jail.

Tyson exchanged telephone numbers with the girl from Rhode Island and they met later that night for what she thought was going to be a nice sightseeing tour of

the bright lights of Indianapolis. Her tour, however, ended in room 606 of the plush Canterbury Hotel where Tyson raped her in an ordeal that has scarred her mentally for life. Tyson proclaimed his innocence throughout the ensuing trial, but it became clear to a watching world that he was a brutish man who took what he wanted when he wanted it. Certainly for the jurors who sat in judgement on him there was only ever going to be one verdict when the ten days of the trial were over – guilty beyond reasonable doubt.

A SHOW TRIAL

From the first day prosecutor Greg Garrison spoke the world knew that this was going to be an incredible trial. Two hundred journalists from around the world were accommodated in an underground storeroom at the courthouse where the trial proceedings were relayed to them on closed-circuit TV. Garrison, setting the scene for his portrayal of Tyson as a predatory beast, said that he had 'lured' her to his hotel room, violated her and discarded her afterwards like so much trash.

The hushed court on the first day of proceedings heard that hours before the attack he had knelt in prayer with the Rev. Jesse Jackson. But after midnight, the lust for the young beauty he had met earlier in the day welled up inside him. Garrison said that the attraction between the former champ and the beauty queen changed from innocence to a nightmare rape ordeal in a split second on July 19 1991.

"She was asleep when Tyson phoned to invite her for a ride around town in his limousine," said Garrison. "He told her he was leaving town the next day. So she gets up and decides to go and see the town with one of her heroes. She was excited. She thought: 'I am out on the town with Mike Tyson!' But then he said something about having to go back to his hotel, something about bodyguards, something about making phone calls.

"On the way into the hotel a 13-year-old girl yelled out: 'Hey, there's Mike Tyson,' and he waved back. Desiree says to him: 'It's great you are doing this,' but he replies: 'Yeah, but it's a pain in the ass.'

"Once in the room she goes and sits on the first chair and he walks through to the living room in the two-room suite. She hears him talking on the phone but doesn't hear what he is saying. He shouts: 'Come in, I want to talk to you.'

"She says: 'I thought we were going to go out on the town.' He replied: 'We will go, come in, I want to talk to you.' When she goes in he is sitting at the head of the bed watching a cowboy show on TV. He says to her: 'Does your family like me?' She says: 'They don't know you.' He then says: 'Well, do you like me?' And she replied: 'You seem nice.'

"And he changed in a second. There was a change in his voice and in his actions. He said to her: 'You are 18 years and one month old and you turn me on.' She says: 'What? Now look, I don't know what you think I came up here for, but you said we would see the sights and I brought my camera. I want to go to the bathroom and then go.' Tyson then held his head in his hands, rubbed his eyes, and said that he would take her back to his hotel after she had been to the lavatory.

"But when she came out of the bathroom he was sitting on the edge of the bed with nothing on but his underpants and he said to her: 'Come here.' Then one of the fastest and strongest men in the world grabbed and spun around this 18-year-old girl as she said: 'What are you doing to me?'

AN UNFAIR STRUGGLE

"He then pins her on the bed and sticks his tongue halfway down her throat. She begs him to get off. A massive forearm pins her down like a ragdoll and he peels her clothes off with one hand. She begs the heavyweight champion of the world to get off her. He pulls her legs apart and she cries out in pain. She is tearful. She is frightened. She hurts a lot and says to him: 'Please, I don't want to have a baby.'

"He says: 'We'll have a baby together.' She says: 'I cannot afford to have a baby. I cannot get any diseases.' Tyson replied: 'I have not got any diseases and neither have you.' And he screams at her: 'Don't fight me, don't fight me!' Like a ragdoll he lifts her up. He exposes himself, drives himself into this 5ft. 4ins. 18-year-old girl. She says: 'You are hurting me. Please don't do this to me.' She is hitting him but she later says it is like hitting a brick wall. He goes

on until he is done. She is crying all the while, begging him to get up."

The courtroom remained transfixed as Garrison described how Desiree tried to make a bolt for freedom when Tyson suggested she sit on top of him for more sex. "She makes a break from the bed," he said, "but he grabs her back and forces himself on her again until he climaxes. Then in an eerie voice he says to her: 'You love me now, don't you?' Tearful, Desiree staggered from the room. Back in her hotel room her

Above: *Desiree Washington, the beauty queen who accepted an invitation to see the sights of Indianapolis with Mike Tyson... and ended up as his victim in a rape without mercy.*

roomate asked: 'What was he like?' And Desiree replied: 'He raped me.'" Garrison said she complained to police a day later and when doctors examined her, they found two wounds "clearly visible 25 hours after the attack. It is beyond reasonable doubt that he callously and viciously raped her."

Tyson's lawyer, a tax expert for his manager Don King called Vincent Fuller, embarked on a weird strategy to try to defend his client from such shattering testimony. Rather than painting Tyson as the victim of a financial sting or a girl who cried wolf because he was not more romantic, he went on the tack of portraying Tyson as a brute. Yes, he was tough, he was crude, he was brutal – but girls KNEW that because he was from the ghetto. His bottom line was that any girl who went into a hotel room after midnight with a hulk like Tyson should have known they weren't

Above: *The gloves and boxer shorts have been swapped for an Armani suit and silk tie as Mike Tyson prepares to fight for something far more important than purses or titles – his freedom and his name.*

"I ASKED HER IF SHE WANTED TO F**K ME THE FIRST TIME I MET HER," HE SAID. "SHE REPLIED: 'SURE – GIVE ME A CALL'"

---

going there to play scrabble. "There is no denial on Mr. Tyson's part that sex took place," he said. "But we will prove that sex was consensual." He argued that Miss Washington had a craving for cash equal to that of his ex-wife Robin Givens, a woman who took him to the financial cleaners after they split up. And he says the fact that Tyson didn't call a cab after the brief encounter led her to concoct the rape story. He added: "Miss Washington left his room in anger – not because of rape, but because of disillusionment."

Tyson did nothing on the witness stand to endear himself to the jurors or the judge. He swore, he spoke in crude terms of what he did to women, he frequently blurted out the F-word. "I asked her if she wanted to f***k me the first time I met her," he said. "She repled: 'Sure – give me a call.' I am very blunt, very crude. That's what I am when I ask for something – I want to know what I am getting." He said that far from being an innocent victim, a Sunday school teacher in her hometown, she "thrust" her telephone number into his hand when he had met her earlier in the day at the beauty contest. He said he made several telephone calls to her hotel before finally getting through to her shortly before midnight. He claimed she told him: "S**t, I'm in bed and have got no make-up." Tyson said: "I told her to just wash her face, comb her hair and just put on something loose. When she came down to the car there was just my driver there and my bodyguard Dale Edwards. I kissed her and she kissed me. We were kissing and touching, you know.

BEDROOM TALK

"We went to the bedroom of my hotel and we started talking. We were talking for about ten minutes, perhaps, and we were touching, my hand was on her leg. Yeah,

> "SHE WANTED SEX.
> WE HAD SEX.
> SHE WAS NOT ON
> THE PILL SO I DIDN'T
> CLIMAX INSIDE HER"

Below: *Camille Ewald, the elderly white woman who raised Mike Tyson as her own son since his teens, was one of the few women in America who stood by him and spoke out for him at his rape trial.*

we were kissing. I slid down the bed to reach her and she's movin' fast, dropping her jacket, getting it off quick. I was kissing her neck, her cheeks, kissing her chest, kissing her shoulders and her nipples. She had taken off her shorts and I had taken my shirt off. She had taken off her underwear and the underwear had dropped to her knees and then I took it all off. I started having oral sex with her. We had oral sex for a little while. She told me to stop, saying 'come up, come up.' That indicated she wanted sex. We had sex. It lasted for 15 or 20 minutes. She was not on the pill so I didn't climax inside her.

"I offered her to stay the night because she and a girlfriend had a 5.00am wake-up call. I said my limo would take her home but that I was not going to walk back down the stairs. She was irritable because I would not walk her down the stairs."

Fuller interrupted his client's monologue to ask Tyson: "At any time did you force Desiree Washington to engage in sexual

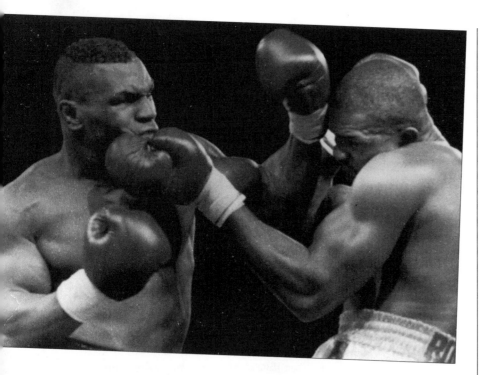

Above: *This is what Mike Tyson did best – hammering opponents into mincemeat with his terrible fury.*

"SOME OF THE THINGS THAT WERE SAID PAINTED ME AS A MANIAC, A GUY GOING CRAZY. BUT I WAS JUST TRYING TO HAVE FUN"

"IT WAS HORRIBLE TO BE IN THIS COURTROOM... TOTALLY UNBELIEVABLE... I AM DEVASTATED... I WAS CRUCIFIED"

intercourse?" Tyson replied: "No, I did not. Never. I did not violate her in any way." "Did she tell you to stop?" inquired Fuller. Tyson responded emotionally: "Never! She never told me I was hurting her, she never said no or anything."

Desiree on the stand was treated with kid-gloves by prosecution and defence alike. She merely re-stated what Garrison had said in his opening arguments and Fuller could do little other than suggest that sex was consensual. There followed a stream of other witnesses, including other beauty queens, all of whom testified as to the lewd and licencious nature of Tyson's comments to the contestants that morning. But it was clear that the proceedings were not going his way. After deliberating at trial's end for nine hours and 20 minutes the verdict came in: guilty of rape.

A STRONG SPEECH

In his last moments as Mike Tyson, free man, before he became prisoner no. 922355, Tyson showed no remorse in the dock. Instead he gave a dramatic 12 minute speech in which he protested his innocence and expressed disbelief at what had happened to him. He said: "I would like to apologise for the things that have been said in this court. Some of the things I agreed with, some of the things I do not agree with. I have been convicted but I did not rape anyone. I did not attempt to rape any-

one. I am sorry – I agree that I did something but I did not mean to do it. My conduct when I went to Indianapolis was kind of crass, I agree.

"Some of the things that were said painted me as a maniac, a guy going crazy. But I was just trying to have fun. I don't know why a complaint was made against me because we talked back and forth and made agreements. The situation happened and I cannot believe she said what she said.

"It is incredible to believe how I could fool her and do these horrific things to her. I am sorry not only for me but also for my family and the people close to me. People said I had been manipulated by money but I read the papers – I can read the papers – and some of the things that were said about me were not very nice. I am not vindictive or ferocious. Things that were said by the prosecution were very distasteful." Then, pointing at prosecution tormentor Garrison he said: "He was on TV. He was on the Barbara Walters show. These flash-in-the-pan media stars making comments on incidents they have no knowledge of. Big man – he was on Barbara Walters. I was hurt. I was humiliated. I expect the worst here today. I don't know if I can deal with it but I am not afraid because I am not guilty. I did not hurt anyone.

"She had no black eyes, no broken ribs. I am not the type. They said I was emotionally disturbed. I don't know what emotionally disturbed is. Charles Manson – I guess he's emotionally disturbed. My life has been incarcerated by this. I am a public figure and this goes worldwide. It was horrible to be in this courtroom, one big dream, totally unbelievable. I am devastated – not just for myself but for the people who support me. I cannot see any good coming out of it. I was crucified. The reason I don't cry is that the people standing behind me are stronger than I. I feel that if I cry I will lose them. I am prepared to deal with this. That's all that I am prepared to say."

As Judge Patricia Gifford pronounced sentence of six years she told him: "I believe there are two Mike Tysons – one capable of kindness and generosity and one that acts in the manner which you did in Indianapolis last year." Tyson, surrounded by four prison guards, rose slowly from his seat. He took off his gold watch and cufflinks, handed them to his lawyer and then walked slowly away from the courtroom and into incarceration.

Yet even as a free man he will be guilty – as the court says he is – or innocent as he maintains he is. Perhaps for Desiree, her sentence is one for life. After the trial she said: "I feel no happiness or elation about this. I am saddened however that Tyson showed no remorse or regret. I thought I would have a sense of relief that it is all over, but I don't. I feel in a sombre mood, almost down. This is still very difficult for me to deal with. I fear it will leave a permanent scar. But I will just have to get on with being a college kid again."

TOUGH TIMES

That has not been easy for Desiree in the years since Tyson has languished behind the bars of the Indiana Youth Centre – an innocuous sounding name for a maximum security jail. There are many in America who feel that Tyson got the rough end of the stick – particularly in the black community. Desiree has been every bit as much a prisoner as Tyson. She can go nowhere without the stares, the whispers, the accusing fingers that she plotted his downfall to get her painted nails into his fortune.

America's blacks, victims of a racist past and present that still pervades all aspects of their society, have branded her a female "Uncle Tom" – black on the outside but white on the inside. She bears the mark of Cain – bringing down a "brother" for "cracker-ass honkies" intent on keeping blacks in their place.

Private detectives have delved into the past which was strictly off-limits at the ten-day trial in February 1992. Resulting allegations suggested that violent rows with her father punctuated her upbringing – that once he tried to drown her after finding out she lost her virginity at 15. It was also alleged that she underwent psychiatric counselling after these rows. And the world also knows that now she plans to sue Mike

AMERICA'S BLACKS HAVE BRANDED HER A FEMALE "UNCLE TOM" – BLACK ON THE OUTSIDE BUT WHITE ON THE INSIDE

Below: *Prison cost Mike Tyson everything – his titles, his respect, his money, his adulation and material comforts like this £3.5 million mansion outside Bernardsville, New Jersey.*

Left: *An artist's impression of Desiree Washington giving firm and disturbing testimony against Tyson.*

Below: *The verdict is in and Mike Tyson leaves the court with his lawyer Vincent Fuller.*

There are no more beauty pageants, like the one where she met Tyson, to be attended. There are no more dances to go to, no movies to share with boyfriends. In statements issued through lawyers she said: "I am the victim yet I am also the guilty one. It seems I am being punished for this. My life was destroyed that day and yet people are always trying to prove Mike Tyson innocent. He knows what he did. I don't hate him, but I do think he has to pay for what he did. God knows that I am paying for what he did. Some people have turned against me. His people have portrayed me as scheming and manupulative.

Tyson for a large percentage of his not inconsiderable fortune. The sum of the parts of that, and other lurid portions of her background, is meant to equal this: that Desiree Washington was sexually experienced, slightly unbalanced, and financially motivated when she walked into room 606 after midnight with Mike Tyson, her hero.

Her detractors say that these allegations show she set him up for a fall.

Rape counsellors and feminists are appalled by the treatment that has marked Desiree out as a social leper. And they point to the effectivness of the campaign to rubbish her by the fact that two of the jurors who convicted Tyson now say they believe she was NOT raped. "It is incredible to think that the weight of public opinion has been manipulated in this fashion," said Renee Dodds, a rape crisis centre organiser in Los Angeles. "She gave her testimony and he was convicted of rape. Now we have all this extra-court kangaroo justice whereby it seems fair and right to trawl through her past to make judgements on her and her motives. The jury decided then that there was no motive on her part. She was RAPED. And now she is being punished for it. Never have I seen less sympathy for a proven victim of rape."

Punishment is how Desiree sees it too. A student at a college in Providence, Rhode Island, she shuns the out-of-classroom activities which she once enjoyed so much.

"But I told the truth that night. I said no and he raped me. I know the support he has in the black community by the fact that I was offered money before the trial to drop the charges. I was offered a million dollars. If I wanted just money why didn't I say yes and not go ahead with it? I had to go ahead with it because I was brought up to do what's right. But my life will never be the same. Never."

A PERSONALITY CHANGE

Friends who know her say she has changed beyond all recognition. The bright, bubbly personality has been transformed into one of sullen introspection. Her parents' marriage broke up shortly after the trial and she lives with her mother, Mary Bell Washington, who does her best to shield her daughter away from the worst excesses of anti-Desiree hysteria. Desiree herself cannot quite grasp that a huge segment of America's black population hates her for what she did. Black activist Nathan Pearson, who points out that he makes no judgement on Desiree, says: "They see her as a person who destroyed a black icon. You don't got much in the ghetto – you got dreams and heroes. Well, she took away a

Above: *The jurors who put the world champ behind bars answer press questions.*

Below: *The famous hands that floored his rivals are prepared for fingerprinting.*

hero when she cried rape. And people think: 'What you doing, child, in a room with Mike Tyson at 2.00am if you ain't there for one thing?' Black people have got enough troubles without blacks turning on blacks. I think that is part of the problem with Desiree and the black community."

In the case of Indianapolis v Tyson, there are no winners – only losers.

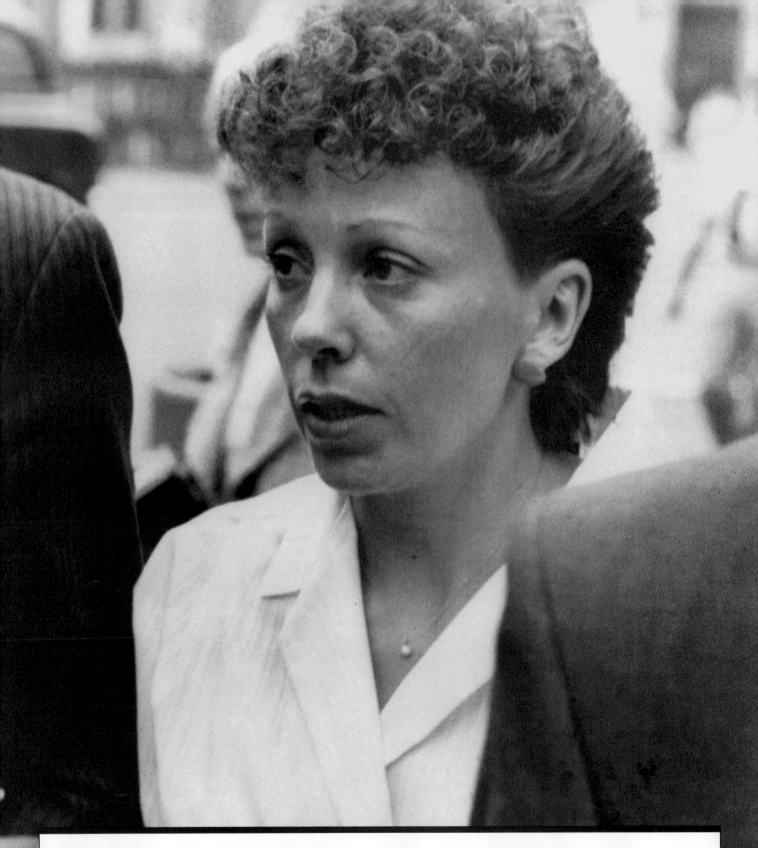

KILLING GAMES
Unsporting conduct

Jayne Scott took a hammer to the head of her lesbian love rival and injured the woman she despised so much she became little more than a wheelchair-bound vegetable. Victim Susan Craker was a deputy headmistress, tangled up in a web of sexual intrigue spawned upon the playing fields of Eton and Windsor.

It was a sensational trial at the nation's premier court – the Old Bailey, London. In the dock stood a woman accused of grievous bodily harm, namely that attractive Jayne Scott had taken a claw hammer to the head of her lesbian love-rival and attacked her with such ferocity that the woman she despised was left as little more than a wheelchair-bound vegetable.

What added even more intrigue to the court case – as spicy and as lurid as Britain had witnessed in many a year – was that victim Susan Craker was a deputy headmistress, tangled up in a web of sexual intrigue spawned upon the playing fields of Eton and Windsor. British police in modern times have had their fair share of dealing with criminal conspiracies, but none seemed as strange, when it was unravelled, as that of the teachers who were linked in a blue-stocking network of lesbianism. "Secret Lust of the Netball Girls!" screamed the headline in one tabloid news-

IT WAS A COURT CASE AS SPICY AND LURID AS BRITAIN HAD WITNESSED IN MANY A YEAR

Opposite: *Jayne Scott, whose jealousy led her to extreme violence.*

Below: *The proximity of the famous Eton school brought unwelcome attention to the area.*

Above: *Sue Craker, pictured before the attack which left her a virtual vegetable.*

GIRLS WHO COMPETED SO VIGOROUSLY ON THE SPORTS FIELD WERE BEDHOPPING, KISSING AND CUDDLING OFF IT

paper when the trial ended with Scott's conviction. The image of the jolly-hockey-sticks mistresses was changed forever in its wake. For those muscular girls who competed so vigorously in cricket, netball and hockey on the field were bedhopping, kissing and cuddling off of it. And their dangerous liaisons were to end with such tragic consequences for Susan Craker.

Jayne Scott was a teacher before she wound up standing before the full might of British justice at the Old Bailey in August 1986. A staff member at the 500-pupil Slough and Eton Church of England Secondary School, she was popular among pupils and staff alike in her position as gym mistress. She taught all the usual sports and served on a netball committee outside school hours. Her victim Sue Craker was not as popular among schoolchildren, probably because of her position close to supreme authority at the school as deputy headmistress. Janita Lake, a pupil who left in the same summer as the attack, said: "Miss Scott was great. She was the sort of woman you could go to and talk about anything with. She enjoyed a laugh and a joke and was everyone's favourite.

But Miss Craker was terrible. If you walked past her she would just give you a hard stare." That was an unfair viewpoint from someone who just knew her as a keeper of rules and discipline. Sue Craker was, at 36, a top all-round sportswoman, dynamic and ambitious, who excelled in cricket, squash and swimming and who was destined for the top of the academic ladder. And also what Janita did not know, nor the rest of the school, or her parents or anyone else save for a select few, was that both women were lesbians. Both kept the fact a secret from each other in the early days, but the world they moved in was small... and gossipy.

THE OBJECT OF DESIRE

Jayne Scott, at 31, was considered attractive by men at her school, but from her earliest years had been attracted to people of the same sex. The terrible tangled web which would lead to the ruination of Craker's life began being woven when she was attracted to married woman Debbie Fox. Debbie was a 34-year-old petite blonde, a sophisticated dresser who worked as credit controller. She was trapped in a "brother and sister" marriage and looked for gratification elsewhere. The court heard how Debbie, who described herself as bisexual, was on the same extra-curricular sporting committee as Jayne – the Slough and Eton Netball League. Debbie was about to split from her husband and had thrown herself into sports as one way of easing the pain of the break-up.

She later revealed: "I met Jayne and for months we just met as friends. But one weekend she invited me to a hockey tournament in Weymouth when she was playing for the Guildford Ladies team. I knew then that my feelings for her had changed,

Left and Below: *Abbots Road and the house where the brutal attack that would lead to Jayne Scott's trial at the Old Bailey took place.*

but nothing happened. It was the first time I had had feelings like this for a woman. I told her I fancied her on a walk home but she said: 'But you're married!' We became lovers after a hockey tournament in Southampton. I took the dominant role." The passionate affair between the two women snowballed... with Debbie sneaking home to her husband after her sex sessions with Jayne.

But Debbie insisted: "Jayne was in no way responsible for the break-up of my marriage. My husband and I had talked about going our own ways long before that. When we split up I moved into a flat with her and we bought it on a joint mortgage."

Like most couples – certainly married ones – they settled into a life that was more routine than roaring passion. Debbie told the Old Bailey that Jayne soon began to rebuff her sexual advances and that they didn't have sex with each other for more than a year. Then, because of her involvement with sports, she met Susan Craker and became attracted to her. Craker was herself involved in a domestic gay situation – she lived with lesbian shoe-shop manageress Kate Potts, 34, and was also on the lookout for sexual gratification from somewhere else. The catalyst for the dangerous liaison between Craker and Fox came when the four gay girls went together on a Riverboat Shuffle – a disco down the Thames organised by the school where the teachers were based. Afterwards, at a house in Windsor, the foursome carried on their own private party.

Fox told the court that she had danced with Kate Potts and Sue Craker but that her own live-in lover Scott turned her down. Yet in a bid designed to arouse passions and jealousies, Debbie later found Craker and Scott with their arms around each other on the sofa. "All this was after you told Jayne you fancied Susan?" asked Richard Cherrill, defending. "Yes," replied Debbie. Then he added: "It was Jayne who brought

THE PASSIONATE AFFAIR SNOWBALLED... WITH DEBBIE SNEAKING HOME TO HER HUSBAND AFTER SEX SESSIONS WITH JAYNE

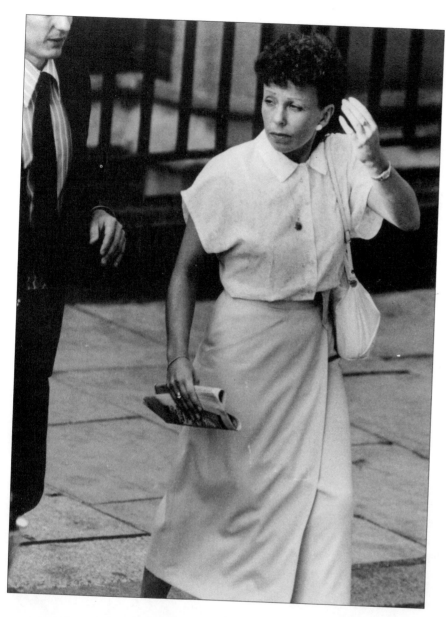

Above: *Jayne Scott summons a taxi outside the Old Bailey after a trying day in the dock.*

IN THE FRENZIED ATTACK,
SUE CRAKER'S HEAD
WAS, LITERALLY,
BASHED IN WITH A
CLAW HAMMER

tions, sleepless nights and long silences." In the six days after Debbie had told of the amorous encounter Scott started demanding kisses and cuddles from Debbie, even though she had rejected her sexual advances for a period of more than a year. "She suddenly wanted more attention from me," said Debbie. "She wanted me to hold her or kiss her."

She also wanted something much, much more, alleged the police. She wanted revenge against the deputy headmistress who claimed her "girl". Their case, denied by Scott, was that she went to Susan's home on August 6 1985 armed with a claw hammer. In an attack, the result of which police described as one of the most frenzied they had seen, Sue Craker's head was literally bashed in. Two gardeners working in the grounds of her home testified at Scott's trial how they heard eerie, moaning noises coming from inside the house… but thought it was someone "mucking around".

Gardener Ian Smith said: "It was like a moaning sound that went on for five minutes. We thought that someone was playing around and so we made the same noises back. Then it just stopped and there was silence." His workmate Nicholas Finney added: "We thought that it was someone having fun. We didn't think anyone was in pain. It was a sort of oohing noise, quite loud so as you could hear it over the noise of the lawnmowers."

A HORRIFYING SIGHT

Ian Scofield, Miss Craker's nephew who lived next door to her in Abbots Road, Barnet, said he rushed around to the house after the attack. He found his aunt wearing only a blouse and pants, groaning and gurgling on the floor amid a large pool of blood. Whatever the gardeners might have been able to do for her in terms of making her comfortable, the damage to her brain had already been completed with the first few blows of the hammer. Jayne Scott, despite her denials to police and to the court, had turned Miss Cracker into a vegetable.

The case was a sensation in Britain and involved hordes of journalists armed with fat chequebooks descending on Eton and Windsor seeking out the juicier background stories that would draw more and more people into the "secret lust of the netball

the sexual side of your relationship to an end by repulsing your advances, was it not?" Again she answered yes… which led events on to the 6 August 1985 when Susan Craker's dynamic world ended.

Days before the attack Jayne Scott had gone to Sheffield to compete in a sporting tournament. During that weekend Debbie and Sue Craker shared an evening of lesbian sex. "We were in Susan's house on our own," Debbie told police. "During the evening we kissed each other several times. At some stage Sue said: 'Shall we go to bed?' I agreed. Sexual contact of a lesbian nature took place between us – Susan taking the dominant role." Such a one-night-stand could have been shared and kept secret forever – but Debbie confessed all to her lover. She said: "She was a very emotional person. There were tears, recrimina-

was not all that I thought it would be. I don't think it was normal for young people in their early twenties. We found our relationship was more like brother and sister than man and wife. I do not think that I got what I thought I would in marrying her. I did not get any early warning signs to tell me she might be lesbian. I think the split came because we had such a hectic social life and did such a lot of sport that we were apart too much. But I never thought of her being a lesbian. I was very young and I'm a lot older now and know a lot more and maybe now I would be able to pick signs out. When all this is

girls" inquiry. No-one was more surprised to find himself thrust into the limelight over the front-page case than Debbie Fox's ex-husband Stephen Fox. He had known nothing of his wife's lesbian affairs until he picked up his national newspaper one morning and read about her all over the front page. He said knowledge that he lost his wife to the charms of another woman hit him "like a bombshell", and that he was reeling from it days afterwards. Stephen, 28 at the time of the crime, had met Debbie when they worked together for an engineering firm in 1977.

They began dating and were married in the picture-postcard church of St. Giles in Stoke Poges in 1979. A financial accountant later in life, he said: "We were too young for marriage really. Gradually the marriage became like a brother and sister relationship. I remember that she was really nice looking. When you are that age you lust after everything in sight, but she was special. I had just broken up from a fairly long-standing relationship and Debbie was attractive, intelligent, quite a female altogether. But we just seemed to drift apart after we got married.

"I had no warning signs of Debbie's love for other women during the time we were together, three years in all. But my sex life

Above: *Susan Craker is surrounded by Fleet Street pressmen after Scott is found guilty.*

Top: *The Old Bailey, London, where Jayne Scott's frenzied attack was set out in gory detail.*

over I shall speak to her. I shall ask her why she did not tell me about what was coming up in court. All I knew was that she said there was a case coming up, but she didn't go into it."

Stephen split from Debbie in 1982 but they remained friends. Their divorce came around by mutual agreement on the grounds of separation – nothing to do with her extra marital affairs with other women. "I don't believe my wife had lesbian lovers

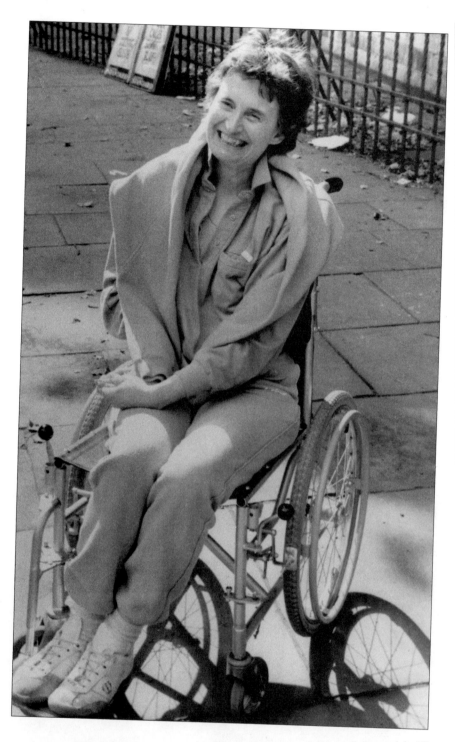

Above: *The verdict was of some comfort for Miss Craker but nothing could give her back her previous life.*

dence against her piled up daily. Kate Potts took the stand to testify how she became a sort of go-between after Scott telephoned her to say that she suspected an affair between Fox and Craker.

Potts' relationship with Craker had fizzled in the weeks before the attack and she now lived alone. "I took the call on August 2, four days before the attack," said Potts. "She asked if she could see me to talk about Debbie and Sue. She just mentioned that she wanted to talk about their relationship. I did not know anything about the relationship. She seemed a bit fraught on the phone and I agreed she could come around about midday.

"When she arrived she was in control but very nervous, very on the edge. She said Debbie and Sue had been seeing each other in the previous week and would I find out what was going on. She said Debbie had stayed with Sue and had explained everything that happened.

"She said she went to see Sue the previous day to ask her to give up the relationship with Debbie. But Sue would not listen to her. I rang Sue while Scott was still in the house. I asked her what was happening and she said it was none of my business. She said she would not be intimidated. When I told Scott what Sue had just said to me it did not ease her at all. She said she and Debbie were going around to Sue's at the weekend and I thought it a very foolish idea and told her so."

A SOLID CONVICTION

The verdict when it came down was greeted with a look of shock and disbelief from the defendant. The jury of ten men and two women returned a unanimous verdict which proved beyond reasonable doubt that the woman from Farnham Royal, Berkshire, was guilty of the crime with which she was charged – grievous bodily harm with intent. Judge Michael Morland told her in the dock of victim Craker: "You all but destroyed her life." He rejected a plea from defence counsel Richard Cherrill for the sentence to be postponed so Scott could be considered for psychiatric treatment. He told her: "You have been convicted of an horrific crime. I accept that you were suffering from depression following your father's death. It's clear that you were

while she was with me," he said. "I am planning to re-marry now and have told my fiancee all about Debbie. She understands that I now just have a friendly relationship with her and doesn't mind if I meet her and take her for a drink. This lesbian thing is quite staggering but it hasn't changed my opinion of Debbie."

Scott steadfastly maintained her innocence, hoping that a lack of forensic evidence tying her to the crime would make the police case come down to her word against theirs. But the circumstantial evi-

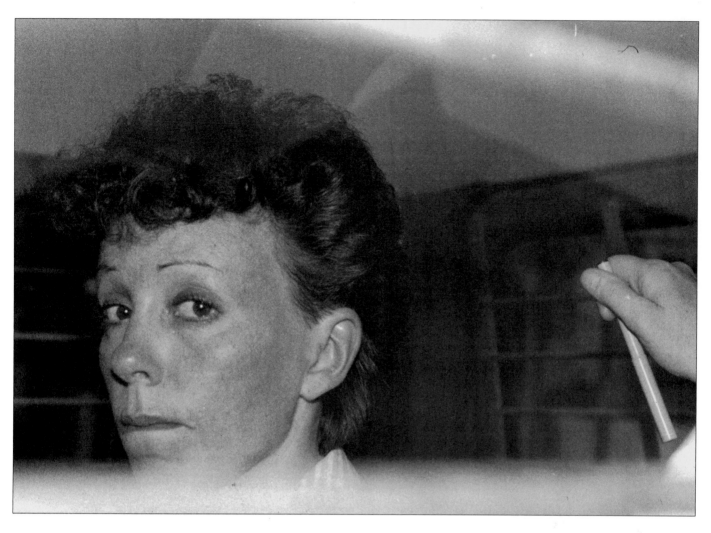

vulnerable to the burgeoning sexual relationship between Susan and Debbie. Your jealousy caused a loss of self control and you deliberately took the opportunity to bludgeon Sue Craker with the claw hammer, all but destroying her life." Scott went to the cells without a glance at the jury of her peers who had convicted her.

Outside the court there was solace in justice for Sue Craker – solace that could only be expressed in the staccato words she is now capable of due to her massive injuries. She told newsmen at the end of the two-week-long trial: "Thank God, thank God. Deserved everything she got... not enough... should be longer. Ruined my life... hope she suffers. Like me. Never forgive, never... Justice... done."

With the ending of the case came the inevitable "backgrounders" in the newspapers – the story-behind-the-story revelations that boosted sales in the sluggish summer months. Police officers involved in the case revealed that they were stunned by the extent of the lesbian network which

spanned the playing fields and sports of the most English of areas.

One unamed officer said: "It was sex in the suburbs all right – only it was all women having it off with other women. It was quite an eye opener!" The police found a network spanning all walks of life and seemed astonished by it – yet those who had known Jayne Scott and the others said their lifestyle was merely one of those "open secrets" which so many know but say little about. Staff at the Monten Sports Centre in Slough, which had been used by the defendant for nine years, giggled behind her back at the passionate affairs that she pursued.

One 26-year-old woman attendant said: "Jayne was a very nice person – but everyone knew she was that way inclined. She wasn't the only one, though. Her sports attracted a lot of 'butch' girls and we knew there was a lot of hanky panky going on. One day the park-keeper opposite told us of a passionate lovemaking session he heard in the ladies' changing rooms!"

Above: *Jayne Scott has one last glimpse of the world before she is taken away in a prison van to begin her sentence.*

"IT WAS SEX IN THE SUBURBS ALL RIGHT – ONLY IT WAS ALL WOMEN HAVING IT OFF WITH OTHER WOMEN"

"HER SPORTS ATTRACTED A LOT OF 'BUTCH' GIRLS AND WE KNEW THERE WAS A LOT OF HANKY PANKY GOING ON"

SOAP IN COURT
Taylforth's Big Blow

The Eastenders soap opera made a household name of Gillian Taylforth. But the flip side of fame brought misery to Gillian when her name appeared in a newspaper linked to a kinky sex act. She went to court to try to defeat the newspaper but ended up being humiliated and beaten in the courtroom.

Fighting a case for libel in the High Court in London can be like winning the pools... or losing at Russian roulette. For the aggrieved party who says his or her good name has been dragged through the mud in a publication there is the chance of great riches if the jury finds in their favour. Jeffrey Archer scooped £500,000 when a jury found he had been libelled by a newspaper which claimed he consorted with a prostitute. Elton John won a £1,000,000 settlement from The Sun newspaper which accepted there was no truth in its allegations that the singer had been with under-age rent boys. The paper caved in before the case was heard, mindful that legal bills – and a vengeful jury which always settles the sums to be paid – could have sent the final reckoning sky-high.

Yet for a person to lose can mean financial ruin. Sonia Sutcliffe, wife of the Yorkshire Ripper Peter Sutcliffe, was saddled with legal expenses close to £250,000

THERE IS THE CHANCE OF GREAT RICHES IF A HIGH COURT JURY FINDS IN FAVOUR OF A LIBELLED PARTY

Opposite: *Gillian Taylforth enters the High Court with her boyfriend Geoff Knights.*

Below: *Day in, day out, Gillian and Geoff Knights had to listen to damning testimony.*

Above: *Gillian hoped that her reputation as a famous actress would rise above that of the often scurrilous Sun newspaper.*

THE SUN CLAIMED SHE HAD BEEN PERFORMING ORAL SEX ON KNIGHTS AS THEIR RANGE ROVER CAR WAS PARKED IN A LAY-BY

when she sued one newspaper too many after an incredible winning streak against the Fleet Street tabloids. It is a risk that is inherent when the action is brought because losing means paying one's own legal costs, plus the side of the defence. And when barristers of the A-Team of the legal profession are involved, such costs are significant. That is why most people mull over the pros and cons of launching a libel action carefully.

One can only assume that Gillian Taylforth, a leading actress in the BBC soap opera *Eastenders* had taken the best advice before deciding to take on The Sun in the High Court. But after a sensational trial which gripped the nation she ended up staring ruin in the face. She had pulled the trigger… and the chamber had been loaded. When the jurors returned to deliver their verdict after pondering on a case she felt certain of winning she suddenly found herself staring a £500,000 legal bill in the

face. Not only that, but it was clear that a jury of her peers had found her guilty of performing a particularly lurid act – which she denied – and that it would go into the history books as fact.

Gillian Taylforth's ire was aroused by a story in The Sun newspaper which claimed she and her lover Geoff Knights had been caught by a police officer in a compromising position; that she was performing oral sex on him as their Range Rover car was parked in a lay-by off of the A1. The allegation was damaging enough to any person, irrespective of their standing in the community. But Miss Taylforth, as Kathy Beale in the super-popular TV series, had more to lose than most. Television is a fickle game and the image of an actress is everything. She is paid £80,000 a year for her role in the show which is watched by 19,000,000 people. This kind of publicity, she knew, was the kind that could destroy her acting career for good.

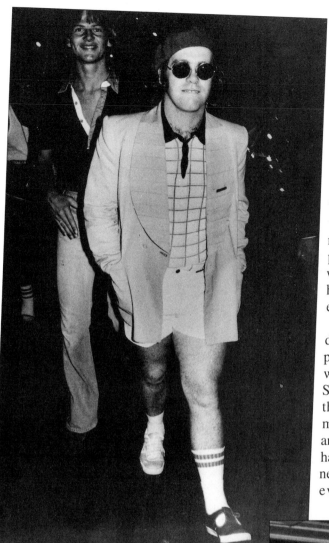

11 days and provide high theatre for Britain in the middle of a drab winter. There would be witnesses, explanations and a final, dramatic 11th hour video produced on behalf of The Sun which would finally clinch the case against her. Newspapers expended acres of space on it and it was the talking point of Britain. Clearly the cost for Ms. Taylforth in proceeding with it was not only financial – it also raked over a story that most people in the country, save those who read The Sun, had never heard of and gave it to an audience of tens of millions.

Court 13 was the setting for the drama in January 1994 and the principles played to the gallery with aplomb. Representing The Sun was George Carman, Q.C., the Torquemada of barristers, a man with a rapier sharp mind and an even sharper turn of phrase. He had gone to battle for and against newspapers in his time, but whoever he was representing had

---

THE CASE RAKED OVER A STORY THAT MOST PEOPLE IN THE COUNTRY HAD NEVER HEARD OF AND GAVE IT TO MILLIONS

Left: *Elton John took £1,000,000 from The Sun over allegations that he had sex with under-age rent boys.*

Below: *Lord Jeffrey Archer with wife Mary. He too went to battle in the High Court to clear his name and won record damages. Gillian Taylforth would not be so lucky.*

The story first appeared in 1992 in The Sun. The implication was that the couple were having oral sex when a police officer chanced upon the vehicle parked in a slip-road off of the A1 at Borehamwood, Herts. It quoted police as saying Knights had been cautioned for an indecent act. The story from Miss Taylforth was simply that she had been leaning over to rub his stomach because he had drunk too much champagne at Royal Ascot and was feeling queasy.

A BIG GAMBLE

It was left to a jury of four women and eight men to prove, beyond reasonable doubt, who was telling the truth. If it was 38-year-old Miss Taylforth she stood to gain a massive amount of money and all legal costs would have to be picked up by The Sun. But a loss could prove catastrophic – yet it was a risk she was willing to take "for my good name". The trial was to last

Above: *Gillian Taylforth with friend Steve McFadden before the verdict that wiped the smile from her face.*

bought the best. Peter Carter-Ruck, himself one of the top libel lawyers in Britain, said: "He is the first choice in any criminal case and certainly one of the leading choices in libel cases. He is extremely thorough in the preparation of his cases and even in cross-examination can get pretty near offensive." Yet no-one ever accused a court of law as being a finishing school for girls – and Miss Taylforth was to find out for herself just how brutal George Carman could be as he hacked away for the truth.

Her evidence was simple: that Knights had suffered a "pancreatic attack" after drinking the champagne and that she was rubbing his stomach to soothe away the pain. "How could anyone think I would stop on the A1 to have oral sex?" she asked the court quizzically.

"It was cheap and really made me feel sick to my stomach." Her QC Michael Beloff, whose fees would eventually top out at around £75,000, tried to suggest that the policeman whose unhappy lot it was to

> MISS TAYLFORTH WAS TO FIND JUST HOW BRUTAL GEORGE CARMAN COULD BE AS HE HACKED AWAY FOR THE TRUTH

stumble across the couple, was doing it for some kind of glory, of making the story up "and revelling in the limelight".

But P.C. Terry Talbot was a man whose evidence was firm and measured in every way. He told the court that he had approached the parked car and saw Taylforth's head "moving slowly up and down" over her lover's lap. He also said he saw Mr. Knight's exposed manhood. Under increased pressure that he was somehow mistaken or otherwise disposed to give inaccurate testimony, the 49-year-old officer said: "If I stood here until Christmas I would not change anything I said or saw."

Indeed, he said he had in fact been too soft on the soap star and should have arrested her and Knights instead of merely cautioning them. That was backed up by his superior, Inspector Francis Monoghan, who said: "The actress should have been arrested along with Mr. Knights for outraging public decency and using abusive language." It was clearly quite a strain on the copper who had twice been commended for bravery in the line of duty. PC Derek Sweeny, a colleague, said after the case: "It was such a terrible thing hanging over him that he was mentally breaking up. He is a very well-thought-of officer and everyone was behind him. Everyone knew he would tell nothing but the truth."

Bringing the case to court also exposed practically every other facet of their lives, including Taylforth's relationship with Knights, a man for whom the term "flash" seems to have been invented. The Daily Mail newspaper went so far as to state: "Knights could have stepped straight from the streets of Walford, fictional home of BBC TV's *Eastenders*. A strapping play-boy wheeler-dealer, he has dated a series of page three girls, has a taste for flash cars and has a number of convictions for burglary, criminal damage and assault."

A BAD HISTORY

Indeed, the litany of his run-ins with the law were seen by libel experts as seriously damaging the couple's standing in the eyes of the jury. Far from seeming a couple with reputations to lose, they began to be perceived as a couple yet to get them. "They became objects of ridicule," said The Guardian. "The jury appeared to be enraptured as the courtroom scenes ranged from moments of humour and emotion to outright sleaze."

The year before the case Knights had punched an *Eastenders* scriptwriter in a brawl after he had claimed an affair with her. The trial for him seemed embarrassing more than anything – especially when it came to a piece of police evidence which he clearly had not remembered anything about.

On the night that P.C. Talbot had interrupted his "stomach rub" he had signed a police caution admitting the sexual offence. The only defence he had for that was that he had drunk a lot of champagne and didn't know what he was signing. He did not seem to enjoy the police version of events which had him outside Borehamwood police station – Miss Taylforth had been allowed to drive home to look after their baby daughter Jessica – where it was alleged he said: "Take your uniforms off and I will fight you outside." The police

IT WAS ALLEGED THAT KNIGHTS HAD SAID TO POLICE: "TAKE YOUR UNIFORMS OFF AND I WILL FIGHT YOU OUTSIDE"

Below: **Gillian in her Eastenders *role with Albert Square market trader Pete Beale.***

said Knights calmed down and agreed to a caution over the sex act with the words: "You know how it is – we had a good day at the races and just got carried away!" He denied it, but the theatre surrounding the case was escalating daily.

The case was proving hilarious for those not directly involved in it. Long a nation used to the nudge-nudge, wink-wink humour of Benny Hill, many newspapers began running daily joke columns, each one playing off the blue humour of the court case. Comedians like Bernard Manning, known for his coarser-than-coarse jokes, said: "Gillian Taylforth asked this scouser if he wanted a blow job and he replied: 'Not if it affects my Giro cheque!'" The Daily Star – a newspaper which forked out £500,000 to Jeffrey Archer six years earlier, ran a Blue Jokes on Gillian half-page which included: "What's the difference between a willy and a German sausage? No? Well, let's go for a picnic!" The jokes were mildly amusing and lapped up by an audience that craved more and

GILLIAN CONFESSED TO
FRIENDS HALFWAY
THROUGH THE TRIAL THAT
SHE WISHED SHE HAD
NEVER BROUGHT IT

Right: *A videotape of Gillian performing an obscene act on a bottle for a joke at a party was to prove crucial in her losing the case.*

Below: *Geoff Knights and Gillian enjoying happier times, in the Range Rover where the sex act was alleged to have taken place.*

THE TAPE DESTROYED HER
CAREFULLY CULTIVATED
IMAGE OF A WOMAN
WRONGED BY THE POLICE
AND A PRESS REPORT

more details of the actress and her "past". But it was no laughing matter for Gillian who confessed to friends midway through the trial that she wished that she had never brought the matter to court.

Perhaps the most hilarious moment occurred when the judge Mr. Justice Drake agreed to a reconstruction of the incident in the car park of the High Court! Miss Taylforth and Knights were in the vehicle to depict themselves on the night in question while a couple of Sun reporters acted out P.C. Talbot's version of events. The Sun then pictured another reconstruction in their newspages the following day. It seemed as if there was no sanctuary left in England from the all-embracing courtcase.

But if the reconstruction was mildly amusing to all involved, the same cannot be said of the trump card of the defence, a video tape which the defence tried in two hours of legal argument to block. Miss Taylforth clearly had no idea what the

video contained when the judge consented to let it be screened and High Court staff moved into Court 13 to fix up the necessary screens and apparatus. It was later learned that the video was taken by a man known as "Herbie". Herbie had called The Sun at the 11th hour claiming that the video would vindicate the newspaper entirely. The Sun claimed that two unidentified men

later handed the video over, no money changed hands and the judge was satisfied that "nothing improper" had occurred in getting the video. It clinched the case for The Sun.

You could have heard a pin drop in the court as the tape was played. It destroyed Taylforth's carefully cultivated image of a woman wronged by both the police and a press report. The video showed her simulating oral sex at a party with a wine bottle and a large German sausage and above the lurid images could be heard her words: "I'd like to state I give good head. I give very good head."

The video was made during a lunchtime party with some showbiz friends at a small theatre in North London. It was a private affair and it would have remained so forever had Gillian Taylforth not chosen to take the newspaper to court. Now the video which she said was "a joke" was being used to damn her. George Carman went in for the kill: "The tacky and cheap video exposed her performance in the witness box as a sham. She is not quite the demure lady.

"Miss Taylforth's daughter Jessica has been waved in and out of the script as if she is the president of the Mother's Union. That is not the whole picture. The reality is that there is another side that has been carefully concealed from you. It is not a shameful side. It is a coarser side. Drunk or otherwise, with friends or otherwise, Gillian Taylforth was behaving in a way that one hopes the majority of women in this country would never behave. And she was doing that because in drink she can be given to a certain coarseness in sexual matters. Of course that doesn't prove she was having oral sex in a car. The words 'I give good head' could be her epitaph." Carman, nicknamed the Silver Fox within the rarified atmosphere of the law courts, had been at his best... or worst.

A SAD FIGURE

It took over five hours for the jury to retire and reach their verdict. When they came back into court Taylforth seemed to crumble when they took their places. Her fingers clutched at a silver charm and the jury avoided her eyes. The foreman stood and said that a majority verdict had been reached. When he said it was for the defendants – The Sun – there was a moan from Miss Taylforth as her sister Janice hissed at a police sergeant who had given evidence: "Satisfied, are you?" Outside the court as the legal minutiae was tied up – namely that Taylforth and Knights were responsible for the estimated £500,000 legal bill – she collapsed and needed to be taken to St. Bartholomew's Hospital by ambulance.

Later, putting a stoical face on a disastrous end to a disastrous case, she said: "I am emotionally drained. If I had known then what I know now I don't think I could have gone through the ordeal of the case. But at the end of the day it is all about clearing your name and that is

what Geoff and I tried to do. I was in deep shock when the verdict came in – I just couldn't breathe. Finding the money to pay these costs will be a serious struggle. It's not going to be easy. My whole character has changed. My faith in human nature has gone. I have come out of this a very, very cynical person. I have always been an open and honest person – but I know now that I have come out of this a different woman. The video was a joke, taken by someone who was a friend from the age of 17. Someone I trusted. I don't know who gave or sold that video. I feel I cannot trust anybody now."

Susan Aslan, a libel lawyer at a London law firm, said: "This has hammered home the point that libels are always risky, when it is one person's word against another. It is like playing Russian Roulette with the jury. There is never more than a 50-50 chance in most cases. I spend a lot of time talking people out of bringing such proceedings." Gillian Taylforth, of *Eastenders* fame, had spun the barrel on the gun... and lost.

"GILLIAN TAYLFORTH WAS BEHAVING IN A WAY THAT ONE HOPES THE MAJORITY OF WOMEN WOULD NEVER BEHAVE"

Below: *Gillian Taylforth leaves hospital accompanied by Knights. She had collapsed at the end of the libel trial that she had lost.*

A BLOODY END
The Death of Dillinger

John Dillinger was a criminal who lived by the gun and eventually died by it. There was no trial for Dillinger, no fancy lawyers to argue that he was the victim of society. He got his comeuppance the way that most said he deserved – violently, shot down after an elaborate FBI plan had come to fruition.

John Dillinger scorched his mark on the depression years in America like a branding iron. He was the most famous and most ruthless desperado of all. So daring were his actions and so successful his evasion of the full might of American crimefighters that laws were passed in Congress to find new ways to end his crime spree. He was rotten to the core, but to the forces of law and order he was becoming that most dangerous type of criminal – a hero to the man in the street.

These were hard times and even though he had murdered wantonly in his escapades and people viewed anyone who was getting their own back at a system which had deserted them as a Robin Hood figure.

Yet this Robin Hood gave nothing away – everything was done for the greater glory and greed of John Dillinger himself and no-one else. When he eventually died in spectacular fashion, outside a movie theatre in Chicago, America's attorney general of the

HE WAS BECOMING THAT MOST DANGEROUS TYPE OF CRIMINAL — A FOLK HERO TO THE MAN IN THE STREET

Opposite: *John Dillinger, Public Enemy No. 1.*

Below: *John Dillinger, in the white shirt second from right, after his 1934 capture.*

Above: *The tools of his murderous trade – weapons used by John Dillinger during his crime career.*

career in 1920, even though his most hair–raising exploits were all carried out in a remarkably short period of time in the early 1930s. John Toland, whose 1963 biography of the outlaw is regarded as one of the definitive works on his crime career, said: "John Dillinger, in the opinion of many, is the greatest folk hero of American crime. He was never mixed up with the vice or gambling rackets. He never tortured or shot his accomplices.

"Working with only a friend, or a small group, he was essentially a loner, an operator who planned and executed daring bank robberies and prison escapes. He came from a modest, rural, midwest background but somehow seemed destined to act out his role in the large cities. The banks that he knocked off were countless and Billy the Kid's exploits today seem child's play in comparison."

A BRUTAL YOUTH

Born in 1902 in Indianapolis, he was marked down as a bad seed by his teachers in school. Shrewd and cunning, ruthless and self centred, one master remarked that he had all the attributes for a career in

times was moved to say: "I find his death gratifying. It has saved the taxpayer a lot of money in a trial, for there can be no question that he would have lied to the end."

The man who would rise to the top of the FBI's most wanted list to become Public Enemy No.1 began his criminal

Right: *President Franklyn Roosevelt signs a tough anti-crime bill aimed at curbing the exploits of Dillinger and his kind. Directly behind him is J. Edgar Hoover, the FBI director who swore to get Dillinger one way or the other.*

crime – which is exactly what he was planning. Dillinger Jnr. burned with all the indignation of his countrymen who grew up poor with little government help. Life was a black and white affair to him – those who had and those who had not. He was most definitely in the latter, but his unique skills would place him in the former. Crime started off as juvenile burglaries and car thefts before he began to home in on those repositories of wealth – the banks. He had briefly held a job in a machine shop when he was 17, but the only items he seemed to fashion on the shop's lathe were replica guns – a skill that would one day stand him in good stead.

In September 1924 he was already on the run for having deserted the Navy after five months' service. With an accomplice he attempted to rob a grocery store in the

small town of Mooresville, where he had moved four years previously. But the store owner, Bertram Morgan, had an alarm wired up to the local police station, a novel device in those days. Soon cops were swarming all over the store and Dillinger

was arrested without a shot being fired. He and his companion were sentenced to serve between ten and 21 years in jail, their term to be determined by their behaviour inside the penitentiary. He twice tried to escape but in 1933, as the nation suffered like a prisoner upon the rack from the ravages of the Great Depression, the state governor took pity upon him and he was granted a pardon. It would go down as one of the great misguided judgements of all time.

A BAD TRAVELLER

Within less than a month he had procured firearms from the Chicago underworld and embarked on his legendary crime spree. With a moll at his side he first hit the pay-roll of a thread-making factory in Monticello, Illinois. Then in July 1933 he took $3,000 in an armed raid at a bank in Montpelier, Indiana. Raids in Daleville, Ohio and Indianapolis followed, each one more daring than the last. In the Indianapolis raid he was seemingly cornered – but some sixth sense told him to bolt for the rear of the building where he found a door unlocked. He walked calmly into the street and mingled with the lunchtime crowds – with the $28,000 in stolen loot still with him.

Above: *The Depression bred the conditions of hopelessness which turned Dillinger into a folk hero in the eyes of many.*

Left: *To the man in the street without a penny, the idea of Dillinger robbing the rich man's banks made him into a Robin Hood type of figure.*

HE WALKED CALMLY INTO THE STREET AND MINGLED WITH THE CROWDS – WITH THE STOLEN LOOT STILL WITH HIM

dollar robbery at the First National Bank in Chicago. It was a murder which shocked America and placed him at the top of the FBI most wanted list.

For three months Dillinger laid low, undergoing rudimentary plastic surgery to change his appearance. His chin was altered to disguise a tell-tale cleft in his chin, a mole on his face had been removed and there had been crude acid-burns applied to his fingertips in a bid to remove the prints. Experts said these would have caused him excruciating pain when done – and for nothing, as it turned out, because upon death his fingerprints were as crystal clear as the day he was born.

Soon it was time for him to go hunting again and he chose a bank in Tucson, Arizona – way out west and far from his usual stomping grounds around America's heartland. But this time it went badly wrong. Heavy bank security and police back-up surrounded him and his cohorts within minutes. There were no shots fired as Dillinger was led away in chains to await his destiny with the electric chair. But, after having been transferred back to Indiana, where most of his crimes had been committed, he staged the kind of spectacular escape that set polite society in Paris, Rome, Berlin and London talking about his exploits as well as all of America.

After the Indianapolis raid he was caught three days later, on September 25, in Dayton, Ohio, and sent to jail in Lima, Ohio, to await the arrival of an FBI investigating team. But members of his gang broke into the jail and murdered sheriff Jessee Sarber to spring him. Dillinger took a shot at the sheriff too. Dillinger now had blood on his hands and knew that there was no looking back.

Any capture in any state would mean extradition to the state where the most serious crime occurred – and ultimately a date with the electric chair. Instead of going underground with his not-inconsiderable reserves of loot he opted instead to increase the tempo of his activities. Raid followed raid – one on a police armoury to steal bullet proof jackets and machine guns, one on a bank that netted $144,000, another bank raid, this time in Wisconsin, where he stole $28,000, and a raid in Chicago. On January 15 1934 in Chicago he shot and killed Patrolman Patrick O'Malley in a $20,000

Above: *Dillinger affects a pose of supreme disinterest during one of the many court appearances he made during his violent life.*

ANY CAPTURE IN THE STATE WOULD MEAN EXTRADITION AND, ULTIMATELY, A DATE WITH THE ELECTRIC CHAIR

DEADLY SKILLS

Remembering his skill learned from the short time spent in the machine shop as a youth he fashioned an authentic-looking gun from wood in the prison workshop. Using some black boot polish he gave the gun a metallic hue. Using this he held up a guard, marched out into the street and was gone! His fame was never higher... the frustration of the authorities to hold down this Houdini of hold-ups never greater. The escape cemented his Robin Hood image in another way. He took two hostages out of the prison gates with him and gave each of them $4 for their cab fare home! This was big money during the Great Depression and was the kind of PR that the forces of law and order despised.

"Events followed swiftly after that," the New York Times wrote breathlessly of his exploits. "They multiplied until his name became a byword for outlawry, his existence a political shibboleth, his career a reason for the passing of laws in congress and the posting of rewards. Spectacular in the way he staged his lawless escapades, devil-may-care in his encounters with the law, he nevertheless brought every possible modern facility into play in his skirmishes. He used fast cars. He had bullet proof vests. His men used machine guns."

Although just two deaths were directly attributed to Dillinger, there had in fact been 16 lawmen killed by his gang members in shootouts and escapes. The law of "common purpose" applied across America and John Dillinger was jointly held responsible for them all.

"HE BROUGHT EVERY MODERN FACILITY INTO PLAY IN HIS SKIRMISHES... FAST CARS... BULLET PROOF VESTS... MACHINE GUNS"

Below: *Chicago, the Windy City, became a playground for such gangsters as Al Capone and John Dillinger.*

In April 1934 he and the gang decided to rest up again in woods in Little Bohemia, Wisconsin. There, amid respectable holidaymakers, the hoods rented a cabin and spent time sunbathing, fishing and playing endless games of cards. But the underworld was talking now and a massive armed task force of agents descended on the quiet wooded area for what they hoped would be the final showdown with Dillinger and his boys. On April 22 there were terrifying gun battles raging all day in the woods. Two lawmen were killed and several of Dillinger's men wounded, but the arch criminal and several others escaped in cars. He had eluded the law once more but he knew that the trap had been sprung due to the lure of the $15,000 reward. The government knew it too and consequently upped the money to $25,000 – around £150,000 by today's standards.

Dillinger decided to retire to Chicago after putting around rumours that he had been killed in the running gun battles in

Above: *The Biograph Cinema on the night John Dillinger was gunned down outside it.*

Right: *The girl whose photo was in John Dillinger's watch: Polly Hamilton.*

DILLINGER LIVED LIKE A PRIVATE, LAW-ABIDING CITIZEN FOR THE FIRST TIME SINCE HE WAS A SCHOOLBOY

Wisconsin. He took the name Jimmie Lawrence, a board of trade clerk, and began seeing an attractive 26-year-old divorced waitress called Polly Hamilton. Polly was hooked on the dashing good looks and casual manner of the man she knew as Jimmie – even more hooked when he bought her a diamond ring and gave her $50 for a visit to the dentist. Polly rented a room from a friend called Anna Sage, a woman who had twice been convicted and pardoned of running a brothel. She had been busted a third time and on this occasion there was to be no let-off; when John Dillinger moved under her roof she was staring at deportation to her native Romania, a prospect she truly dreaded.

In this period Dillinger lived like a private, law-abiding citizen for the first time

since he was a schoolboy. He knew the great manhunt was still on, but he severed his contact with underworld pals and kept a low profile. He enjoyed leisurely meals, movies in air-conditioned cinemas and going to nightclubs with Polly. He was pondering a move to Mexico and made tentative arrangements to fly there on the morning of July 23, unaware that he would be dead 24 hours before departure time, the pieces of silver on his head too tempting for someone to resist.

A SERIOUS MANHUNT

FBI Director J. Edgar Hoover had sent special agent Sam Cowley to Chicago after receiving information that he had fled there. Hoover said to him: "Stay on Dillinger. Go everywhere the trail takes you. Take everyone who was ever remotely connected to the gang. Take him alive if you can but protect yourself." But a situation that had no connection to the FBI or the chase was about to bring the case of Public Enemy No.1 to its climax.

Anna Sage, the woman who was facing deportation, had learned through her own contacts in the criminal fraternity who the board of trade clerk living with Polly really was. She was not only tempted by the large reward – she was tempted by the possibility of cutting a deal with the immigration authorities intent on deporting her from

America . After negotiating with policemen whom she knew she was finally granted an audience with senior officers at a secret meeting on the shore of Lake Michigan late at night. Satisfied that the lawmen would both pay her the reward money and use their clout to stop her being deported, she ratted on the gangster.

Sunday July 22 was a hot and muggy day in Chicago, so hot that 23 people would die from weather-related problems. The cinemas were a favourite spot in the city because of their air conditioning. Sage had told the police that Dillinger and Polly were planning a trip to the Marbro movie

theatre. Or possibly the Biograph. At 7.00pm Sage telephoned the FBI to say: "He's here. He's just come. I am going with them. Probably the Marbro or the Biograph. I don't know." She hung up, leaving the agents scrambling to cover both theatres. Special agents trained in marksmanship covered both of them, all entrances and exits. They wanted him alive, but if there was trouble he would be gunned down like a dog. The case had a unique aspect to it already – so keen were the FBI on maintaining security that they didn't even tell the Chicago police of the operation they were mounting.

Above: *The bullet-ridden body of John Dillinger is examined by lawmen and the plain curious at the local morgue after he was gunned down.*

could only bolt for it. In a low crouch he ran into the alley at the side of the cinema. The gun was in his hand now and before he had gone 20 paces the barked commands to halt were being shouted ater him.

Two agents opened fire on him, one bullet hitting his left side, the other tearing into his back and exiting through his right eye. He was stone dead before he hit the hot cobblestones.

Dillinger died a few blocks from the garage where the Al Capone gang had wiped out rivals in the infamous St. Valentine's Day Massacre. As agents went into the Biograph to telephone Hoover in Washington with the good news, Dillinger's body was taken to the Cook County Morgue for an autopsy.

It was there that the extent of his plastic surgery became clear – and also how ineffective his fingerprint mutilation had been. The acid had failed to do its work and the whorls of all his dabs came out crystal clear; it was the concrete identification the FBI needed that they had their man. A few minutes after he had been deposited at the morgue Sgt. Frank Reynolds of the Dillinger squad – a man who had spent two years hunting him – came in. He was so glad to see his nemesis dead that he shook the hand of the corpse. Meanwhile, outside

But the presence outside the cinema of so many plainclothes men aroused the suspicion of the manager, fearful that he was to become the victim of another box-office hold up. He telephoned the police, who arrived just as Dillinger was exiting the Biograph at 10.30pm, having watched *Manhattan Melodrama* starring Clark Gable and William Powell. The picture ended with the villain, Gable, walking to the electric chair.

ANIMAL CUNNING

Dillinger's feral senses stirred as he saw men flashing identification badges to other men outside the theatre and his hand reached inside his jacket pocket for the loaded Colt automatic nestling there. He knew something was up and knew that he

Above and Right: *Before and after. His death mask after he was shot and how he looked before he paid for plastic surgery with the loot from his bank raids.*

ONE BULLET HIT HIM ON HIS LEFT SIDE, THE OTHER TORE INTO HIS BACK AND EXITED THROUGH HIS RIGHT EYE

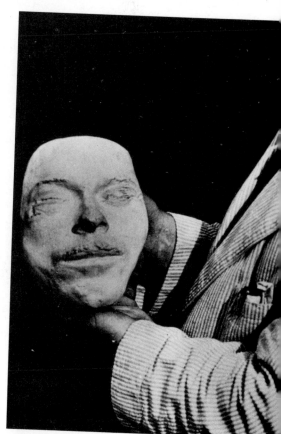

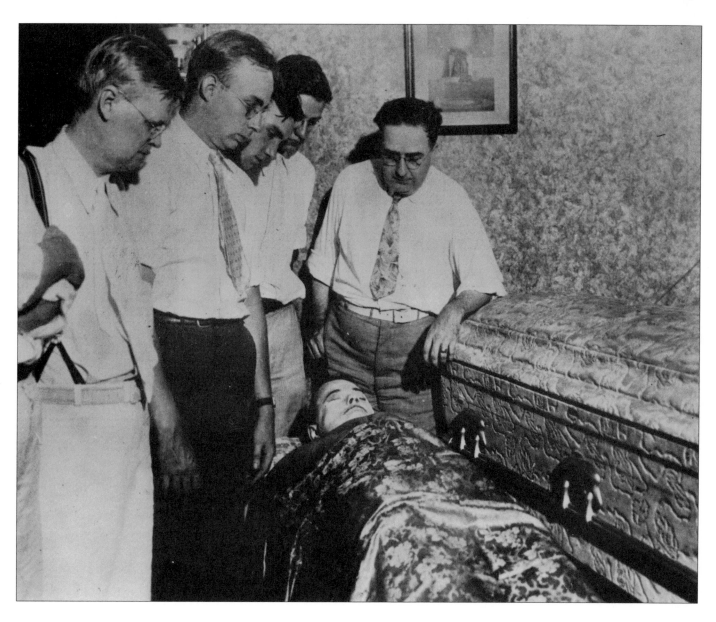

the theatre, women dipped handkerchiefs in his blood, even the hems of their skirts, to remind them that they were there the night the greatest gangster of them all finally got his just desserts.

SOLO MOURNER

"So it is really true?" asked the old man as he opened the door to his farmhouse home. "Are you sure there is no mistake?" Perhaps John Dillinger Snr., father of the slain gangster, was the only true mourner that night. Federal agents knocked on his door to inform him of his son's death just hours later.

"I prayed it would not happen," said the old man at his home in Mooresville, Indiana. "The thing I have prayed for all these months has happened, he's finally

Above: *Lying in state in his home town of Mooresville, Indiana. The glory days for the gangsters were over with the death of Dillinger.*

WOMEN DIPPED HANDKERCHIEFS IN HIS BLOOD, EVEN THE HEMS OF THEIR SKIRTS.

dead. If you live life like he lived it I guess that the best he could have hoped for was a quick death. At least this way there won't be folks sitting in judgement on him. Because I am sure he knew what their verdict would be… guilty."

Dillinger's grave in Mooresville became the object of curiosity hunters down the years. His father, fearing that someone would dig up the body, poured concrete laced with scrap iron over it to deter the more ghoulish souvenir hunters, those who would not be happy with a handful of earth or a posy of dried flowers.

It has been hacked about during the passage of time, but no-one has yet penetrated through that barrier. The greatest gangster of them all has lain undisturbed since he was interred – a peace and tranquility in death that he never knew in life.

DE LA BECKWITH
Third Time Unlucky

Byron De La Beckwith was a man who was born with hate in his heart and racist mumbo-jumbo in his mind. For more than 30 years he had managed to get away with the murder of a rising civil rights leader in the deep south but changing times and new attitudes brought him to justice... and jail.

Byron De La Beckwith was a man born with hate in his heart and bigotry burned deep in his soul. In America's old south he was raised a "Klucker" – the slang term among non-disciples for the Knights of the Ku Klux Klan, the white supremacists who strayed far beyond fancy dress in bedsheets and pointy hats to wreak their own brand of evil.

As organised terrorists who believed only in the supremacy of the white race they were – sometimes still are – responsible for bombings, lynchings and other murders. Not that they ever saw it as murder. Negroes to them – particularly back in the 1960s when the civil rights movement was "interfering" in the way the Dixieland states did things – were the lesser race, a breed for whom there could be no human compassion or decency.

They saw their extermination as the next best thing to where they once had them – under the heel of their boots. And nowhere was the stifling heat of oppression, the cruel vindictiveness of America's own brand of apartheid, more virulent and more apparent than in the city of Jackson, Mississippi, in 1963.

On a sultry June night Byron De La Beckwith murdered a young civil rights worker whose only calling was to bring basic human dignities to blacks denied them long after the last bugles had blown across the battlefields of the civil war. Byron De La Beckwith walked free from court where he was tried for the young man's murder – and walked free a second time months later. But the shot that snuffed out Medgar Evers' life was destined to be heard down three decades. And finally its ricochet got the murderer who is now serving life behind bars after scoffing at justice for 30 long years.

It was hot in Jackson on that June night as bugs danced around the humming street lights and creaking air conditioners across town struggled to keep ahead in the fight against the high temperature and humidity.

THE SHOT THAT SNUFFED OUT MEDGAR EVERS' LIFE WAS DESTINED TO BE HEARD DOWN THREE DECADES

Opposite: *Byron de la Beckwith, racist murderer.*

Below: *Beckwith in 1963, six years after the 'good ole boy' network of racist police, judges and jurors had saved his hide.*

Medgar Evers was in his second floor office overooking Lynch Street, clearing up paperwork in his job as the field secretary of the Mississippi branch of the National Association for the Advancement of Coloured People. These may have been Camelot days in Washington with the Kennedy administration working fast and furiously to dismantle the bureacracy of discrimination which existed across the deep south, but Evers was a front line warrior in the battle; it was he who protested at the separate lunch counters in restaurants and stores for blacks and whites, the "no blacks" signs at hotels, the signs which forbade humans of different colour from drinking from the same water fountain.

As an officer in this war he was used to harassment and threats, and often without joking said that the most valuable weapon in his arsenal was his Oldsmobile which he often used to escape from hostile towns where the local good ol' boys didn't take kindly to uppity niggers like him. Before his death he said: "Someone's been following me wherever I go. And I am getting

Above and Below: *Beckwith relied on the racism of his fellow white men to get him off the hook. Here the all-white jury enters the court-room on the first day of the original trial.*

plenty of calls. They say I am going to end up dead soon. One man who called was obviously holding a pistol. He spun the cylinder so I could hear it was a revolver. Then he said: 'This is for you.' I said to him: 'Well, when my time comes I am ready.' And I am. If I die it will be in a

good cause." It was just eight nights later that his prophesy came true. After he finished up his paperwork he drove to his home in the still night, looking forward to seeing his wife and three small children who were waiting up for him. As he walked to the front door of his home a hunting rifle used usually to shoot deer cracked in the still night and he fell before he had got the key into the lock. At 37, he had become one of the martyrs in the war against racism, dead in the heat of the night on June 12 1963.

"You have got to understand," said Robert Moses, a former leader of the black action group The Student Nonviolent Coordinating Committee, in attempting to explain away why there was no justice for him following his death, "that Mississippi in 1963 was a police state. It was a state where its elected officals promoted racism and all the terror that went along with it. Medgar worked right in the middle of this terror, surrounded by all the violence used by the state to keep people in line."

A BORN FIGHTER

Yet Medgar was born to lead his people in the fight for justice. One of the defining moments of his life came when, as a nine-year-old boy in his hometown of Decatur in the same state, he witnessed the KKK lynching of a black man wrongly accused of raping a white woman. He recalled: "He was a friend of my daddy's and we saw him strung up. The man's clothing remained in the field where it stayed a very long time. For ages his clothes were still there, slowly rotting in the wind and the rain, long after he had been cut down and buried. I used to see them whenever I went hunting and I always remembered.

"I made a pact to myself then that I would grow up and try my best to stop this ever happening again." After a spell in the U.S. Army he returned to Civvy Street. He attended a black agricultural college but was denied entry to the University of Mississippi law school because of his colour. Ironically he was instrumental in dismantling the college's system of apartheid the year before he was killed.

It was in 1954 that he first joined the NAACP and his first job was persuading scared negroes to go to city halls to register

Above: *This was the lot of many blacks in the deep south – no trial, no jury, no judges. Just a lynching.*

HE BRAVED MOBS WHO SPAT ON HIM AND BULLIES WITH BILLY CLUBS AT THE CROSSROADS INTO TOWN WHO SMASHED HIS CAR UP

to vote – bastions of white supremacy that most feared to go near, let alone enter. He braved mobs who spat on him, bullies with billy clubs at the crossroads into town who smashed his car up and then smashed his face up; he endured the taunts and the threats and the abuse with only his dignity and his sense of right intact. He recalled picking up an elderly black hitch-hiker who kept his eyes down on the floor of the car for the whole journey as he kept repeating over and over in a mantra fashion: "Yessir, the best friend a negro man ever had was a southern white gentleman. Yessir." Medgar said: "I had to tell him it was not a view I shared. And I said I aimed to make it my life's work to prove him wrong."

That dream died on that hot still night because Medgar Evers, visionary, had col-

Above: The Ku Klux Klan, racists who continued to haunt, persecute and murder blacks in the deep south long after the Civil War was over.

DE LA BECKWITH HARBOURED FANTASY NOTIONS OF BEING AN HEIR TO A GREAT CONFEDERATE GENERAL

lided with the philosophy of Byron De La Beckwith, bigot. A self confessed white supremacist, working as a fertilizer salesman, De La Beckwith was a decorated World War Two veteran who served in the bloody battle for the Japanese-held island of Tarawa as a trained sniper. Hunting in the woods around Jackson, he kept his eye in and boasted to friends that he was able to hit a running deer at 1,000 yards. Picking off a member of the race he despised at a distance of 30 feet would have been no problem at all.

De La Beckwith harboured fantasy notions of being an heir to a great Confederate general and his home in Greenwood, 90 miles from Jackson, was cluttered with the self-glorifying paraphenalia of the obsessive. He had Dixieland stars-and-bars flags, a field-grey kepi and a musket rifle as used by an infantryman at the watershed battle of Gettysburg. He also stockpiled the litera-

ture of hate – pamphlets that he handed out at shopping centres warning against the perils of "race mixing". On one occcasion he wrote to his local newspaper: "When you get to heaven you will find me in the part that has a sign saying 'for whites only'. And, if I go to Hades, I am going to raise all hell over Hades until I get to the white section. I do believe in race segregation like I believe in God. I shall make every effort to rid the United States of America of race integrationists until the day I die. There can be no place for the mongrel negroid races defiling and diluting the blood of American whites."

Such a diatribe in a newspaper in any "normal" town would have instantly brought the author to the attention of the local police department with a strong warning to officers to keep a close watch on the person responsible. But in the twisted atmosphere of Jackson, De La Beckwith was a friend of many policemen, many of

it an unreasonable question, was immediately excluded, but there can be no doubt that most of the 12 good men and true who were to sit in judgement on De La Beckwith were just as bigoted as he was. De La Beckwith denied he had killed Evers, but used the dock as a pulpit to preach his gospel of hatred.

He said that he was at home 90 miles away when the killing occurred – and produced three upstanding police officers to testify that they had seen him in Greenwood just like he said. The first trial in 1964 ended in a hung jury and a mistrial was declared. There was a second trial the same year with the same result.

At the end of the second courtroom hearing De La Beckwith had practially become a folk hero to the white racists of Mississippi. He was even greeted outside court by the Governor of the state, Ross Barnett, who shook his hand and wished him well!

Such endorsement of his actions later encouraged De La Beckwith to run for the position of Lieutenant Governor, but the majority of voters had the good sense to reject him and his rantings.

THE JFK ADMINISTRATION PLEDGED THE FULL WEIGHT OF FEDERAL LAW TO PURSUE MEDGAR EVERS' KILLER

Left: *Medgar Evers, a devoted family man and a rising star of the civil rights movement that sought to bring equality and liberty to all negroes in America.*

Below: *Evers, with the 'End Brutality' sign around his neck, is arrested in Jackson, Mississippi, shortly before his murder.*

whom shared his not-unique outlook about black people. That is why the investigation into the death of the most prominent civil rights worker in the state of Mississippi was not pursued with anything that could be termed vigour.

PRESIDENTIAL BACKING

Four days after his death, as the JFK administration pledged the full weight of federal law to pursue his killer, Evers was laid to rest in Arlington National Cemetery, the final resting place for American heroes which would later that year receive the body of the president, himself a victim of another sniper with another rifle.

The local police were slow to act but a federal investigation team was soon on the scene and all clues pointed to the man who couldn't bear blacks in his world. The bullet found in the victim matched his rifle, he was seen in Jackson that day, the gun disappeared shortly afterwards and De La Beckwith's car tyre marks were found in town near to where Evers was slain. He was charged with murder but the first trial turned into a celebration of racism.

An indication of how things were going to go came on day one of the trial when the prosecutor, William Waller, asked prospective jurors: "Do you think it is a crime to kill a nigger in the state of Mississippi?" Anyone who seemed to hesitate, or to think

The verdicts were, of course, of little surprise to Evers' widow Myrlie and his three small children. They had been taught by Medgar to lie on the floor if they heard gunfire at their home – once the target of a firebomb attack and all had lain prostrate with fear in their house the night he died at midnight on the doorstep.

"I wanted justice," said Myrlie, "but I was pragmatic enough to realise that it would probably never come. He grinned in court, gesticulated, used the word nigger like a hammer to bash us with.

"He was disgusting, and lining up on his side were all the forces of the state. I thought that I will die and my children would die without ever seeing justice done for him."

Above: *John F. Kennedy, president, right, speaks with brother Robert at the White House about bringing down the deep-rooted racism that infected so much of America.*

"HE GRINNED IN COURT, USED THE WORD NIGGER LIKE A HAMMER TO BASH US WITH. HE WAS DISGUSTING"

Byron De La Beckwith went back to his salesman job and married twice more in his lifetime. He was always unrepentant to the last about his racist ways, declaring that God would ultimately justify his segregationist views. But he couldn't leave it all to God. In 1979 he was arrested with bomb-making equipment and maps marking the home of a prominent Jewish leader in New Orleans – Jews, in the twisted philosophy of Byron De La Beckwith, having as little right to life as negroes. During his time in jail he couldn't resist talking to anyone who would listen about his twisted feelings on the "lesser races"… and about how he had gotten away with murder back in 1964.

SPECIAL RESEARCH

While he was doing his boasting a man who was nine-years-old at the time of Medgar Evers death was doing his research. Bobby DeLaughter had never even heard of the name of the dead man until he finished law school 13 years later. And then he became engrossed by the case, by the searing injustice of it all which he thought blemished all Mississippians and all southerners as being violent, racist rednecks. When he graduated he swore to himself that he would do everything in his power to re-open the case – and he did. "The big problem," he said, "was evidence 30 years after the fact. The murder weapon had disappeared, for instance, and I was keen to get it back.

"One day I recalled that my father-in-law, a Mississippi judge named Russell Moore III, had once shown me a rifle he kept in a closet. 'This is from one of the old civil rights cases,' said Judge Moore, unaware at what a trophy he really had, and indicating that he had taken the rifle home as a souvenir. By the time I remembered that he had shown it to me he was dead, so I went around to my mother-in-law's, checked the same gun and found that it matched the one on the records for De La Beckwith. Everthing was starting to fall into place. Police ballistic records were intact so it was a valuable piece of evidence to have." By now the boy who was nine when it happened was a man burning for justice on the staff of the district attorney's office. It was in his power to bring a new case and he intended to.

The key to getting trial number three came in 1990 when six new witnesses stepped forward to say that De La Beckwith had boasted to them during the years since the killing of how he was the hitman – of how he waited in bushes outside his home until he showed up and pulled the trigger.

The most compelling testimony came from Mark Reilly, a 36-year-old prison hospital guard in Baton Rouge, Louisiana, who guarded the suspect in 1979. Mr. Reilly, in a sworn affadavit which he later repeated at De La Beckwith's February 1994 trial, said: "He boasted of having killed 'that uppity nigger', and said that he had influence in Mississippi that protected him from ever being found guilty or of being prosecuted again."

As well as this damning testimony came even more concrete proof – De La Beckwith's fingerprints on the telescopic sights of the hunting rifle that had turned up again after so many "lost" years.

De La Beckwith was a man living in a timewarp, an anachronism in the modern age who believed that the juries who judged him in the heat and dust of 1963 would be around to listen to his bilge in 1994. He relied on the testimony of the three police officers – two of them now dead, one who turned up in person – to again place him 90 miles from the murder scene when the killing was carried out. Such evidence was seen as suspect to say the least in the enlightened 1990s, especially given the ballistic evidence. The only thing which marked this trial out as different from the others was De La Beckwith's silence in the dock. Although an unrepentant racist still, he acquiesced to his lawyer's demands to stay silent throughout the week-long trial.

THE FINAL VERDICT

At 10.33am on February 5 1994 the Civil War which had started in 1861 finally ended in Mississippi when jurors filed back into the courthouse from which Byron De La Beckwith had twice mocked justice and declared him guilty of murder. Eight blacks and four whites had judged him this time and there was no return to the "good ol'boy" days of the 1960s. The six witnesses, said the jurors afterwards, who told of

DE LA BECKWITH BOASTED OF HOW HE WAS THE HITMAN – OF HOW HE WAITED IN BUSHES AND PULLED THE TRIGGER

Below: *Mrs Evers weeps at the graveside of her slain husband during his funeral.*

his boasting, had sealed it for them. In six and-a-half hours they found the twisted old man guilty "beyond reasonable doubt'.

Two women in the front of the court were most affected by the verdict. One was the widow of Medgar Evers, one the third wife of Byron De La Beckwith. "He didn't do it, he's innocent," said Thelma Beckwith, tears streaming down her face for the man who had cheated justice – and the death penalty – for so long. Now, because of a change in the law, he couldn't be sentenced to die, just a life sentence instead. "Yes! Yes!" screamed the widow who has heard the shot that claimed her husband's life for 30 long years. "It's been a long journey," said Myrlie Evers, looking to the sky. Then she addressed a long-dead hero with the words: "I've gone the last mile, Medgar – but it was worth it. This will send a message to all racists who hide behind sheets and hoods.

"It won't bring you back, honey. But I hope it makes you rest in heaven a little easier."

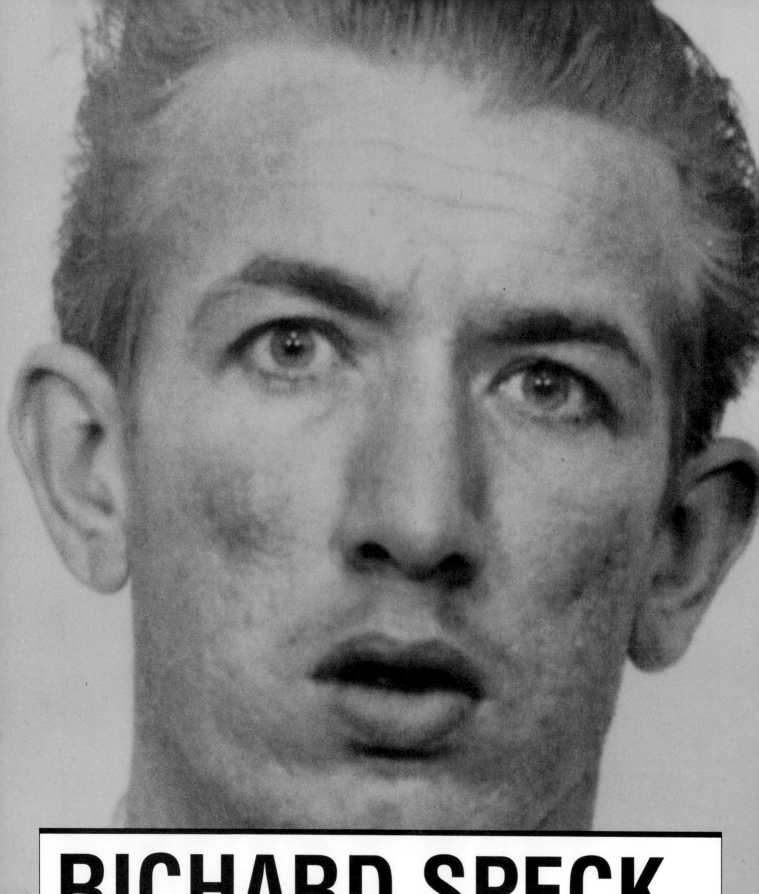

RICHARD SPECK
The Nurse Killer

Rarely has a human being sunk so low as Richard Speck, who unleashed a night of horror on a nurses' hostel in Chicago, turning a peaceful dormitory into a human abattoir, killing eight carers sadistically and mercilessly. It was described as "the crime of the century" by horrified experts.

Richard Speck died on Thursday December 5 1991 at the age of 49. He passed away in the prison wing of the Statesville Correctional Centre in Joliet, Illinois, after apparently suffering a heart attack. The death of just another con in America's overcrowded prison system is not usually a signal for prime-time news and massive coverage in the daily papers. But Richard Speck was a man who made history – a man who brought the term "mass murderer" and "thrill killer" into the American lexicon.

On a hot July night in Chicago this aimless drifter, his arms tattooed with the legend "Born to Raise Hell", broke into a nurses' hostel, tied up eight nurses and one by one systematically killed them, raping one in the process. Only one young woman escaped the night of incredible bloodlust, living to see the monster who slaughtered her friends say in court "not guilty".

But there could never be any doubt what the verdict would be – a resounding guilty in less than 55 minutes of deliberation. Speck was sentenced to death for his crime but the state, in a moment of mercy which he never afforded his pleading victims, commuted his sentence to life imprisonment. Jack Wallenda, a 65-year-old retired Chicago detective who had helped catch Speck, was one of those both gladdened and saddened by his passing – glad that he had gone, sad that he had not been executed. "He died an easy death as far as I am concerned," said Wallenda. "I had hoped that sucker would suffer a long time. The pain he caused the families of those dead girls was beyond belief."

James Fox, a professor at Northeastern University in Boston, Massachusetts, said of him: "The word mass-murderer was hardly in our vocabulary until Richard Speck. The idea that one person could indiscriminately slaughter innocent people was virtually unknown until July 14 1966." On that day Speck the nonentity, the loner, the misfit, earned himself a place in history for all time.

Chicago was hot and humid on that night. The searing summer heat pulsated throughout the city, forcing people into air-conditioned bars or cinemas for relief.

HE TIED UP EIGHT NURSES AND, ONE BY ONE, SYSTEMATICALLY KILLED THEM, RAPING ONE IN THE PROCESS

Opposite: *The wild, wild face of Richard Speck.*

Below: *Blood spatters the floor in the nurses' hostel. Rumpled bed clothes and abandoned slippers testify to frantic struggles for life.*

*Above: **The innocent facade of the hostel where Speck claimed his victims.***

Others simply stayed at home by their fans or AC units if they were lucky enough to have them. Choosing to stay home too were nine student nurses, most of them sleeping after long spells on duty at the South Chicago Community Hospital. All was quiet at their house, Jeffrey Manor, a two-storey townhouse, with only the whirring of the electric fans breaking the silence. But they had an appointment with lethal destiny that night – a man out to satisfy his murderous impulses.

Speck was born a misfit and died one. Born in Kirkwood, Illinois, on December 6 1941, his early childhood was marked by brutality at the hands of his drunken father and neglectful mother. By the time he was 20 he had notched up some 20 arrests for burglary, disorderly conduct and public drunkenness. Speck's family moved to Dallas when he was six and he was, by the time he was a teenager, "well known" to the police. He married a 15-year-old named Shirley Malone when he was 20 and

> IN A BLUR OF NARCOTICS AND BOOZE HE TOOK SOLACE IN SQUALID STRIP BARS AND ENCOUNTERS WITH PROSTITUTES

fathered one child, but his drinking and his violence increased and she left him, taking their daughter with her. Speck always threatened to kill her if he ever found her in Texas – and police would later say that the only victim he raped in the nurses' home bore a remarkable resemblance to the woman who left him.

A LOW-LIFE TALE

He added drugs to his alcohol dependency as he drifted from Texas back to Illinois. In a blur of narcotics and booze he took solace in squalid strip bars and cheap encounters with prostitutes that left him feeling bitter and angry towards all women. Later one would recall: "He liked to talk dirty and make sly remarks that all women were whores. I think he probably hated all women." On the rare occasions that he worked he became a crewman aboard the barges plying the Great Lakes between the USA and Canada, using his wages to buy knives – a lasting obsession up until the day he was caught – and liquor.

Although he would end up in jail for life for killing the nurses, police believe his hatred of women led him to kill at least three others, bringing his human harvest to a grand total of 12. The first to die was Mary Pierce, a barmaid and divorcee who rejected Speck's lewd advances at the Monmouth bar where she worked. On April 10 1966 she disappeared and her body – nude and strangled – was discovered three days later. On April 18 a 65-year-old woman was robbed and raped by a man matching Speck's description, but the ore barge he worked on had sailed away before he could be quizzed.

On May 3 he was back on dry land and rushed to hospital for the emergency removal of his appendix and, while there, befriended a young nurse whom he invited to go swimming. She went with him but later told police: "He had so much hatred in him – he was against everybody and felt that everybody was against him. He was very unhappy." Unhappy enough, police now believe, to murder three more young girls on July 2. He had been dismissed that day for being surly to the skipper of an ore boat and went on a bender back on shore. That day three young girls disappeared at Indiana Harbor. They had been wearing swimsuits and their clothes were discovered in the back of their parked cars. They were never seen again and police believe that Speck's monstrous lust claimed them in a bizarre training run before he moved on to the nurses in Chicago.

> "HE HAD SO MUCH HATRED IN HIM – HE WAS AGAINST EVERYBODY AND FELT THAT EVERYBODY WAS AGAINST HIM"

Below: *Police Superintendent Oliver Wilson holds up the wanted picture of Speck at a news conference before he was captured.*

A MIXTURE OF HEROIN AND
BOOZE, SCORED FROM A
JUNKIE, LED HIM OUTSIDE
THE NURSES' HOME
SHORTLY AFTER MIDNIGHT

Below: *The skid-row hotel where Speck was found.*

Speck washed up in Chicago on July 10, virtually penniless and in search of work. He went to the National Maritime Union seeking a passage on a vessel bound for New Orleans. He was told to return in two days' time to fill out an application form, but left behind his name and the telephone number of his sister where a message could be left for him, even though he was living in a sleazy hotel not far away. A mixture of heroin and booze, scored from a junkie on nearby Dearborn Street, led him outside the nurses' home at shortly after midnight on July 13. Brandishing a knife and a pistol he waved them in the face of 23-year-old Filipino student nurse Corazon Amurao. "I'm not going to hurt you," he lied. "I am only going to tie you up. I need some money to move to New Orleans."

He moved through the house and put Corazon in a room where three nurses were sleeping. He made them get up then herded the four into another bedroom where two more were asleep. Three more came home from dates within an hour until he had nine captives, all trussed up and lying on the floor. Bound and gagged in front of him, the girls looked with wide-eyed terror as he sat on the edge of a bed menacingly running his finger up and down the blade of his knife. The killing was about to begin.

Twenty-year-old Pamela Wilkening was untied first and led into another room where she was stabbed in the chest and strangled with a strip of sheet. He went back next for 20 year-old Mary Jordan and 21-year-old Suzanne Farris, guiding both women into a different bedroom. There he stabbed Jordan three times – in the heart, neck and eye – before butchering Farris with multiple stab wounds and strangling, then shredding her underclothes with his blade which he left laying around her.

Nina Schmale, 24, was next. Speck ordered her into an adjoining bedroom, slashing her throat and strangling her to death. While he was engaged in his berserk quest for blood the nurses left alive were wriggling under the beds in the room in a bid to avoid detection, but only Corazon, who had answered the door, would survive.

THE ONLY HIDING PLACE

She had wriggled under a bed in a darkened corner and was forced to watch in silence as Valentina Paison, 23, and Marlita Gargullo, 22, were the next to die. Paison died with one deep stab wound to the throat while Gargullo was stabbed four times and finally finished off by strangulation. Patricia Matusek, 22, died next after she was viciously kicked in the stomach and strangled to death. It was Gloria Davy, the last victim, who police said bore an uncanny resemblance to the wife he hated so much. She was the only one subjected to rape for close to half-an-hour before she too was murdered.

At 5.00 am Corazon, in a state of almost paralytic shock, listened for noises and decided that he had finally gone. She rolled out from under the bed and walked into one of the adjoining rooms… to see the girls that only hours before she had been joking and laughing with butchered like farmyard animals. She ran to the balcony in hysterics and yelled: "All my friends are dead! He killed them all!" A couple who were walking their dog just below thought that she was a potential suicide jumper and beseeched her not to take her life. One of them telephoned for the police who broke in the door of the boarding house… and discovered the horrific massacre within. "The man had behaved exactly like a fox in a poultry house," said a police officer at the scene. "It was killing for the joy of killing."

It was some five hours after she had been treated for deep shock that Corazon Amurao was able to tell police about the killer – that he stank of alcohol, that his face was pock-marked and that he bore tattoos that told he was 'Born to Raise Hell'. The knots that were tied on the victims told police two other interesting things – that the killer was possibly a seaman and an ex-convict, because he had expertly tied the hands to face away from each other behind the girls' backs, much in the way that a pair of handcuffs works. Corazon was also able to recall that the murderer had spoken of getting money to go to New Orleans.

Routine police enquiries were all

Above: *Corazon Amurao, the Filipino nurse who lived through the night of murder, hearing her friends die one by one at the hands of Speck.*

Left: *Mrs Margaret Lindbergh, Speck's mother, arrives for the start of his trial.*

Left and Right: *Valicentia Passon and Pamela Wilkening, two of the first victims.*

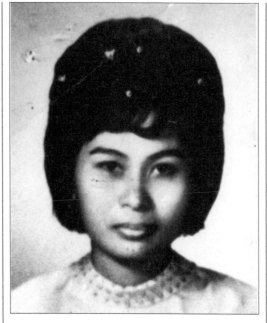

SOME KIND OF FERAL SIXTH-SENSE MADE SPECK BREAK THE APPOINTMENT HE HAD TO SHOW UP FOR THE JOB

Left and Right: *Susan Parris and Patricia Matusek, two more of the nurses who were beaten, raped, strangled and stabbed by the maniac Speck.*

HE PRESSED A HUNTING KNIFE AGAINST THE THROAT OF THE BARMAN, SAYING: "THIS HAS KILLED MORE THAN YOU KNOW"

that were needed to get on Speck's trail. The seaman's mission where he had gone for work was nearby and there the police found staff who confirmed the presence there of a tattooed, pock-marked man who had been seeking passage on a ship to New Orleans – together with a name and a telephone number for him.

One of the clerks there also explained how the drunken Speck had boasted of "going to spy on nurses" who he had heard sunbathed with little on in the grounds of the house. The police rang the number of Speck's sister declaring that a job was now available for him and he called back three hours later – during which time Corazon

had identified him from his photo attached to the application form. But some kind of feral sixth-sense made Speck break the appointment he had to show up for the job.

Police in return began trawling the seedier hotels where sailors and derelicts traditionally stayed. One hotel was found in North Dearborn Street but he checked out half-an-hour before they arrived. On 15 July he had been in a bar where he pressed a long-bladed hunting knife against the throat of the barman, professing to all around in the rough pub: "This has killed more than you know!" A policeman was called the same night to another cheap hotel after a prostitute had complained of a

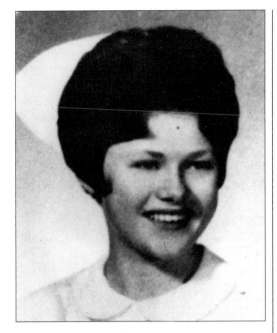

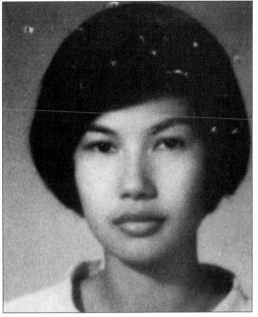

Left and Right: *Marlita Gargullo and Mary Jordan. Surviving nurse Corazon Amurao heard their death cries from her hiding place beneath a bed.*

HE SLASHED HIS WRISTS AND KNOCKED ON A NEIGHBOURING DOOR FOR DRINK, COLLAPSING AT THE FEET OF A STUNNED GUEST

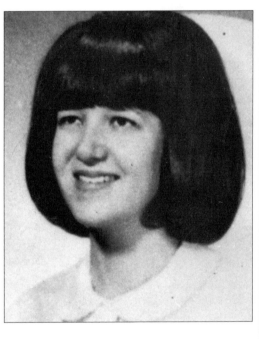

Left and Right: *Nina Schmale and Gloria Davy, the other two victims, making a total human-harvest of eight in all for the crazed killer.*

lunatic with a gun and a knife threatening her life. But crossed wires led the unsuspecting beat officer to confiscate the weapons, let the drunk off with a warning and Speck was allowed to go free!

He was caught after a televised appeal the next day. Speck had gone to the Starr Hotel in West Madison Street where he was spending money stolen from his victims. But he needed the money for the room and was penniless for the drink that he so desperately wanted to stop himself shaking. At midnight, whether suffering from some remorse or alcohol withdrawal symptoms, he slashed his wrists and knocked on a neighbouring door for drink, collapsing at the feet of a stunned guest. Twenty minutes later he was in the emergency room at a hospital where a surgeon recognised the "Born to Raise Hell" motif that had been part of the police TV broadcast. Police were called, he was under arrest and his trial came in April 1967.

Speck's behaviour at his trial was extraordinary. He showed great charm to the pressmen, laughing and joking, earning himself such plaudits as "remarkable" and "witty" from the city's scribes. He pleaded not guilty, hoping to scare the sole surviving witness to the slaughter with a fixed stare and a nonchalant air. There was little forensic evidence to fix him to the scene of

HE PLEADED NOT GUILTY, HOPING TO SCARE THE SOLE SURVIVING WITNESS WITH A FIXED STARE AND A NONCHALANT AIR

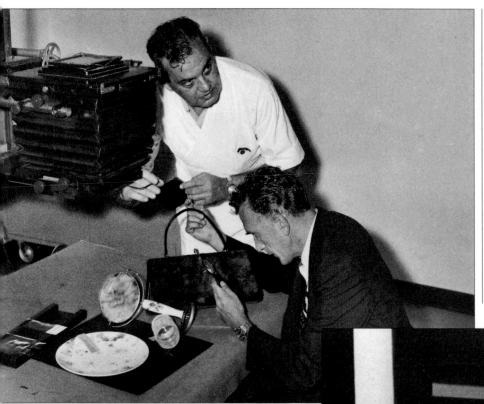

"Eight people and that effeminate homosexual." Speck said he and the second man chose the house in which the nurses lived by accident. And he said that after the killings he later killed his "accomplice" by shooting him in the face six times before dumping his body. Joseph De Leonardi, the Chief of Detectives who had led the hunt to capture him, said: "It is the rantings of a madman. There was no accomplice. Speck forgot that one of his victims survived. She testified at his trial there was only one man – and there was. There can be only one release from eternal suffering for the families of his victims – that is when he dies."

In 1987 Speck actually applied for parole – a bid that sent shock waves through America. Having pleaded not

the crime – and claimed he had been on a drinking bender when the attacks took place. But there was too much circumstantial evidence. He was sentenced to a total of 600 years in jail by a jury who came back in record time for someone accused of so many crimes. He looked at the jury and said: "No problem."

A STRANGE CONFESSION

It wasn't until 1978 that Speck had a change of heart and admitted to the Chicago slaughter – but in a weird twist only to seven of the eight murders. He said that they would still be alive had one of them not spat into his face and that the last killing was carried out "by an effeminate homosexual accomplice". In a rambling interview given to the Chicago Sunlife he said: "Yeah. I killed them. I stabbed and choked them. If that one girl didn't spit in my face they would all be alive today. She spit in my face and said she'd pick me out of a line-up... I just blew it. I can't even tell you what she looked like. She got stabbed in the heart."

Speck said that before the killings he and his accomplice drank whisky and he shot heroin into his arm. "I never shot heroin before so eight people got killed," he said.

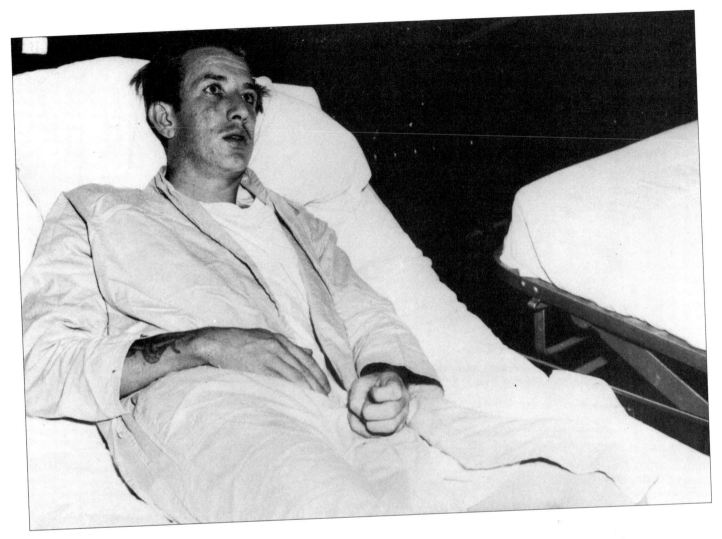

guilty to the murders, then having changed his story to admit them, the act of seeking freedom was almost more than the families of the dead girls could take.

"The parole of Richard Speck would devalue life since he took the lives of eight individuals who became nurses because they valued and loved the lives of others," said Ellen Stannish, a classmate of the girls. "We have lived with fear, shock, loss and sorrow since that day he has struck. The only consolation to us is that he is behind bars. Granting him parole would be too much to take."

Not only classmates and family but ordinary Americans were sparked into action. People who had never written a letter of complaint before found themselves angrily addressing the Governor of Illinois in a bid to block his release. Lena Wilkening, the mother of one slain student, said: "A mass murderer like that is always a mass murderer. He must stay there until the day he dies. You can't punish him enough because he snuffed out eight lives and murdered five

Above: *Speck, the tell-tale tattoo showing on his arm, in a prison medical ward before his trial.*

Opposite Top: *Forensic experts go to work on the personal belongings of the murdered nurses to pin the crimes on Speck.*

Opposite Below: *The madman has his day in court, but it doesn't save him from a guilty verdict.*

"THEY WENT LIKE LAMBS TO THE SLAUGHTER. YOU CAN SEE WHY THIS WAS CALLED THE CRIME OF THE CENTURY"

---

of their parents too – the strain of knowing what he had done to their loved ones killed them as surely as if he had strangled and stabbed them too."

Gayle Shines, an assistant district attorney for the city, was instrumental in getting parole refused. "They went like lambs to the slaughter," he said. "You can see why this was called the crime of the century and why he was convicted, beyond reasonable doubt by a jury of his peers, of it. A parole is a matter of clemency and grace, not a right. We say that Speck should die in prison and be buried in a prison grave.

Eventually, he did, but the legacy of the mass killer lives on in the American psyche. "I think what Speck did succeeded in turning us into a paranoid society," said Chicago criminal psychiatrist Marvin Ziporyn, who examined him at length before the trial. "Thank goodness the jury had the good sense to convict him first time around, otherwise he could have gone on drifting and killing. Then his acts of wickedness could have been tenfold."

A TIME TRIAL
The Baronet's Tragedy

Aristocrat Sir Trevor Dawson ended his life when his financial empire collapsed and he became depressed at the prospect of being unable to care for his family. A jury had to decide the crucial question of whether he died before or after midnight – a verdict on which depended a small fortune.

Merchant banker Sir Trevor Dawson was the kind of man who embraced life with gusto. Rich, handsome, talented, he had amassed a fortune and liked nothing better than to spend it. Among the set who inhabited Whites Club in London, the Cavalry and Guards, Bucks, the MCC, the racecourses of Ascot and Epsom and certain discreet gaming establishments, he was known fondly as "The Galloping Major".

Betting was a serious business to Sir Trevor; he thought nothing of placing £1,000 bets on rank outsiders with long odds, or of cheering himself up when the nags invariably lost with bottles of vintage Dom Perignon champagne at £50 a time.

"Life," he once said, "is for living to the max, and I intend to do so." His lavish tastes were reflected in a number of expensive possessions – there was a leather-upholstered, air-conditioned American Cadillac with the number plate TD1. There

RICH, HANDSOME, TALENTED, HE HAD AMASSED A FORTUNE AND LIKED NOTHING BETTER THAN TO SPEND IT

Opposite: *Sir Trevor Dawson was born into a life of privilege.*

Below: *The London home where Sir Trevor was to end his life.*

Above: *Sir Trevor in happier times when he was a financial wizard in the city.*

THERE WERE SUITS BY SAVILE ROW TAILORS AND A SOCIAL LIFE THAT READ LIKE A WHO'S WHO OF THE SMART AND FASHIONABLE

was the £350,000 Belgravia flat, in Eaton Square to be precise, one of the prime addresses in England. There was a cottage in the countryside, suits in the closet by the finest Savile Row tailors and a social life that read like a who's who of the smart and fashionable throughout the land. There were, outwardly, no blots on the horizon of this wealthy and privileged man.

But Sir Trevor's financial affairs were something of an iceberg by March 1993. His friends and family saw only the tip of them and presumed that all was well. Beneath the calm surface, however, was fomenting a financial maelstrom that he had no control over. For years he had risen through the ranks of the City of London with ease and grace… before a scandal in 1981 sent a stunning reversal of fortune through his glittering lifestyle. He was by then the investment chief of bankers Arbuthnot Latham and found himself at the centre of unwelcome attention from members of Scotland Yard's Fraud Squad. It was alleged that he took personal advantage of his position in the bank to funnel share profits through the Manchester-based stockbroking firm of Halliday Simpson to private clients' accounts.

Halliday Simpson ceased trading and the scandal caused Sir Trevor's company an estimated £350,000 at least, although there were rumours in certain quarters of the square mile of the city that it was double that amount. In the "old boy" network of London banking there was nothing that Sir Trevor could do but resign.

The resignation changed something within him. Over time he lost his easygoing ebullience and charm and seemed more and more to carry the weight of the world upon his shoulders. He began to frequently tell friends that there "is nothing left to live for". He had many friends and continued to frequent the clubs and haunts. But he sensed that people merely tolerated him, rather than embracing his company. He was, after all, tinged with scandal and in the rarified world in which he moved there were many who considered him the bearer of the mark of Cain.

A MYSTERIOUS AFFAIR

A diabetic and overweight, he continued to drink, but frequently became disoriented. In 1982 he was found lying seriously injured beneath a footbridge at Heathrow Airport. No-one ever got to the bottom of what happened but police believed he jumped from the overpass in a failed bid to kill himself. But he recuperated and returned home to a family whose love for him had not diminished… and to a bank balance that clearly had.

The years of high living had taken a toll on the finances of the galloping major and he began to worry about the future for his 26-year-old spastic son and his wife Caroline. He had parted from Lady Dawson after the financial scandal which forced him from the city, but they remained close friends and were constantly in touch with one another. The old soldier had made enormous amounts of money during his lifetime, but a lifestyle which kept up Cadillacs, Belgravia apartments and country cottages – together with gambling, drinking and dining – needed regular injections of cash, and that was running out. He had not been wise in his investments and the net result was impending financial doom. It led him to attempt suicide once more with an insulin overdose, but all he succeeded in doing was collapsing his lung, putting him on the critical list once more before he made a full recovery.

LIFE MIRRORS ART

In the play *Death of a Salesman* by Arthur Miller, the central, tragic character Willy Loman sees death as the only way out to provide for his family. Loman's logic is that, whereas most families need their husbands and fathers, his needed the money that the insurance on his death could provide. No-one knows whether or not Sir Trevor Dawson had ever read Death of a Salesman, but certainly the path he eventually chose mirrored that of the fictional Loman. The disgraced ex-banker had over £100,000 in life insurance policies, policies that he knew would relieve the great financial stress that was beginning to bear down on his family.

On February 14, Valentine's Day, his chauffeur Harold Munton, who had been with him for many years, dropped him off at the Belgravia flat at 6.00pm at night with instructions to come for him the next day. Once inside the flat he uncorked a bottle of champagne and sat in his favourite armchair where he composed a letter to his wife which read: "There was no other choice if you and Michael were to have any independence and security. I love you and will be with you always." Then Sir Trevor Dawson, a man who served his country in peace and war, took his own life by placing

Above: *White's Club, London, one of the bastions of the elite to which Sir Trevor Dawson belonged.*

Below Left: *Sir Trevor was a man for whom the best things in life meant everything – like champagne-soaked days at Ascot.*

HE HAD NOT BEEN WISE IN
HIS INVESTMENTS AND
THE NET RESULT
WAS IMPENDING
FINANCIAL DOOM

Above: *Sir Trevor and his wife Lady Caroline on their wedding day.*

Dr. Paul Knapman, the Westminster Coroner, spoke gravely to the five men and four women who would decide whether or not the tragic baronet had met the deadline. He told them: "Ladies and gentlemen of the jury, this case assumed rather more than incidental importance in determining death. A number of insurance matters involving considerable sums of money may hinge on the date that you decide he died.

"But you must not be swayed by any sympathy for any particular point of view. Just stick to the facts. Sir Trevor knew perfectly well that his life insurance policies expired before the dawn of February 15. In common parlance, he needed to do it – to take his own life – before midnight."

A DATE WITH DEATH

The policies that would have become worthless on that morning totalled £137,500. Three were with Phoenix Assurance, valued at £20,000, £20,000 and £65,000, and one with National Provident for £32,500. All were fully paid and fully redeemable if the insured party died before their expiry on February 15.

First to testify was Sir Trevor's chauffeur Harold Munton who described his former boss as an old-school gentleman. "I dropped him off at 6.00pm and I couldn't detect anything was wrong. The next morning I went into the flat at 11.30am and I found him dead in an armchair. There was a message waiting for me that said: 'Call ambulance on 999.'" The court heard from police how a half-empty champagne bottle was found in the drinks cabinet together with an empty glass at Sir Trevor's side.

Pathologist Professor Keith Simpson, Britain's most eminent expert in his field for some three-plus decades, testified next that the cause of death was asphyxia and that no foul-play was detected. In suspicious cases he said he always takes the temperature of the body.

The body cools at a certain rate after death and the temperature indicates at what time the person died. In this case no temperature was taken, although police surgeon Dr. Roger Durston said that he could have been dead "for many hours". It was a nugget of information not lost on the jury who saw the tearful Lady Dawson in court as she sat intently listening to evidence.

a plastic bag over his head. His weak lungs soon gave out and he suffocated to death.

After such a death in Britain there must be an autopsy and a full inquest presided over by a Crown Coroner. For the death of Sir Trevor Dawson, the inquest would take on immense importance for his widow – because her husband had killed himself either before midnight on the 14th or in the early hours of the 15th. If he had died before midnight, insurance policies that expired that night would be valid and redeemable. If he had died after midnight then his Lomanesque gesture would have been totally in vain. It was left to the nine good men and women of the Coroner's Court to decide such a weighty burden when they assembled to hear the last details of Sir Trevor Dawson's end at the inquest held at Westminster on March 23 1983.

> "IN COMMON PARLANCE, SIR TREVOR NEEDED TO DO IT — TO TAKE HIS OWN LIFE — BEFORE MIDNIGHT"

The jury heard that three days before he ended his life, Sir Trevor had called his secretary, Miss Pamela Gleason, and asked her for the expiry dates on one of the policies. Mr. Graham Read, his insurance broker, confirmed the policies, their amounts and the day they expired. Mr. Read said Sir Trevor had written to him about extending his policies. "He said he had had pneumonia and was considering extensions because he was not sure of his health."

Lady Dawson, dressed in black, spoke softly and eloquently before the jury when she was called into the witness box. She said: "My husband and I parted after his business difficulties but we kept in touch by letter and telephone two or three times a week. The last time we met he was very worried about Michael's welfare. Michael is severely retarded and needs constant care. He used to be looked after by my in-laws but they have since died. My home in Wiltshire is owned by the bank and I have to be out of there by March 31."

Ultimately the jury had just the pointer from the police surgeon and Lady Dawson's tragic circumstances to guide them. The Coroner had made it plain that

LADY DAWSON, DRESSED IN BLACK, SPOKE SOFTLY AND ELOQUENTLY BEFORE THE JURY WHEN CALLED INTO THE WITNESS BOX

Below: *Lady Caroline, Sir Trevor's widow, after the timetable verdict was brought in.*

they should not be swayed by personal feelings, although it would be ludicrous to imply that feelings of humanity towards a widow and her disabled son did not exist. After less than an hour of deliberations the jury filed into court to say that Sir Trevor Dawson had taken his own life BEFORE midnight. He had met the deadline – and now Lady Dawson was able to pursue the insurance companies for payment.

MORE HARD WORK

Later her solicitor, Mr. David Long, told pressmen outside the court: "We are grateful to the jury for its decision but this is not the end of the road by any means. We don't foresee any further court action but the next step is to ask the insurance companies for payment." China Cottage, her home near Marlborough that was owned by Barclays Bank, could be saved now. The solicitors said that they would ask the bank to delay its action in re-possessing the property while they pursued negotiations with the insurance companies.

Ultimately, it is unclear whether she received her money; the law on insurance was vague. Bernard Chandler, Secretary of the Life Offices Association, an industry professional body, said: "There are no set guidelines about whether an insurance company will meet a claim in a case of suicide. It depends on the company and the client and the contract which is drawn up between them. Some have suicide clauses, others have a clause saying that no money will be paid if someone commits suicide within a year of the policy's start."

The court's decision was a milestone victory. Crime author Larry Hackett commented: "It was a victory for humanity and common decency. If you look at the plain facts, those jurors did not know any more than the man in the moon about what time Sir Trevor Dawson finally expired. It could have been one minute to midnight or ten minutes to five on the morning that the insurance polices ran out.

"But thanks to grace and intelligence they let a widow facing financial hardship seek out what was owed to her on those policies. British justice has been frequently criticised in recent years, but I don't think anyone can fault the integrity or common-sense of British jurors."

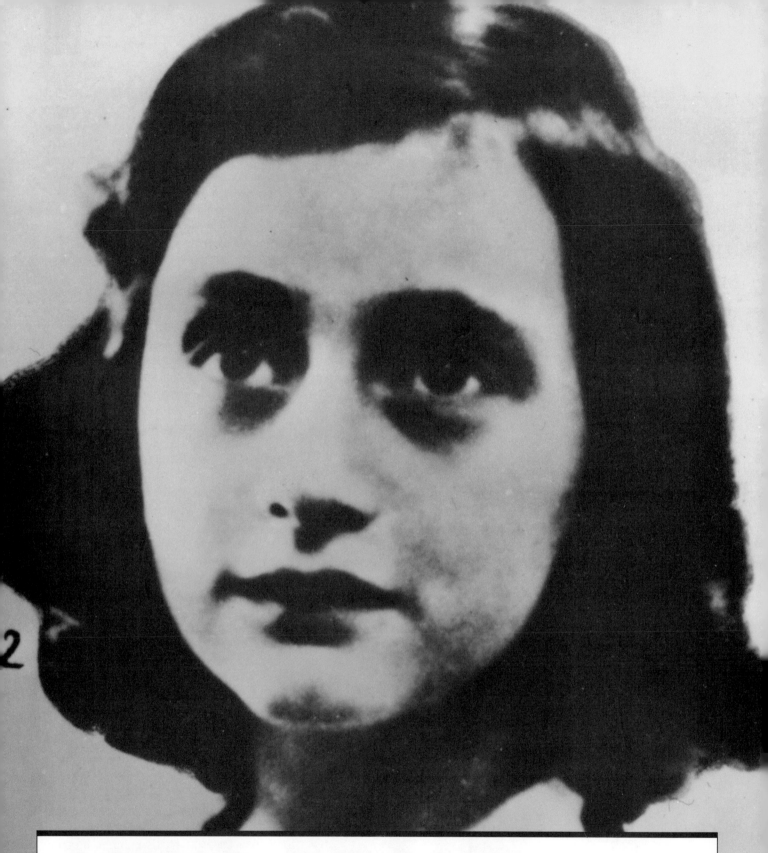

ANNE FRANK
Bringing Nazis to Book

Anne Frank was a Jewish schoolgirl whose eloquent jottings in her diary spoke to a generation that lived beyond the Holocaust that consumed her and her family. Nazi revisionists tried to degrade her memory by branding her diary a fake. It was left to a Nazi hunter to prove them wrong once and for all.

Anne Frank was just an ordinary little schoolgirl, her head filled with dreams and optimism when the Nazis marched into her country in 1940. Because she was Jewish she was forced into hiding with her family, occupying a secret loft in Amsterdam for over two years to escape the trains that took her people east to places like Auschwitz, Dachau and Majdanek. Places for which there was only a one-way ticket. In those years in hiding Anne Frank changed from a naive schoolgirl into a compassionate, sensitive thinker who confided her innermost feelings in a diary. That diary was discovered at the same time she and her family were – on the dreaded day of August 4 1944 when the S.S. came for them. Anne was to die in the Bergen-Belsen concentration camp before the war's end, another painful statistic in the Nazi catalogue of death.

A year after her death in March 1945 her father, who had survived the concentration

SHE WAS FORCED INTO HIDING WITH HER FAMILY, OCCUPYING A SECRET LOFT IN AMSTERDAM FOR OVER TWO YEARS

Opposite: *Anne Frank, whose diary became a document of massive historical importance.*

Below: *A close-up of some of the pages of Anne's diary which is now taught in schools around the world.*

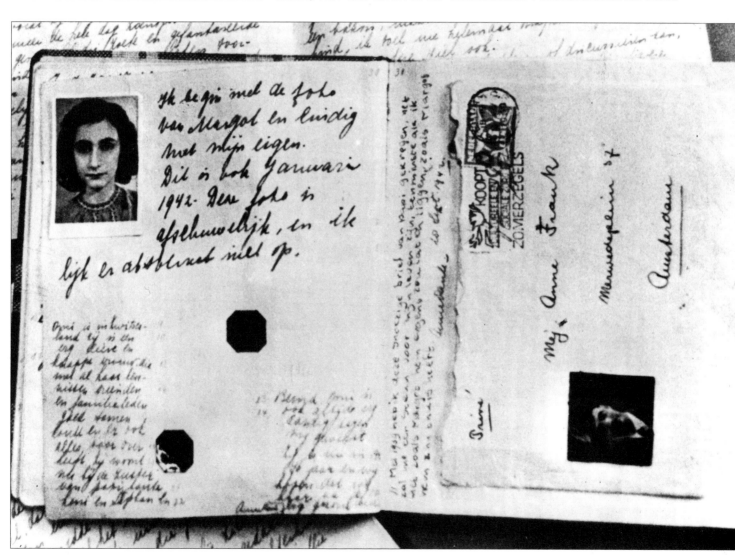

Above: *The house where Anne and her family hid from the Nazis for two years is now a shrine to visitors from all over the globe.*

Right: *Adolf Hitler and his Nazi cronies at a party rally in Nuremberg. His bizarre racial policies sent innocent girls like Anne to his extermination camps.*

camps, returned to the loft that had given him and his family sanctuary for so long. The diary that the S.S. man had held in his hands as they were marched away lay on the floor, alongside the other pathetic relics of what had once been a happy family life. Soon it was published as *The Diary of Anne Frank*, a book that touched the heartstrings of mankind and shone as a beacon of hope for the human soul. The diary was published in 32 languages, became a stage play and a Hollywood picture and is now taught as literature to scoolchildren around the world who can only wonder at her immense bravery and compassion as she struggled to live normally under the most abnormal circumstances.

Anne Frank was proof positive of the horror that the Nazis inflicted on subjugated peoples. But after the war certain anti-semitic elements in Austrian society began to question the veracity of her journal. Just like the "big lie" revisionists who like to pretend that the Holocaust itself was a figment of the allies' imagination – that there was no extermination programme – so the neo-Nazis in postwar society tried to pretend that Anne Frank had never existed.

The smear on her name began in 1958 in Linz, Austria, where anti-semitic demonstrators interrupted a stage performance of *The Diary of Anne Frank*. Leaflets hurled in the aisles of the city's Landstheater read: "The play is a fraud. Anne Frank never existed. The Jews have invented the whole story because they want to extort more restitution money. Don't believe a word of it! It's a fake!" To people like Nazi hunter Simon Wiesenthal, the camp survivor who lost 89 relatives in the Holocaust who devoted himself to tracking down surviving war criminals, the demonstration was a ghastly affront to his sensibility and an appalling victory for facism if it was left to go unanswered.

NAZI APOLOGISTS

Simon Wiesenthal spoke to a meeting of Viennese youth days later and what he heard shocked him. The diary? A clever fake, they insisted. The mass grave she is interred in? Where is the proof, they countered. "Proof," said Wiesenthal. "One would have to produce proof – irrefutable

---

THE BOOK TOUCHED THE HEARTSTRINGS OF MANKIND AND SHONE LIKE A BEACON OF HOPE FOR THE HUMAN SOUL

proof that would convince these young sceptics. One would have to tear one single brick out of the edifice of lies that had been constructed then the whole structure would collapse. But to find that one brick... Something occurred to me as I spoke to a young man who doubted its authenticity. Suppose the Gestapo officer who arrested

Above: *Hitler appeared to be capable of kindnesses to individual children.*

Below: *Children at Vittel concentration camp, France, after liberation by the US Army.*

Anne Frank were to be found. Would that be accepted as proof? 'Yes,' he said reluctantly. 'If the man himself admitted it.'" Simon Wiesenthal set out to find that man, to prove beyond all doubt to those who glorified the sick world of Adolf Hitler, that Anne Frank lived.

A DIFFICULT SEARCH

It was to prove an enormous detective hunt. Since Anne's father had returned to the attic to find the diary many years had elapsed, people had died, records were sketchy. Paul Kraler, a former employee of Anne Frank's father, who took over the company when Jews were forbidden to run businesses, recalled to Wiesenthal that the Amsterdam Gestapo had told him a man named Silvernagl had arrested the family. Yet no such name existed in Austria, so Wiesenthal assumed the v might be a b.

At first he searched in all the known S.S. records for a man named Silbernagel, adding an e to the name too, concentrating on the kind of low-ranking individual who might be ordered to do something as routine as an arrest of hiding Jews. He hired private detectives who ran background

Above: *The reality of Hitler's superman policies – the living among the dead at Belsen concentration camp.*

mation while constantly trying to keep tabs on the bigger fish like Eichmann and Mengele who had escaped justice at war's end. He was on the verge of giving up in 1963 when he visited the Anne Frank house in Amsterdam for the first time. He touched the walls that she had touched, drank in the atmosphere of the place where a frightened family had sheltered from the most appalling regime that had ever gained power in a civilised country. He knew then that his search must go on.

On a second visit to Amsterdam the same year he consulted with two officials of the Dutch Insititute for War Documentation. Wiesenthal shared information about missing war criminals and the documents which he worked from, sources, spies, etc., but there was no fresh evidence about the possible wherabouts of a possible S.S. man possibly named Silbernagel.

As he was getting ready to leave the meeting one of the men handed him a 1943 photostated copy of the official S.S. telephone directory for Holland. With the words "here is something to read on the plane that should keep you awake" he had unwittingly handed him the solution to the Anne Frank puzzle. Wiesenthal later

checks on the Silbernagels listed. Many showed up but they were either dead, had never been in Holland in service during the war or had rankings too superior to the kind of task alloted to the man who arrested Anne Frank.

For five years the enquiry trundled on, with Wiesenthal struggling for new infor-

---

FOR FIVE YEARS THE ENQUIRY TRUNDLED ON, WITH WIESENTHAL STRUGGLING FOR NEW INFORMATION

HE WAS ON THE VERGE OF GIVING UP WHEN HE VISITED THE ANNE FRANK HOUSE IN AMSTERDAM FOR THE FIRST TIME

Right: *Hitler, at the beginning of his conquest, addresses a Viennese crowd on the glories to come.*

revealed in his memoirs *The Murderers Among Us*: "The flight to Vienna lasted about two hours. I settled back in my seat and looked through the Gestapo directory. I was almost asleep when I turned to the page headed 'IV Sonderkommando'. Under 'IV B4 Joden' I read: 'Kempin, Buschmann, Scherf, Silberbauer.' I was now wide awake! Section IV B4 had handled the round-up and transportation of Jews to death camps. If anyone had tipped off the Gestapo about Jews hiding in Holland the report would inevitably reach this section. All of a sudden the plane seemed to be very slow. I could hardly wait to get to Vienna. I knew that most officials of this section had been recruited from police forces in Germany and Austria."

A STRONG CLUE

Wiesenthal was certain that he was on the trail of the man who arrested Anne and her family and put the mis-spelling of the officer's name down to a mistake. Deciding to chance his hand with a massive bluff, he rang Dr. Josef Wiesinger, head of the department within the Austrian Justice Ministry which handled war crime cases. "I told him," said Wiesenthal, "rather boastfully I'm afraid, that I had found the Gestapo man who had arrested Anne Frank. 'He's a Viennese policeman called Silberbauer,' I said."

Wiesinger did not call the bluff of the world's most famous Nazi hunter; instead he agreed to go through records and asked Wiesenthal to get back to him at a later date, although he did not hold out much hope of finding someone "who was posted somewhere else in Europe 19 years ago."

Wiesenthal, whose own offices were in Vienna – he preferred to work there because of the massive support the Viennese had given to Hitler during his rise and subsequent years at the top – did not know if his gamble would pay off. But it did – and in spectacular fashion.

He began to worry that something was being kept from him – a certain edginess in the voices of officials, a certain reluctance to say at what stage the enquiry was. Then, on November 11 1963 the Volkstimme paper, official organ of the communist party of Austria, broke a sensational story about police inspector Karl Silberbauer

pending an investigation into the arrest of Anne Frank and her family. It mooted the possibility of a war crimes trial. It seemed that Wiesenthal was not the only man on his tail; communists – a group that suffered heavily under the Third Reich – had also been pursuing the guilty man.

Wiesenthal believes that a communist sympathiser who also happened to be a member of the police force leaked the news of the Justice Ministry enquiry to some of his left wing colleagues, thus providing the communist paper with a scoop of quite staggering proportions.

Silberbauer became an instant recluse behind the curtains of his modest apartment home in Vienna, refusing to talk with the hordes of journalists who turned up to try

Above: *Adolf Hitler became a religious deity for many Nazis. Yet the only gospel he preached was one of hatred and murder.*

WIESENTHAL WAS CERTAIN THAT HE WAS ON THE TRAIL OF THE MAN WHO HAD ARRESTED ANNE AND HER FAMILY

Left: *Otto Frank, the father of Anne, who survived the Holocaust to find his little girl's diary.*

to talk with him about that infamous appointment with destiny he had kept all those years ago. Wiesenthal gave his address later to a Dutch newspaperman who managed to get a few well chosen words from the suspect. He said: "Why pick on me after all these years? I have been railroaded. I only did my duty. We have just bought some new furniture on instalment – how on earth am I going to pay for it now?" That is what it had come down to for a former proud member of Hitler's super-race – paying the bills for hire purchase home fittings.

SELFISH FEELINGS

"Don't you feel sorry sometimes for what you did?" asked the journalist, hoping to elicit some human response other than self-preservation from the man. "Sure I feel sorry," replied Silberbauer, "and sometimes I feel downright humiliated. Every time I take a streetcar now I have to buy a ticket like everybody else. I can no longer get by on my police pass. I bought her little book last week to see if I am in it, but I am not. I suppose I was the first person ever to touch it, to see it. Maybe I should have picked it up off the floor. Maybe then no-one would ever have heard of me."

Silberbauer didn't even come close to the division one of Nazi war criminals. He was, in what the journalist Hannah Arendt summed up in Adolf Eichmann, the epito-

> "WHY PICK ON ME AFTER ALL THESE YEARS?" SAID SILBERBAUER. "I HAVE BEEN RAILROADED. I ONLY DID MY DUTY"

Right: *Anne Frank's statue in Amsterdam, a memorial to a little girl whose courage equalled that of 10,000 men.*

> HE HAD PROVED BEYOND REASONABLE DOUBT – BEYOND ANY DOUBT – THAT ANNE FRANK HAD EXISTED

me of "the banality of evil". Wiesenthal was not particularly interested in what happened to Silberbauer – his success came from the fact that the man who had arrested Anne Frank had been found.

Wiesenthal learned that Silberbauer – in accordance with postwar dictates set by the victorious allied powers – had submitted to a de-Nazification tribunal before he could reclaim his pre-war police job. Enquiries from his superiors found he was not responsible for deporting the Franks and therefore not guilty of war crimes. He kept his job, his pension, his rights.

Yet Wiesenthal was able to go back to the pimply youths who became heady with the martial music and imagery of the Third Reich, and say to them that here was the man who confessed to arresting a real family with a real daughter who wrote a real book that shamed them and their kind. He had proved beyond any doubt that she had existed and, by extension, that the Holocaust that had snuffed out her young, unfulfilled life had also existed.

Silberbauer didn't matter a jot. But the establishment of the fact that he had walked through the door and arrested them mattered enormously when it came to fighting the propaganda of the new Nazis.